RKO Radio

The publisher gratefully acknowledges the generous support of the
Ahmanson Foundation Humanities Endowment Fund
of the University of California Press Foundation.

RKO Radio Pictures

A Titan Is Born

RICHARD B. JEWELL

University of California Press

BERKELEY   LOS ANGELES   LONDON

University of California Press, one of the most distinguished university presses in the United States, enriches lives around the world by advancing scholarship in the humanities, social sciences, and natural sciences. Its activities are supported by the UC Press Foundation and by philanthropic contributions from individuals and institutions. For more information, visit www.ucpress.edu.

University of California Press
Berkeley and Los Angeles, California

University of California Press, Ltd.
London, England

Library of Congress Cataloging-in-Publication Data

Jewell, Richard B.
    RKO Radio Pictures : a titan is born / Richard B. Jewell.
        p.   cm.
    Includes bibliographical references and index.
    ISBN 978-0-520-27178-4 (cloth : alk. paper)
    ISBN 978-0-520-27179-1 (pbk. : alk. paper)
    1. RKO Radio Pictures—History.   I. Title.
    PN1999.R3J46   2012
    384'.80979494—dc23

                                                        2011047718

20   19   18   17   16   15   14   13   12
10   9   8   7   6   5   4   3   2   1

For
Lynne and Annie
and
John and Vernon

Contents

List of Illustrations   ix

INTRODUCTION   1

1. "MASTER SHOWMEN OF THE WORLD": PREHISTORY
   AND THE FORMATION OF THE COMPANY   8

2. "IT'S RKO—LET'S GO": THE BROWN-
   SCHNITZER-LEBARON REGIME (1929–1931)   20

3. "FAILURE ON THE INSTALLMENT PLAN, A TICKET AT A
   TIME": THE AYLESWORTH-KAHANE-SELZNICK REGIME
   (1932–1933)   40

4. "ALL THIS IS VERY DISTRESSING TO ME": THE
   AYLESWORTH-KAHANE-COOPER REGIME (1933–1934)   65

5. "HE FEELS THE COMPANY IS UNSETTLED": THE
   AYLESWORTH-McDONOUGH-KAHANE REGIME
   (1934–1935)   94

6. "AN AWFULLY LONG CORNER": THE SPITZ-BRISKIN
   REGIME (1936–1937)   115

7. "PLAYTHING OF INDUSTRY": THE SPITZ-BERMAN
   REGIME (1938)   149

8. "THE COMPANY'S BEST INTEREST": THE
   SCHAEFER-BERMAN REGIME (1939)   168

9. "QUALITY PICTURES ARE THE LIFEBLOOD OF THIS
   BUSINESS": THE SCHAEFER-EDINGTON REGIME
   (1940–1941)   191

10. "CROSSING WIRES": THE SCHAEFER-BREEN
    REGIME (1941–1942)   223

Appendix: "The Whole Equation of Pictures"   257

Notes   273

Selected Bibliography   305

Index   311

Illustrations

1. Joseph P. Kennedy, the famous Bostonian   11
2. David Sarnoff, president of the RCA Corporation and the true father of RKO   17
3. William LeBaron, the first production chief of RKO   23
4. David O. Selznick, the wunderkind head of RKO production   45
5. *Rockabye* (1932)   57
6. *The Most Dangerous Game* (1932)   70
7. *Little Women* (1933)   77
8. *Of Human Bondage* (1934)   87
9. *Down to Their Last Yacht* (1934)   91
10. *Roberta* (1935)   100
11. *Becky Sharp* (1935)   104
12. *Top Hat* (1935)   109
13. *Sylvia Scarlett* (1936)   119
14. *Shall We Dance* (1937)   124
15. Samuel Briskin, head of production at RKO   125
16. *Mary of Scotland* (1936)   129
17. *A Damsel in Distress* (1937)   144
18. *Bringing Up Baby* (1938)   163
19. *Room Service* (1938)   165
20. George Schaefer, RKO corporate president   172
21. *Bachelor Mother* (1939)   182
22. *They Knew What They Wanted* (1940)   210
23. *Suspicion* (1941)   232
24. *The Magnificent Ambersons* (1942)   240

Introduction

"RKO—isn't he a wrestler?" asked one of my students when I told him I would be teaching a class on RKO during the following semester.

"No," I said. "It's an old movie studio that had a particularly interesting history."

"Oh," he responded, and quickly walked away.

As the years fall away since the general public recognized only one kind of screen entertainment, the name RKO Radio Pictures has less and less resonance. Most of the company's competitors during the "golden age" of American cinema—Paramount, Warner Bros., Universal, Twentieth Century–Fox, Columbia—remain familiar, their ubiquitous corporate logos gracing all manner of moving-image entertainment. But the RKO organization stopped producing motion pictures in 1957 and is now remembered principally by a small coterie of nostalgia buffs, film historians, and cinema students required to learn a bit about the industrial aspects of old Hollywood. This is a pity because RKO's abbreviated lifespan has a great deal to teach us about the movie business, corporate management, and the very special era when the company was making its product.

RKO was, in fact, one of the major corporations that dominated film commerce from the late 1920s until the mid-1950s. Along with four elite competitors, MGM, Paramount, Warner Bros., and Fox, it was vertically integrated—the company operated a studio to produce its product, a worldwide distribution arm to market it, and a chain of theaters where its films nearly always played. During its lifetime, it released more than one thousand feature motion pictures, including some of the most famous titles in cinema history. And yet today, most of what we know about RKO comes indirectly from general texts on American film; biographies of David Selznick, Katharine Hepburn, Fred Astaire, Ginger Rogers, Lucille Ball, Orson

Welles, Howard Hughes, and other well-known individuals who worked there; studies of musicals, comedies, horror films, film noir, and other genres that were RKO specialties; and analyses of famous individual pictures such as *King Kong* and *Citizen Kane*. I am in a unique position to argue that this company deserves additional attention, having already written a book on the company that was published almost thirty years ago.[1]

I am proud of *The RKO Story*, but its authorship was a frustrating experience. The book contains an overview of the company's development, plus short descriptive reviews of all the films the studio produced or released. It is a handsome volume with lots of photo illustrations and was designed to sit majestically atop coffee tables all over the world, though I attempted to make it the most carefully researched and accurate book of its kind. But I had much more to say about the company—information that was impossible to include because of the format and space limitations. Thus, I always knew that someday I would return to the subject and write a different sort of corporate history, one that would focus on the constantly changing leadership of RKO.

Executive turnover was in fact the distinguishing feature of its twenty-nine-year existence. Unlike the executive setup at most of the other major companies during the studio system era, RKO's management was never stable. New corporate presidents or production heads, or both, arrived every few years, making RKO the most unsettled and erratic of motion picture enterprises. Each new leader focused his attention on the goal of making RKO a vital and profitable corporation, and each one reacted to a variety of internal and external pressures that affected his job performance. This book centers on them—their personalities, philosophies, management styles, and efforts to succeed.

Movie folk—even the executives—tend to be dreamers. They dream of running a company that produces "quality" products that will be applauded by the most erudite and sophisticated members of the audience, yet will simultaneously generate millions of dollars in box-office revenues. Most do not believe these two types of product are mutually exclusive. RKO came late to the business, so its executives were always struggling to catch up with the established companies in order to realize their dreams. Still, they had confidence they could challenge the other studios if only RKO could corral a unique stable of performing talent, or pull together the best producers, directors, and writers in the business, or discover the next technological breakthrough that would propel the corporation past MGM, Warner Bros., and the others. None ever saw his dreams become reality, but their lives were certainly not failures. New stars, innovative productions, surprise hits emerged from the seven hundred–plus films that the company produced, as well as flops and fizzles and other disappointments. This is a history that contains many peaks and valleys, and a story of the men who steered the vehicle called RKO through them.

My research on RKO began in the 1970s and was aided immensely by two very generous men: John Hall and Vernon Harbin. In 1977 John was placed in charge of RKO's West Coast archive, which was then housed in a building on Vermont Avenue in Los Angeles. The archive had been off-limits for many years, but John opened it up and welcomed scholars from around the world to access its contents. That little building on Vermont contained a treasure trove of film history. One of the fortuitous aspects of the studio system for film scholars was its bicoastal structure. Because the corporate president and the heads of distribution and exhibition were headquartered in New York while all the production work took place in Hollywood, a continual flow of letters, telegrams, and memoranda between the two coasts resulted. These archival documents, along with internal studio correspondence, provide the crucial skeleton of this book, as well as that of my forthcoming second volume of the company's history.

John Hall was pleased with my work and even allowed me photocopying privileges, so I began to amass my own miniversion of the archive. It was, indeed, fortunate that I copied so many documents, because after John's untimely death, the archive was broken apart. Some of the material was donated to UCLA, some ended up at Warner Bros., but most was transported to Atlanta, where, I'm told, the documents reside in a warehouse closed to all except a few select employees of the Turner/Warner Bros. organization.

Vernon Harbin "built" the archive that John Hall so openly shared with others during that wonderful period in the late-1970s and 1980s. Vernon became an RKO employee in the early 1930s. His first task was to forge Richard Dix's signature on publicity photographs, but he soon worked his way up to an executive position. He continued to labor for the studio, with time off for military service during World War II, until its demise, spending most of his years in the Commitments Department. Even after the studio stopped making movies, Vernon was retained by RKO General, which owned the theatrical rights to the old RKO films. Vernon oversaw the studio's paper holdings, answering questions, renewing copyrights, and fielding queries about the possibility of remaking specific productions. To do his job thoroughly and accurately, he spent part of his time reorganizing the files from the studio's many departments, and despite his lack of archival training, he did an exceptional job of arranging the materials in a comprehensive and comprehensible fashion.

Vernon became a close friend and collaborated with me as consulting editor on *The RKO Story*. He pointed out many important documents in the archive, but his greatest asset was his extraordinary memory. Whenever I got a fact wrong or misinterpreted an event in the studio's history, Vernon would gently straighten me out. He died not long after John Hall, and I miss them both.

Unquestionably the most important item I copied from the Vermont Avenue archive was a ledger entitled "Statistics of Feature Releases—June 1952," which belonged to C. J. Tevlin, a studio executive who worked for Howard Hughes when he was running RKO. This ledger contained the production costs, domestic and foreign film rentals, and profits or losses of all RKO feature films up through the end of 1951. Accurate information of this kind is difficult, in many cases impossible, to find for most of Hollywood's classical-era movie companies. Whenever I report financial data related to individual pictures in this study, they are derived from the Tevlin Ledger.[2]

The reader may wonder why it has taken me so long to return to my work on the studio. After I completed *The RKO Story*, I decided to put the organization aside for a time and pursue other projects. Little did I know that those projects would be superseded by academic administration, wherein I would labor for most of the next twenty years. During that period, I occasionally revisited my cache of documents and published articles related to the studio's history, but I was an indifferent scholar at best while I was department chair of Critical Studies and subsequently associate dean of the University of Southern California School of Cinema-Television. Now, finally, I have come back to RKO Radio Pictures with renewed enthusiasm and a determination to make this two-volume study the capstone of my career.

As any student of historiography understands, there are many different kinds of histories. The one that you are about to read is a *business* history. It focuses on the men who attempted to make RKO a financial powerhouse and judges them largely on their success or failure to accomplish that job.

Of course, theatrical motion pictures have always been more than just a business. They are also an art form, a technological phenomenon, a medium of communications, and an influential conveyor of popular culture, and RKO certainly made important contributions in each of these areas.

Unfortunately, the scholarship related to Hollywood and its films is often unbalanced, emphasizing artists and artistic achievements while ignoring or even attacking the industrial basis of all production. What many scholars tend to downplay is one simple fact: the films they admire or believe are worth discussing would never have been produced if executives had not believed they would make money for their companies.

Choosing to approach the history of RKO from a business perspective sometimes places me in the awkward position of presenting negative assessments of films and individuals I admire. But just because a movie is aesthetically brilliant and stands the test of time does not mean it was a boon to the company that made it. Many of the greatest cinematic works failed at the box office when first released. From a business perspective, such artists as Howard Hawks and Orson Welles and such films as *Bringing Up Baby* and *Citizen Kane* were bad news for RKO, and the problems they spawned will be detailed in this study. There are plenty of other scholarly works that analyze the excellence of such films; this book considers them from a different point of view—as commercial products expected to generate substantial revenue.

Now that I have clarified the kind of history I am presenting, I need to offer the following disclaimers. This book focuses on RKO and its principal product: feature-length motion pictures. After years of research, I am convinced that Hollywood companies like RKO rose and fell, thrived, survived, or expired based on the financial performance of their features. Therefore, certain particularly influential feature motion pictures and the individuals responsible for them are emphasized. But there were other important components of the organization's business model, especially its worldwide distribution network and its chain of affiliated theaters. The functioning of RKO distribution and exhibition and the people who worked in these areas play roles in the narrative, but they will not receive as much attention as the feature production end of the corporation.

The company's short films are barely noted. Over the years, RKO produced hundreds of shorts, mostly comedies starring Leon Errol, Edgar Kennedy, and others. They were licensed to theaters for a nominal price. Directors Mark Sandrich and George Stevens, among others, honed their craft in the shorts unit before graduating to feature film making, but the shorts were always a very small component of RKO's business equation. So was its newsreel, the RKO Pathe News, which the company acquired in the 1931 merger with Pathe. Beginning in 1935, RKO also started distributing the *March of Time*, short informational documentaries made by Time, Inc., and, until Walt Disney partnered with RKO, it offered theater owners cartoons produced by the Van Beuren Corporation. None of these shorts is unimportant, but there is only room for passing mention of them in this history.

For those unfamiliar with the structure and operations of a classical-era movie studio like RKO, I suggest they begin by reading the book's appendix. In it, I have summarized how the organization functioned, broken down by production, distribution, and exhibition and by its most important departments. Included are the names and job titles of a number of the company's crucial employees. Although RKO must have seemed like one giant revolving door to most of its executives, it was home to a legion of stalwart staff members who spent the lion's share of their careers working for the company. They deserve more credit than I am able to provide them for their never-ceasing efforts to propel RKO to the top. A reader knowledgeable about the studio system approach to film business should skip the appendix and proceed directly to chapter 1, though I hope you will eventually take a look at it for additional information about the company and its workforce.

I have received significant support for this project. I am particularly grateful to the Academy of Motion Picture Arts and Sciences for naming me an Academy Scholar and providing a generous grant that helped broaden my research, enabling me to visit additional archives containing valuable documents. My own academic home, the Critical Studies Department of the USC School of Cinematic Arts, chaired by Tara McPherson and later Akira Lippit, allocated funding for some of these excursions as well. I also spent a good deal of time catching up on many books and articles, published since I conducted my initial RKO research, that touch on the company's history. In this regard, I want to thank Erin Hoge and Jennifer Rosales, two USC graduate students who located and pulled together important material for me. Kristen Fuhs and Eric Hoyt did this and more; their superior research skills enriched the project in more ways than I could ever describe.

Of the works I consulted, one in particular stands out: Cari Beauchamp's *Joseph P. Kennedy Presents.*[3] Exhaustively researched and beautifully written, this book answered a multitude of questions about Joseph Kennedy's activities with Robertson-Cole, FBO, Keith-Albee-Orpheum, and Pathe and about the role he played in RKO's formation. Its contributions to my project will be obvious in chapters 1 and 2. Thank you, Cari, for your brilliant work and for saving me an enormous amount of time.

I must also express my gratitude to Mindy Gordon of the Rockefeller Archive Center; Harry Miller of the Wisconsin Center for Film and Theatre Research; Barbara Hall, Val Almendarez, Faye Thompson, and Linda Mehr of the Academy of Motion Pictures Arts and Sciences Margaret Herrick Library; Shawn Guthrie, grants coordinator of the Academy's Film Scholar Committee; Patricia Hanson of the American Film Institute Library; Ned Comstock and Steve Hanson of the USC Cinematic Arts Library; Dace Taube of the USC Doheny Library Special Collections Department; and Leith Adams and Steven Bingen of Warner Bros. for their many kindnesses and contributions.

The fingerprints of two academic reviewers contracted by the University of California Press may be found throughout this manuscript. I am indebted to the anonymous reader and particularly to Thomas Schatz of the University of Texas for their excellent suggestions.

Mary Francis of the University of California Press deserves special mention for her investment in me and RKO and her unwavering encouragement. Like a good producer, she began to cultivate the project a couple of years before I received the Academy recognition and has shepherded it through to its final form. Eric Schmidt, Kim Hogeland, Suzanne Knott, and Steven Baker of UC Press also provided a good deal of expert assistance as we moved through the process.

Others who have had a salutary impact on my work through the years include Lawrence Bassoff, Irwin Blacker, Drew Casper, Hugh Hefner, Tom Kemper, Arthur Knight, Lisa Majewski, David Malone, John Mueller, Woody Omens, Frank Rosenfelt, John Russell Taylor, and the brilliant students I have been privileged to teach. Finally, I owe a massive debt to my patient wife, Lynne, and vivacious daughter, Annie.

Once in a great while, an author stumbles upon a quote that seems to justify, in an especially felicitous way, precisely what he hopes to accomplish. In December 1952, RKO was passing through one of its many turbulent periods. Journalist and film historian Terry Ramsaye noted the dramatic events taking place, ruminated on the company's roller-coaster past, and offered the following suggestion:

> ROMANTIC ASSIGNMENT—The intricate and excitingly fantastic week-to-week, sometimes day-to-day, sometimes hour-to-hour, developments in the current chapter of the affairs of RKO suggest that some competent writing-researcher might do a fascinating history of that corporation.
> . . . .
> Everything that has happened in the motion picture industry has happened to what we call RKO—so far. It is a story of the vitality of an industry close to the people.[4]

1. "Master Showmen of the World"

*Prehistory and the Formation
of the Company*

The roots of RKO can be traced back to 1883. In that year, the vaudeville showman B. F. Keith opened a variety theater in a fifteen-by-thirty-five-foot remodeled store in South Boston, Massachusetts.[1] Keith's theater was a success and he decided to expand. When he died in 1914, he controlled a nationwide circuit of vaudeville houses that could, and did, book entertainers on tours of more than a year's duration. Keith built his theatrical domain through expansion of his Keith houses and by amalgamating them with the Albee circuit.

During the early years of the twentieth century, the movies were generally regarded as a vulgar, low-class form of entertainment. Vaudeville theaters, like those in the Keith-Albee group, used films mainly as "chasers" to clear a house of patrons between shows.[2] *Birth of a Nation,* the films of the great silent comedians, and such early stars as Mary Pickford and William S. Hart gradually changed the attitudes of even the most educated and cosmopolitan members of the public. Movies grew in popularity while vaudeville diminished in attractiveness. In some variety theaters, movies received equal billing with the live performers.

The leaders of Robertson-Cole, a British company whose primary business was exporting Roamer automobiles, decided to pursue a serious foothold in the movie business in the early 1920s. They purchased thirteen and a half acres on a site called Colegrove in Hollywood in 1920 and constructed seven buildings, including three production stages. This studio would become the West Coast headquarters of RKO eight years later. Harry Robertson and Rufus Cole had already dabbled in the distribution of motion pictures made by various Hollywood producers. Intrigued by the notion that their company could realize greater profits by producing its own films,

Robertson and Cole began making movies on the new lot before the facilities were even finished.

Robertson-Cole's next-door neighbor at the time was the United Studios, a rental facility where First National and other producers shot films. A few years later, Paramount bought the property; thereafter, Paramount Pictures and RKO Radio Pictures would exist side by side, separated only by a wire fence, throughout RKO's history.

The first Robertson-Cole feature production was *Kismet* (1920). Personally overseeing the release of *Kismet* in Boston was Joseph P. Kennedy, who had formed a company to distribute R-C pictures in the New England area in late 1920.[3] The thirty-two-year-old Kennedy's foray into the movie business must have been viewed as something of a lark by his family and acquaintances. A graduate of Harvard with financial expertise in everything from balance sheets to stock pools, he appeared headed for a career as a prominent Boston banker. Indeed, he had already succeeded in this arena, becoming "America's youngest bank president" when he assumed control of Columbia Trust at twenty-five.[4] He also worked for the prestigious banking and brokerage firm Hayden, Stone during the period when he was looking after the distribution of R-C movies.

But Joe Kennedy did not become involved in film distribution because he needed a stimulating side interest to take his mind off the dull realm of ledgers, accounts, and portfolios or because he adored the movies. Kennedy jumped in because he smelled money. As would soon become apparent, he had contempt for the business acumen of nearly all the people he encountered in the rapidly expanding film industry and believed he could squeeze more dollars out of their efforts than they even imagined were there. He was right.

Kennedy was appointed to the Robertson-Cole board of directors in 1921. This gave him access to company balance sheets, which he soon realized were "a joke."[5] Two years later he resigned from the board and sold his New England distribution franchise, but he would not forget what he had learned about the precarious financial condition of the organization.

That condition did not improve. In 1922 Robertson-Cole underwent reorganization, including a name change to Film Booking Offices of America, Incorporated. British banking interests took control of the company in 1923. Pat Powers was placed in charge of production, and, for a time, the lot on Gower Street was known as the "Powers Studio," though its releases were still labeled "R-C Pictures." Powers's productions were decidedly second-class, mostly B films and serials, though it did turn out an occasional middling drama featuring such actors as Pauline Frederick, Sessue Hayakawa, and Billie Dove. Film Booking Offices also continued to distribute independent films made by Chester Bennett Productions, Tiffany Productions, Hunt Stromberg Productions, and other companies. It even released *Haldane of the Secret Service,* directed by and starring Harry Houdini for the Houdini Picture Corporation.

Powers was succeeded by B. P. Fineman in 1924. Fineman had experience as an independent producer for First National, but his R-C pictures were no better than Powers's. With the industry growing rapidly as evidenced by the construction of huge theaters in many cities, the formation of new "supercompanies" like Metro-Goldwyn-Mayer, and the emergence of stars like Charlie Chaplin, Douglas Fairbanks, Rudolph Valentino, and Harold Lloyd to delight audiences, R-C remained mired in a quicksand composed of equal parts bad management and poor productions.

In 1926 Kennedy made his move. He offered the rock-bottom sum of $1 million for the whole company, and the British bankers who owned R-C accepted. They had little choice, for the company was deeply in debt. But Kennedy understood something they failed to recognize. He would not need to pump in large sums of new capital or even appreciably improve the studio product to turn things around. Utilizing handpicked lieutenants E. B. Derr, Charlie Sullivan, and Pat Scollard to implement his policies, the new president reduced personnel, streamlined operations, and instituted other money-saving programs that stabilized the company in a short period of time.[6] Hollywood insiders marveled at his accomplishment, leading the trade papers to publish stories for the next several years extolling Kennedy's managerial genius.

Joe Kennedy referred to his new company as FBO (after Film Booking Offices) and installed Edwin King as head of production. Though rarely a candid person, Kennedy admitted that his venture was not ready to compete on the same level with Paramount, Fox, or MGM. "We are trying to be the Woolworth and Ford of the motion picture industry rather than the Tiffany."[7] To those who worked at the studio, FBO must have seemed more like the Cheyenne of the industry. Westerns were its specialty, starring Fred Thomson, Bob Custer, Tom Tyler, Yakima Canutt, Ranger the dog, and others. Among the other employees of R-C and FBO during the early years were a number of directors who would later contribute to RKO's history: Christy Cabanne, Wesley Ruggles, William Seiter, Al Santell, Sam Wood.

In the same year Kennedy took control, the first rumblings of the sound revolution were heard in Hollywood. Warner Bros. premiered *Don Juan*

Figure 1. Joseph P. Kennedy, the famous Bostonian who functioned as a highly compensated midwife at the birth of RKO Radio Pictures. (Courtesy of the Academy of Motion Picture Arts and Sciences)

in New York in August 1926 with a synchronized musical score and sound effects. The film, starring John Barrymore, and the series of sound shorts that accompanied it were received enthusiastically, convincing the Warners to continue their sound film experiments. When *The Jazz Singer* opened fourteen months later, it transformed Al Jolson into an instant movie star and enabled the studio to assume a leadership position in the first great technological breakthrough since the invention of the medium. In 1928 the company released the initial true "talking picture," *The Lights of New York.* The enormous success of that film, along with the popular Movietone sound newsreels distributed by the Fox Film organization around the same time, demonstrated to even the most skeptical executive that he better start building sound stages if he wanted his company to survive.

What does this have to do with RKO? Everything—for RKO was a child of the sound revolution.

But Joe Kennedy was not thinking about the role he would play in the coming of sound—yet. Dissatisfied with the continuing lackluster films pouring forth from his lot on Gower Street, he replaced Edwin King with William LeBaron in 1927. Bill LeBaron was an educated and savvy show business veteran in his early forties. He had served as editor of *Collier's* magazine, written several plays produced on Broadway, and worked on films for Famous Players–Lasky starring Gloria Swanson, Richard Dix, and others.

FBO's product under LeBaron would improve, but only fractionally, because Kennedy continued to keep a tight grip on production expenditures. The studio's biggest star of the late '20s continued to be cowboy hero Fred Thomson. The rest of its films featured lesser-known performers and rarely cost more than $75,000 to produce. This apparently did not discourage Kennedy, who took a presentation credit on most of the releases and billed himself and his colleagues as "Master Showmen of the World" in FBO advertisements. Nevertheless, in July 1928 the company's reputation was such that it placed a notice in *Motion Picture News* declaring that the rumor that FBO planned to "produce pictures of an inferior quality" was absolutely unfounded.[8]

There is no evidence to suggest that Joseph Kennedy had been paying much attention to sound film developments. But when new business opportunities presented themselves, he was quick to take advantage. In January 1928 Kennedy announced that the Radio Corporation of America, the General Electric Company, and the Westinghouse Electric and Manufacturing Company (allied companies at the time) had acquired "a substantial interest" in FBO Pictures Corporation.[9] The original announcement stated that RCA's new sound reproduction and synchronization method not only would be used in FBO films but would also "be available to the entire motion picture industry."[10]

While Warner Bros. and, to a lesser extent, the Fox Film Corporation were industry leaders in the introduction of sound pictures, the company that stood to make the most money was not one of the movie studios. It was A.T. & T., which "through its subsidiaries, Western Electric and Electrical Research Products, [had] captured the entire market for sound equipment."[11]

This did not sit well with David Sarnoff, the young and ambitious leader of Radio Corporation of America. He also understood that substantial income could be generated by the manufacture, installation, and maintenance of sound equipment, both within production facilities and in theaters. Engineers at RCA had developed their own sound-on-film system, which they felt was competitive with the system offered by A.T. & T. They trademarked their system "Photophone."

Photophone, however, had obstacles to overcome. Since nearly all of the important movie companies had signed agreements to use Western Electric equipment exclusively, Sarnoff and the other RCA executives had to find a way to wedge their products into the new market. They needed a foothold within the industry and they found it in FBO. RCA planned to use the movie company to showcase Photophone and as a base camp from which to launch an attack against the near-monopoly of Western Electric. Part of the following first notice of the plan is of particular interest in light of the subsequent formation and development of RKO: "This is the first time that any great industrial organization so closely related to the motion picture business, has ever become a directly interested associate of any motion picture company. It is one of the first times in the history of all business that two organizations representing distinct industries, have associated themselves to further the common interests of both industries."[12] The contention that radio and the movies were related and shared common goals and interests would become a constant corporate refrain in RKO's early years.

February 1928 brought another tantalizing announcement. Joe Kennedy stated that he was joining the Pathe Film Company as an advisor.[13] Despite Kennedy's denials that this meant a merger of FBO and Pathe, Pathe's class A stock nearly doubled in one day.[14] Kennedy emphasized that he would simply be a business advisor to Pathe, without remuneration, and was taking on the job because of his long friendship with J.P. Murdock, the president of Pathe.

The next few months seemed to indicate the veracity of Kennedy's remarks. FBO and Pathe did not merge, at least not right away. But another merger did occur involving FBO. First, the Orpheum circuit of vaudeville theaters amalgamated with Keith-Albee. Almost before the ink was dry on this deal, the newly formed Keith-Albee-Orpheum purchased a significant interest in FBO. As the *Motion Picture News* declared, this transaction completed "a combination . . . that is a tremendous power in the motion picture industry."[15] It was obvious what the author meant. Now, in addition to the financial support and technical expertise of RCA, FBO could count on "assured bookings [for its pictures] in practically 700 theatres which make up the Keith-Albee-Orpheum circuits and affiliated houses in America and Canada."[16] This comment, however, contained one significant misstatement. Many of the vaudeville houses would not be converted into sound film theaters. In actuality, the original chain of K-A-O motion picture theaters would number fewer than two hundred.

B. F. Keith's expanded theater empire retained much of its original thrust and purpose. Vaudeville performances continued for a few years as a significant element in the K-A-O houses. But there was no doubt about the general direction of entertainment trends. The movies were taking over, and live shows were moving swiftly into the background. Within ten years, nearly all the surviving K-A-O theaters would be film palaces exclusively.

By midsummer 1928 the Hollywood movie companies were engaged in a feverish rush to convert to sound. MGM, First National, Paramount, and other companies were building sound stages, installing equipment in theaters, and looking for properties that would make suitable "talkies." FBO was more conservative. Joseph Kennedy advocated a go-slow policy: "The expense that the industry will have to undergo because of talking pictures will be very excessive. . . . It behooves the utmost care and caution in handling this new invention so that it is properly and judiciously placed before the public, and not induce expenditures out of all proportion. There are too many concerns in this business within 6 or 7 percent of going in the red for any wild flinging about of money at present. That is far too small a margin."[17]

William LeBaron echoed his boss's remarks. After decrying the "hysterical" responses of some film people to the coming of sound, LeBaron observed that the silent cinema would probably never disappear completely:

> I believe . . . that there will eventually be three distinct forms of entertainment. First, there will be the legitimate stage play with the human person and voice; second, the talking picture or all talking picture program; and third, the old reliable form of a good silent picture program, during which the patron as [sic] to exert but one sense—the sense of seeing. This enables the patron to relax, where on the other hand, either the stage play or the talking picture brings into use both hearing and sight. The silence and relaxation afforded by the silent drama is one of the chief reasons for its tremendous success.[18]

Thankfully, LeBaron's abilities as a studio head were somewhat superior to his understanding of the pleasures derived from visual entertainment and the psychology of human perception.

The RCA engineers did not proceed so cautiously. They were making impressive strides toward the perfection of the Photophone equipment. In August 1928 an important breakthrough was announced. David Sarnoff informed the press that "complete interchangeability of sound picture films made by Movietone and Photophone processes had been achieved."[19] This meant that films synchronized with Western Electric's optical sound system would be fully compatible with Photophone's projection and sound reproduction equipment and vice versa. Theater owners would not have to worry about whether their system would work with each individual film.

At first, there was some skepticism about RCA's claim. But when FBO's first partial "talkie," *The Perfect Crime*, opened at the Rivoli in New York, Sarnoff was proven correct. The picture, synchronized by Photophone equipment, was run on a Western Electric projector with no technical difficulties.[20]

The fall of 1928 was a time of extraordinary ferment in the film business. Many of the choicest rumors involved Joseph Kennedy and the FBO situation. After several months of speculation about Kennedy assuming the presidency of Pathe, the trade papers reported that he would instead take over First National.[21] This seemed to indicate that FBO and perhaps Pathe, as well, would amalgamate with First National. One week later, however, the entire deal had come undone. Disagreement over complete versus partial authority annulled the arrangement. Kennedy wanted complete autonomy, but the First National board of directors refused to give up all its power.[22]

If Joe Kennedy had been able to gain control of First National, he would have created his own superstudio by merging it with FBO, Pathe, and K-A-O. Now that this was no longer possible, he began to consider exiting the movie business and, of course, how he might realize significant monetary rewards for his short sojourn in Hollywood. David Sarnoff provided the answer.

Kennedy had been working with Sarnoff long enough to know that he coveted FBO and K-A-O. Thus, in October 1928 Kennedy began to put together a deal that would deliver the movie studio, its distribution arm, and the K-A-O chain of theaters to RCA. Consummated late in the month, the transaction made Kennedy a rich man and gave David Sarnoff a vertically integrated movie company whose product would demonstrate the quality of RCA sound equipment, as well as complement his growing radio and radio equipment businesses.[23] Published reports indicated that Keith-Albee-Orpheum and FBO Pictures would now stand together as one giant, $300 million corporation.[24] The stated purpose of the new enterprise was obvious: "to produce, distribute and exhibit perfected synchronized pictures made by RCA's Photophone system."[25]

The merger was confirmed on October 23, 1928—the birthday of RKO. On that day, the venture was officially named the Radio-Keith-Orpheum Corporation, and David Sarnoff became chairman of its board of directors.[26] According to an industry trade journal, Radio-Keith-Orpheum appeared to have unlimited potential: "This new organization will be, at its outset, one of the most powerful and potentially most promising in the amusement industry. The consolidation of an established producing unit with a string of theatres and an important synchronizing company, possessed of existing discoveries and equipped for future research, is a matter of outstanding importance to motion picture circles."[27] David Sarnoff stated that "he did not know who would be president of the new company and he did not know when he [the president] would be appointed, or announced." Employees of the various companies were assured that there would be "a minimum of unsettling of the present personnel."[28]

The new corporation's executive positions were filled in the final month of 1928. Some were surprised when Kennedy did not become the first leader of RKO. Instead, Hiram Brown, whose experience included the public utilities field and the leather industry but nothing remotely related to show business, was named president of the Radio-Keith-Orpheum Corporation. David Sarnoff explained his selection of Brown:

> The Radio-Keith-Orpheum Corporation is building upon a foundation that has no exact parallel in the amusement field. The new company is associated with the Radio Corporation of America and its subsidiary, the RCA Photophone Company; with vaudeville by ownership of the Keith-Albee-Orpheum Corporation; with motion picture production, through acquisition of the FBO Productions Company; and with broadcasting, through the cooperation to be given by the National Broadcasting Company.
>
> The existing personnel of the enlarged Radio-Keith-Orpheum Corporation already includes the entertainment, picture production and theatre experience necessary to the successful operations of the company. It is evident, therefore, that the primary requirement for the administrative task involved in such a combined effort . . . calls for great coordinating and executive ability. The board of directors believe that the company is fortunate in obtaining the services of an administrator whose capacity has been so thoroughly proven in other fields.

Figure 2.   David Sarnoff, president of the RCA Corporation and the true father of RKO. (Courtesy of the Academy of Motion Picture Arts and Sciences)

Mr. Brown will have the advice, support and aid of all the directors. It is my own expectation to maintain an active interest in the affairs of the company and to work closely with Mr. Brown.[29]

Hiram Brown's entry into the entertainment field was not greeted with such unbridled enthusiasm by Martin Quigley, publisher of the *Exhibitors*

Herald and Motion Picture World. While admitting that business executives like Brown could "enrich" the industry, Quigley cautioned Brown to study "the regrettably large number of instances outside executives have come into the industry with little regard and little respect for things as they are, and for the personalities who occupy leading positions in the industry."[30] Quigley's advice was quite sensible. The movie business bore little resemblance to the leather trade or public utilities; indeed, it was a unique industry with demands that rarely cropped up in other professional fields. Hiram Brown needed to do plenty of homework to catch up with the seasoned executives who ran the other Hollywood companies.

Joseph I. Schnitzer became the president of the film production company, still named FBO at the time. Schnitzer, unlike Brown, was well acquainted with the movies. He had begun his career as manager of the Des Moines branch of the Pittsburgh Calcium Light & Film Company during the early days of American cinema. After serving as general manager of Universal, he was president of Equity Pictures from 1920 to 1922. From there he moved to R-C, then FBO, where he was the ranking vice-president when the merger was announced.[31] Although Schnitzer had supervised film production at various points in his career, he would cede this responsibility to William LeBaron, who was retained as production chief. In addition, Lee Marcus was named vice-president of FBO and B. B. Kahane, its secretary-treasurer. Both of these men would play more important roles than Schnitzer in RKO's subsequent history.

Joseph Kennedy resigned as president and chairman of the board of FBO and also gave up his chairmanship of the K-A-O board. To outsiders, it probably appeared that Kennedy was tiring of the vicissitudes and wacky personalities of the movie business. In the midst of the whirlwind negotiations of 1928, Kennedy had organized a new company around Gloria Swanson called Gloria Productions, Incorporated. Erich Von Stroheim was engaged by Gloria Productions to direct Swanson in *Queen Kelly*, resulting in one of "the costliest misadventures of the twenties."[32] The picture, whose budget ultimately ballooned to approximately $800,000, turned out to be unreleasable.

But the real reason Joe Kennedy would play no active role in RKO's future was that David Sarnoff did not trust him. Sarnoff had spent enough time with Kennedy to recognize that the man from Boston was a profiteer. Kennedy's personal fortune, which the RKO deal had enriched by more than $4 million, was his only concern.[33] Sarnoff wanted to work with builders, men with vision determined to make this new company into an outstanding success. He sought executives with values that mirrored his own. Joe Kennedy did not fit the mold.

The formation of RKO was unique in Hollywood history, but it did not take place in a vacuum. The year 1928 will be remembered as a time of frantic conversion to sound *and* the beginning of a consolidation trend that led to the dominance of eight major movie companies. The basic thrust of these companies was theater acquisition. Warner Bros., for example, bought the Stanley circuit in September 1928. The deal gave the Warners two hundred theaters and was worth $100 million.[34] Paramount, Fox, and MGM (the last through the Loew's organization) also increased the number of outlets for presentation of their product, for the belief at this time seemed to be that no company could control too many houses. The accumulation of theaters continued in 1929 and was not even completely quelled by the stock market crash in October of that year. Many of these corporations (including RKO) would regret their profligate acquisitiveness when the Great Depression finally started to pummel the movie business.

Initially, FBO's subpar production history appeared to be of little concern to David Sarnoff. He understood the company had always made movies on the cheap, and he was prepared to give LeBaron a budget sufficient to create better product and upgrade its reputation. Indeed, Sarnoff had big plans. Although he had created RKO primarily to make RCA a player in the sound equipment business, he believed that someday a giant entertainment octopus would emerge from the arrangement, combining talking pictures, vaudeville shows, radio broadcasts (RCA controlled NBC), and television (then in the experimental stage at RCA) into a mutually symbiotic package. A man of extraordinary vision, David Sarnoff could foresee the world of show business conglomerates that dominate public entertainment today. Unfortunately, he could not foresee the economic cataclysm that would soon bring the bullish business environment of late-1920s America to a shocking conclusion; the stock market crashed during the week in which RKO was celebrating its first birthday. Soon afterward, Sarnoff found himself working day and night to lead RCA through difficult times, able to pay only cursory attention to RKO. Lesser men would pilot the new movie concern through the Depression.

2. "It's RKO—Let's Go"

The Brown-Schnitzer-LeBaron
Regime (1929–1931)

On January 25, 1929, FBO ceased to exist. The film production enterprise was renamed RKO Productions, Incorporated. "Officials of the old FBO company," the *Exhibitors Herald-World* reported, "were elated at the change in name, feeling that the new title carries with it some of the glory and prestige of the gigantic Radio-Keith-Orpheum organization, of which RKO Productions is such a prominent part."[1] Three weeks later, it was announced that the studio's product would be trade-named "Radio Pictures." RCA's determination to foster the new enterprise and to remind people that it had brought the company into existence was implicit in both the name and the logograph adopted. The logo at the beginning of each RKO release showed a giant radio tower bestriding the world and beeping out its Morse code signal of "A Radio Picture."

On February 9, 1929, the *Exhibitor's Herald-World* ran a slick four-page advertisement for the new "production machine."[2] It was one of the most hyperbolic ads ever created by an industry that has always wallowed in hyperbole. The graphics depicted a bare-chested, godlike figure towering over a modern metropolis and pointing his index finger at "RADIO PICTURES" on the adjoining page. The text proclaimed: "A TITAN IS BORN . . . eclipsing in its staggering magnitude and far-reaching interests any enterprise in the History of Show Business."[3] The superlatives continued: "one mammoth unit of showmanship . . . fulfillment of daring dreams . . . colossus of modern art and science." *Rio Rita,* "Florenz Ziegfeld's gorgeous smash hit," was accorded a full page in the ad as the company's preeminent production of the 1929–1930 season. The spread was charmingly inflated, meant to convince the world that RKO's auspicious future was practically guaranteed.

Now that his titanic company was up and running, David Sarnoff began his crusade to forge a close relationship between radio and the movies. "Radio has traveled far afield since its establishment as a wireless telegraphic service," he said. "It is on the ocean, aboard ship, in the home; it is now entering the theatre through the development of talking motion pictures. Electrical science has finally synchronized sound and motion on the screen."[4]

In his weekly trade paper column, Martin Quigley echoed the enthusiasm of Sarnoff and his associates: "Great results may be expected from the active entrance into motion picture affairs of the tremendously successful Radio Corporation of America. This vast organization will contribute much to the motion picture industry. In the linking together of the great forces of radio and the principal radio company, with the motion picture, there will be common advantages to both parties, with especial advantages to the public."[5]

The ballyhoo about the new "Titan" glossed over one fact that would cause controversy for years to come. Radio and the movies could never be total allies. Both were primarily mediums of entertainment and both competed, and would continue to compete, for the time the public could devote to leisure activities. The American family that stayed at home to listen to its favorite programs on one of NBC's two networks (the "Red" and the "Blue") instead of venturing out to the local movie house cost film companies significant revenues. And what would happen, some movie insiders wondered, if television became a commercial reality? RCA engineers were actively developing "radio with pictures" for the home. Sarnoff, via RCA, NBC, and RKO, kicked off an aggressive program to join radio and the movies in 1929, but the link wedding these two enterprises would not be easy to forge.

A schizophrenic production climate prevailed in Hollywood at the end of the 1920s. While most studios rushed ahead with sound films, silents remained important because the majority of the world's theaters were not yet "wired." In its first year, Radio released pictures that were 100 percent talking, pictures that were 100 percent silent, talking pictures in silent versions, and silent pictures with music and sound effects added. By the end of 1929, the studio reported it had distributed thirty "dialog" films and fifteen "silents," although some of the "dialog" pictures and some of the "silents" were the hybrids mentioned above.[6]

Without question, however, the studio was committed to sound pictures. And the most spectacular type of sound film in 1929 was the musical. The opening of *Broadway Melody*, MGM's "all-talking, all-singing and all-dancing drama" early in the year at New York's Astor and Holly-wood's Grauman's Chinese Theaters broke all house records.[7] This con-firmed industry-wide speculation that moviegoers would be captivated by lavish examples of this new genre. *Broadway Melody* was based on an original screenplay, but most of the musicals that followed were adapta-tions of Broadway hits: Universal's *Show Boat*, Paramount's *The Cocoa-nuts*, and RKO's first important feature, *Rio Rita*.[8]

RKO's belief in the musical was expressed by Joseph Schnitzer in Feb-ruary. After mentioning *Rio Rita, Syncopation, Hit the Deck*, and *Dance Hall* as examples of RKO attractions soon to be available, he boasted: "We've given William LeBaron carte blanche to make the biggest film musical shows that the public has ever been called upon to witness. They'll get there first and they'll clean up for exhibitors."[9] A sum of $10 million was earmarked for the 1929–1930 production program, signaling "the begin-ning of the great strides which Radio Pictures will take."[10]

Schnitzer must have felt fortunate to have Bill LeBaron running pro-duction at the studio. LeBaron had written several musical plays, includ-ing the Broadway hit *The Echo*. But LeBaron couldn't give his undivided attention to the film musicals. He had other responsibilities, such as over-seeing the expansion taking place at the studio. On January 29 he informed the press that a new soundproof stage would be built and all the standing stages on the lot soundproofed. In addition, three new projection rooms would be constructed, resulting in a total expenditure of $250,000.[11] In March, another quarter-million dollars was appropriated for the new mu-sic department building and the wardrobe and property units. The RKO "Ranch" became a reality later in the year. The studio leased five hundred acres in the San Fernando Valley near Encino to be used for the construc-tion of large standing sets and for filming exterior scenes in action pictures such as Westerns. Later, it would purchase this property. When the expan-sion program concluded, the company had spent $2 million.[12] The studio lot now contained ten production stages, an administration building, an office building, a dressing room building, an editing and projection build-ing, plus four other buildings and a restaurant.

LeBaron and his fellow executives also had to contend with rumors of further mergers involving RKO in 1929. In February, Hiram Brown stated emphatically that RKO was "in business to stay." He continued, "There is no truth to rumors we are to submerge our corporate identities with those of other companies."[13] In June, RKO and Paramount announced that they would form Radio-Keith-Orpheum (Canada) Ltd. The new company was purely an exhibition venture, set up to handle the theater operations of

Figure 3. William LeBaron, the first production chief of RKO. (Courtesy of the Academy of Motion Picture Arts and Sciences)

the two entities in Canada. But the deal sparked a new round of conjecture regarding an alliance of the two companies in the United States and around the world. After all, their Hollywood properties made them next-door neighbors. Again, the rumors were denied by RKO executives.[14]

To strengthen its theater position, RKO purchased the Proctor chain of vaudeville houses—eleven theaters in New York and New Jersey.[15] Later in the year, six Pantages theaters on the West Coast became affiliated with RKO exhibition. Several of the other companies were even more acquisitive. By November, Paramount had added more than 250 theaters to its holdings during the year, Fox had acquired more than 400, and Warner Bros. had gained a substantial number.[16]

The first RKO sales convention was held in June 1929 at the Drake Hotel in Chicago. The executives, declaring that the company "in less than four months [had] assembled an impressive array of stories and authors," listed thirty productions for the 1929–1930 season, with each "to be of major importance."[17] Besides the musical "specials" *Rio Rita, Hit the Deck,* and *Vagabond Lover,* featuring radio star Rudy Vallee, a number of specific titles were announced that would never be produced. For instance, *Upperworld,* to be written by Ben Hecht, author of the profitable *Underworld* for Paramount in 1927, did not become a 1929–1930 release, nor would it show up in subsequent seasons.[18] Failure to deliver on these kinds of commitments upset many company salesmen who promised their theater customers that the titles would be forthcoming. But nothing could be done about it; the production process was hardly an exact science and some projects simply didn't pan out.

Bill LeBaron also expended considerable energy building up the RKO stock company. Given his theatrical roots, LeBaron might have been expected to draw on the New York stage for new talking picture talent. Several of the other companies were doing just that, convincing actors comfortable with dialogue, such as Paul Muni, Claudette Colbert, Edward G. Robinson, the Marx Brothers, Bette Davis, James Cagney, and Spencer Tracy, to move to Hollywood. But while the RKO studio chief cast adrift many of the performers from his FBO productions, he did gamble that established silent-film stars would continue to be box-office magnets in the talkies. Richard Dix and Bebe Daniels were the biggest names among the initial RKO acting contingent, which also included Olive Borden, Betty Compson, Rudy Vallee, and Sally Blane. In addition, silent directors Wesley Ruggles, William J. Cowan, and Mal St. Clair were placed under contract, and, in keeping with RKO's commitment to musicals, Bert Kalmar, Harry Ruby, and Vincent Youmans would be the first composers or lyricists to work for a company that would later employ some of the most famous figures in the musical world for its Astaire-Rogers pictures. Luther Reed, who would oversee *Rio Rita,* was considered the studio's leading writer-director, and LeBaron promised to take time away from his administrative duties to contribute to the writing and production of certain RKO films. His first personal production would be *Rio Rita.*

This looked like a strong nucleus around which to mold a production enterprise. But 1929 was the key transitional year between silent and sound movies, and a good deal of uncertainty prevailed. Many of the important stars of the 1920s, such as John Gilbert, were already losing their hold on the public. Others would quickly rise to take their places. Richard Dix won a poll as the "most popular male star of the era" in 1929, but no one could be sure his popularity would continue in the new talking picture milieu.[19] Ominously, both Dix and Daniels had been released by their former studios. Likewise, who could say if established silent directors such as Mal St. Clair and Wesley Ruggles would be able to master the complicated requirements of sound motion pictures? The assembling of RKO personnel was, thus, a very provisional operation.

But no one seemed worried. In September 1929 a nationwide sales drive was launched with the slogan, "It's RKO—Let's Go!"[20] Six weeks later, shortly after the release of *Rio Rita* and around the time the stock market crashed, company leaders felt so confident, they renewed William LeBaron's contract for three years at a salary of $4,000 per week. According to trade paper reports, the new arrangement made him one of the highest-paid executives in the motion picture industry.[21]

LeBaron's reputation was made by *Rio Rita,* a smash hit from its first day of release. Shortly after Joseph Schnitzer was named president of RKO's film production arm, he had purchased the screen rights to Flo Ziegfeld's musical success for $85,000.[22] The play had opened in New York in February 1927 and, following sixty-two weeks on Broadway, had become a roadshow attraction throughout the country.[23]

The New York premiere of the film in October 1929 represented the high point of the year for the new studio. Joseph Schnitzer described it in a wire to musical director Victor Baravalle: "Too bad you could not have witnessed the opening of *Rio Rita* last night. We had most brilliant audience ever assembled for picture opening and thing went off with a bang. Everybody raving about it in New York."[24] Schnitzer's comments were reiterated by Douglas Hodges of *Exhibitors Herald-World* when the film opened in Los Angeles. Calling *Rio Rita* "a triumph in many ways for many people," Hodges lavished praise on LeBaron, star Bebe Daniels, director Luther Reed, comedians Bert Wheeler and Robert Woolsey, and production and costume designer Max Ree.[25] Audience members agreed, contributing almost $1 million in profits to the fledgling company.

But Hiram Brown and Joe Schnitzer should have been less exhilarated and more circumspect before they offered Bill LeBaron his munificent new contract. *Rio Rita* was in fact a "false positive" that blinded them to the fact that their new company was not off to such an auspicious start. The film itself was essentially a stodgy recording of the stage play, its success attributable to the public's initial love affair with sound movies and especially with the novelty of musicals. A better reading could be gleaned from RKO's other 1929 releases, which were a thoroughly undistinguished lot. Nevertheless, the numbers looked good. RKO corporate profit for the first year was $1,669,564, and David Sarnoff must have been quite pleased with his creation.

In February 1930, Radio-Keith-Orpheum stock was considered one of the best buys on Wall Street. One broker conjectured that the company's theaters would entertain 500 million customers during the year, and the stock could possibly show earnings of $10 per share.[26] Most Wall Street professionals expected that the economic downturn begun by the crash of October 1929 would not last long, while few Hollywood insiders paid the slightest attention to the onset of hard times. Why should they have?— their coffers were overflowing. Warner Bros. realized a profit of $17 million in 1929, while Paramount reported $7 million in earnings, Fox $3.5 million, and MGM $3 million.

Industry experts realized that a large portion of the extraordinary earnings from Warner Bros. was attributable to their sound innovations. They therefore began to consider what might be the next crucial technological breakthrough and how they could profit from it. If they beat their competitors to the next revolutionary innovation, they might realize even more income than the Warners had. Color films seemed to be one possibility, but another concept intrigued company leaders even more: the wide screen.

In November 1929, RKO acquired the rights to a "wide stereoscopic film" process invented by George K. Spoor and P. J. Berggren.[27] Joseph Schnitzer announced that RKO would soon begin the construction of sets and the installation of new cameras and accessories at the studio and expected to have a feature completed within three months. The studio's initial commitment to musicals had a great deal to do with the decision. If the Spoor-Berggren process worked, it would enable RKO to shoot big musical shows "in their natural perspectives, showing complete choruses, the full width of a 52-foot screen or even larger, and full 30-feet high, with all the action of a stage production as naturally as it is seen in three dimensions behind the footlights."[28]

RKO was not alone in mobilizing this idea. Fox, MGM, Paramount, and naturally, Warner Bros. were also working feverishly on their own wide-screen experiments.[29] RKO continued its tests with the enlarged image during the early months of 1930. Three special Spoor-Berggren cameras were delivered to the Hollywood studio for use in several proposed pictures.[30] But by late March, enthusiasm for the new technology had waned. The trade papers speculated that RKO was dropping wide film altogether.[31]

At least one widescreen RKO picture did reach a few select theaters. This was *Danger Lights*, a railroad story that opened in New York in December. Although the Spoor-Berggren process did provide a greater illusion of depth and added excitement to action sequences, there were many drawbacks. Chief among these was the prohibitive cost of the 63.5-millimeter film and cameras. In addition, the technique was not yet perfected; figures in screen-center were always in focus, but those on the sides and in the background appeared fuzzier than normal. The cost of the special equipment needed to project the film represented the final impediment.

RKO was not the only company to reembrace the standard format. Fox tried its "Grandeur" film in newsreels and *Happy Days* and *The Big Trail*, then decided there was no advantage to it. Likewise, MGM's "Realife" process was scrapped after the release of *Billy the Kid*. The 65-millimeter "Vitascope" process that Warner Bros. tried out also joined the ranks of the quickly forgotten, though expensive, experiments. In late November 1930, *Variety* ran the following postmortem: "Burial services are all that remain to end the wide film era which never really was born. Producers are satisfied that the public won't go for it. Furthermore any increase in the width of celluloid is too expensive a proposition all round."[32] Widescreen movies would reappear twenty-two years later; the reception would be more enthusiastic the second time around.

Despite RKO's much reiterated promise to pull together the best production talent in the business, only one potential star was signed in 1930: Irene Dunne. She had gained a reputation as an attractive musical performer in the Broadway production of *Show Boat* and was expected to step rapidly into musical comedy roles at the studio.[33] Hardly an overnight sensation, Dunne did not become a major asset for several years, at which time she was no longer exclusively bound to the company.

Another signing that appeared to have considerable potential involved radio comedians Amos 'n' Andy. Their tenure at RKO, however, represented one of the fastest revolutions of the wheel of fortune in show business history. Following a policy begun with Rudy Vallee (*The Vagabond Lover*, 1929) that reflected David Sarnoff's belief in radio-film synchronicity, RKO signed the well-known personalities (Freeman Gosden and Charles Correll) and starred them in *Check and Double Check*. The movie was so successful that the pair were rated RKO's top stars at the end of the year.[34]

In studying the pattern of gross receipts, however, the company decided that *Check and Double Check* had no "holdover" value whatsoever.
Apparently, audiences turned out to see the two white men in blackface
out of pure curiosity. Studio executives determined that, having viewed
the radio comedians once on celluloid, audience members had little interest in additional adventures featuring the duo. According to *Variety,* they
were "freaks of the screen, good for one film only."[35] RKO's "biggest" stars
of 1930 were dropped by the company with minimal fanfare.

One comedy team that did succeed was Bert Wheeler and Robert Woolsey. They had emerged from the vaudeville circuit and played secondary
roles to Daniels and John Boles in *Rio Rita.* Audiences liked them, prompting LeBaron to feature the pair in a series of wacky comedies. At the end
of 1930, *Variety* called them "head and shoulders above any other featured
draw on the Radio lot."[36] This suggested that the value of the company's
principal stars, Bebe Daniels and Richard Dix, was diminishing rapidly.

RKO's product did not showcase them, or any other members of the studio's thespian group, very well. Its output consisted primarily of musicals,
comedies, domestic dramas, and an occasional "socially important" film like
The Case of Sergeant Grischa. Most were lambasted by critics and paled
when compared to equivalent MGM, Warner Bros., and Paramount productions, but they were not all failures at the box office. *Check and Double
Check* earned $260,000 in profits, and *Hook, Line and Sinker,* an early
Wheeler and Woolsey effort, made $225,000; indeed, more than half of the
1930 releases were profitable, though none approached the blockbuster status of *Rio Rita.* The full impact of the Depression had not yet penetrated
America, and the tastes of the new talking picture audience were less than
discriminating.

But, besides the mediocre product moving through theaters bearing the
RKO logo, there was another ominous sign that business conditions were
about to change for the company and not for the better. *Dixiana,* a top-
budget musical starring Daniels and made by the same team that had
turned out *Rio Rita,* ended up as the year's biggest loser ($300,000).

In October, *Variety* reported that vaudeville programs in RKO theaters
were apparently carrying the company.[37] All but one of the theaters featured variety shows as well as films, and considering the poor quality of
the company's pictures, there seemed to be no other explanation for its
continued profits. Joseph Schnitzer, not oblivious to the situation, began
reading scripts and plays and promised to take a more active interest in production matters. By the end of a gloomy year in which banks began failing

throughout the country, Hollywood rumors started to circulate that Schnitzer would replace LeBaron as head of production, though why anyone felt he could do a better job remains a mystery.[38]

Undeterred by the shriveling economy, RKO executives continued to act as if their company would soon be the flagship of the industry. They agreed to two huge financial commitments in 1930 that would affect the corporation for years to come. The first involved a giant office and retail complex in midtown Manhattan—Rockefeller Center.

Begun just as the United States was sinking into economic purgatory, the Rockefeller venture was a grandiose gamble that would eventually take its place among New York's most famous landmarks. By the time its patriarch, John D. Rockefeller, Jr., drove the last rivet into the twelfth building in 1939, the center had also become another of the famous family's successful investments. But it might never have become a reality if David Sarnoff had not decided to relocate to the uncompleted complex: "For an annual payment of $4.25 million, RCA and its affiliated companies—NBC, RKO, RCA Victor, Photophone—would take control of one million square feet of office and studio space; four broadcasting-equipped theaters; and naming rights to [the] entire western part of the development."[39]

Because Sarnoff was the first leader of a major company to make a commitment to Rockefeller Center, he would be rewarded by having his favorite brands displayed prominently throughout. The dominating, seventy-story central structure would be named the "RCA Building"; it would contain the broadcasting studios for the NBC networks and a large portion of the entire complex would be called "Radio City." In addition, RKO would have a building named in its honor, though, like RCA, it would not be the sole tenant. The original plan also called for four theaters to be operated by RKO.[40] The largest would be devoted solely to variety entertainment and seat seven thousand; the others would present talking pictures, musical comedy productions, and dramas. The film theater was supposed to seat five thousand people.

David Sarnoff could still afford to be an optimist at this point. The 1930 RCA annual report revealed gross income of $137,037,596 and net profit of $5,526,293. RKO was one of the reasons Sarnoff's company was doing well, and he was also undoubtedly pleased to reveal that RCA Photophone "had equipped 1,690 theatres in the United States and 635 theatres in foreign countries with its system of talking picture reproducing apparatus" during the year.[41] In addition, Sarnoff was using his leverage in the new industry to institute lawsuits against Western Electric's near-monopoly on studio sound equipment. Eventually its leaders would back down, allowing the studios that had signed exclusive agreements with Western Electric to shop around.[42] Several of them ended up switching to Photophone.

Although RKO's executives had little choice concerning the move to Rockefeller Center, there is no evidence they expressed any resistance to Sarnoff's plan. Indeed, Hiram Brown enthusiastically predicted a number of future benefits:

> In leasing and operating a theatre devoted to variety, a second devoted to sound, a third devoted to musical comedy, and a fourth to dramatic productions, the Radio-Keith-Orpheum Corporation is providing itself with facilities for the greatest possible development of its business; it proposes to use the technique of all the arts in the creation of its entertainment programs and it will obtain this first hand under this new plan.
>
> In the entertainment center now to be established, RKO will be able to tap the creative talent developed by the variety, musical comedy and dramatic stages and by the air. It will have the opportunity to test the audience's reaction to any musical or dramatic production before deciding to place it before the country on the screen. The association of motion pictures with the sister arts of radio, electrical recording and other forms of entertainment, can only result in raising the values and standard of the screen.[43]

The logic of President Brown's statement is suspect. Why did RKO need to make a substantial financial commitment to Rockefeller Center in order to "test" performers and properties for possible movie presentation? Couldn't the company simply send story experts and talent scouts to vaudeville presentations and to the openings of plays for evaluative purposes? All its competitors did. And what was to prevent the representatives of those other companies from attending Radio City theaters and signing the best talent or bidding for the best plays? Despite Brown's remarks, it appeared rather obvious that the only tangible benefit RKO might derive from the arrangement would be income generated by the theaters.

The second set of negotiations resurrected rumors that had been dormant for more than a year. They involved a potential merger between RKO and Pathe. Although original announcements in 1928 indicated Joseph Kennedy was joining Pathe as an unpaid advisor, Kennedy had quickly taken control of the company. And with a few deft managerial moves he appeared, once again, to have turned a struggling movie enterprise around. The price of Pathe stock had doubled, though Kennedy was less impressed than most investors. While they were buying, he was selling company shares.[44]

At first, speculation concerning a merger between RKO and the Pathe Exchange was flatly denied by both parties. In February 1930, E. B. Derr, executive vice-president of Pathe, stated that "any discussion of an amalgamation between these two film companies has been pure rumor and such a plan has never been under actual consideration."[45]

In May, a press release indicated that Joseph Kennedy was giving up active management of Pathe, though he would remain chairman of the board of directors. It was claimed that the company had shown "marked improvement" under his leadership.[46] In truth, the "improvement" had ended some time before this. The cost of converting to sound production, the business downturn, and the company's lack of a theater chain were pulling it in a southerly direction. Joe Kennedy knew he needed to unload this albatross as soon as he could. So he went back to David Sarnoff.

One can understand why Sarnoff and Hiram Brown might have viewed Pathe as an attractive acquisition. The Pathe Corporation had a long and distinguished history in the movie business. American operations had begun in 1905 when J. A. Berst opened a New York office for the production of features and short subjects by the French concern. The company pioneered the newsreel and, over the years, its newsreels gained wide popularity. Indeed, the famous crowing Pathe rooster logo became a symbol of excellence in the visual news field.[47] Pathe also owned a studio in Culver City and leased an adjacent tract of land, known as the "40 acres," where standing sets could be constructed. Since RKO's Gower Street lot was small with very little room for expansion or the erection of exterior sets, the additional studio space would be a welcome addition. Finally, Pathe also had that precious commodity that William LeBaron had failed to develop in his first years as RKO production chief—movie stars. Constance Bennett, Ann Harding, Helen Twelvetrees, and William Boyd did not reside at the top of the fan magazine polls, but they were bigger names than anyone under exclusive contract to RKO.[48]

What is more difficult to understand is why Sarnoff once again overpaid for a company fronted by Joe Kennedy. After the transfer of papers comprising the FBO and K-A-O deal, Sarnoff had learned that Kennedy's sales pitch had considerably overstated the financial health and value of the companies he was purchasing. Yet he allowed Kennedy to outfox him a second time.

RKO's first offer was sensible; it entailed an exchange of stock that would have cost the corporation no hard cash. But after Pathe's directors refused the plan, RKO agreed to pay a fixed sum. The purchase price was approximately $5,000,000, with a cash down payment of $500,000 and the rest to be paid in 6 percent notes. They would mature in five equal annual installments beginning January 1, 1932.[49] The agreement was finalized on January 29, 1931.

There may have been one additional reason David Sarnoff jumped into the transaction without taking a careful look at what he was buying. Throughout 1930 and early 1931, constant maneuvering threatened to upset the balance of power among the major Hollywood companies. For a time, it appeared MGM and Fox would form an alliance. Then rumors began to spread of a Fox-Warner deal, and several other combinations were proposed. If any one of these mergers became a reality, some industry executives theorized, the new giant studio would dominate the film business, making it nearly impossible for less-powerful outfits to compete. RKO-plus-Pathe was more formidable than just RKO—at least that was the thinking. Because of the worsening Depression and the threat of government action against a monopoly, no "megastudio" arrangement was ever concluded. And RKO quickly discovered that its absorption of Pathe had come at a most inopportune time.

Just how RKO and Pathe would be integrated was a mystery at first. In February 1931 the executives decided to operate RKO Pathe (the new name) as an autonomous unit within the corporate structure. Lee Marcus, who would later superintend RKO's low-budget production unit, was made president of RKO Pathe Pictures, Incorporated. His initial task was "reorganization," which translated into wholesale downsizing. The *Motion Picture Herald* reported that "echoes of the standard, routine and customary statement that everybody's job was safe had hardly died to a whisper when the volleys of the firing squad began."[50] No major shake-up occurred in the newsreel arm of the company. In fact, "Pathe News and Reviews" was made a subsidiary corporation with Courtland Smith in charge.[51] Smith, a former newspaperman, had organized Fox Movietone News and worked on the development of the sound newsreel.

Charles R. Rogers signed a contract to head production at the Culver City plant. He had begun as an independent distributor in Buffalo, then tried the theater business awhile before migrating to Hollywood, where he became a producer. He specialized in Westerns starring Harry Carey and Ken Maynard and was credited with discovering the team of Jack Mulhall and Dorothy Mackaill. The company announced that his budget would be "at least $10,000,000," and twenty to thirty features would be forthcoming, as well as 158 shorts and weekly issues of the newsreel.[52] Once again, however, the heady plans would quickly be sabotaged, this time by forces largely beyond the control of the RKO leaders.

The commitment to Rockefeller Center and the Pathe merger were not the only signs that RKO management still believed the company could be an industry pacesetter. Early in 1931, it released its first epic production, *Cimarron*.

Joseph Schnitzer had purchased the movie rights to Edna Ferber's novel about the birth of the state of Oklahoma for $115,000. Bill LeBaron then assigned Howard Estabrook to write the adaptation and Wesley Ruggles to direct. From the beginning, *Cimarron* was conceived as a special project, but it continued to grow in scope until it far surpassed anything the studio had ever attempted. Final costs amounted to $1,433,000; the combined budgets of *Rio Rita* and *Dixiana* were less than that.

The completed picture received near-unanimous approbation from the tough New York critics.[53] Even Franklin D. Roosevelt, then governor of New York, penned an appreciation: "It is not often that I really wax enthusiastic over a picture, but I think a really big thing has been done in the production of 'Cimarron.' There are so many millions of our present population who have no real conception of the great drama of the opening up of Oklahoma and of Cherokee Strip, that this representation will, for many years to come, have great historic value, even long after it is a 'best seller.' "[54]

A giant advertising campaign accompanied the film throughout its American release, and its reputation grew. It was included among the "Ten Best" of 1931 by both the National Board of Review and *Film Daily*. The climactic accolade came when *Cimarron* received the best picture "Oscar" awarded by the Academy of Motion Picture Arts and Sciences. No other RKO picture (except *The Best Years of Our Lives*, a 1946 Samuel Goldwyn production distributed by RKO) would ever win the coveted statue. Movie companies, however, run on box-office receipts rather than kudos, and here the movie failed its makers. The mammoth production cost was simply too much to recoup; *Cimarron* was carried on the studio books at a loss of $565,000.

The hugely disappointing financial performance of *Cimarron* signaled the end of RKO's short-lived period of prosperity. The corporation reported net profits of $3,385,628 for 1930, but late in that year box-office admissions began to plunge and red ink replaced the black on its balance sheets. Company executives did not express alarm, but they did begin to look for ways to make better, more audience-pleasing pictures.

Early in 1931, Joseph Schnitzer offered the unoriginal theory that production problems were actually story problems. He outlined the following cost-efficient procedure for the development of better material: "We will pay the free-lance writer so much down for an idea submitted and which we approve. Later on we will pay so much more for the story's development. And upon its completion we will make the final payment."[55] This, apparently, is one of the earliest formulations of the so-called step-deal that became popular during the post–studio system era. RKO, however, did not implement the concept with any effectiveness in 1931; instead, it invested in literary properties that were then adapted to the screen by studio writers, or it combed the files looking for silent scenarios to remake as sound vehicles. Only a few new ideas made it into production.

By midyear, everyone in Hollywood recognized that the movies were not "Depression-proof" after all. RKO's leaders had placed their new company in a particularly vulnerable position. The theater expansion of 1929 and 1930 now seemed ill-advised because most houses were losing money. Its productions were among the least appealing in the industry; the studio was spending an excessive amount of money on its pictures, but not getting much value on the screen. There was also something of a war going on between William LeBaron and Joseph Schnitzer concerning who would have the final say in production decisions.

Friction had also developed between Lee Marcus and Charles R. Rogers at RKO Pathe. The economy-minded Marcus became alarmed by the costs of Rogers's initial pictures and the fact that some of his films had begun shooting without finished scripts or final budgets. On May 1, 1931, Rogers wrote Marcus defending his approach. He asked the RKO Pathe president to get the accountants off his back, because "we are not manufacturing shoes and hats. After all, we are producing pictures and it is simply impossible to give definite final budgets until we are almost ready to start shooting." He begged his boss "to have confidence in our judgment out here . . . in order that we may give you the kind of product we are striving for."[56] But Marcus was right to express concern, for his studio was fast becoming a major burden to the corporation.

In June 1931 Hiram Brown arranged a loan of $6 million from the Chemical National Bank to keep RKO Pathe afloat. Marcus's cost-cutting policies and Rogers's productions were not paying off; the subsidiary was losing between $10,000 and $50,000 per week. Reasons offered for the difficulties included a "low inventory" of completed pictures, "markedly increased operating costs of the newsreel under the new regime," and "payments from income to Pathe Exchange, Inc."[57] The operating costs were figured to be $100,000 weekly. However, Marcus and Herman Zohbel, treasurer of RKO, did not appear to be overly distressed. With new capital assured, they predicted that the company would be running in the black by August 15.[58]

They were mistaken. In October, business was so grim that all the Hollywood companies began calling for a reduction in admission prices throughout the nation.[59] RKO Pathe continued to be a millstone around the corporate neck, and something had to be done. A partial solution was reached in early November; the separate distribution systems of the two studios would be merged, saving an estimated $2 million a year.[60] Not surprisingly, this was the first step in a process that would eventuate in the disappearance of RKO Pathe. The move was also the first in a startling series of events that would continue into early 1932.

The next major surprise was the signing of David O. Selznick as the company's new production head in November 1931. Selznick was an enfant terrible. Son of pioneer producer Lewis J. Selznick, from whom he had learned a great deal about filmmaking, Selznick had weathered stormy tenures as a producer for MGM and Paramount. Nevertheless, he did an exceptional job of selling himself to the chairman of the RKO board, David Sarnoff. Sarnoff decided to give Selznick a chance, even though the twenty-nine-year-old had never run a studio before.[61] It was a brilliant, though poorly timed, decision.

In the beginning, no one was quite sure how Selznick would function. Uncertainty arose from the fact that LeBaron was still on staff and Charles Rogers remained the apparent head of RKO Pathe production. Indeed, Rogers, who was in New York when the Selznick deal was completed, must have received mixed signals from upper management about his position. He sent a wire to his second-in-command at the studio, Harry Joe Brown, asking him to "correct the erroneous impression" that Selznick would have oversight of all future production.[62] Brown dutifully copied Rogers's wire and circulated it to all the RKO Pathe department heads. In it, Rogers stated emphatically he would continue "in complete charge of all RKO Pathe pictures with the definite understanding that I am not to supervise any . . . Radio Pictures and Selznick is not to supervise any . . . RKO Pathe Pictures."[63] By late December, however, David Sarnoff had clarified the situation. Selznick would indeed be supreme commander of production at both RKO and RKO Pathe, while the others would fade into the background or soon be looking for new jobs. Charles R. Rogers was the first to go.[64]

Selznick was hired to make superior, successful pictures, a scarce recent commodity at the company. During 1931, RKO and RKO Pathe had released fifty films. Thirty-three were unprofitable and two broke even. Of the winners, only three posted profits of $100,000 or more. *The Common Law,* starring Constance Bennett, and *Cracked Nuts,* featuring Wheeler and Woolsey, topped the list, each bringing home a profit of $150,000. But

Beau Idea lost $330,000, *Friends and Lovers* $260,000, *Rebound* $215,000, and *Fanny Foley Herself* and *The Woman Between* $200,000 each, while five other pictures generated losses of at least $100,000 apiece. And let us not forget the mammoth box-office belly flop of *Cimarron*. It was a horrible year for company product, which helps to explain why Sarnoff decided to take a flier on the inexperienced Selznick.

The fact that RKO's talent cupboard was inadequately provisioned made Selznick's new job even more daunting. The reputations of the RKO Pathe actors had not been bolstered by their 1931 films, and LeBaron continued to strike out in his efforts to attract or develop any star personalities for the Gower Street lot. Appearances in *Cimarron* did lift the careers of Richard Dix and Irene Dunne a bit, but character actor Edna May Oliver probably profited more from the picture than either of them. By the end of the year, she was ranked third behind Dix and Wheeler and Woolsey in the hierarchy of RKO players.[65] A concerted effort was under way to make her the equivalent of MGM's surprisingly potent star, the elderly but vibrant Marie Dressler.

Bebe Daniels left RKO for Warner Bros. during the year, prompting LeBaron to sign Dolores Del Rio. But, otherwise, 1931 was characterized by the wholesale dismissal of many creative personnel. The financial crisis cost the jobs of producer Myles Connelly, directors Harry Hoyt and Paul Stein, and writers Tim Whelan, Anthony Coldeway, Charles Whittaker, and Graham John.[66] Although the studio was not exactly a ghost town when he took over, Selznick would at least have considerable latitude in building his own production team.

Besides Selznick, one other important executive became associated with RKO in 1931. Ned E. Depinet had worked as sales manager for Universal, First National, and Warner Bros. before accepting the position of vice-president and general sales manager of RKO Pathe in February.[67] In a company that became notorious for its executive revolving door, the baronial Depinet would demonstrate remarkable longevity. He soon took control of RKO's distribution arm and remained one of the company's most engaged and visible administrators for more than twenty years.

Depinet and David Selznick's new jobs would be further complicated by their company's frightful financial situation. During the month Selznick was hired, reports that RKO was in danger of total collapse began to circulate. B. B. Kahane, RKO's general counsel, attempted to explain what had happened: "Up to and including May of 1930, RKO boasted of an average daily bank balance of $800,000. Little did we think then that economic conditions and business activities within the company would make it so difficult in May and again in September of 1931 to secure financing." Kahane added that current problems necessitated the procurement of at least $4 million by January just to continue operations. In addition, extra money was required to cover obligations that would come due early in the year. RCA had already advanced $1 million to RKO, but this was only a stopgap.[68]

RKO leaders quickly developed a strategy to salvage the infirm "Titan."[69] Stockholders were asked to approve a recapitalization plan that would give them one new share of RKO stock for four old ones, thereby reducing capital stock by 75 percent and clearing the way for issuance of new stock and ten-year 6 percent debentures totaling $11,600,000. RCA agreed to underwrite the debentures. If stockholders rejected the plan, the company would, almost certainly, fall into receivership.

As expected, several minority stockholders were not enthusiastic. Some considered the deal a stratagem by which RCA planned to acquire total control of the movie organization. Despite management statements that RCA naturally wanted to aid a company it had created and that RKO would be no prize package for RCA, a number of stockholders filed suits and petitions for receivership. Their stock was not worth much, but they could not comprehend the logic of trading four of their RKO shares for one new one.

In early December, Hiram Brown invited twenty newsmen to his office and publicly accepted the blame for RKO's precipitous decline. In addition to the production of bad pictures, Brown listed such disparate causes of company trouble as "the warm summer spell and protracted hot period of 1931, [and] the British going off the gold standard."[70] *Variety* advanced the idea that Brown's biggest mistake was failing to select "showmen as his closest advisors."[71] The same story chastised RKO's leadership for remaining nonchalant about its dreadful productions for almost two years. The decision to place someone new in charge of the studio was considered long overdue.

A majority of RKO stockholders eventually decided that the refinancing plan was best for the future. The plan was ratified during the week of December 12, with the company to receive $11,600,000 on January 2, 1932.[72] As guarantor of the advance, RCA would secure more than one-half the stock and over three-quarters of the debentures; there was no question that David Sarnoff now controlled RKO.[73] Still, the film corporation was no bargain, as both RCA and RKO executives constantly reminded the press. Its stock had plummeted from a high of 50 to a low of 1⅞ in less than two years. A great deal of work would be required just to prop the studio back on its feet.

Watching as RKO's leaders churned their way through the year-end financial imbroglio, exhibitors began to wonder if both RKO and RKO Pathe would deliver product as promised. Some conjectured that the films might be rushed and inferior due to the crisis situation. Lee Marcus assured the theater owners that the companies would discharge their obligations and that there would be "no foolish economies sacrificing either negative quality or distribution efficiency."[74] Despite such promises, RKO production ended 1931 under a very dark cloud. Before most Americans, including President Herbert Hoover, realized what was happening, their country had plunged into a frightening depression. Millions of workers lost their jobs, thousands of businesses failed, and the combined profits of the eight major film studios fell from more than $50 million in 1930 to $6.5 million in 1931.[75]

And, thus, the Radio-Keith-Orpheum age of innocence came to an abrupt end. From a beginning filled with glorious possibilities, through a period of aggressive growth when its theaters prospered and many of its bad pictures made money, RKO awakened in late 1931 to a problematic future. The corporation reported a net loss for the year of $5,660,770 with $3,716,865 of the deficit stemming from production operations.[76] From this point on, nearly every year of the company's history would be a struggle. Only during the movie-crazed World War II era would studio executives be able to smile and watch the profits pour in.

Is there a simple explanation for the poor quality of studio product during RKO's first three years? No, but some tentative answers may be suggested. Beginning with William LeBaron and including its producers, directors, and stars, most of RKO's formative production personnel had earned their reputations in the silent cinema and were slow to adapt to the new medium. Even though studio personnel worked in such talkie-friendly genres as the musical and the gangster film, their efforts were labored and constipated compared to Paramount's *Applause, The Love Parade*, and *Monte Carlo* on the one hand, and to Warner Bros.' *Little Caesar* and *The Public Enemy* on the other. Another problem was the complete failure of RKO to develop any stars during the three years. The attempts to make talking-picture luminaries out of such silent performers as Bebe Daniels and Richard Dix were unsuccessful, and no new faces were discovered or promoted with the exception of Irene Dunne.

RKO's initial leaders made few sagacious decisions during their three years in power. Future administrations would not have the same opportunities that were presented to Messrs. Brown, Schnitzer, and LeBaron; instead, each new RKO executive would be expected to build something great upon the faulty foundation laid down by these gentlemen.

3. "Failure on the installment plan, a ticket at a time"

The Aylesworth-Kahane-Selznick Regime (1932–1933)

A scene that would be repeated all too frequently during RKO history played out during David O. Selznick's first few months as production head. "Reorganization" was the objective—a general realignment and housecleaning intended to get the company on the right track. Many changes were made, the most dramatic coming in the executive ranks.

Early in 1932, it appeared Hiram Brown and Joseph Schnitzer would continue at the top of the RKO totem pole. Schnitzer announced that he planned to move his office back to New York, leaving production matters on the West Coast completely in Selznick's hands.[1] Schnitzer had spent most of 1931 overseeing (some said interfering with) picture making in Hollywood. In February, Hiram Brown was given a vote of confidence by the RKO board of directors, and it seemed that the status quo would indeed be maintained.[2]

But "status quo" did not have the same definition at RKO as it did at other organizations. In April, Schnitzer resigned to enter independent production.[3] Soon after, Brown was replaced by Merlin Hall Aylesworth, the president of the National Broadcasting Company.[4] Brown, it was announced, would continue to serve RKO in an "advisory capacity." He stayed on as a lame duck through the summer, then left the industry forever.

David Sarnoff was the impetus behind the shake-up. As chairman of RKO's board and president of its parent company, the head of RCA had been highly influential from the very beginning. But now that RCA had gained even stronger control of RKO, Sarnoff appeared determined that no more missteps occur. The tall, eloquent Aylesworth was said to be a master organizer with an exceptional flare for public relations; Sarnoff fully expected him to be as successful in guiding RKO as he had been with NBC.

Merlin "Deac" Aylesworth had grown up in the Midwest. He attended several colleges, eventually receiving a law degree from the University of Denver.[5] After practicing law in Fort Collins, Colorado, from 1908 to 1914, he became chairman of the Colorado Public Utilities Commission. In 1919 he accepted the post of managing director of the National Electric Light Association. Aylesworth surrendered this position in 1926 to become the initial president of the National Broadcasting Company, the nation's first coast-to-coast radio network. The incredible aspect of his appointment as president of Radio-Keith-Orpheum was that he planned to devote only half his time to the position. He would retain the presidency of NBC, spending mornings on RKO business and then devoting his afternoons to the broadcasting concern. Aylesworth was supposed to have boundless energy, but the arrangement still raised plenty of eyebrows in Hollywood. RKO, struggling to make money as the United States continued its economic free fall, deserved full-time attention.

The corporation promoted one of its own to replace Schnitzer as president of the production company. Benjamin Bertram Kahane was a "theater man," having begun with the Orpheum circuit in 1919. Later, he worked for Keith-Albee and was secretary and director of the Keith-Albee-Orpheum Corporation when RKO was formed in 1928. He became the first secretary-treasurer of RKO. Like Aylesworth, Kahane held a law degree, which prompted the company to appoint him general counsel in 1929. Kahane's new office was set up at the Hollywood studio; there he would soon become a mediating figure attempting to satisfy the financial needs of Selznick's filmmaking operation while placating New York executive concerns about production expenditures.

Other important executive posts were handed to Ned E. Depinet, now vice-president in charge of distribution, and Harold B. Franklin, the new president of the theater division (Keith-Albee-Orpheum). Lee Marcus was invited to stay on in the vague position of liaison officer between the studio and the home office.

In one year, RKO leadership had been revamped from top to bottom. The new setup had not come inexpensively, however. Several of the former executives held long-term contracts; the only way to dispense with them was to make settlement deals, and these deals dug deeply into RKO's cash reserves. For example, in May, David Selznick convinced B. P. Schulberg of Paramount to hire former production chief William LeBaron. But RKO still had to pay LeBaron $1,500 per week until his contract expired in 1933.[6] The company had been paying LeBaron $3,500 per week since Selznick arrived, even though he had no real function within the production schema. This was, therefore, considered a successful—though costly—arrangement.[7]

One of the reasons Sarnoff had placed Merlin Aylesworth in charge of RKO quickly became obvious. Aylesworth's mission was to unite the entertainment spheres of radio broadcasting and movie production. The idea had been paramount in the formation of RKO, but little of consequence had been made of it during the first three years. Shortly after assuming the RKO presidency, Aylesworth stated that the "picture business and radio business must be co-ordinated" and that radio "should be used to exploit motion pictures." He also announced plans to erect a broadcasting studio on the RKO lot and assured movie executives that radio was no threat to the picture business: "People will never stay at home. They will always seek entertainment elsewhere. Radio programs plugging the idea, 'Go to the theatre' will serve to get people out of their homes and into the motion picture theatres."[8]

The leaders of the other companies were not only dubious but downright antagonistic. Everyone was suffering because of the recent chilling drop in box-office attendance. The lure of "free" radio amusement had to be partially responsible, and thus, radio had become something of a villain in Hollywood circles. Aylesworth's remarks raised questions about his true allegiance. Would he really use NBC to boost the movies and get people back into a picture-going routine—or would he employ RKO to strengthen broadcasting? Deac Aylesworth seemed to think he could do both.

In June, RKO's leader journeyed to Hollywood to present his philosophy of mutual cooperation. A luncheon sponsored by the Academy of Motion Picture Arts and Sciences introduced him to the industry moguls. In his speech, Aylesworth promised that radio could work for the studios, that radio's great "lung power" should be exploited to bring people back to the theaters. He emphasized that there was more than enough business for both concerns and that radio had not ruined the newspapers as had been feared at one time. He also stated that television was still a long way off because there was, as yet, no demand for it.[9]

Unfortunately, Aylesworth coupled his remarks with an excessively gloomy analysis of the current motion picture industry. He predicted that all the companies could be in bankruptcy within ninety days unless drastic measures were taken. He blamed the "ridiculously high salaries" of stars and executives and the overabundance of both theaters and poor pictures for the calamitous state of affairs.[10]

The Hollywood establishment was not impressed. Here was a man whose movie experience amounted to fewer than three months, who was running a company in considerably worse shape than most of their studios, yet had the audacity to predict apocalypse for the entire business. An editorial in the *Motion Picture Herald* criticized Aylesworth for his bad timing and negativity:

> Words such as these are scarcely spoken across a conference table of industry without first a cautious survey of those in the room. That the responsible head of a corporation in the peculiar responsibility of RKO . . . should as daringly become the herald of disaster and ruin in the presence of the American press pertains to an order of logic which he alone, if anyone, can explain.
>
> . . . .
>
> Mr. Aylesworth, in his speech, is selling the motion picture short. . . . He is in the position, as president of RKO, of inviting the public to spend its money at the box office for entertainment merchandise produced under what he sets forth as a condition next akin to bankruptcy. He asks the American picture-going public to buy failure on the installment plan, a ticket at a time.[11]

Aylesworth's impolitic speech won few friends and even fewer supporters for his radio-movie cooperation plan. Speaking in San Francisco two weeks later, he flip-flopped from despair to optimism, predicting that radio would ultimately revive the theater business. He cited a "growing spirit of mutual cooperation between radio broadcasting companies, the theatres and studios" as the basis for his belief that attendance would soon begin to increase.[12]

Aylesworth's Hollywood remarks were too frank, but they were based on reality—specifically the dire financial condition of his new company. Even before he assumed his RKO post, the company catchphrase for 1932 had become "cost-cutting." If the studio hoped to survive a steadily worsening depression, every identifiable strip of fat would have to be pared. A 10 percent salary cut was put into effect for all company employees in January.[13] In February, RKO revealed its plan to eliminate RKO Pathe, merging that production unit with Radio Pictures. This not unexpected decision meant that the Gallic gamecock, long a Pathe trademark, would be seen in future only on company newsreels.[14] The RKO Pathe studio in Culver City was soon closed to effect further savings. It reopened in May, principally as a rental lot available to independent producers.

Despite these efforts, along with belt-tightening procedures in the theater organization, RKO continued to operate in the red. A net loss of

$2,166,713 was reported for the quarter ending March 31.[15] B.B. Kahane then embarked on the unpleasant job of eliminating every inessential aspect of studio operations.

This meant that David Selznick's decisions would be subject to intense scrutiny. But Kahane took an immediate liking to his brilliant young production head, and they soon became a supple and effective team. Selznick's first few months were spent completing pictures set in motion by the previous regime, such as *The Lost Squadron* and *Bird of Paradise,* and preparing the 1932–1933 program. This program would be Selznick's first as studio head; thus, he was determined to make it as impressive as he possibly could.

In April, Selznick abolished the established policy of using "supervisors" or "associate producers" to oversee individual films. Considering the supervisor to be "just another mind to convince, to compromise with and to argue with," Selznick decided to watch over the pictures himself as they would all reflect on him.[16] By that time, David Selznick was working closely with two assistants who would help him in this herculean undertaking— Merian C. Cooper and Pandro S. Berman.

Merian Cooper was a former military man, aviator, and explorer who had made two famous documentary films in the 1920s, *Grass* and *Chang.* The documentaries, shot in some of the most primitive, treacherous regions on earth, so excited Jesse Lasky of Paramount that he hired Cooper to produce *The Four Feathers.* The adventure saga starring Richard Arlen and William Powell turned out well, and Cooper's Hollywood career was launched. David Selznick became friendly with Cooper while both were working at Paramount. Impressed by Cooper's exuberance as well as his production abilities, Selznick invited him to come to RKO and soon offered him opportunities to begin producing films again. Ernest B. Schoedsack, a cameraman and director who had functioned as Cooper's partner since the days of *Grass* and *Chang,* also joined the company.

Pandro Berman was only twenty-seven years old, but he had worked in the movie industry for several years as an assistant director, script clerk, and editor before William LeBaron allowed him to begin producing movies. His initial RKO pictures were *The Gay Diplomat* and *Way Back Home,* neither remotely noteworthy. Thus, Berman fully expected the ax to fall shortly after Selznick took over; indeed, he heard rumors that the New York executives had told Selznick to fire him. Berman was, therefore, shocked when Selznick kept him on as his second assistant and eventually allowed him to resume his producing career.[17]

The immensity of the task facing these men became clear when the company sales convention was held in May.[18] Delegates learned that sixty-two

Figure 4.   David O. Selznick, the wunderkind whose tenure as head of RKO production would be short-lived but memorable. (Courtesy of the Academy of Motion Picture Arts and Sciences)

features would be completed by RKO. The count included pictures that would fill out the rest of the 1931–1932 season, as well as the 1932–1933 offerings, but the figure still looked highly challenging. Unable to attend the convention, David Selznick sent the following terse message: "We are facing a big job and a big responsibility. Anything further I have to say will be said with what I trust will be box office product."[19] The tone of the statement suggested grim determination on the part of the new head of production.

David Selznick would not be required to supervise sixty-two different productions, which must surely have been a relief to him. The reason the company decided to back off of its commitment was, however, deeply disconcerting. Despite all the economizing measures, RKO was still losing alarming amounts of money when summer arrived. This initiated a high level of concern about the progress of production from corporate president Merlin Aylesworth. Soon, B. B. Kahane found himself in the uncomfortable position of middleman between Selznick, who was trying to make the best possible pictures at the least expense, and Aylesworth, who was not always satisfied with the results.

Intimations of a baleful future were contained in a June 4, 1932, letter from Kahane to Selznick. After discussing the distressing "Consolidated Profit and Loss Statement," Kahane continued: "I wish I could write you an optimistic letter and point out some signs of an early improvement in business conditions generally, but the gloom is very thick and black. . . . There is no doubt that the conditions facing the industry are critical. The next six months will be crucial ones and it will be a case of the survival of the fittest." Kahane also expressed regret that he and Selznick had taken over at such an inopportune moment: "I am sorry, David, that you and I, in what is virtually our first year, have these external problems and difficulties to add to the task we have of getting product of quality and merit, produced at a proper cost. It would be so much easier if we did not have to be concerned so much about cost and if we had no worry about our cash requirements being filled. But we must face conditions as they are."[20] Conditions now required the production of forty pictures on a total budget of $9,548,000, or an average expenditure of $238,000 per picture.[21] If RKO's financial status did not worsen and the pictures were solid, Kahane believed the company could make money on such a program.

While Selznick made pictures, B. B. Kahane continued to whack away at studio expenses. On July 11 he wired Aylesworth that overhead had been slashed by $254,000 and, by year's end, savings of $1.4 to $1.5 million could be expected.[22] Among the economies were a reduction of the writers' payroll by $3,000 per week, a reorganization of the prop department that was expected to result in savings of $6,868 per picture, and elimination of certain crew personnel on productions, cutting $40,000 per year. Kahane promised even more reductions and assured his boss that "these savings are being accomplished without impairing quality or detracting from production value. Morale at studio is good and Mr. Selznick is cost conscious and is co-operating with us fully."[23]

Not everyone viewed the cuts so positively. One of the most disturbing new policies was a rule allowing only one take of any scene to be printed.[24] To print more than one take, directors or editors would have to secure approval from a number of different individuals. This policy remained in effect for years and resulted in several ingenious gambits on the part of directors who wanted more latitude to view what they had shot.

Kahane also started looking for ways to rid RKO of some of its highest-paid employees. He was instructed by Aylesworth to study the contracts of all those making large salaries and come up with some plan for reducing the obligations. On July 25, Kahane wrote Aylesworth concerning his findings. The letter provides insight into the "relative worth" of most of the current talent. Constance Bennett, the highest-paid RKO actress, would be more than willing to release RKO from her contract, according to Kahane, because she could certainly make an even better arrangement with one of the other studios. Therefore, unless the company was willing to forfeit its biggest star, nothing could be done about her. Kahane was certain Ann Harding would accept a cut in salary if the company agreed to extend her contract and "give her the right to approve the stories upon which her pictures are based."[25] But since he felt dubious about the contract extension and was firmly opposed to giving Harding story approval, there appeared little chance of a concession.

Three secondary players were reported to be on the way out. Robert Armstrong was making $2,000 per week, a salary deemed "excessive," and would not be renewed when his contract expired on October 18. Kahane thought that Helen Twelvetrees was "virtually through with us" and reported that Ricardo Cortez had failed to develop "a box-office following."[26] But Kahane decided to postpone a final decision about Cortez until just before his contract expired in October. Cortez was then making $1,750 per week.

Among the directors and writers, the only ones felt to be receiving too much money were Wesley Ruggles and Howard Estabrook, the *Cimarron* duo. Although no specific comment was made, it appears implicit that these two holdovers from the former administration were dispensable.

This kind of candid dissection of company personnel may seem cold-blooded, but it was absolutely necessary as the company's financial condition approached a very dangerous plateau. Analyses of this kind would become even more frequent in the future.

Despite the frenzied studio economizing of B. B. Kahane and cuts to Selznick's production budget, RKO continued to lose significant amounts of money. The net loss for the first half of the year amounted to $1,375,170.[27] One problem was vaudeville, formerly a financial asset that had become a decided liability. In the Brown-Schnitzer-LeBaron days, the popularity of vaudeville shows in RKO theaters partially compensated for the company's poor pictures. Now the studio was making better movies, but the variety programs no longer seemed to appeal to customers. In late August the company eliminated vaudeville shows completely in thirty-one of its houses. Harold Franklin, head of RKO's theaters, estimated the move would result in increased gross profit of 237 percent.[28]

Conflict between Aylesworth and Selznick began to develop in late July. Aylesworth wired Kahane refusing Selznick's request to hire Sam Jaffe as studio production manager because he considered the salary requirement exorbitant.[29] He also criticized the studio's failure to complete productions on time (in order to meet distribution dates that Depinet and his staff had promised exhibitors) and mentioned cost overages on certain pictures.

When the telegram arrived in Hollywood, Kahane gave it to Selznick who immediately responded in a heated memo. With respect to Jaffe, Selznick stated emphatically that he considered him the best production manager in the business, a man who could save the company hundreds of thousands of dollars in production costs. The refusal to hire Jaffe because of his salary demands represented, according to Selznick, the worst kind of "false economy": "We would be justified in overpaying a man a great deal in salary, for he could save a yearly overpayment to him in the course of a month's production in any major studio. This, believe me, is not theory or conjecture; it is fact."[30]

He also lamented the inability of New York executives to understand that the studio "daily bulletin" contained only *tentative* release dates for pictures. "I cannot tell you, and neither can anybody else, how long it is going to take me to lick this story or that script," Selznick explained. He concluded the memo with a defense of his administration's performance: "I do not know who in New York is back of Mr. Aylesworth's worries or criticisms. . . . I am both surprised and sorry, because I had hoped, and, indeed, thought, that he was fairly well impressed when he was out here. But I should like you to know that I have no apologies whatsoever to offer for the job we have done; on the contrary, I am proud of it."[31]

Kahane enclosed Selznick's memo in his reply to Aylesworth, dated July 26. His letter amplified Selznick's remarks. He included lists of features and their planned release dates, showing that only three of the last fifteen had been delayed. In addition, Kahane reminded his boss that movie production is unlike other industrial undertakings:

After all, the production of pictures is not like the manufacture of some staple commodity—there are many delays that are inevitable and unavoidable—and some lee-way must be allowed. Knowing our cash condition and realizing how "close to the handle" we must work, I have impressed upon Mr. Selznick the necessity of doing all he possibly can to meet release dates punctually and I am sure we can count on his complete cooperation, but New York must not expect every production to come through exactly as scheduled.[32]

In regard to individual films going over budget, Kahane declared that this also was inevitable, but indicated the averages would be made up by bringing in other films under budget. Thus, the entire program would not cost more than the $9.5 million allowance. *The Conquerors* and *Hold 'Em, Jail* were mentioned as films that would definitely exceed their budgets.

Aylesworth digested the information, along with some other reports he had received, and then dispatched a wire to Kahane designed to impress on him and Selznick the necessity of pinching every penny. He also attempted to mollify Selznick by praising him for giving the company "much better product." Then Aylesworth outlined the seriousness of the current situation: "Fighting as we are here for reduced expenses in the entire RKO organization, we must necessarily strictly limit our expenditures in the studios. . . . Confidentially I had great difficulty in obtaining sufficient monies from our board to carry on our operations at this time due to the general feeling that past experience made it almost impossible for us to carry on successfully and that the present business depression did not warrant a continuation of any business on past financial performances."[33]

The wire continued the complaint about overages on several pictures, and gently scolded Selznick for certain films that were not, in any sense, superior to the shabby efforts of the former regime. *Roar of the Dragon, Roadhouse Murder, Westward Passage, Girl Crazy,* and *Young Bride* were mentioned. Finally, Aylesworth conveyed the news that he had asked for a postponement of the August board of directors meeting, hoping that more definite financial progress could be demonstrated in September or October.

Once again, Kahane asked Selznick to reply. The forthcoming memo was more tempered than his previous effort. After once again explaining that budget overruns on certain pictures would be balanced by reducing the estimated costs of others, Selznick accepted blame for most of the poor films Aylesworth had mentioned. He rationalized the failures thus: "However, conceding . . . that all five of the pictures mentioned are poor, I should like to say that there will always be poor pictures from every studio. Nobody can hit the bull's eye every time, and if out of every group of pictures we send east, one or two of them do not live up to expectations, or are even complete clucks, we would still have the highest percentage of good pictures that any studio has ever turned out."[34]

To prove his point, Selznick listed twelve recent MGM blunders that had been all but forgotten because of the successes of *Grand Hotel* and *Letty Lynton*. After stating that he appreciated "the spirit of Mr. Aylesworth's wire, and know what he is up against," Selznick promised to "conscientiously do everything in my power to cut costs and ease the financial situation."[35] Kahane once again forwarded Selznick's memo with a cover letter assuring Aylesworth that the program would be completed within budgetary limitations.[36]

Apparently, Merlin Aylesworth was beginning to feel that Ben Kahane had become overly supportive of Selznick. He prefaced his next telegram to Kahane with a reminder that "as president of the picture company you must always assume position of New York executive as well as general manager at Hollywood."[37] The implication was that Kahane better start bearing down on Selznick because things were not developing as promised. One aspect that particularly upset Aylesworth concerned A pictures and B pictures. Sometimes the demarcation line between A and B product was indistinct, but usually there was no doubt about the designation of a picture. The RKO program called for forty pictures, alternating regularly between As and Bs. So far, nine pictures had been finished, and Aylesworth was shocked to discover that only one represented the B class. At that rate, the studio would surely exceed its production budget. After instructing Kahane to press Selznick while keeping both the production head and Merian Cooper "inspired," Aylesworth reported that "the next three or four months are the vital period and will tell the future story of RKO and Radio pictures."[38]

Kahane's reply emphasized comprehension of the obligations of his position, of the problems at hand, and of the necessity to produce the correct number of movies within budgetary limitations. Since box-office receipts had fallen even more, he promised to shoot for a $9 million program, rather than one costing $9.5 million:

> I have made all this clear to Mr. Selznick and Mr. Cooper and not a day goes by that we do not discuss the cost of the pictures in production and being prepared for production, as well as commitments, overhead and other factors affecting cost. I go over every preliminary production estimate and if it is in excess of the appropriation I will not pass it

unless I am satisfied that the overage is justified and, if justified, can be made up by reducing the appropriation on other productions.[39]

Kahane was telling Aylesworth that he was doing his job. Significantly, however, the letter contained no mention of the A versus B problem.

Fall arrived, but the movie business could not pull out of its tailspin. RKO's board of directors decided to cut the production budget by $1 million, necessitating the elimination of four pictures from its program. Aylesworth was worried about the new budget and conveyed his feelings to Kahane:

> The entire motion picture business is in precarious position, and the business interests that furnish money have lost confidence in Hollywood production. With all our complications of entering Radio City which is most important to future of Radio Pictures and RKO and with determined successful attempts to cut theatre expense and general RKO expense, it is absolutely essential we show our board of directors we can live up to our word. If we do this successfully, I have no doubt of the future of RKO and Radio Pictures.[40]

Although President Aylesworth was giving most of his attention to financial issues, he had not set aside his commitment to the prospective alliance between radio and movies. There is no evidence his efforts had as yet had any effect on the other studios, but he made sure RKO was doing its part. In August the studio launched an extensive advertising campaign around the joint radio-film exploitation of a mystery called *The Phantom of Crestwood*.

The idea worked as follows: The studio would release Bartlett Cormack's original screen story throughout the United States on October 14. Beginning August 26 and continuing weekly for six weeks, the NBC radio network would present a dramatization of *The Phantom*. The final episode, however, would not be broadcast; instead, listeners would be encouraged to submit their own endings to the story. Awards totaling $6,000, including a first prize of $1,500, would be parceled out for the best dramatic solutions. The winning ending would not, unfortunately, end up in the picture; there would not be enough time to shoot it, since RKO planned to open the film shortly after the final radio broadcast.

The *Motion Picture Herald* was enthralled by the concept: "The ramifications of the campaign will be tremendous. Radio set owners, motion picture fans, newspaper readers, fan magazine readers—and inevitably, all persons with whom these vast potential audiences come in contact, will learn about the picture well in advance."[41] The results of the advertising gimmick, however, were less than earthshaking. The big problem was the story, which had no real freshness to it. *The Phantom of Crestwood* was just another convoluted murder mystery, and its film version starring Ricardo Cortez, Karen Morley, and Pauline Frederick did not excite the audiences of the time. The radio serialization may have helped somewhat—the movie made a modest profit—but it was not deemed worthwhile to offer a sequel to the experiment.

Later in the year, the necessity of reducing the size of the program spawned a new idea in the minds of the Hollywood executives: unit production. This concept was a variation on the United Artists model. A group of independent units might be signed to produce a fixed number of pictures. Financing would be shared by RKO and the independents, with profits to be divided after RKO's standard distribution fee was subtracted. This would assure the company a steady stream of films to meet its exhibitor commitments, while reducing the cash expenditures for production. It would also enable the head of each unit to devote all his time and energy to a limited number of pictures. This appealed to Selznick, who was beginning to tire of managing an entire slate of productions. "A production schedule of forty or more features is too much for one man to supervise in one season," he said.[42]

B. B. Kahane liked the idea. He argued for the unit concept in a letter to Aylesworth dated November 1, 1932:

> I am convinced that in a plan of decentralized production lies the industry's best chance to control costs and schedules and improve the quality of product. For such a plan to be successful, the producers in charge of the independent units must be reliable men of experience and ability and they must have some of their own money invested in their productions, or, if they cannot be induced to share in the cost, they must operate under an arrangement which will penalize them if they exceed their budgets or fail to meet release schedules.[43]

Kahane further explained that no one, in his opinion, would work as hard on a straight salary as he would if he had a stake in the outcome of his efforts. Although convinced of its efficacy, Kahane cautioned that unit production "should be worked out slowly and gradually and without a sharp disruption of the present administration."[44] Pandro Berman, Walter Wanger, and King Vidor were mentioned as potential unit heads.

Remarkably, the year 1932 would be one of the most vital in the history of RKO for talent acquisition, thanks to David Selznick's keen instincts. Despite intense pressure to produce successful pictures, Selznick devoted considerable time to building a solid production team. He turned out to be an astute judge of character as well as capability.

George Cukor, for example, moved to RKO from Paramount, along with Cooper and Schoedsack. Cukor had been part of the influx of New York theater veterans lured to the movie capital by the arrival of sound. After serving as dialogue director for Universal on *All Quiet on the Western Front,* he had been given an opportunity to direct by Paramount. One of his early assignments, *One Hour With You,* resulted in open conflict between the neophyte Cukor and two of Paramount's most powerful men— B. P. Schulberg, then head of production, and Ernst Lubitsch, the company's most famous director.[45] Thus, when Selznick asked him to come aboard at RKO, Cukor was happy to accept. And Paramount seemed pleased to have RKO take over Cukor's contract.

Another individual who would soon become an important RKO employee, Kenneth Macgowan, was signed by Selznick as story editor in January 1932. A cultured gentleman, Macgowan had enjoyed some success as a producer of plays in New York. In short order, he would migrate from the story department to producing pictures.

Without doubt, the company's most serious personnel problem was in the acting arena. The RKO stock company was woeful when Selznick took charge. Even formerly potent stars like Constance Bennett and Ann Harding had been adversely affected by appearances in poor pictures. Selznick knew he would have to build stars; company finances were not in any shape to discuss contracts with expensive talents. If he could sign unknowns to long-term arrangements, then groom them quickly, the production head might be able to pull together a coterie of stars at a modest expense. In light of this approach, the signing of Katharine Hepburn seems a logical, though still rather daring, move.

Hepburn had gained some attention for her New York stage work by the time Selznick and Cukor became interested in her for *A Bill of Divorcement.* In late May, a screen test was made of the actress in New York. She and her agent were both unsatisfied with the results, but the RKO executives decided to look at the test anyway. Lee Marcus was not impressed. He wired Selznick in June stating, "Her salary is one thousand per week which is all out of proportion to her capabilities and experience."[46] Cukor felt differently: "With David Selznick, . . . I saw a test that she'd done in New York. She was quite unlike anybody I'd ever seen. Though she'd never made a movie, she had this very definite knowledge and feeling right from the start."[47]

Selznick evidently concurred, for he overruled Marcus and signed Katharine Hepburn on June 22. The agreement called for one picture to begin production within sixty days, with three weeks guaranteed at $1,250 per week. If the company was pleased with her work, the options in the contract could keep Hepburn in RKO pictures exclusively for five years thereafter. She was, however, free to do theatrical work when not toiling in Hollywood.[48] As B. B. Kahane told Aylesworth, the salary investment in the actress was "comparatively very little if Hepburn makes good."[49]

Late in the year when David Selznick's continuation with RKO became an open question, he nevertheless kept pursuing new talent. He became interested in a dancer who had gained recognition in a stage act featuring his sister Adele as his partner. Once again, Selznick ordered tests to see if the subject photographed well. After viewing the film, Selznick recommended the signing of the performer in this wire to New York story editor Katharine Brown, who doubled as a studio talent scout: "Definitely interested in Fred Astaire for lead in musical to be directed by Sandrich if we can get him on reasonable terms, for period of years; possibly allowing him time off to do play if this becomes absolutely necessary. Conceding that his ears and chin are drawbacks, his personality seems to come through and feel we might be able to drum up considerable publicity interest if we sign him."[50]

Fred Astaire did not sign his first contract with RKO until 1933. As he correctly recalls in his autobiography, the initial commitment was for one picture, three weeks guaranteed at $1,500 per week. With just a trace of bitterness, he stated: "The only risk the studio took at signing was the total sum of $4500. If I had failed, I would have been dropped."[51]

One other 1932 personnel matter involved new contract negotiations with Wheeler and Woolsey. In October, Kahane offered the team $50,000 a picture against 10 percent of the gross receipts, but they held out for a guarantee of $75,000 a picture. Kahane considered this figure too risky. One of his letters reveals how carefully such matters were factored:

> We cannot get away from the fact that the grosses from the Wheeler-Woolsey pictures have steadily and drastically declined, each successive release being less than the preceding one. The fluctuation is from a high of $932,000 to as low as $469,000. . . . It may be that we can develop another team of comedians and build them up to popularity and this would be better than paying Wheeler and Woolsey what seems to be a prohibitive salary in view of the declining grosses . . . and considering also that it has been the history of comedy teams that they go down rather than up in popularity as time goes on.[52]

An agreement was eventually reached between RKO and the comedians. Although details are unclear, the two would continue to appear in Radio Pictures for several more years.

Whether David Selznick would be around to offer them guidance became an open question. His initial agreement with RKO had expired in October, but he continued to work while new terms were discussed. Kahane was in favor of keeping Selznick on and giving him a raise of $1,000 a week and a participation in the profits of the company's films if he continued to oversee all production, or a percentage of the profits of an independent unit if he decided to head one up.

David Selznick had cut filmmaking costs while producing pictures that were, on the whole, both critically and financially superior to those of his predecessors. He had also attracted promising new talent to the company, including Merian C. Cooper, who was then producing a special picture that was the talk of the town. Selznick was so enthusiastic about it that he was squeezing the budgets of other productions to ratchet up the film's special-effects budget. His staff members were still considering different possible titles; they would eventually decide to call it *King Kong*.

Nevertheless, Selznick would still shoulder the blame for a number of 1932 disappointments, even some films started before he arrived. The first two Dolores Del Rio films, *Girl of the Rio* and *Bird of Paradise*, lost $230,000 and $250,000 respectively. And the Ann Harding–Laurence Olivier vehicle *Westward Passage* posted a $250,000 loss. On the plus side, *Bring 'Em Back Alive*, a feature documentary starring adventurer Frank Buck was a nice surprise; RKO's fees for distributing the indie brought the company $155,000 in profits. And Katharine Hepburn's debut became the second most profitable film of the year.

A Bill of Divorcement starred John Barrymore, but Hepburn made an indelible impression under George Cukor's direction. Selznick described the way the first audience responded to her screen introduction:

> Not until the preview was the staff convinced we had a great screen personality. During the first few feet you could feel the audience's bewilderment at this completely new type, and also feel that they weren't quite used to this kind of a face. But very early in the picture there was a scene in which Hepburn just walked across the room, stretched her arms, and then lay out on the floor before the fireplace. It sounds very simple, but you could almost feel, and you could definitely hear, the excitement in the audience. . . . In those few feet of film a new star was born.[53]

When the picture was finished, Selznick feared that RKO's New York office would not publicize and advertise it properly. He dispatched the following memo to several company officers, including Ned Depinet of distribution, Harold Franklin of theaters, and Robert Sisk of advertising:

> Seldom in my experience have I heard such industry enthusiasm for a picture as for "A Bill of Divorcement." . . . I think there is great danger of our under-estimating it, under-advertising it, and underselling it; and I urge that everything possible be put behind it. I know that one or two executives . . . felt that magnificent as it was, the picture was, perhaps a bit above the heads of the audience. I cannot at all subscribe to this conclusion. . . . I have too often in the past seen executives mistaken in stating that "this is box office" and "this is not box office" to believe that any picture of the outstanding quality of "A Bill of Divorcement" does not have every chance to be successful. And even if it is correct that the picture is "too good for our audiences" (and I, personally, don't think there is such a thing), I do not think we should arrive at this conclusion in advance of its presentation to the public.[54]

Selznick was right—the film, which cost $250,000 to produce, turned a profit of $110,000.

Late in the year, however, two costly mistakes combined to undermine Selznick's credibility. *Rockabye,* the final film released under the RKO Pathe logo, was a weepy paean to mother love. RKO bought the rights to Lucia Bronder's play from Gloria Swanson, then rushed it into production because of certain commitments to exhibitors and to Constance Bennett. George Fitzmaurice, who had directed Rudolph Valentino's last film, *The Son of the Sheik,* and two of Greta Garbo's early talkies, was borrowed from MGM. Selznick felt the ideal leading man would be Leslie Howard, but he was unavailable. Joel McCrea, a member of the stock company, seemed the logical choice. Selznick, however, decided McCrea was not "the sensitive mental type" and negotiated a deal with Paramount to use Phillips Holmes instead.[55]

Production went forward without significant problems, but the finished film was a stunning disappointment. B. B. Kahane sheepishly wrote M. H. Aylesworth to explain what had happened:

> The Constance Bennett picture, "ROCKABYE," . . . was previewed while I was in New York and reports had come to me that it was quite bad and that "retakes" were necessary. Upon returning to the Studio I saw the picture myself and was shocked to see how bad it had turned out. As you probably know, we borrowed one of Metro's ace directors, George Fitzmaurice . . . and it is incredible that a director of Fitzmaurice's reputation could bungle a production in the manner he did. I understand that patrons who saw the picture at the preview laughed at scenes in the picture that were intended to get tears.[56]

Believing that release of the film would do "irreparable injury" to both the studio and Connie Bennett, Selznick decided to replace Phillips Holmes

Figure 5. *Rockabye* (1932). Director George Cukor coaxes a performance from June Filmer as Constance Bennett and Joel McCrea look on. Cukor had replaced the film's original director, George Fitzmaurice. (Courtesy of the University of Southern California Cinematic Arts Library)

with Joel McCrea and bring on George Cukor to direct two weeks of retakes. A good deal of rewriting was also part of the salvage effort. *Rockabye* was repaired to the satisfaction of Selznick and Kahane and eventually released, but it was still one of the studio's most feeble efforts. It completed its run a $215,000 loser.

Equally disillusioning was the promised Richard Dix–Ann Harding "super-special," *The Conquerors*. Although Selznick sent memos around discouraging the comparison, here was a film with the same kind of historical breadth and epic sweep as *Cimarron*.[57] Selznick, however, voiced concerns because the cost of *The Conquerors* would be some $800,000 less than that of the Richard Dix–Irene Dunne production. He felt audiences might unfairly compare the less expensive picture to the Academy Award winner.

The studio hired William Wellman to direct from Robert Lord's screenplay, which was based on a story by Howard Estabrook. The finished film encompassed life in the United States from 1870 to the early 1930s. Its central figures were one American family (headed by Dix and Harding) whose three generations triumph over a variety of hardships and lay the foundations of a great midwestern banking institution in the process. Thematically, the film hammered home the notion that after each of its periods of economic crisis, America has not only recovered but forged ahead to greater prosperity. It was obviously designed to provide a tonic to cheerless Depression audiences.

Kahane and Selznick viewed the results with unrestrained enthusiasm. Kahane wrote Ned Depinet on October 4 that *The Conquerors* "should be one of the big pictures of the year."[58] Selznick topped that by predicting it would be "one of the biggest pictures ever made."[59] A Thanksgiving release was chosen, and the initial reviews and attendance were gratifying. Business, however, fell off quickly; it soon became obvious that *The Conquerors* would be a failure. Selznick testily blamed the advertising department for inadequately exploiting the picture.[60] Whatever the causes, *The Conquerors* ultimately was recorded in RKO's ledgers at a loss of $200,000.

David Selznick's contract was a priority for RKO's New York executives, but they had other important matters on their minds as well. The first structure completed in Rockefeller Center was the RKO Building. When it came time to move there, however, the beleaguered company could not pay for all the space it had leased. Neither could RCA afford all the square footage it was supposed to occupy in its tower, so David Sarnoff entered into negotiations with the owners to reduce both commitments. In addition, the opening of the Radio City theaters was fast approaching.

Originally, RKO was supposed to manage four theaters, but the executed plan, thankfully, reduced the number to two. The showpiece of the complex was Radio City Music Hall, a 6,200-seat palace at 50th Street and Sixth Avenue intended for the presentation of stage shows and vaudeville entertainment. Complementing the Music Hall was the RKO Roxy, a 3,700-seat auditorium for movies at 49th and Sixth that would also feature live performances, though not of the same magnitude as those offered by the Music Hall.

Samuel Lionel "Roxy" Rothafel, a showman and radio personality of near-legendary fame, was chosen to direct the operations of both theaters. Rothafel had already worked his magic on a number of New York houses—the Regent, the Strand, the Rialto, the Rivoli, and the Capitol—transforming them from lackluster halls into popular venues and all within six years.[61] At the time he was signed to take charge of the new Radio City theaters, he was running a Broadway theater named after him, the Roxy. Rothafel was renowned for the histrionic presentations he had designed and directed for his theaters, but they had always complemented film screenings. Radio City Music Hall would be different, he said, "This is the first time in my career that I have attempted to do anything without moving pictures. We will not have movies in the Music Hall. We have traveled all over the world to secure talent for it."[62]

Signed to assist Roxy at the Music Hall were music director Erno Rapee, art director Robert Edmond Jones, and Florence Rogge, Martha Graham, and Russell Markert in charge of dancing.[63] December 27, 1932, was the day chosen for the grand opening of the Music Hall, with the RKO Roxy scheduled to present its first movie two nights later. One of the most beautiful theaters ever built, the RKO Roxy would, unfortunately, always be dwarfed by its grandiose sibling. It offered a perfect venue for motion picture presentations.

The great evening arrived and Roxy was ready. The packed house at the Music Hall included such luminaries as William Randolph Hearst, Will Hays, Charlie Chaplin, Amelia Earhart, Leopold Stokowski, Fannie Hurst, Ethel Barrymore, Gene Tunney, Noel Coward, Irving Berlin, Rose Kennedy, and numerous members of the Rockefeller family led by the patriarch of the Center, John D. Rockefeller, Jr. David Sarnoff and Merlin Aylesworth were also on hand to see the show in America's grandest theater. They would all be subjected to nearly five hours of "diversion":

> The opening Music Hall program offered, in addition to numbers by the orchestra and resident ballet and chorus, Taylor Holmes in a musical dramatic sketch, aerialists, comedy by Sisters of the Skillet, Doctor Rockwell and H. Ray Bolger; Fraulein Vera Schwarz of the Berlin Opera, the Tuskegee choir, an allegorical dance by Harold Kreutzberg, excerpts from "Carmen" featuring Titta Ruffo, Coe Glade, Aroldo Lindi and Patric Bowman, the Martha Graham dancers, Weber & Fields and a concluding minstrel number with DeWolf Hopper acting as a master of ceremonies.[64]

Reports indicate that the audience, captivated at first by the scope and sheer magnificence of the Music Hall, became progressively bored, then exhausted with the overblown extravaganza. By the end of the nineteenth and final act at 2:30 the next morning, most of the seats were empty. The journalistic reviews were mixed, but some hinted it would take spectacular shows to make the Music Hall work, considering the darkened times.

It quickly became obvious that the Music Hall was not going to work at all; indeed, it became a disaster unprecedented in show business history. A total of $180,000 was lost during its first sixteen days with admission prices set at $2.75.[65] The solution was to change over to motion pictures as the prime attraction, with stage performances and vaudeville in support. This made the RKO Roxy, which had presented RKO's *The Animal Kingdom* as its premiere attraction, a rather obvious redundancy. Less than two weeks after its opening, the brand-new Roxy was slated to close pending determination of future policy.

Terry Ramsaye analyzed the fiasco in brutal detail, bestowing his heaviest sarcasm on RKO:

> If the seating capacity of the Radio City Music Hall is precisely 6,200, then just exactly 6,199 persons must have been aware at the initial performance that they were eye witnesses to something tremendously more astonishing than the opening of the world's biggest theatre. It was the unveiling of the world's best "bust."
>
> Carefully utilizing every imposing modern resource from money to metallurgy, with the single exception of plain common sense, RKO and its executive control have attained a negative triumph beyond compare in the history of the amusement industry.[66]

After outlining RKO's other corporate misadventures, Ramsaye fixed Merlin Aylesworth in his sights as chief architect of the nightmare:

> It has been somewhat more privately than publicly said that Mr. Aylesworth had little option about assuming the RKO presidency if he were to continue in his happier job as president of the National Broadcasting Company. But, anyway, he did take the additional responsibility, and what he has done about it, and had caused to be done about it, is about as apparent as the Grand Canyon—with about the same cubic content of nothing.[67]

Columbia's *The Bitter Tea of General Yen*, directed by Frank Capra, was the first film to play the Music Hall, with admission prices scaled down to a range of 35 to 99 cents. Stage shows continued, but Rothafel fell ill and disappeared for several months, while Robert Edmond Jones and three members of the administrative staff resigned. Aylesworth, Franklin, and other RKO functionaries held a series of meetings to determine the best plan for RKO's newly leased theaters. Reversing an earlier decision, they announced that the RKO Roxy would not cease operations; *The Animal Kingdom* would continue to screen for an indefinite period.[68]

When the initial arrangement was made, the RKO executives must have been thrilled by the idea of having these extraordinary new houses as the flagships of their theatrical empire. Now the concept had gone very wrong, and they also had to deal with the office space problem. David Sarnoff would eventually negotiate a reduction in both the amount and cost of RKO space in its new building at 1270 Sixth Avenue, plus better terms for managing the theaters. But part of the arrangement was the transfer of 100,000 shares of RKO common stock to the Rockefellers.[69] Now this powerful family owned a stake in the future of the company, and its members would not always remain passive investors.[70]

David Selznick did not attend the opening of the Music Hall, but some of the patrons' idle conversation that evening must have been about him. One day before, *Time* had published a story claiming he had resigned as vice-president in charge of RKO production.[71] It pinpointed a disagreement between Selznick and other RKO officials about implementation of the "unit plan" as a major factor in his decision. The story was, in fact, premature; Selznick continued to work, and contract talks dragged on during the first month of 1933.

This was a particularly bad time for RKO and, by extension, for Selznick's negotiations. The Rockefeller Center debacle was capped by rumors that the company might have lost as much as $10 million in 1932. The eagerly awaited *King Kong* was still in production with costs mounting steadily. And by the end of January the movie enterprise was scraping bottom; the dreaded condition of equity receivership now appeared to be a certainty.

The sticking point that ultimately aborted Selznick's RKO career was not directly related to any of these difficulties. Nor were his salary demands; the company offered him $2,500 per week plus 20 percent of the net profits of the pictures he produced, which Selznick apparently felt was generous.[72] The one aspect of the arrangement that he could not abide was specified in President Aylesworth's final telegram to Kahane concerning the contract: "It must also be specifically understood that the final approval of the story and budget for each picture shall be subject to your written approval and my telegraphic confirmation. In other words, you, as president of Radio Pictures, must have veto power and final authority subject to my confirmation with respect to story subject and budgets."[73] Selznick had informed Kahane in January that he would not accept anything less than total autonomy concerning these matters: "I could not consider accepting the possibility of any veto power on the part of anybody on stories which I might select. This is in all due respect to you [Kahane], but is a matter of policy under any change from which I do not think it possible for a production head to function properly."[74]

It is conceivable that Deac Aylesworth had lost faith in his production leader by this time—that he made this demand knowing it would provoke Selznick to resign. During the remainder of his time as corporate president, Aylesworth never demonstrated an inclination to ride herd on studio matters. Or perhaps he simply wanted to force Selznick to acknowledge his position and authority—to make certain the headstrong young man understood he was subservient to the company's leader. It is even possible that RKO's corporate president had developed a personal dislike for Selznick, who was arrogant, quick-tempered, and sorely lacking in the political skills that were Aylesworth's specialty. Whatever Aylesworth's motivation, the negotiations reached a dead end and were broken off. In early February, Selznick composed a memo to Kahane in which he indicated he could have accepted Kahane's authority. The idea of oversight from three thousand miles away, however, was intolerable: "But an authority in addition to your own on production matters, that of New York—was something else again. I consider that it would be completely impossible for any production head to operate if he had to submit himself to what Mr. Aylesworth demanded—the approval by himself of every script and budget."[75]

The remainder of the memo, written on February 3, 1933, but never sent, included other biting references to Aylesworth and also Selznick's overwhelming disappointment with David Sarnoff. Sarnoff, according to Selznick, had made various promises and given certain assurances, then backed Aylesworth against him at the crucial moment.[76] David Selznick left RKO with a bitter taste in his mouth.

Aylesworth allowed Selznick to slip away just as he was hitting his stride as a production chief. His 1933 releases, including *Topaze*, which was named "Best American Film of 1933" by the National Board of Review of Motion Pictures, could hold their own against product coming from the other studios. Their pictures, however, were completely overshadowed by the most famous film RKO would ever make: *King Kong*.

Begun in August 1932, *King Kong* was not released until after Selznick departed RKO. Known at various times in its production history as *The Beast, The Eighth Wonder,* and *Kong,* the picture was unquestionably the creation of Merian C. Cooper. As described by the movie's star, Fay Wray, Cooper was "a fascinating combination of high imagination, an implicitly rebellious nature, a political conservative, an intellect, an adventurer, and a visionary."[77] He conceived the idea and codirected (with Ernest B. Schoedsack) as well as producing. Cooper's own love of adventure and Barnum-like qualities were captured in the character of Carl Denham (played by Robert Armstrong), who leads the expedition that ultimately transports the giant ape to New York City.

Selznick actually had little to do with the picture, as he readily admitted.[78] But when he and Kahane saw how the film was developing, they ferreted out extra funds to pay for the pioneering special effects that turned *King Kong* into a sensation. Considering the financial situation at the time and the growing strain between the studio and the New York office, this was no small feat. When finally completed, the film had exceeded its original budget by $300,000.

As reports spread about *Kong*, telegrams were dispatched weekly from the distribution department to the studio asking when it would be ready. Everyone understood how much the company needed a major hit. The entire industry also knew that something unique was in the works at RKO; MGM executives even offered to buy the picture for $300,000 to $400,000 more than its production cost. Kahane informed Aylesworth but refused to sell.[79]

The movie finally premiered in early March at both the Radio City Music Hall and the RKO Roxy. It was an instant success. The openings in other parts of the country were equally spectacular. Sid Grauman wired Cooper after its first night at the Chinese Theater in Hollywood: "Never saw greater enthusiasm at any premiere in my past experience of presenting premieres as that of *King Kong*. First time in history of any picture where applause was so frequent and spontaneous. . . . Every person leaving the theatre tonight will be a human twentyfour sheet."[80]

King Kong eventually earned $650,000 for RKO, an impressive figure but not as much as originally hoped. Its later, highly successful reissues suggest that the picture would have fared better if it had been released at a time other than the darkest hour of the Depression. Nevertheless, *King Kong* was like a desperately needed blood transfusion to RKO's corporate body. The film did not save David Selznick's job, nor did it stave off receivership, but it convinced the world that the beeping-tower studio still belonged in the movie business.

David Selznick had gone back to work as a producer for his father-in-law, Louis B. Mayer, at MGM when *King Kong* began its triumphant theatrical run. He was surely pleased for his friend Cooper, but sad that he no longer occupied the most important office on the Gower Street lot. Back in November 1932, when Selznick's RKO contract negotiations had just begun, Mayer offered him the job, which must have been tempting since MGM was the most stable and prosperous studio in Hollywood at the time. But Selznick sent Mayer a long letter refusing the position: "Should RKO wish to continue with me on terms that are mutually agreeable, I feel that I owe them my allegiance. They gambled, and gambled heavily on me. They have permitted me to spend many millions of dollars entirely as I have seen fit. I think I have learned a great deal, and that they, as well as I, are entitled to the benefit of this learning."[81]

After explaining that he was inspired by the idea of making a success of RKO, despite the company's evident difficulties, Selznick ended his missive with additional words of gratitude: "[P.S.] RKO had an amazing faith in me at a time when my previous employers did everything to run me down, and when very few other companies in the business had even an appreciable respect for my ability. Notably, MGM did not change in its disrespect for these abilities from the time I left its employ about six years ago, until a few months ago. Faith, I feel, should be returned with faith."[82]

Thus, Selznick sincerely wished to remain with Radio Pictures, but Aylesworth's intransigence drove him to MGM. No one can say what would have developed had David Selznick continued to function as RKO production chief. But the record of films he brought forth during the following eight years—including *Dinner at Eight, David Copperfield, Anna Karenina, A Tale of Two Cities, A Star Is Born, The Prisoner of Zenda, Intermezzo, Gone With the Wind,* and *Rebecca*—is unequaled in American film history. David Selznick could have given RKO precisely what it needed— a continuity of tasteful, intelligent, and profit-making productions. But Selznick was jettisoned, and the studio never found a comparable replacement. Merlin Aylesworth's decision to drive Selznick away, and David Sarnoff's complicity in the decision, would be one of the most devastating mistakes in the history of RKO.

4. "All this is very distressing to me"

*The Aylesworth-Kahane-Cooper
Regime (1933–1934)*

B. B. Kahane and Merlin Aylesworth were prepared for the departure of David Selznick. They had decided in January that if negotiations with Selznick failed, they would ask Merian C. Cooper to take charge of production.[1] When the opportunity was presented, Cooper first asked Selznick's permission. He felt considerably indebted to Selznick, who had brought him to RKO and supported him throughout his association with the studio. Selznick had no objections, and Cooper accepted the position. Merian Cooper had a big job ahead of him, for at that very juncture the "Titan" was entering equity receivership.

On January 27, 1933, Judge William Bondy of the United States District Court in New York appointed the Irving Trust Company as receiver of the Radio-Keith-Orpheum Corporation. The action came after three separate petitions for receivership were filed in New York, Newark, and Baltimore.[2] The specific circumstance that forced RKO into receivership was its default on some $3.5 million in gold notes, issued to raise operating capital, which came due on January 1, 1933. When the company could not make good on these obligations, court intervention became a certainty. Paramount, a company that reported a deficit of $21 million for 1932, went into receivership at precisely the same time. Warner Bros. and Fox were also tottering on the brink of disaster. The former piled up losses of $14.1 million, and the latter $17 million in the same year. RKO's final corporate loss for 1932 was $10,695,503.

Information disclosed in the subsequent hearings revealed that the theaters were the primary contributors to the company's financial plight: "In spite of subsequent economies which have been effected, profitable operation of these theatres under present business conditions has proved impossible because of the burdens of excessive rents and fixed charges," said

Aylesworth. "A number of these theatres could be profitably run if necessary revisions of rentals and other fixed charges could be effected," he continued. "We hope that a reorganization of such theatres can work out such reductions."[3] *Business Week* referred to the Paramount and RKO situations as retribution "for boom-time financing and new-era purchases."[4]

What was receivership and how would it affect RKO? Put simply, the laws of receivership for corporations were roughly equivalent to the laws of bankruptcy for individuals. When a huge organization could not pay its obligations, wrote prominent attorney Louis Nizer, the "question is not only how to relieve the corporation of its debts but how to permit it to retain its beneficial property, operate its business and divest itself of obligations which are draining its assets."[5] These problems now became the responsibility of the court: "When a corporation goes into receivership the court takes over the administration of its affairs. The receiver is the hand of the court. He is not an agent of the corporation; he is the officer of the court to receive, collect, care for and dispose of the property which has come into the court's custody. The object of the receivership is to avoid the immediate, forced sale of the corporation's property to satisfy pressing creditors."[6] Thus, with the protective wings of the court shielding RKO from its creditors, the company could begin a retrenchment and reorganization that would, it was hoped, lead to a settling of its accounts and the establishment of profit-producing conditions.

Irving Trust Company, a powerful New York banking concern, thus became the agent of the court for RKO. Its job would be to participate in the formulation of economizing and reorganization plans, not to run the corporation. In effect, Irving Trust became the guardian and conscience of the company, constantly prodding RKO executives to set their house in order. A. H. McCausland was named chief representative of Irving Trust with respect to RKO's affairs.[7] Since the theaters were of major concern, the film production company, as well as distribution and the newsreel unit, were exempted from the receivership action.[8] However, when a condition as serious as this grips any corporation, all of its subsidiaries are affected. Radio Pictures was expected to contribute significantly in the all-out drive to get Radio-Keith-Orpheum back on its feet.

One of the questions that must have occurred to many RKO stockholders was why RCA hadn't bailed the movie company out rather than allowing it to collapse into receivership. In fact, RCA was also passing through a difficult time. In May 1930, the U.S. Justice Department had sued RCA, General Electric, Westinghouse, and other companies, charging them with violations of the Sherman Antitrust Act. The goal was to pry these large affiliated organizations apart, opening up competition among them and offering more opportunities for smaller companies to enjoy success in the electrical and electronics marketplace. David Sarnoff was actually in favor of divestiture, but only on his terms.[9] He would work tirelessly for the next two years to make certain that RCA emerged from the action with its core businesses intact and with reasonable working capital to move forward.

He accomplished his goal, and RCA became a freestanding corporation in November 1932. But while he was concentrating on the task, the Depression was lashing his company just like most others. After years of making money, RCA reported a $3.5 million loss for 1931 and would also post deficits in 1932 and 1933. Its common stock, historian Robert Sobel writes, "collapsed from an unadjusted $572 per share in 1929 to $55 in 1930, and then sank to $10 in 1931, as the most spectacular success story of the Bull Market was followed by the Bear Market's most dismal flop."[10] Thus, David Sarnoff was in no position to ride to RKO's rescue. He had his own battles to fight.

B. B. Kahane's commitment to trimming studio costs picked up momentum after the onset of receivership. It would not be said that Radio Pictures had failed to help alleviate the crisis. On February 13 Kahane dispatched a letter to Aylesworth outlining a variety of money-saving moves.[11] Eight highly paid individuals, including writer Howard Estabrook, montage specialist Slavko Vorkapich, and production manager Sam Jaffe, were being dismissed. This alone would save $7,500 a week. The writers' payroll had been cut in half in less than six months, picture costs were being reduced, and average weekly overhead was $9,243 less than it had been during the first six months of 1932. Most important, long-range commitments to stars, directors, writers, stock company players, and the like had been cut back from a figure of $2,172,610 on November 1, 1931, to $731,340 as of January 1, 1933. "The Studio was never in such good condition so far as commitments are concerned," wrote Kahane.[12] All this looked marvelous from an accounting standpoint, but how would it affect the quality and commerciality of RKO productions?

In March, around the time that Franklin D. Roosevelt became the thirty-second president and immediately declared a four-day bank holiday, the Hollywood studios banded together and imposed substantial salary cuts on their employees. Merian Cooper explained the circumstances in a telegram to Katharine Hepburn: "Present nationwide bank situation has so curtailed incoming available cash and has so frozen bank deposits that not one of major companies is in position to carry on as at present this shortage of money has stopped flow of funds necessary to continue production. . . . Only alternative to closing is have every employee in every branch accept fifty percent reduction of salary for eight week period commencing March sixth. Employees in all studios have voted unanimously to accept such cut."[13] The situation was not quite as Cooper described it. Many employees refused to accept the cut in pay, forcing the studios to close down for a few days while negotiations were conducted.[14] The workers were finally convinced to accept an amended proposal, and pay cuts were imposed on the more highly compensated wage earners. In mid-April, the studio made good Cooper's promise and restored full salaries.[15] There is no record of how much RKO saved during the period, but the figure must have been substantial.

By this time, all the companies had formulated strategies designed to help them ride out the hard times. MGM, whose parent, Loew's Inc., boasted a small but well-positioned chain of theaters, powered its way through the rough days. Its star-studded pictures with top-notch production values remained highly popular during the Depression, a period in which it posted enviable corporate profits every year. Even in the horrific year of 1932, MGM made $8 million.

Warner Bros. and Columbia, two of the most carefully managed of the majors, became even more cost conscious. The Warners closed or sold a number of theaters and imposed strict budgetary procedures at the studio. By 1935 the corporation was back in the black, and it would continue to make solid profits for the rest of the period. Harry Cohn tightened a leash around Columbia operations that was already remarkably short. Functioning without theaters and stars, making mostly B pictures and a few As directed by Frank Capra and others, the Cohn studio never posted a loss during the era. While its profits were always modest ($1.8 million in 1935, its best year), Columbia was arguably the most stable of the dark decade's movie companies.

Fox and Universal had more difficult battles. After losing $21 million in 1931 and 1932, Fox reduced payroll in every area as well as pruning underperforming houses from its large theater chain. This enabled the company to post modest profits in 1933 and 1934, but the big turnaround would not come until 1935, when Joseph Schenck took charge as corporate president of the newly formed Twentieth Century–Fox and Darryl F. Zanuck became head of production. Schenck's enlightened managerial skills and Zanuck's excellent story sense and ability to develop stars (such as Shirley Temple, Alice Faye, Tyrone Power, and Don Ameche) enabled the studio to post impressive profits every year except 1940 (a $500,000 loss) until the beginning of World War II. Like most of these companies, it would fare even better after that.

Universal, like Columbia, specialized in B pictures and shorts, with a few A pictures sprinkled in. But it was never run with the same commitment to frugality as Harry Cohn's shop, at least not while Carl Laemmle and his production chief son, Junior Laemmle, were in charge. To fend off catastrophe, the company placed its small theater chain in receivership in 1933 and then sold off the houses. Nevertheless, the Laemmles were still forced out in 1936, but their immediate successors did not do much better. The company lost money every year from 1932 through 1938. Then, a new regime headed up by former RKO employees Nate Blumberg and Cliff Work began to produce more popular pictures. From 1939 on, Universal became a solid if unspectacular profit center.

Under Aylesworth, RKO undertook a careful assessment of its theater operations, but Merian Cooper did not, as expected, implement unit-independent production at the studio. Louis B. Mayer of MGM adopted this model following the illness of his renowned executive producer Irving Thalberg in 1932 and the arrival of David Selznick on the lot in 1933. But Cooper evidently decided he could carry the load, and Kahane announced that the 1933–1934 program would comprise as many as fifty-two features, with the studio prepared to produce almost all of them: "I believe there will not be very many independently made pictures on our new program," said Kahane. "The bulk will be produced in our studio under the supervision of Mr. Cooper and his staff of associate producers. We may arrange deals with outside producers if they have the proper stories, personalities, and so on. We might arrange to release pictures as would be financed by outside producers, or we might even aid in the financing. But we have no definite intention of going out for independent productions."[16] Nevertheless, it was privately hoped that Cooper might use his considerable contacts to lure someone, such as John Hay Whitney, into an independent filmmaking arrangement with RKO.[17]

Cooper's production plan was to work closely with a group of associates who would oversee the individual productions. He promised not to micro-manage their efforts.[18] Chief among the associate producers would be Pandro Berman. Merian Cooper's contract, finally signed in May, gave him a salary of $1,500 per week plus 20 percent of the net profits resulting from the distribution of the pictures produced by him or under his supervision.[19] Berman was so highly regarded by Cooper that the production chief granted him one-eighth of his own profit participation and convinced the studio to

Figure 6.   *The Most Dangerous Game* (1932). Producer Merian C. Cooper, actors Joel McCrea and Leslie Banks, and directors Ernest B. Schoedsack and Irving Pichel pose with the film's hunting dogs. Less than a year after this photograph was taken, Cooper would be placed in charge of filmmaking at the studio. (Courtesy of the Academy of Motion Picture Arts and Sciences)

add another $2\frac{1}{2}$ percent. Thus, Berman now would receive 5 percent of the studio's net profits plus a salary of $1,250 a week. Kahane considered Berman well worth the expense, telling Aylesworth, "I have a very high regard for his judgment, showmanship and ability."[20]

By June, RKO could report some progress in its reorganization. Careful scrutiny of the theaters had resulted in the elimination of twenty-eight nonpaying houses.[21] Still, Harold B. Franklin had to admit to President Aylesworth that "the gross of RKO Theatres . . . has shown a decline in the excess of 40%."[22] One of the biggest, still-unresolved problems involved the Radio City theaters. RKO's leases on the Music Hall and RKO Roxy terminated automatically when the corporation went into receivership. However, a new lease with slightly better terms was immediately agreed to, and RKO continued to operate the mammoth houses. An insufficiency of attractive pictures, high operating expenses, and the continued downturn in general film patronage resulted in losses of $210,000 through May 27.[23] Scuttlebutt again indicated that the RKO Roxy would close. The Rockefellers, apparently, would not permit this; instead, the theater was turned into a second-run house with admission scaled down to a forty-cent top.[24]

Specifics of the 1933–1934 program were revealed at the company's sales convention in late June. One of the interesting bits of information was that RKO planned to drop Westerns completely from its program. The popularity of Westerns had fallen of late, and most of the studios were cutting back in this area.[25] RKO had made a series of very cheap B Westerns between 1931–1933 starring Tom Keene, but Cooper felt it was time to eliminate them.

On the other hand, musicals were poised to make a comeback. That staple of the early years of the company had been in disfavor until recently. The new trendsetter was *Forty-Second Street*, a Warner Bros. backstage story that became an unqualified success and sparked renewed interest in the genre. In late May the *Motion Picture Herald* predicted "a veritable deluge of screen musicals" would be produced during the next few months.[26] RKO was not going to be left behind. *Melody Cruise* opened at about the time the convention commenced and appeared to be a box-office hit. The next effort would be an "aerial musical" entitled *Flying Down to Rio*.[27]

Those in attendance at the sales convention learned that the hoped-for independent arrangement between Merian Cooper and financial tycoon John Hay Whitney had been concluded. Whitney's Pioneer Pictures would complete the "first Technicolor special," to be personally supervised by Cooper and released through RKO.[28]

Production hummed along after the convention. One of the methods Cooper employed to create decent pictures at minimal cost was called "pre-editing."[29] "Pre-editing" simply meant that more time and effort went into preproduction, thus eliminating unnecessary scenes that would probably be cut anyway. This saved time and footage and, logically, production expenses. The key to the concept was having a complete and polished script ready well in advance of the start of a picture.

Even though the studio executives knew they would not be able to lure high-priced talent to RKO in 1933, some upward movement was made in this area. The signing of Fred Astaire, a move first recommended by David Selznick, represented the company's major coup, though no one realized it yet. Francis Lederer, a Czech performer who had starred in films made in Germany and France, also arrived at the studio. It was hoped he could help balance the RKO pool of contract actors, which was heavily weighted with females at the time.

John Ford moved into an office on the lot to shore up the directing department. The initial agreement called for one picture (*The Lost Patrol*).

Later in the year, B. B. Kahane signed Ford to handle three additional films. The terms were quite favorable to the studio. They differed on each picture, but basically Ford would earn a small salary and a percentage of the gross receipts after each production returned twice its negative cost.[30] This was considered a fine deal for RKO, as other studios had paid Ford as much as $50,000 per picture to direct. During this period, Ford and Merian C. Cooper would forge a lasting friendship; after World War II, they formed an independent company together called Argosy Pictures.

Ford was sorely needed, because RKO lost its best director in 1933. After Selznick accepted his producing position at MGM, he convinced George Cukor to join him. RKO let Cukor go, with the proviso that he would return later in the year to direct *Little Women*. The commitment was honored, Cukor directed the picture during the summer, and the results were beyond RKO's fondest hopes. Only then did the executives realize what a mistake they had made, but nothing could be done. George Cukor would be an MGM employee for most of the remainder of his career.

With respect to stars already under contract, Constance Bennett came in for the strongest scrutiny in 1933. In June it appeared that Darryl Zanuck's new Twentieth Century Company might steal Bennett away from RKO. B. B. Kahane reported the situation to Aylesworth and then made the following recommendation: "Despite the fact that Bennett is probably slipping in popularity and is a 'tough dame,' our need for personalities is such that we ought not to lose her. After all we have made a large investment, paying her the big salary we have for all these years and no matter what the story is a Bennett picture is readily accepted by exhibitors as an 'A' picture and is given 'A' playing time."[31]

By November, Bennett's appeal had declined so drastically that Kahane changed his mind. The film that convinced him was *After Tonight*, an espionage story that performed poorly at the box office. Kahane wrote Ned Depinet that even though the company had promised two more Bennett pictures, he doubted even one should be made: "If it is a fact that Bennett can no longer gross enough to get us out of a $300,000. or $325,000. negative, I do not think we ought to make a picture with her even though we have sold one. We can replace the picture on the program with another Harding, or possibly get another set-up to take its place that will be more attractive to exhibitors."[32]

Constance Bennett left RKO but would continue to make movies for other studios. She never regained the level of stardom she had enjoyed earlier in her career, though she was hardly as "washed up" as Kahane believed her to be. If nothing else, this story illustrates the all-encompassing faith that studios held in the star system. A true star could bring the people in to see the most insipid story—or so it seemed. But when a star lost her magnetic powers, it was felt, little could be done to bring her back to public favor. No one seemed to consider the notion of carefully choosing the proper vehicles to showcase an actor's talents and withholding her from anything not appropriate. After all, the studios had commitments, and so a Constance Bennett would be rushed through one film after another to fulfill them.

The one important executive who joined the company in 1933 was Joseph R. McDonough. A former executive vice-president of RCA, McDonough was appointed general manager of Radio-Keith-Orpheum.[33] McDonough had been employed by RCA since 1924, working his way up the company ladder from its accounting department. By the early 1930s, he had become one of David Sarnoff's favorite adjutants. McDonough had a reputation as a tough, shrewd businessman with excellent organizational abilities. His job would be to help with the RKO reorganization, and also to relieve some of the pressure on Merlin Aylesworth. Aylesworth was still trying to juggle the twin orbs of RKO and NBC, a task beyond anyone's capabilities. As McDonough became acquainted with his new job, he would take on more and more of Aylesworth's duties.

Not long after J. R. McDonough joined the team, RKO's leaders were jolted by the news that Merian Cooper had suffered a heart attack. B. B. Kahane described the state of affairs to McDonough on October 5, 1933: "I understand the doctors have told Mr. Cooper that if he will remain completely quiet for three weeks or so and then take it easy for the following three weeks, he will be all right. It will take time to rehabilitate the muscle which has caused the heart trouble. During the latter three weeks of the six week period, I understand that Mr. Cooper will be able to be consulted about business affairs . . . but the doctors think he ought not to return to the Studio until six weeks or so have passed."[34] Pandro Berman agreed to fill the gap until Cooper returned.

RKO tried to keep the news of Cooper's illness quiet—without notable success. David Selznick heard that his friend was seriously incapacitated and might not be able to go back to work for a long time, if ever. He then began probing to discover if RKO would like him to return as production chief. Selznick was, apparently, unhappy at MGM, where L. B. Mayer and Irving Thalberg still dominated company affairs. Kahane wrote McDonough that Selznick desired to return to RKO, then added that this "is a 'crazy' business and most of the 'nuts' are out here."[35] The comment apparently alluded to the wild rumors about Cooper's condition, but Kahane still asked McDonough to consult David Sarnoff about Selznick's interest. McDonough later replied that Selznick "is definitely 'out' as far as we are concerned," and thus RKO once again fumbled an exceptional opportunity.[36] Under the circumstances, however, no other action could have been contemplated, because everyone fully expected M.C. Cooper to be back at work in a few weeks.

They were wrong. Even though his recuperation progressed according to plan, Merian Cooper had been frightened by the attack and decided to continue resting until December.[37] RKO officials had little choice but to grant him the requested disability leave. The situation alarmed them even more than the initial heart attack had. Perhaps Cooper would never return. Even if he did, would he be able to oversee a full program of pictures? The company had to prepare itself for any eventuality.

Oddly, J.R. McDonough then decided to conduct an informal survey to ascertain if Cooper was actually well suited to his position. It would have been more sensible to vet Cooper thoroughly before offering him the job, but the necessity of a rapid switch in production heads had evidently made this impractical. Ben Kahane was asked for his assessment of the man. The only fault Kahane found with Cooper involved story development: "My main concern with Mr. Cooper is that he has been responsible for the absolute waste of thousands of dollars on writing and story costs. We have had to charge off an unusually large amount of money this year because of scripts not turning out satisfactorily and having to be abandoned, and we still have a number of stories that I do not think will be made, and in connection with which we have incurred very substantial writing costs. I would estimate that we would have to charge off at least another $200,000. on the present program."[38]

Other industry insiders provided McDonough with more sweeping criticism of Cooper's abilities. Terry Ramsaye called him a "capable but inconsistent producer": "His chief value is and always will be in the production of an occasional picture of a special type. He is miscast in the chief executive position of a large studio, and probably would be ready to admit this." Leland Hayward, an agent who represented Katharine Hepburn and Fred Astaire, among others, was even harsher: "Cooper is essentially a trick picture producer. He is not well grounded in dramatics and not equipped to supervise the operations of a full studio output. His particular value to any motion picture company is in production of three to five adventure and novelty type pictures per year. He is of a restless nature, not in the best of health, and physically incapable of withstanding the terrific grind connected with the production of forty to fifty pictures a year." Three unnamed Paramount executives concurred with the other appraisals, stating that Merian Cooper "is not a good executive, does not possess any particular artistic ability and . . . his efforts are most productive when confined to trick pictures."[39]

The opinions were somewhat surprising because Cooper's initial performance at RKO looked quite good. His pictures were being made less expensively and returning greater profits than those of his predecessors. *Melody Cruise* earned $150,000 and pointed the way toward more RKO musicals; *One Man's Journey*, a surprise that cost only $150,000 to produce, made a profit of $157,000; and *Morning Glory* would eventually win Katharine Hepburn her first Academy Award and generate $115,000 in earnings. Most happily, *Little Women*, released around the time McDonough was conducting his survey, turned into an immediate blockbuster.

David Selznick had initiated the *Little Women* project in the fall of 1932. His original concept involved modernizing the Louisa May Alcott novel, but he rapidly had his mind changed for him. Selznick described the circumstances in a wire to Ned Depinet: "In connection with 'Little Women,' I was personally very strong for modernizing this story until I was flooded with protests from women who had read the book, whereupon I had the questionnaire put on the radio to determine whether I was wrong. The protests I received plus the response on the radio, clearly indicated to me that it would be almost as great a mistake to modernize this story as it would be for example, to modernize 'A Tale of Two Cities' or 'Uncle Tom's Cabin.' "[40]

After Selznick left RKO, Merian Cooper kept the project alive. Although this type of film was not Cooper's forte, he assigned former studio story editor Kenneth Macgowan to produce and supported his efforts wholeheartedly. MGM honored its promise, allowing George Cukor to return to RKO and direct the film, and extra money was obtained to upgrade the cast. The filming proceeded a bit slower than anticipated, and the picture went over budget, but it was still a relatively smooth, trouble-free production. Before shooting was even completed, enthusiasm began to build. In July, Cooper wired Ned Depinet: "Just want to emphasize . . . that LITTLE WOMEN looks to me from rushes like our most important picture of the year, and think it should be sold as such. If big exploitation campaign is put behind the picture, I think it is liable to be better than any of you all realize. Would suggest emphasizing . . . the four little women, namely Katharine Hepburn, Joan Bennett, Frances Dee and Jean Parker. The four of them together are as charming as anything that has ever been on the screen, and Hepburn gives an even better performance than in MORNING GLORY. . . . Certainly it should be sold as big as KING KONG, if not bigger."[41]

The high hopes were confirmed when RKO previewed *Little Women* on October 30, 1933. Audience response was thunderous, and reviewers in *Variety*, *Hollywood Reporter*, and the *Los Angeles Times* raved about the production.[42] It opened at the Radio City Music Hall in November, breaking all house records. The *Motion Picture Herald* reported that on Saturday of the first week, at one in the afternoon, "3,000 people waited in the street, with 1,000 'standees' in the lobby. Thirty mounted policemen were called to keep crowds in order."[43]

Although Cooper was at that time recuperating from his heart attack, he deserved much of the credit for the movie's success. Selznick wired to congratulate him, and Cooper wrote back:

> My only good point in the picture was deciding to shoot the works on it . . . and in letting no one bother Cukor regardless of how many days he was behind shooting time; also in insisting on getting as many motion picture names as possible, regardless of the cost, and not stinting in anyway [sic] on its physical production.
>
> As you and I both know, the chief credit in any picture basically goes to the director and the writers, and certainly no one could have done a better job than George. You proved yourself right in backing him against the field, and he is undoubtedly one of the greatest directors in the picture business.[44]

Little Women was received enthusiastically wherever it played, eventually earning profits of $800,000 on a remarkably lean production cost of $424,000. The lift it provided to RKO's seven-thousand-plus employees cannot be overstated. Robert Sisk, for example, reported to Ned Depinet that the picture had "put new life" into the sales force in the Chicago exchange: "The stories they all tell of what it has meant to them in combating sales resistance, etc., were most interesting."[45]

The film also revived interest in the "classics" and costume pictures; all the Hollywood studios soon began scrambling after such properties. *David Copperfield* and a host of other 1930s features can be viewed as the progeny of *Little Women*.

And, for once, RKO's timing was impeccable. The movie industry had come under fire in 1932 and 1933 for presenting a variety of sexually titillating (Mae West was the chief exponent) and violent (the gangster genre) films that many Americans considered despicable and dangerous. Their wrath would ultimately force the Motion Picture Producers and Distrib-

Figure 7. *Little Women* (1933). Shooting a scene with the crew and cast members Douglass Montgomery and Katharine Hepburn. The grinning, bespectacled man on the right is director George Cukor. (Courtesy of the Academy of Motion Picture Arts and Sciences)

utors of America (familiarly known as the Hays Office) to create the Production Code Administration in July 1934, a censorship department run by Joseph Breen to make certain subsequent studio product conformed to the 1930 Production Code. *Little Women* was just the kind of film the industry critics felt should be produced; they proclaimed it, sent their children to see it, and made it a part of school curricula, enabling RKO to reap the financial rewards.

Katharine Hepburn probably benefited from the success of *Little Women* more than any other individual. The picture confirmed that in a very short time she had become RKO's most prominent star. Recognizing her new status, the strong-willed young actress had her first clash with company executives in November 1933.

On the morning of November 14, she finished work on a film directed by John Cromwell entitled *Spitfire*. There were still a few scenes to be done, but since the scenes were not considered essential and since the studio had promised Hepburn she could leave for the East Coast on that day, it was determined to close the picture down. Hepburn, however, had different ideas. Kahane described what transpired to J. R. McDonough:

> Hepburn stated that the additional scenes ought to be made and that if we decided to omit them she would never return to Hollywood. When it was pointed out to her that this would be a breach of her contract and that she could be enjoined from working on the stage or in pictures, she replied that she realized this but was satisfied to give it all up and "get married and raise a couple of kids." For the extra day's work to do the scenes in question, she demanded $10,000. She said that if we desired to do so we could withdraw the participation which we recently voluntarily gave her, and that she realized in demanding $10,000. now she might be jeopardizing a possible $25,000. or more, but that she had made up her mind that if she worked one minute after the 15th she would have to be paid $10,000.[46]

Part of Hepburn's disenchantment apparently related to her salary (roughly $2,000 per week, when she worked), which, she realized, was well below her current value to RKO. The company had given her a small percentage of the profits of *Spitfire* as an act of good faith, but this evidently was less than satisfactory.[47] Now she had the president of the studio over a barrel, and he buckled. Kahane authorized the additional scenes and a $10,000 payment to Hepburn.

Hard-nosed J. R. McDonough was outraged by Hepburn's "gun-play," as he put it. He fired off a letter to Kahane, criticizing him for giving in and instructing him to immediately withdraw the actress's participation in the film's profits: "I do not agree with you that not paying Hepburn's demand would have jeopardized the biggest asset the company has. I believe we have now jeopardized the asset by submitting to her first demand. If you will remember when you were in New York I hazarded the guess that Hepburn would employ such arbitrary tactics against us. I believe our submission to the first of her demands has allowed her to open a breach which from now on she will attempt to widen at every opportunity."[48]

Kahane argued vociferously against further alienating the actress by withdrawing her percentage of profits, but McDonough held firm. A letter was sent to Hepburn advising her not to expect any more money from the film. Interestingly, fourteen months later Hepburn coyly inquired when she would be receiving a check for her percentage of the profits of *Spitfire*. The request was made directly to McDonough, who crumbled and coughed up a check for $10,445. B. B. Kahane must have smiled when he received a carbon of McDonough's congenial letter to the star, informing her that any subsequent payments would be made on a monthly basis.[49]

Despite the Hepburn dustup, the end of 1933 contained mostly good news. A second report on the RKO receivership situation, filed in November, noted that a reduction of $5 million in RKO's net loss was expected, and that 58 of the 162 wholly owned RKO theaters had been abandoned.[50] In addition, business at the Radio City theaters had jumped in the fall. Operations for the month of September actually showed a profit before rent of $90,580.87. The report also mentioned that the Cooper production regime had substantially reduced the cost of pictures produced by the Hollywood studio. The report concluded: "Encouraging progress has been made in reducing operating expenses, which has been reflected in improved results in operations, despite the disruption of organization and morale consequent upon the receivership and the decline in theatre attendance during the period of bank closings and moratoria throughout the country. . . . Despite the absence of borrowing and the maintenance of a full motion picture production schedule, consolidated cash reserves have not been depleted to any considerable extent."[51] These were encouraging signs, to be sure.

In December, Merian C. Cooper announced that he was fully recovered and ready to return to the helm. The positive news flowing from Hollywood had clearly trumped the negative assessments of him contained in the McDonough survey; no one seemed inclined to dump Cooper as production chief.

Around the middle of the month, Merian Cooper went to New York to show the board of directors he was a healthy man. A memorandum prepared for the board outlined his production philosophy and his plans for the future.[52] His avowed production preference was, as the experts had predicted, films with a "minimum of dialogue and a maximum of spectacle." These pictures, he argued, were more universal in expression and therefore fared better in the world market than other types of productions. He recommended the following as an example of a spectacular story with the "epic universal quality" he was talking about: "For example, an African *Covered Wagon,* showing the British trek to open up Rhodesia, with Zulus, instead of Indians; lions, elephants and other animal hazards to the settler, instead of deserts, mountains, etc. of Western United States. There are literally hundreds of such pictures which can be made with universal appeal and with a maximum of action and a minimum of dialogue, equally good for the United States, England and the rest of the world."

While admitting that such pictures would be expensive, he reminded the board that *King Kong* and *Little Women* would not have been made if the studio had been locked into a "rigid appropriations system." In addition to revealing his personal preferences, Cooper stated that first priority for the new year would be getting picture production back to an annual rate of forty-eight films. The average had fallen to twenty-eight due to Cooper's illness, and he quoted figures showing that the studio could not make money on only twenty-eight pictures. The costs of studio and distribution overhead alone would absorb all the profits.

This last piece of information is revealing. It shows that RKO had to release a certain number of movies each year to have any hope of success. It was costly to run a studio, a worldwide distribution organization, and a chain of theaters. Without the constant product—on the order of one new picture a week—overhead alone would swamp the enterprise. Given this business model, it seems obvious that expediency was likely to take precedence over quality in the thinking of a studio head. Harry Cohn, Columbia's resident mogul, explained the situation to a young film editor in his own unique style: "Listen, kid, . . . I make fifty-two pictures a year. Every Friday the front door opens on Gower Street and I spit a picture out. A truck picks it up and takes it away to the theatres, and that's the ball game. Now, if that door opens and I spit and nothing comes out, you and everybody else around here is out of work. So let's cut out the crap about only good pictures. How many of those pictures I spit out do you think that I think are any good? . . . I run this place on the basis of making one good picture a year. . . . The rest of them I just have to keep spitting out."[53] One marvels that, working under such demanding conditions, the studios were able to produce as many engaging motion pictures as they did.

In his presentation to the board, Merian Cooper also emphasized his economizing efforts. He had scaled back average shooting time on pictures from 30.8 days (the Selznick figure) to 22.6 days, with corresponding reductions in the cost of production. He offered the following figures:

Negative Costs

LeBaron:	Average of 43 pictures	$342,000
Selznick:	Average of 33 pictures	$293,000
Cooper:	Average of 28 pictures	$204,000

Estimated Profit or Loss

LeBaron:	Average of 43 pictures	Loss $60,000
Selznick:	Average of 33 pictures	Loss $11,000
Cooper:	Average of 28 pictures	Profit $94,000[54]

The comparisons, based on production records beginning with the 1930–1931 program, reflected favorably on Cooper. It should be noted, however, that some of his productions had been initiated by Selznick and the production chief had been ill and absent from the studio for several months; thus, he was not entitled to full credit for the studio's apparent turnaround.

Cooper and the RKO board had plenty to celebrate on New Year's Eve 1933. Shortly before, *Flying Down to Rio* had opened at Radio City Music Hall, and it was selling a lot of tickets. Lou Brock, the head of the shorts unit, had been allowed to produce the first big company musical since *Dixiana* because he had handled *Melody Cruise* successfully earlier in the year. Thornton Freeland took care of the direction.

At the request of Ned Depinet, postproduction was rushed so that *Flying Down to Rio* could open in New York during the holidays. After the film was previewed on December 6, Kahane sent Depinet the following telegram: "Previewed *Rio* last night. Although if we had time could improve picture by additional cutting decided not to hold picture any longer. Think novelty of production plus beautiful music of Vincent Youmans and smartness of whole production should give us fair amount of success. Incidentally Fred Astaire steals picture and think properly handled we have created another new and fresh screen personality."[55] Ben Kahane underestimated the potential of his new musical. *Flying Down to Rio* would turn out to be more than a "fair success"; it brought in profits of $480,000.

Although those profits were sorely needed, this exuberant entertainment would ultimately be more important to RKO for establishing Astaire in movies and introducing the Astaire-Rogers partnership. Astaire received fifth billing but was given ample opportunity to display his talents. As Kahane stated, he overshadowed the nominal stars of the picture, Dolores Del Rio and Gene Raymond. And in the captivating "Carioca" number, a team was cemented that would be RKO's class act for years to come: Fred and Ginger.

Merian C. Cooper returned to work at the studio in January 1934. He approached his job with gusto, bombarding producers and directors with memoranda about the necessity of volume production; about shooting schedules, proper picture length, omission of unnecessary sets; and about meeting tentative start dates.[56] The year 1933 had indeed shown significant improvement for his company. Corporate losses were $4,384,064—less than half the deficit of the previous year. The production company's losses had been reduced even more dramatically, from $4,426,177 in 1932 to $300,134 in 1933.[57] Thus it appeared that with Cooper back in charge, conditions would stabilize and continue to improve. This feeling of equilibrium was short-lived, however.

In early February, Cooper's health started to fail again, and he immediately resolved to take an extended vacation in the Hawaiian Islands. This precipitated a major studio restructuring. At first, it was reported that Cooper had resigned.[58] Two weeks later, however, the trade papers divulged that he would return to his position after the Hawaiian holiday. Pandro Berman would once again provide supervision while Cooper was away. In addition, conferences between Merlin Aylesworth, J. R. McDonough, and the studio executives in Hollywood resulted in the naming of McDonough as president of RKO Radio Pictures. Ben Kahane, who had occupied the position, was made president of RKO Studios, a subsidiary. Ned Depinet was also given another promotion; he now became president of the RKO Distributing Corporation. According to Aylesworth, the purpose of the new setup was to change "the form of the operating organization so that executive activities might be coordinated in Hollywood."[59] Kahane's job would continue much as before, with McDonough assuming some of Kahane's administrative duties as well as taking responsibility for all of Aylesworth's managerial functions. This would free Aylesworth to devote himself exclusively to the company's financial problems. Plans called for McDonough to divide his time between the New York office and the Hollywood studio.[60]

The first few months of 1934 also produced some interesting developments in RKO's relationships with Fred Astaire and Katharine Hepburn. Astaire had gone to England after the completion of *Flying Down to Rio.* He was appearing in the London stage presentation of *The Gay Divorce* when he began to receive the pleasing news that *Rio* was a hit. Something else that he heard vexed him, however. He wrote agent Leland Hayward on February 9, 1934:

> What's all this talk about me being teamed with Ginger Rogers? I will not have it Leland—I did not go into pictures to be teamed with her or anyone else, and if that is the program in mind for me I will not stand for it. I don't mind doing another picture with her but as for this team idea it's out! I've just managed to live down one partnership and I don't want to be bothered with any more. I'd rather not make any more pictures for Radio if I have to be teamed up with one of those movie "queens."[61]

Astaire's comment about having "live[d] down one partnership" referred to the fact that he and sister Adele had been a very successful dance act before she suddenly retired, leaving him to founder for a time. Astaire dispatched another letter to Hayward three days later telling him to "squelch the idea of teaming me with Rogers."[62] Astaire had received several more clippings about the "new team" in the interim.

Leland Hayward responded to his client reassuringly:

> I don't think R.K.O. have any intention of teaming you with Ginger Rogers. When Pandro Berman came through New York on his way West from Europe the last trip, I talked to him several times about the "The Gay Divorce" which they were negotiating for at that time, and told him you were not terribly keen to play forever and ever with Ginger Rogers. Pandro said there was nothing obligatory about having you do same, that she was popular, pretty and good in her pictures, but if you felt so vehemently about not having her with you, they probably would not use her. However, they have no intention of making it a permanent team.[63]

Hayward once again conveyed Astaire's feelings to Pandro Berman, who wired back: "Tell Astaire hold his water regard to teaming. He is not yet ready to be a star in his own right and if we want to bolster him with good support for next few pictures think he should thank us. Ginger Rogers seems to go rather well with him and there is no need assume we will be making permanent team of this pair except if we can all clean up lot of money by keeping them together would be foolish not to."[64] Berman's remarks proved prescient. Astaire's distaste for the teaming notion lessened when the pair became a giant success and he began to receive a percentage of their films' profits. Nevertheless, the dancer would continue to pressure the studio bosses to allow him to make films with other actresses.

The Hepburn matter also came up in February. Now that she had become a star, a renegotiation of her contract was in order. The parties were apparently close to an agreement when she discovered that RKO had exerted some pressure on Paramount to prevent her from making a series of personal appearances in its theaters. This so infuriated the actress that she fired off a personal letter to RKO charging that the two companies were acting in "illegal restraint of trade." She ended the epistle by candidly remarking: "In many respects, I would greatly regret it if my contract with you was broken because of your fraud, collusion, or unfair business tactics, because my association with your operating personnel has been most pleasant and I would leave them with genuine regret. I propose, however, to stand upon every right which I possess, for I have noticed that your company is not at all meek in taking a position, whether it is right or wrong."[65]

Once again, Katharine Hepburn proved to be a tough-minded, volatile businesswoman. While Fred Astaire had Leland Hayward take care of all his studio disputations, Hepburn, who was handled by the same agent, did not hesitate to involve herself personally in the fray. If a lesser player had behaved in this fashion, the studio would undoubtedly have fired her. But Hepburn was too valuable. Kahane set about appeasing her, and a satisfactory contract was eventually worked out. From this point on, RKO would be very careful in its relations with Katharine Hepburn. The studio officials now understood that she had much in common with the iconoclastic, often impetuous characters who were becoming her screen specialty.

Hepburn's close ally at the studio, Pandro Berman, kept the wheels turning while he waited for RKO's official production head to come back to his office. In early April, however, J. R. McDonough received the following news from Merian Cooper:

> I regret to say my return looks quite a time off. I did splendidly out here at first—swimming four or five times a day, and really having a marvellous vacation. Unfortunately, I got caught in the flu epidemic with half the rest of Honolulu, and have to start all over again recuperating. At any rate, am not going to start drawing salary this time until I feel 100% efficient—or anyhow 97.2%. I think you should know, however, that it does not look as if I shall be back to work in April, as I had hoped.[66]

David Sarnoff received a copy of a similar letter from Cooper to Aylesworth and scribbled "All this is very distressing to me" on it.[67] The company executives wanted Cooper back so production could move ahead without further disruption. On April 16 Merlin Aylesworth cabled congratulations to Cooper, whose wife (former RKO actress Dorothy Jordan) had given birth to their first child. Aylesworth added the following suggestion to his cablegram:

> Hope you can return to Hollywood with your family as soon as possible. Honestly believe if you can get back to the office, the work can be so arranged that you can guide the program without getting into detail which pulled you down before. Three or four hours a day twice a week to start with and short days for the first month or two should put you on your feet. . . . Your wise counsel is much needed at RKO Radio Studios and this doesn't mean full responsibility until you are in good health.[68]

Cooper did return in May. J. R. McDonough was then on the West Coast and reported his impressions of the man in a telephone conversation to A. H. McCausland of Irving Trust. According to McDonough, Cooper looked healthy but his behavior seemed erratic. "One day he wants to make any number of pictures and the next day he decides he had better not make any," said McDonough.[69] McDonough informed Cooper that he could not go on working half of the year, that RKO management needed some assurance of his intentions. Cooper gave them his decision by electing not to continue in full charge of production. Instead, an agreement was concluded for him to produce two special films for the 1934–1935 program. The first of these would be *The Last Days of Pompeii*, inspired by the Bulwer-Lytton novel.[70]

Thus, Merian C. Cooper retired after sixteen months as RKO's nominal production head. He had actually functioned in the position for less than half of that time. Pandro Berman, who had reluctantly filled the gap, agreed to continue running filmmaking operations. It was well known, however, that Berman disliked the job and wished to have his own autonomous unit so that he could devote all his energy to ten or so pictures a year.

During the time Cooper was on leave, Berman had grown frustrated by the company's penny-pinching. Nearly all the films he had been allowed to put into production were undistinguished, low-budget projects. These pictures would enable the studio to meet its exhibitor commitments, but Berman knew they would reflect on him and not flatteringly. Berman was also piqued that RKO had practically abandoned the field of bidding for choice literary properties. He became so concerned that he dispatched a telegram to J. R. McDonough in March, imploring him to purchase the Broadway hit *Roberta* for the 1934–1935 season no matter what the price: "Think you can get it for sixty or sixty-five thousand and while you passed up all important properties of the year . . . feel I have reached time where we are desperate and moreover that in *Roberta* we will have property that is far more valuable than anything that has been purchased this year by other companies. We cannot make a go of this business without competing once in a while and this is the time to do it."[71]

B. B. Kahane also had concerns, which he had expressed to McDonough during the previous week. After mentioning *Where Sinners Meet, Let's Try Again, Murder on the Blackboard, We're Rich Again*, and other titles as examples of the mediocre offerings on the studio schedule, he asked McDonough to approve an extra $50,000 for the $175,000 budget of *Down to Their Last Yacht*.[72] This Lou Brock musical production might, according to Kahane, qualify as a class A picture if the extra money were forthcoming. McDonough agreed to the extra funding, but the results were not at all what Kahane hoped.

Stingaree and *Of Human Bondage* represented the only films that Pandro Berman had confidence in. The former, set in Australia, starred Richard Dix and Irene Dunne in a singing role. Berman remarked that he "could have wished for better work . . . in connection with writing and direction," but still expected *Stingaree* to be a "money picture." He was not as certain about Somerset Maugham's *Of Human Bondage*, at least from the money-earning standpoint: " 'Of Human Bondage' from the rushes looks very big. It will probably be one of the best pictures we have ever made. Its box-office I cannot vouch for as it will depend entirely upon whether the public will accept a fine realistic picture which has as its principal star Leslie Howard."[73]

Berman was right. The film, directed by John Cromwell, became one of the most powerful dramas of the year and made a star of Bette Davis, who had been borrowed from Warner Bros., but it would not bring home any profits.

Another of Berman's difficulties was a scarcity of good associates. Since he had forsaken individual productions for overall program supervision, he was left with Kenneth Macgowan, Lou Brock, and a few lesser names to turn out films. Brock, promoted to features after the successes of *Melody Cruise* and *Flying Down to Rio*, had become temperamental and was causing both Berman and Kahane unending grief. Each of Brock's pictures was going over budget. Kahane described the new Brock policy to McDonough:

> Berman and I have had to adopt a new rule with respect to Brock's productions. First of all, we do not feel we can assign him more than one picture at a time. Secondly, we will assign him a writer and let him work on the script until he has brought in a satisfactory script and the Production Department brings in an estimate that is within the appropriation, and will not allow him to make any commitments for directors and members of the cast. This is far from an ideal way of proceeding with productions.[74]

Kahane concurred with Berman that the RKO "producers staff is really extremely weak" and mentioned that they had been "desperately trying to find some available producers who can be relied upon."[75] He and Berman had been unsuccessful, principally because the company could not afford to pay the necessary salaries for reliable, experienced men.

In mid-June, not long after he became the studio's official production leader, Pandro Berman's frustrations boiled over. He addressed a vitriolic memorandum to B. B. Kahane complaining about interference he was receiving—especially from McDonough—and about the studio's policy of lending out such stars as Irene Dunne and Ann Harding.[76] Not only was RKO receiving nothing but vague promises in return, Berman admonished, but the policy was destroying production schedules as well. Berman, who

Figure 8.   *Of Human Bondage* (1934). Actors Leslie Howard and Bette Davis, with crew members and director John Cromwell (wearing hat and positioned next to the actors in the photo). The film made Davis a star, but not for RKO. She had been borrowed from Warner Bros. for this production. (Courtesy of the Academy of Motion Picture Arts and Sciences)

was then only thirty years old, seemed to feel RKO had betrayed him personally:

> I honestly do not see what benefits can come to the company in my being called Executive Producer, which is a ridiculously empty title under the present circumstances. The Company has never adopted these tactics when they were dealing with men who had no interest but a selfish one, and men who spent the company's money blindly for personal glory. Why the company should decide now to thwart every move of one who is most conscious of its desires for economy and efficiency, as well as quality, I cannot understand. I have not asked for this position, but was forced into it against my will out of a sense of loyalty and a desire to be helpful to those I thought my friends.[77]

Pandro Berman asked for an immediate "show-down" on the matter.

Kahane was apparently infuriated by the memo. He shot back a reply the following day, relieving Berman of production oversight and granting his request to head his own unit. Kahane prefaced the memo with references to "nervous and mental strain" that seemed to have affected Berman, and then proceeded to counter every charge the young executive had made. The policy of lending stars to other studios was not disruptive to production, Kahane argued, and RKO had benefited from it. He cited the acquisition of John Boles from Fox for two pictures. With respect to McDonough, Kahane interpreted the situation quite differently than Berman had: "You also claim that you are getting interference from Mr. McDonough. What you call interference, Mr. McDonough does not consider interference at all. As President of the Company and with responsibility as such, Mr. McDonough intends to continue to get into matters of production and discuss stories, properties and policies with you and other producers when he is here."[78]

It is hard to determine who was right about the interstudio lending arrangements. But Berman had a valid gripe about McDonough, notwithstanding Kahane's rationalization. McDonough emerges, in his letters and memoranda and in the descriptions of others, as a strong-minded organization man, an efficiency expert who certainly had his place within the RKO structure. But to thrust this individual into a creative post where he could directly influence the company's production policies seemed foolhardy. J. R. McDonough had no training and no experience in this area; he had, in fact, been working for RKO less than a year. And yet suddenly he found himself in a position to pass judgment on story selection, casting, and other vital matters. No wonder Pan Berman was upset.

Later in June, *Time* magazine called RKO "Hollywood's most mismanaged studio" in an article discussing Berman's resignation as production chief.[79] The story also reported that Benjamin Bertram Kahane himself would take charge. Thus, a new regime was born in the summer of 1934. It would have approximately the same longevity as its two antecedents.

Before Merian Cooper stepped down, Merlin Aylesworth had reembarked on his campaign for a radio-movie symbiosis. The latest idea involved a new NBC radio program. *Hollywood on the Air* would emanate weekly from the RKO studio and feature a stock company composed of RKO players.[80] The movie company had fronted a similar program, called *RKO Theatre of the Air*, in its early days, but it had not been successful. Even though the talent lineup for this new offering was definitely second-class (Chick Chandler, Tom Brown, Thelma White, Dorothy Grainger, and others), and though stars of the first magnitude would participate only occasionally, industry opinion was largely negative. The *Motion Picture Herald* announcement of the show trumpeted: BROADCASTERS ORGANIZE RAID ON HOLLYWOOD FILM TALENT.[81] In June, Hollywood columnist Victor Shapiro reported that exhibitors were upset because "any broadcast by film folk keeps patrons at home."[82]

Aylesworth was unmoved by the criticism. At about the same time *Hollywood on the Air* was being launched, he ordered the studio to begin developing a picture featuring a number of radio talents. The tentative title was *The NBC Revue of 1934*, though it was later changed to *Radio City Revels* in order to provide additional exposure to the entertainment complex.[83] Fred Astaire and Ginger Rogers were projected as the stars of the film with Joe Penner, Block and Sully, and other NBC favorites making appearances. Something like the Paramount "Big Broadcast" films was envisioned. The studio failed to put the package together in 1934, but the idea continued to hold high priority for several years.

The films turned out during Merian Cooper's convalescence periods and the month when Pan Berman was officially in charge were, as Berman predicted, an undistinguished lot. Even though produced inexpensively, most did not make a profit. One of the biggest disappointments was *Man of Two Words* because it introduced Francis Lederer to American audiences. Far short of the star-making vehicle RKO officials were seeking, this odd picture about an Eskimo thrust into British culture ended up losing $220,000. *Stingaree*, which Pandro Berman had predicted would be a "money picture," lost $49,000; *Of Human Bondage*, which garnered many positive reviews, lost $45,000; and four other films lost more than $100,000 each. The most distressing of the four was *Down to Their Last Yacht*.

Producer Lou Brock assured his RKO downfall through his mismanagement of this production. As mentioned previously, Kahane had squeezed extra funding out of McDonough for the film and had put the producer on notice concerning his less-than-professional approach to his job. But Brock did not pay much attention, for the picture quickly trampled its own budget. Kahane was particularly enraged by Brock's signal disregard for proper authorizations: "For instance, the budget called for twenty-one dancers for a period of two weeks and nineteen dancers for a week and a half. You [Brock] actually used fifty-six dancers and I am informed that you ordered the additional dancers and committed the company to the obligation without . . . any proper authorization. Similarly, you engaged forty singers instead of twenty-eight as provided for in the budget."[84]

In the same memo, Kahane stated emphatically that Brock was not "to engage any people, add any scenes, make any expenditure, or incur any obligations not called for by the approved budget unless you first obtain from Mr. Berman or myself authorization or approval."[85] Much can be forgiven an indulgent producer if his efforts are successful. And both *Melody Cruise* and *Flying Down to Rio* had done well. But Brock's luck ran out with this picture. Kahane described his reaction to the previews in a letter to Ned Depinet: "At both sneak previews of the picture the reaction of the audience was unusually unfavorable. I never felt so sick at heart and disappointed at the reactions given any picture as was given 'Down to Their Last Yacht.'"[86] Brock and others at the studio tried to repair the damage with additional editing and sound work, but the movie was beyond help.

Directed by Paul Sloane, this Depression-inspired tale of former millionaires forced to live on their yacht and work for a living, which somehow devolves into a South Seas adventure, quickly became known around the lot as the worst film RKO had ever made; the company was fortunate it lost only $198,000.

Although *Spitfire* was the biggest success ($113,000 profit) of this group of pictures, it actually turned out to be more disastrous in the long run than *Down to Their Last Yacht.* Lula Vollmer's play *Trigger* was purchased by RKO with the intention of starring Dorothy Jordan as uninhibited mountain girl Trigger Hicks. When Katharine Hepburn learned about the property, she became enamored of the character and used her influence with Pandro Berman to secure *Trigger* for herself.[87] John Cromwell was assigned to direct, and the film was made in late 1933. Production culminated in Hepburn's celebrated "$10,000 holdup," described earlier in this chapter.

Spitfire kicked off public disenchantment with Katharine Hepburn that would grow throughout most of the rest of the decade. Her portrayal of Trigger Hicks must surely be the worst performance of her career. She was completely miscast as the uneducated, poverty-stricken mountain girl

Figure 9. *Down to Their Last Yacht* (1934). The crew shooting one of the musical numbers includes producer Lou Brock, who is wearing a suit and standing underneath the camera crane. This unfortunate movie would abort Brock's RKO career. (Courtesy of the University of Southern California Cinematic Arts Library)

who mixed quaint oaths with hymn singing and rock flinging at the very people for whom she prayed. Hepburn's uneven rendition of a southern accent came off as laughable and nearly unintelligible. It was a terrible mistake on her part to want to play the role, and a terrible mistake on Pandro Berman's part to let her do it. Apparently, she felt challenged by a character whose background was the exact opposite of her own wealthy, educated New England upbringing. And Berman and the other executives perhaps believed that the essence of Trigger Hicks was rebellion mixed with vulnerability, qualities Hepburn had mined successfully in earlier roles. Whatever the justifications, *Spitfire* proved to be a miscalculation that would plague RKO and its best actress for years to come.

In spite of the deficient productions, the company continued to make progress in its efforts to pull free of equity receivership. The reduction in 1933 losses and a consolidated profit of $498,131 for the first quarter of 1934 indicated RKO was slowly working its way out of debt.[88] No formal plan of reorganization had yet been presented to the court, however.

When President Franklin Roosevelt signed new bankruptcy laws into effect on June 7, 1934, Radio-Keith-Orpheum became the first corporation to file for relief under the statutes.[89] Paramount joined its neighbor, filing a similar petition a few days later. The new code, known familiarly as 77B, did not materially affect the receivership situations of either company.

The state of affairs at Radio City also showed improvement. On the first anniversary of the change to film programs at the Music Hall, RKO announced that more than six million people had attended the theater during the year.[90] Two million additional admissions had been purchased at the RKO Roxy box office. The theaters had booked films from several studios, but RKO pictures had predominated. Attendance records still belonged to *Little Women*, which played the Music Hall for three weeks and then moved into the RKO Roxy for four more. Hepburn's other vehicles *Christopher Strong* and *Morning Glory* had also enjoyed successful runs at the Music Hall.

J. R. McDonough accepted S. L. Rothafel's resignation as managing director of the Music Hall in January 1934. The Music Hall had been one long nightmare for Roxy since the ill-fated premiere. After recuperating from illness, he returned to work but encountered considerable pressure from RKO theater executives who felt his stage shows were overly extravagant and "too long" and "lacked humor." Rothafel disliked this kind of criticism and quit, though he defended himself to the end: "The budget at all times was adhered to. At no time were the stage shows in excess of the budget allowance."[91]

It was also decided to change the name of the smaller theater, though this had nothing to do with Rothafel's departure. The RKO Roxy became known as the RKO Center because of pressure from the owners of the original Roxy Theater, who did not appreciate the fact that the Rockefellers and RKO had stolen Roxy away from them and were using his (their) name on the Radio City theater.

Even though company finances were clearly improving, the Aylesworth-Kahane-Cooper period had not stabilized RKO. In fact, the company was more wobbly when the era ended than when it had begun. Merian C. Cooper's physical condition was largely to blame. With Cooper in absentia throughout much of his regime, studio production plans were constantly in flux and employee morale was certainly affected by this. The receivership situation compounded the insecurity. Although respectable progress was being reported, what if the studio's fortunes suddenly suffered another reversal? Considering the lousy pictures released in the first half of 1934, this was conceivable. Even if one preferred not to consider the possibility that RKO might go out of business, the effects of receivership were already depressing enough. The company had ceased bidding for the most prestigious properties and had suspended signing top-flight talent to long-term agreements. Its creative arm had begun to stagnate, to fall further behind MGM, Warner Bros., and other companies in the quality of its product. After a much ballyhooed debut, the "Titan" studio was now considered barely a notch above Universal, Columbia, and the poverty row companies. Fortunately, the Astaire-Rogers musicals were about to catch fire; they alone would lift the Radio film brand back to importance during the next several years.

5. "He feels the company is unsettled"

The Aylesworth-McDonough-Kahane Regime (1934–1935)

Except for the emergence of Fred Astaire and Ginger Rogers as vital stars, very little of consequence transpired at RKO during the last half of 1934. J. R. McDonough set up a permanent office in Hollywood, and B. B. Kahane began devoting himself to specific production problems and decisions. Company executives decided to maintain a low profile concerning the studio's new organizational structure. The fact that Kahane was now functioning as production chief received only passing mention in RKO publicity. Perhaps this was a face-saving strategy for Kahane, former president of the production company, who now appeared to be saddled with two separate jobs (he was still president of "RKO Studios"). In fact, McDonough would run the studio and both men would be involved in production planning.

After Kahane took charge, he rapidly formalized the RKO equivalent of MGM's unit system of production. This meant that each staff producer would be responsible for a set number of features with Kahane maintaining overall supervision. In essence, this represented only a slight variation on the approach that had existed during Merian Cooper's periods of convalescence, except that each producer's group would be relatively autonomous. All productions were financed by RKO, however, and Kahane and McDonough therefore had the authority to step in and influence the process whenever they felt such action necessary.

Pandro Berman headed the list of associates; he was given a unit of thirteen pictures containing most of the studio's important, high-budget presentations.[1] Kenneth Macgowan was assigned six films, and Merian Cooper a minimum of two. The balance of the program would be divided among Richard A. Rowland, Cliff Reid, Glendon Allvine, H. N. Swanson, and former Robertson-Cole production head B. P. Fineman. Most of the B productions were supposed to be made by these individuals. Lou Brock was also mentioned, but his cavalier attitude and mishandling of *Down to Their Last Yacht* had already aborted his RKO feature career.[2]

In June the company held its sales convention at a familiar site, the Drake Hotel in Chicago. A program of fifty features for the 1934–1935 season was unveiled, along with a commitment to "clean" motion pictures. Moral rectitude on the Hollywood screen was still a hot issue at this time, thanks primarily to the recently formed and bellicose Catholic Legion of Decency. Corporate president Merlin Aylesworth assured the participants that "RKO has made clean pictures in the past and will continue to make them."[3]

Katharine Hepburn and Irene Dunne, considered the company's top stars, were scheduled to appear in three "specials" each. Such RKO veterans as Ann Harding and Wheeler and Woolsey maintained their positions on the program, but one name associated with RKO from its earliest days was missing. Richard Dix's performance in *Stingaree* had failed to resuscitate his career; the studio elected not to renew his contract.

Directors assigned 1934–1935 pictures included John Cromwell, John Ford, and newcomers Mark Sandrich and George Stevens. Both had done fine work in the shorts division and been promoted to features.

The association with Pioneer Pictures had not yet yielded any movies for RKO to distribute, but the plan was still alive. The goal remained production of the first feature in three-strip Technicolor. At that time, Pioneer was working on a short, *La Cucaracha*, designed to serve as a test of the feasibility of a feature undertaking. Merian Cooper's *The Last Days of Pompeii* was mentioned as the probable choice for the full-length color experiment.[4]

Little else of consequence was revealed at the convention. RKO's production machine would continue to roll along, largely under its own momentum, without any noteworthy changes for the rest of the year.

The condition of equity receivership also remained relatively unchanged. Some of the theater problems were ironed out, and termination of the management of the Radio City houses was effected. Actually, the RKO theater division desired to continue running the Music Hall and RKO Center, but when the company's lease expired on September 1, terms agreeable to both RKO and the Rockefeller interests could not be reached.[5] The studio would still supply many films for presentation in the theaters, but actual operations now fell to the Rockefellers and their man W. G. Van Schmus. This turned out to be a good move for the Rockefellers because the two houses became more and more popular as the decade drew on. Once again, RKO's timing was poor.

A plan of reorganization for Radio-Keith-Orpheum was finally initiated in November. Federal judge William Bondy, observing that "RKO had begun to show a profit for the first time in many months," instructed the trustees to commence formulation of a reorganization plan "if the company's earnings continue their improvement."[6] Nevertheless, the end to receivership was not yet in sight; it would take considerable time to come up with a viable plan.

The most important RKO release of 1934 was *The Gay Divorcée*. Fred Astaire had not originally wanted the studio to buy the stage hit in which he had starred. In November 1933 he wrote Katharine Brown, RKO's New York story editor: "I'm anxious to do my next picture—but hope they will not make it 'Gay Divorce.' I'd really rather not do that story even though it has worked out so well for me in the theatre. So much of it is held up by 'hoofing,' which of course cannot be done as advantageously on the screen. Hope you'll use your influence to make them get an original story, especially for the next thing I do."[7]

Pandro Berman saw the play in London, convinced Astaire it would make an excellent screen vehicle, and prevailed upon the New York executives to purchase the rights. Although Clare Luce and others were discussed as possible female leads, Ginger Rogers got the role—Astaire's objections notwithstanding. A final *e* was added to the movie title to satisfy the Hollywood censors, whose Catholic sensibilities decreed that a divorcée might be "gay," but a divorce must always be viewed as a sad and serious matter.

Production commenced in the summer of 1934 with Berman in charge rather than Lou Brock.[8] Nevertheless, the old bugaboo of escalating costs reared its head and the final figure was about $100,000 over budget.[9] The overrun was rapidly pardoned when the film opened in October. Ned Depinet wrote J. R. McDonough an ecstatic memo calling *Divorcée* a "smash hit" and quoting comparative figures to show that the film was doing considerably better than *Flying Down to Rio* had done.[10] It eventually made a profit of $584,000.

The Gay Divorcée was significant for several other reasons. The romantic misunderstanding that fueled the plot became a basic formula for most of the later Astaire-Rogers efforts, the dance numbers were extraordinary, and the supporting characters (Edward Everett Horton, Alice Brady, Erik Rhodes, and Eric Blore) added humorous subplots that complemented the story's romantic thrust. Finally, the fundamental Astaire-Rogers production team coalesced on *The Gay Divorcée* with producer Berman and Mark Sandrich, who would direct a majority of the films, heading the group. Other important members were studio art director Van Nest Polglase, who took overall responsibility for the quintessential art deco design of all the pictures, musical director Max Steiner, cameraman David Abel, and editor William Hamilton. According to dance critic and historian Arlene Croce, choreographer Hermes Pan also contributed, but received no credit.[11]

The importance of *The Gay Divorcée* to RKO cannot be overemphasized. At this point in its history, the studio desperately needed a first-class attraction, something to lend prestige to Radio Pictures as well as assure a box-office windfall. It had been hoped that Katharine Hepburn would emerge as a powerful star, able to sustain the company with her considerable talent, but now it appeared she would never become one of Hollywood's truly magnetic personalities. Hepburn was a great actress, but she was not destined to be a great draw for RKO. The team of Fred Astaire and Ginger Rogers, on the other hand, was rapturously embraced by the moviegoing public almost overnight. *The Gay Divorcée* proved to RKO that its new musical duo could become a topline attraction—something so alluring that exhibitors would scramble to book all the company's pictures in order to receive two or three Astaire-Rogers "specials" a year. The studio had finally stumbled upon a ticket to class and cash that would sustain it for years to come.

RKO's remaining 1934 releases hardly raised a ripple within the industry. *Anne of Green Gables*, starring a fresh-faced teenager formerly known as Dawn O'Day, was a sleeper hit, generating $272,000 in profits. Miss O'Day was convinced to change her theatrical moniker to Anne Shirley, the Lucy Maud Montgomery–created heroine she played in the film, and she would hold on to that name for the rest of her career. Most of the other Radio Pictures, however, lost money—though not very much. Even the company's holiday picture, the $648,000 *The Little Minister* starring Katharine Hepburn, failed to break even. It came up $9,000 short.

As a new year commenced, the zeitgeist in America seemed cautiously positive. The Depression had eased, and in New York and Hollywood, major studios were charting an increase in movie attendance, thanks partly to such stratagems as double features and "give-away" nights. With business conditions improving, all the companies had decided to produce more pictures, and RKO was no exception. This severely strained existing studio facilities, as J. R. McDonough explained in a letter to Merlin Aylesworth:

> We have been renting the Pathe facilities to independent producers because it is so far distant from this studio that we cannot afford to use it unless we set up separate production units there. Our own ranch is

not used much because of its great distance from the studio and also because of its lack of dressing room facilities, restaurant facilities, etc. The result is that we are confined largely to the use of this Gower Street studio as to RKO productions. Its ten stages do not afford us enough room to keep pictures constantly in work. I mean by that it seems impossible for us to keep a steady flow of pictures shooting due to the difficulty of preparing some pictures while others are shooting.[12]

McDonough requested an appropriation of $150,000 to $200,000 to build two or three additional stages. This expansion, he believed, would provide the necessary "elbow room" and pay for itself in two or three years.[13] It took longer than McDonough had hoped, but finally the RKO board of directors allocated $500,000 for the project. The work was completed in 1936, adding to the RKO physical plant three sound stages, dressing rooms, an electrical storage building, scene docks, a number of film vaults, and a three-story office building.[14]

As usual, the first half of 1935 was spent mapping out plans for the 1935–1936 season. J. R. McDonough took an active part in the formulations. In January he wrote Merlin Aylesworth stating that he intended to de-emphasize "over-sweet sentimental" stories such as *Anne of Green Gables,* *Laddie,* and *Freckles.* Although *Anne of Green Gables* had been especially profitable and McDonough expected the two other films to do well, he believed this type of screen entertainment was approaching the end of its cycle. Perhaps taking a page out of Merian Cooper's script, McDonough expressed the opinion that RKO should "concentrate as much as possible on the adventure, fast moving, quick dialogue type of story from now on."[15]

"Mac" McDonough had overlooked a crucial factor. RKO still did not have the requisite thespian talent to specialize in adventure pictures. With the exception of Astaire, who was hardly the *King Solomon's Mines* type, the studio's important stars were all female: Katharine Hepburn, Irene Dunne, Ginger Rogers, Ann Harding, and Barbara Stanwyck, the last of whom had joined RKO on a non-exclusive basis. Richard Dix did return to the company for B-picture roles in 1935, and Francis Lederer was still under contract, though no one seemed to understand how best to harness his talents. This suggested that fast-paced, action movies would probably be confined almost exclusively to B-unit productions.

Indeed, RKO would continue to aim its A pictures at female audience members, and chief among those productions would be its pace-setting musicals. Pandro Berman's fierce determination to secure *Roberta* for RKO was the first to pay handsome dividends in 1935. The picture elevated the careers of Astaire, Rogers, and Irene Dunne and brought $770,000 in earnings into RKO's account.

Even before he made *The Gay Divorcée*, Fred Astaire had heard about the play. He wrote Merian Cooper: "There is a show called 'Roberta' which I am told would make a suitable thing for me with of course some revision. The part is that of a football player who falls heir to a gown shop in Paris called 'Madame Roberta' & he goes over there to take charge of the business. As I could hardly be a football hero—it has been suggested to me that the character could be changed to that of a track star or something to suit my size."[16] The part that Astaire mentioned was eventually played by Randolph Scott, who did have the physique of a football player. Astaire took the role of Huck Haines, dancing bandleader of the "Wabash Indianians."

After filming was completed, the studio executives became convinced they had another big hit on their hands. Ned Depinet, visiting the West Coast in February, wired Jules Levy about the sneak preview: "First batch preview cards last night's ROBERTA came in and unanimously favorable, lauding picture to skies. . . . Comparisons odious but I think ROBERTA better all round entertainment and stronger box office attraction than DIVORCEE."[17]

Jerome Kern, who had written the original play with Otto Harbach, concurred with Depinet's appraisal. He telegrammed Berman: "Thanks for wonderful evening. It certainly was unique experience to find motion picture version of one of our plays something to be proud of instead of otherwise. Every department of the studio concerned in *Roberta* is to be congratulated."[18] The picture opened in March at the Radio City Music Hall and quickly became one of the big hits of its day.

Roberta bogged down into an interminable fashion show near the end. The only point of interest concerning this sequence was the appearance of Lucille Ball as one of the models. This apparently represents the first RKO appearance of the actress whose company would, more than twenty years later, purchase the entire studio for the production of television programs.

Not long after the debut of *Roberta*, RKO neighbor Paramount Pictures pulled free of receivership. Its plan for reorganization was accepted early in the year, thus ending the company's court supervision on April 5, 1935.[19] RKO's receivership lingered on, however, despite definite evidence of progress. A disclosure of financial operations for 1934 revealed a small loss ($310,575) that compared quite favorably with the $4.4 million deficit of the year before.[20] RKO Radio Pictures, the film production company,

Figure 10.   *Roberta* (1935). Fred Astaire (right) and his assistant Hermes Pan
discuss the choreography of one of the movie's musical numbers. (Courtesy of
the University of Southern California Cinematic Arts Library)

actually showed a profit of $570,378 for the year.[21] Without question, RKO
had made impressive headway toward rehabilitating its corporate and financial operations.

   But the corporation still needed some financially responsible group to
step forward and propose a workable reorganization plan. Apparently, Wall
Street insiders had always expected RCA to do this, since it continued to

hold a controlling interest in RKO. But David Sarnoff was not inclined to bail out the RCA offspring again. Memories of the unproductive 1931 intercession were still too fresh. Therefore, by midyear, other financial groups began to consider the opportunities inherent in the RKO situation. Leading the interested parties were the investment banking house of Lehman Brothers, which had been concerned with RKO financing for some years, and Floyd B. Odlum's Atlas investment trust.[22] Atlas had already participated in the Paramount reorganization. The fact that RKO reported a net profit of $388,002 for the first twenty-one weeks of 1935 made the company seem more attractive as an investment.[23]

At the midpoint of 1935, RKO released the most anticipated feature film in years—the first three-strip Technicolor special, *Becky Sharp*. *Becky Sharp* had been incubating since 1933 when John Hay (Jock) Whitney and his cousin Cornelius Vanderbilt (Sonny) Whitney formed Pioneer Pictures at the suggestion of their friend Merian C. Cooper. The Whitneys were not really interested in making motion pictures; as the company name suggested, they hoped to blaze new trails in the entertainment industry. Color film seemed the next logical step in the evolution of the cinema, prompting the Whitneys to decide to produce the initial feature in the "perfected" Technicolor process.

Color was actually nothing new. The *Motion Picture Herald* listed fifty different color processes that had been utilized with varying degrees of success since the silent era.[24] Technicolor had been available to movies since the early 1920s, and many films had been produced, either partially or wholly, in the company's two-color process. RKO's own *Rio Rita* and *Dixiana* were among those pictures.

But all the earlier processes—including those of Technicolor—had been flawed. They failed to produce vivid and realistic color images. Technicolor finally solved the problem, developing a technology that offered filmmakers the full spectrum of color possibilities. When the three-color process first became available in 1933, Walt Disney quickly adopted it for some of his cartoons. His color Silly Symphonies were well received, and it seemed only a matter of time before someone completed a "natural color" feature. But, to the chagrin of Herbert Kalmus, the president of Technicolor, no one stepped forward. The problem was the added expense.

Several of the RKO executives were less than enthusiastic about three-strip Technicolor. Both Pandro Berman and B.B. Kahane expressed serious hostility; they believed that "color would not add enough value to the negative to compensate" for the additional costs involved.[25] They also apparently worried about the possibility that public enthusiasm for three-color pictures might bring the black-and-white era to an end—just as the success of *The Jazz Singer* and *Lights of New York* had mandated the conversion to talkies. If this happened, the average budget of RKO features would skyrocket. To begin with, three times as much film had to be shot, and processing and printing charges were also higher. The extra expenditure would vary from picture to picture, but there was no doubt that color would add at least 15 percent to production budgets.

The two men at RKO who embraced color filming were Merian Cooper and Kenneth Macgowan. Since Cooper was ill throughout much of the *Becky Sharp* germination period, Macgowan became liaison between the studio and Pioneer Pictures, as well as the film's line producer. Because of Cooper, RKO had agreed to distribute the finished picture. The company really had nothing tangible at stake; the Whitneys were putting up all the money for production. RKO provided only studio facilities and Macgowan's services.

The first important decision facing Jock Whitney and Macgowan involved the choice of a property. It had to be something exemplary, a story with enough cachet and substance to merit special treatment. *Hamlet, Joan of Arc, Tristan and Isolde, The Three Musketeers,* and *The Last of the Mohicans* were some of the titles considered before *Becky Sharp* finally won out. The film would be based on Langdon Mitchell's play, which had been adapted from Thackeray's classic novel *Vanity Fair.*

While discussions concerning the crucial property dragged on, Macgowan convinced Whitney to make a short film as a kind of trial run. Respected set and costume designer Robert Edmond Jones—present in the early days of Radio City Music Hall—was hired as art director. He worked closely with director Lloyd Corrigan on *La Cucaracha,* completed in the summer of 1934. The short was a flimsy tale about a Mexican girl (Steffi Duna) whose perseverance enables her to win the affection of a handsome dancer. Nevertheless, the film showcased the new Technicolor beautifully and would ultimately win an Academy Award as Best Short Subject (Comedy) of 1934. *La Cucaracha* fulfilled its purpose, as Macgowan wrote Whitney: "As things turn out, it seems to me the making of 'Cucaracha' was really very fortunate. We have learned far more about the difficulties and costs of a feature than we ever could have with ordinary tests or even with the shooting of one sequence from our intended picture."[26]

Jock Whitney was pleased and decided to proceed. After *Becky Sharp* was chosen and Miriam Hopkins signed to play the lead, a director had to be hired. When the decision making ended, the job belonged to Lowell

Sherman. The actor-director had not made a film on the RKO lot since *Morning Glory* (1933).

Production began in December 1934, and quickly devolved into an unending nightmare. At first, the bright lights required by the color camera aggravated the eyes of the actors, especially Miriam Hopkins. Then Sherman developed pneumonia and, to everyone's shock, died in early January.[27] The showbiz veteran, who had played the villain in D. W. Griffith's *Way Down East* as well as directing Mae West in *She Done Him Wrong* and Hepburn in *Morning Glory*, was only forty-nine years old.

Rouben Mamoulian, hired as Sherman's replacement, threw out his predecessor's footage and started over. About two weeks after this, Hopkins came down with pneumonia and was taken to the hospital. She recovered, but her absence delayed the picture considerably.[28] The budget continued to escalate, and problems kept cropping up even after the completion of shooting. Postproduction work revealed that the soundtrack was deficient, forcing the rerecording of much of the film and necessitating further delays in its release. Macgowan wrote Whitney: "It is a bitterly ironic fact that in a picture in which we thought we would have to worry about color, we have ended in spending three weeks of time and considerable money and a good deal of heart-ache over sound."[29] The final cost of *Becky Sharp* was $1,094, 811.[30]

The release of the picture in June caused a near-unanimous double-edged response from critics. The quality and artistic usage of color received unqualified praise, while the dramatic elements of the film were considered woefully deficient. The public's response mirrored that of the critics; there was no box-office stampede. Consequently, black-and-white cinematography would remain the industry standard, although other studios would employ three-strip for occasional special features in future years. RKO did not join them until 1945, when it produced *The Spanish Main* as its first Technicolor feature.[31]

Since RKO had invested nothing, its distribution of *Becky Sharp* produced a profit of $112,000. The Whitneys and Pioneer Pictures, however, must have taken a pretty sound financial beating on the experiment.

Both Merian Cooper and Kenneth Macgowan left RKO in 1935. Cooper did complete his promised pictures, *She* and *The Last Days of Pompeii*, but neither one looked or performed like *King Kong*, so there was no resistance to his exit. Pioneer Pictures was expected to continue making films for RKO release, especially after Cooper became executive vice-president of the company later in 1935. But after its second Technicolor production,

Figure 11.   *Becky Sharp* (1935). William Faversham, director Rouben Mamoulian, and Frances Dee in front of the mammoth Technicolor camera. The film was the first feature made in three-strip Technicolor. (Courtesy of the University of Southern California Cinematic Arts Library)

the feeble adventure-musical *Dancing Pirate,* was released in 1936, the company was folded into David Selznick's new independent enterprise, Selznick International Pictures.

Kenneth Macgowan departed in August to accept a position with the newly formed Twentieth Century–Fox organization. He was a hard worker as well as a man of intelligence and refinement, and such RKO productions as *Topaze, Little Women, Wednesday's Child,* and *Anne of Green Gables* reflected his inherent taste. RKO would miss his gentlemanly demeanor and his production ability.

To bolster its withering staff, RKO promoted several employees to producer status. Edward Kaufman, a former staff writer, became a producer. Lee Marcus was given overall supervision of B pictures in addition to his short film duties. And Robert F. Sisk started producing movies. He had served for some years as the company's head of publicity.

RKO's only talent acquisitions of consequence in 1935 were composer Irving Berlin, who would work on a non-exclusive basis with the Astaire-Rogers series, and French-born opera singer Lily Pons. Kahane and McDonough were evidently influenced by the success of Grace Moore, another operatic star, in *One Night of Love* and other Columbia releases. They hoped to duplicate Harry Cohn's accomplishment with vehicles especially tailored to Pons's talents. Unfortunately, the studio leaders discovered too late that Grace Moore's popularity was ephemeral. Arriving just as the public was tiring of Moore, Lily Pons failed to develop into a box-office attraction. Berlin, however, would contribute significantly to the company's musicals.

Fred Astaire adored Irving Berlin, one of America's premier songwriters. He must have been thrilled when RKO hired him. Nevertheless, the dancer's relations with the company grew strained in 1935. His extraordinary rise to the top—making him, without question, RKO's leading male star—meant that a contract renegotiation was in order. Company officials were quite willing to work things out, but Astaire became skittish because of continuing uncertainty about RKO's future leadership. He conveyed his feelings to agent Leland Hayward, who spelled them out in a letter to B. B. Kahane:

> He [Astaire] feels the company is unsettled, due to the recent acquisition of a certain amount of it's [sic] stock by new interests. He feels that working in pictures as he does is such a personal relationship with the people in charge of the company, that to undertake to do this at some future date at which time it is now unknown who will be running the company or who will be making the pictures, is asking too much of anyone in his position. He might have a complete understanding as to his work, his efforts and his ambitions with the people now running the company, only to find at some future date that the new owners and operators would feel entirely different.[32]

It is possible to interpret this as a ploy on the part of Astaire and Hayward to secure better terms from RKO, but their motives were likely pure. Astaire was a perfectionist, a man who cared deeply about his art, and it is completely in character for him to have misgivings about a company as unstable as RKO. After all, his future depended on the studio just as, to a significant extent, RKO's future depended on him. The contract discussions were held in abeyance until the leadership questions could be sorted out.

The only true breakthrough of 1935 came in the directing department. George Stevens had been an RKO employee for several years following his apprenticeship with comedy producer Hal Roach. Like Mark Sandrich, he began work in Lou Brock's short film unit, where he cranked out comedies starring Grady Sutton, Edgar Kennedy, and others. The shorts earned him a chance to direct a Wheeler-Woolsey film, *Kentucky Kernels,* but it was a Katharine Hepburn picture that fueled his move from B productions to As. A telegram from Pandro Berman to Ben Kahane reveals that it was Berman's idea to use Stevens on *Alice Adams:* "Have inspiration on *Alice Adams.* Believe George Stevens man to do this job. Think I can handle Hepburn. Great idea for the company and fully confident he can develop in this picture as Sandrich did in *Gay Divorcee.* If you are willing gamble a little with me on this, please advise."[33]

When considered in the context of Hepburn's career, Berman's gamble was a large one. After *Spitfire* and the disappointing financial performances of *The Little Minister* ($9,000 loss) and *Break of Hearts* ($16,000 profit), Hepburn needed to play an appealing character in a popular film to rejuvenate her status. Booth Tarkington's Alice turned out to be an inspired choice, and Stevens guided Hepburn and the other elements of the production with verve and humor. The film not only earned $164,000 in profits but revitalized Katharine Hepburn's career as well and rocketed Stevens to the top level of RKO's directorial ranks.

An even greater surprise than Stevens's firm handling of *Alice Adams* was John Ford's brilliant direction of *The Informer.* Little was expected of the film version of Liam O'Flaherty's novel. It was made on a frugal budget ($243,000) as the first of Ford's new three-picture RKO deal. The subject matter proved ideal for the director, a close student of Irish literature and history, and the resulting film became the most prestigious that RKO had ever produced. The Dudley Nichols screenplay, Ford's creation of the constricted, fog-shrouded ambience of Dublin during the Black and Tan occupation, and Victor McLaglen's stunning portrayal of gutter Judas, Gypo Nolan, elicited hosannas from critics all across the country. The National Board of Review named *The Informer* Best Film of 1935, and it won four Academy Awards: Direction (Ford), Adaptation (Nichols), Male Performance (McLaglen), and Musical Score (Max Steiner). MGM's *Mutiny on the Bounty* somehow managed to grab the Best Picture Oscar, although that film won no other major awards.

The Informer performed erratically on its first run. Subsequent releases, buttressed by the flood tide of critical encomia, turned the picture into a very solid moneymaker. A final tally revealed profits of $325,000.[34]

The good news became even better in September. *Top Hat* kicked off the 1935–1936 program, and RKO would never have a more auspicious Labor Day release. The film today is considered the quintessential Astaire-Rogers musical with its bewitching score by Irving Berlin; supple direction by Mark Sandrich; delightful supporting performances from Edward Everett Horton, Helen Broderick, Eric Blore, and Erik Rhodes; exceptional art design by Van Nest Polglase and Carroll Clark; and its plot of incredibly elaborated romantic misunderstanding—a prime example of the Astaire-Rogers formula.

That plot was concocted by Dwight Taylor and Allan Scott. After a first reading, Fred Astaire was less than impressed. He wrote Pandro Berman:

> In the first place—as this book is supposed to have been written *for me* with the intention of giving me a chance to do the things that are most suited to me—I cannot see that my part embodies any of the necessary elements except to *dance-dance-dance.*
>
> I am cast as a straight juvenile & rather a cocky and arrogant one at that—a sort of objectionable young man without charm or sympathy or humor.
>
> I cannot see that there is any real story or plot to this script.
>
> It is a series of events patterned *too closely* after *Gay Divorcee,* without the originality & suspense of that play.
>
> I have practically no comedy of any consequence except in the scene in the cab.
>
> I am forever pawing the girl or she is rushing into my arms.[35]

Astaire's criticism continued at length, but apparently Berman was able to calm the star during personal conferences. Some additional polishing brought the script up to acceptable standards.

Production was completed in early summer 1935, enabling the studio to get the picture ready for release as the first offering of the 1935–1936 season. Ned Depinet had often expressed a desire for a major hit to kick off the company's new program. With a blockbuster lead, the distribution department would have a much easier time selling the entire slate of RKO films to exhibitors. Depinet's dream came true with *Top Hat.* It launched a big sales year and even brought four separate lawsuits from exhibitors claiming they should be able to play the film as part of their 1934–1935 commitment. Actually, the exhibitors had a plausible argument. The company had promised two Astaire-Rogers films, *Roberta* and *Radio City Revels,* in its 1934–1935 contracts. Since *Radio City Revels* was not produced, the theater owners felt entitled to *Top Hat* without having to book the entire RKO product for the new season. Nevertheless, a judge in Ohio ruled in the studio's favor: " 'Top Hat,' in the opinion of Judge Skeel, is a 1935–36 feature picture by reason of its production number and also its national release date, it having previously been agreed that the motion picture season opens officially on September 1st. 'Top Hat' was released September 6th."[36]

Top Hat became an immediate and unprecedented (for RKO) smash hit. It easily surpassed all the attendance records of the Radio City Music Hall, bringing in over $244,000 in two weeks.[37] W. G. Van Schmus, managing director of the huge palace, wrote Pandro Berman in appreciation:

> I want to congratulate you from the bottom of my heart for this great achievement. I expressed myself to Mac [J. R. McDonough] when he was here and also saw Fred Astaire . . . and told him of our great pleasure. I wish you would kiss Ginger Rogers on both cheeks for me and tell her that I agree with the critics of the New York papers who stressed her performance and placed her on equal partnership in this wonderful team. There is something so thoroughly human about her performance it appeals to the *people*. Fred Astaire, of course, has his top position and nobody can take it away from him.[38]

Indeed, *Top Hat* secured a top position for both Astaire and Rogers. In late December, the duo was accorded fourth place on the *Motion Picture Herald*'s list of the "biggest moneymaking stars of 1934–35."[39] It was the first time any RKO performers had appeared in the Top Ten.

Fred and Ginger were definitely moneymakers. It is arguable whether *Top Hat* represents the best of the Astaire-Rogers efforts, but the film certainly was their most successful. It earned a profit of $1,325,000, thus making it the top box-office attraction produced by RKO during the 1930s.

The 1935 releases also included some flops. The Merian Cooper adventures *She* and *The Last Days of Pompeii* lost $180,000 and $237,000, respectively. *She,* the H. Rider Haggard fantasy about eternal youth, had been analyzed by the RKO story department in 1932. A reader named Twitchell reported: "Viewing this story, even in the light of a 'horror' possibility, I fail to see that it possesses the slightest value to the screen today. It is so old fashioned, so highly improbable, so stilted, that I don't think anything could be done with it to make it worthwhile. *NOT RECOMMENDED.*"[40] Nevertheless, Cooper was convinced *She* had exciting possibilities and prevailed upon J. R. McDonough to purchase the rights from Universal for $20,000.[41]

To include some additional moments of excitement, such as a glacial avalanche, Cooper transplanted the story from Africa to the Arctic. For the role of She-Who-Must-Be-Obeyed, Cooper chose Helen Gahagan, a virtual unknown to motion picture audiences.[42] Direction was handled by Irving Pichel and an architect named Lancing C. Holden, the producer apparently being fond of directorial teamwork.

Production proceeded in a tense atmosphere. Cooper feuded with J. R. McDonough throughout the making of this picture and *The Last Days of Pompeii.* At one point, Cooper asked McDonough if he could exceed the original budget for *She* by about 10 percent. McDonough held firm: "I

Figure 12. *Top Hat* (1935). Director Mark Sandrich directs Ginger Rogers and Fred Astaire as they dance on the famous Venice set of this highly successful musical. (Courtesy of the Academy of Motion Picture Arts and Sciences)

know you have told me for some time you would like to spend from $40,000 to $50,000 more on the picture than your contract permits. My answer to that is still the same, namely, I expect you to make for RKO in accordance with your contract the great picture you promised us for $500,000."[43] The friction between McDonough and the producer may have been a significant factor in Cooper's decision to leave RKO.

The Last Days of Pompeii was better than *She,* but it cost substantially more ($818,000 versus $521,000) and also lost more. The plot bore no resemblance to Sir Edward Bulwer-Lytton's novel of the same name, other than the climatic destruction of the city by erupting Mount Vesuvius. Instead, the Ruth Rose screenplay, based on a story by James Creelman and Melville Baker, was heavily influenced by Cecil B. DeMille's religious epics, especially *The Sign of the Cross.* One of the disappointments of the picture was the relatively meager level of its spectacle. The scenes in the gladiatorial arena were less than dynamic, and the special effects simulating the devastation of Pompeii were not up to the usual level of Willis

O'Brien and his team of wizards.[44] Considering that the budget was higher than *King Kong*'s, this is hard to understand. The ultimate responsibility for the picture's nonsuccess, however, must reside with Cooper and the film's director, Ernest B. Schoedsack. They failed to achieve the proper mixture of DeMillean decadence and sanctimony that made films of this type almost certain winners. *The Last Days of Pompeii* turned out to be considerably less than sensational.[45]

Among the year's other disappointments were *Enchanted April*, an Ann Harding picture that lost $260,000; *Jalna*, which lost $174,000; *Village Tale*, which ended up $159,000 in the red; and Lily Pons's debut, *I Dream Too Much*, which dropped a sobering $350,000 as the final release of the year. Still, when compared to 1934, the quality of RKO releases had taken a giant leap upward in 1935.

Evidently, David Sarnoff was not particularly impressed by the company's improving product or its prospects. In October he signaled his desire to get out of the moviemaking business when the Atlas Corporation and Lehman Brothers purchased half of RCA's controlling interest in RKO, with an option to buy the other half within two years.[46]

Atlas was Floyd Odlum's company. Low-key, bespectacled, and publicity-shy, Odlum was nevertheless a highly successful tycoon. Investment analyst and business historian Kenneth L. Fisher has called him the "original corporate raider."[47] Through Atlas, Odlum invested in companies that he felt were undervalued by Wall Street. At the time he made the deal with RCA, Odlum controlled a number of different enterprises, including the Foreign Power Company, United Fruit Company, and the Italian Superpower Corporation. He was no stranger to the movie business, either; besides Paramount, Atlas Corporation held investments in Warner Bros., Fox, and Loew's Incorporated (MGM).[48] Odlum knew that his first priority would be development of a reorganization plan to remove RKO from the onus of 77B. He assigned the task to favored associate N. Peter Rathvon, who was then a vice-president of the Atlas Corporation.[49]

Rathvon's job would not be easy. There were still many large claims against the company, including one of $8,700,000 from Rockefeller Center. The *Motion Picture Herald* reported: "The huge Rockefeller Center claim arises out of RKO's liability under leases for the Music Hall and Center Theatre, which held RKO liable for the unamortized cost of the theatres in the event of a default under the lease. Although allowance of the claim at $8,700,000 is being contested by Irving Trust Company, as trustees for RKO, factors in the reorganization are reported not hopeful of obtaining any appreciable reduction in the amount."[50] The story neglected to mention that the claim was also based on the original lease for office space in the RKO Building, a portion of which the company never occupied. Rapid revamping was predicted by the new RKO investors, but the Rockefeller claim plus other complications would cause receivership to drag on.

Sadly, vaudeville presentations in the RKO theaters could not help the situation. The combination of variety acts and movies had been declining for years, its anachronism speeded by radio and talking pictures; the controversial double-feature policy in most of the nation's theaters proved lethal. Many of them simply replaced the live acts with a second film. Thus, vaudeville sank to its lowest point, continuing to exist only in the largest cities. The Loew's circuit, which five years before had scheduled shows in thirty-six of its houses, used vaudeville regularly in only three theaters in 1935. RKO held out longer than most of the other chains. It still featured stage bills in Chicago, Cleveland, Cincinnati, Dayton, Rochester, Boston, and other cities, but dropped the Brooklyn, Detroit, and Schenectady combinations.[51] During the next twelve months, many of these houses would adopt film programs exclusively, as vaudeville faded from the American scene.

The entry of Floyd Odlum into RKO's business affairs presupposed a shake-up of the company's officers. The first step was the naming of Leo Spitz to the presidency of Radio-Keith-Orpheum. Merlin Aylesworth moved upstairs, replacing David Sarnoff as chairman of the RKO board of directors. *Newsweek* reported that Spitz's closest friend was John Hertz, a partner in Lehman Brothers, but also stated that film exhibitors considered him "the country's foremost authority on how to turn movie house losses into profits."[52] A native of Chicago trained as a lawyer, Spitz had served as a counsel to the Balaban and Katz theater chain and to the advisory board of Paramount. His advice concerning the reduction of long-term theater leases and methods for cutting expenses was credited with making that company's reorganization possible.[53]

Odlum's decision to hire Spitz took place without consultation. He did not bother to discuss it with the receivership trustee or Sarnoff or the Rockefellers or any of the other interested parties.[54] This was a mistake, for the friction it caused ignited a small fire that would flare up again and again for years to come. RKO affairs were now the concern of several different very powerful individuals who would rarely agree on the best course of future action.

Upon assuming the RKO post, Leo Spitz "let it be known that the company's operating organization would not be disturbed, at least pending a study of its corporate needs, and that the survey would be as much for reorganization purposes as to familiarize himself with operations."[55] He left for Hollywood in mid-November to study studio operations firsthand. Spitz remained for about a month, meeting the heads of the major companies and consulting with J. R. McDonough, B. B. Kahane, and other members of the West Coast staff.

By the end of the year, the executive line-up was complete. Samuel Briskin was named vice-president in charge of RKO production. Briskin came to RKO from Columbia, where he had been general manager of Harry Cohn's studio for eight years. Before that, he had worked in the sales department of C. B. C. Film Corporation, the company that became Columbia. Since much of his industry experience had been outside the creative sphere, Sam Briskin's production abilities were hard to predict. Leo Spitz evidently hoped for a smooth transition. B. B. Kahane, J. R. McDonough, and Ned Depinet were all slated to remain with RKO, although their precise future duties were amorphous at this point. Each was made a vice-president of the corporation.[56]

December 23 was Sam Briskin's first day on the job. He described it in a telegram to Leo Spitz: "Herewith first days report. Arrived studio ten thirty a.m. Left six. Spent day informally discussing matters with Ben [Kahane] and Mac [McDonough]. Expect continue do this for balance week per your suggestion. This should make everybody happy as fits in with your plans."[57]

Briskin would soon discover that the studio was not in as good a condition as he had hoped. After Floyd Odlum entered the company's affairs in October, McDonough and Kahane became hesitant to make contracts, approve purchases of story material, and so on.[58] The two men realized that changes would likely occur and deemed it imprudent to effect any major commitments. Thus, it would take Briskin several weeks just to get the machinery back up to speed. Once again, RKO's penchant for periodic transformation was interfering with its ongoing production activities.

Meanwhile, although Deac Aylesworth had been kicked upstairs, he was still pursuing his crusade to link radio and film. He traveled to Hollywood late in the year when a newly completed National Broadcasting Company studio, strategically located next door to the RKO plant, was dedicated in gala ceremonies. Will Hays, Al Jolson, May Robson, and Jack Benny also participated in the celebration, which was broadcast throughout the country.[59] Aylesworth recognized that a more conducive atmosphere for movie-radio cooperation now existed in the film capital. Recent months had witnessed MGM's use of a broadcast hookup to plug *The Broadway Melody of 1936*, with Paramount following suit for its *Big Broadcast of 1936*.[60]

Believing that his message of "wedlock" between radio and screen would be received more warmly on this occasion, Merlin Aylesworth proclaimed: "Those engaged in production for the screen will now have opportunity to offer their talent directly through the medium of radio. . . . It will carry the entertainment of the world's greatest personalities into the forgotten corners of the earth."[61]

Nevertheless, there was still some opposition to Aylesworth's position. If motion picture stars appeared regularly on radio broadcasts, it seemed logical that this could diminish their box-office appeal and subtract from nightly theater attendance. Martin Quigley, ever mindful of the plight of exhibitors, editorialized in the *Motion Picture Herald:* "Radio competition is not a theory but a fact. Whether it is liked by the industry or not, it is here and doubtlessly is going to stay. We do not regard the situation as one warranting violent alarm, but neither do we construe the circumstances as justifying any high note of exultation on the part of Hollywood. . . . Before this we would like to have seen some evidence that what is called co-operation in this case means something like a reasonable division of benefits between the two high contracting parties."[62] The theater owners who subscribed to Quigley's journal were undoubtedly pleased that Aylesworth's last radio experiment, the *Hollywood on the Air* program, had bombed, largely because none of RKO's major talent could be convinced to appear.[63] The program was no longer on the air.

Merlin Aylesworth would not have much input into the next phase of RKO's history. Floyd Odlum had become the company's principal figure, and he had placed his own men in its key positions. It might, however, have been advantageous for Odlum to have adopted a more measured approach before making changes. Besides not alienating other important behind-the-scenes powers by hastily appointing Leo Spitz as president, Odlum might have taken a closer look at studio operations. The McDonough-Kahane collective he was uprooting had turned in a very creditable performance in 1935. The year-end corporate statement showed profits of $684,733.[64] It was the first time RKO had made money since 1931, and film production deserved a large portion of the credit.

Still, it would be unwise to lavish too much praise on B. B. Kahane and J. R. McDonough. Under their associate producer system, the creative work was basically farmed out to others, especially Pandro Berman. And Berman had an extraordinary year, numbering *Roberta, Alice Adams,* and *Top Hat* among his several successes. Certainly Kahane and McDonough had input on story selection, casting, and general production matters, but they were not like David O. Selznick in 1932—they did not scrutinize every element of company product as it took shape. Thus, it is difficult to determine just how responsible the two men were for the happy results of 1935.

All of this, in the final analysis, is mere academic speculation. Floyd Odlum liked what he saw happening in the industry: 1935 was the best year since 1930, with all the studios posting profits except Universal. He believed RKO to be a good investment and was in a position to shuffle the RKO corporate deck, considering neither McDonough nor Kahane vital to the hand he wished to play. Berman, however, was untouchable. His unit would ride out the administrative retrenchment intact and completely unaffected.

6. "An awfully long corner"

*The Spitz-Briskin Regime
(1936–1937)*

The initial period of Odlum stewardship turned out to be particularly troublesome. Management shake-ups, now seemingly regular company events, had always proved disruptive, but this one churned the waters more than most. Leo Spitz and Sam Briskin were both mystery men as far as RKO's employees were concerned, and their unfamiliar personalities magnified the usual trepidation that accompanied executive realignment. The situation was different from that created by the promotion of M. C. Cooper or J. R. McDonough or B. B. Kahane into positions of authority, because each of these men had prior service with the company. Spitz and Briskin did not.

Morale at the studio fell to a low point in January 1936, amidst rumors that Sam Briskin planned a thorough housecleaning. The problem was such that B. B. Kahane sent Briskin a memo asking him for a statement "to correct the impression . . . that the studio is due for one of the biggest shake-ups in film history."[1] It is not possible to determine if Briskin actually complied. The rumors were, however, unfounded; no indiscriminate firing squad appeared on the scene, and RKO continued to function with essentially the same team of employees as before.

Nevertheless, difficulties beset the studio throughout 1936. Among them would be relations with the company's biggest stars, the production of a group of disappointing pictures, and the continuing inability of the organization to free itself from the stigma of receivership. It soon became apparent that 1935 had been a felicitous year for the company, but not a stepping stone to greater accomplishment. Even though the business climate throughout America continued to warm, and a couple of the RKO releases would generate large profits, the new year and the new regime would not revitalize the company.

Sam Briskin had developed a reputation as a tough, stubborn, aggressive executive at Columbia Pictures. His no-nonsense approach had helped pull Columbia up from poverty row to a position of respectability. He was, in the words of director Frank Capra, a "hit-first type."[2]

Briskin faced numerous challenges in his new position. Pandro Berman's unit could be counted on to handle the company's most important product, but otherwise, Sam Briskin found himself with an untidy situation on his hands. Most of the films in progress when Briskin took over the studio were mediocre efforts designed to fill out the 1935–1936 program. Except for Berman's *Follow the Fleet*, none of these pictures turned out to be particularly successful. Several promised A efforts—such as *Sylvia Scarlett, The Witness Chair,* and *The Lady Consents*—fell far short of top quality, thus raising the ire of exhibitors who had booked the RKO product for the full year. Briskin refused to accept the blame for this situation, but admitted he had not been able to do much about it. Writing company sales manager Jules Levy in April, he stated:

> I fear that there is nothing to do but to complete the program and plan ahead sufficiently in advance for next season to have plenty of A pictures that are really A's, and to release them in such a manner that at least every fourth, fifth, or sixth picture will really be an A. . . . You will have to bear with me and remember that these things were either prepared or in work when I entered the Studio, and, therefore, there was nothing to do but to salvage the money already invested, except in such cases where it looked absolutely hopeless, and make the best of the situation.[3]

Even though Briskin had to rely on Pandro Berman for a substantial percentage of the A films, he had minimal oversight of Berman's unit. Leo Spitz had taken an immediate liking to Berman and promised him that he would have to answer only to the corporate president. Berman, perhaps inspired by *Mary of Scotland*, which he felt was going to attract excellent reviews as well as substantial audiences, began thinking of producing additional highbrow entertainment. He consulted Spitz about the idea rather than Briskin, making a strong case for the purchase of an antiwar play, *Idiot's Delight*, by enumerating the box-office successes of such Warner films as *A Midsummer Night's Dream, The Petrified Forest,* and *The Story of Louis Pasteur*.[4] Spitz wrote back, promising to try to purchase *Idiot's Delight* (he was unsuccessful—MGM won the bidding war for the property), even though he felt the reports on the Warner Bros. pictures were greatly exaggerated. Nevertheless, he told Berman he was committed to "quality product" if "made in such a manner as to have wide appeal."[5]

Meanwhile, Briskin was dealing with a number of vexing personnel problems. One of them almost cost the studio its most valuable performer. As mentioned previously, Fred Astaire had misgivings about his future with RKO. The company was too volatile to suit him, and he felt ill at ease with the new leadership. Negotiations on his new contract stalled in late January because some of the clauses he insisted on were considered impossible by Briskin, Spitz, and others. Chief among those clauses was one that would have given Astaire the right to name the leading lady in each of his pictures.[6] He was still hoping to cut the cord that tied him to Ginger Rogers.

Astaire at this time had two years of obligation remaining to RKO. Thus, when it began to look as if no compromise were possible, Briskin started formulating plans "to crack through with as many pictures as possible in the next two years, even if it meant carrying one or two on the shelf after his [Astaire's] contract with us was up." The RKO lawyers were instructed to go over Astaire's present contract carefully to determine how many pictures could be required of him. In the course of this scrutiny, a question arose concerning "whether or not because of the peculiar wording of the contract" the studio had to begin photography on the next Astaire picture (eventually entitled *Swing Time*) by February 12, 1936, or breach the agreement.[7] The RKO legal staff decided it would be sufficient to start dance rehearsals by that date. Since the film was not ready for principal photography (there was not even a script yet), Sam Briskin breathed a sigh of relief. To be safe, though, he sent the contract to Mitchell, Silberberg and Knupp, a law firm on retainer to the studio, for an opinion. Briskin was shocked by their reply: there was no doubt in their minds that if RKO failed to commence photography by February 12, Fred Astaire would have just cause to terminate his obligations to the company.

Briskin, in concert with the lawyers, came up with a plan to avert the disaster. Taking into account Astaire's perfectionist character, the company informed him that shooting on the new picture would begin on February 12 without the customary rehearsal period for dance routines. The ploy worked. In a letter to Leo Spitz, Briskin described Astaire as jumping "clear out of his skin" and agreeing quickly to an alteration in the contract: "We succeeded to-day in getting a letter which, in the opinion of our attorneys, unquestionably protects our rights under the contract and eliminates our worries as to a breach. Incidentally, we ascertained that Astaire and his managers were aware of this clause in the contract and were quietly praying and hoping that we would not attempt to start photography of the picture."[8]

The battle did not end there. On February 16 Alfred Wright, Astaire's attorney, sent the following letter to RKO:

> Upon the direction and with the authority of Mr. Fred Astaire . . . I hereby notify you that, because of your failure to submit for his approval, the advertising used in connection with the pictures produced by you in which he appears . . . , because of your continued and continuing violations of the provisions of his contract resulting from using or licensing the use of his name and photograph in advertising other than in connection with motion pictures in which he appears, and because of your failure to pay to him the amount of money due under the terms of his agreement with you . . . , and for each of said reasons Mr. Astaire has elected to and does hereby terminate his said contract (as amended) with you and I hereby notify you of his election so to do.[9]

The studio responded by sending Astaire a check for $10,000 (owed him for his participation in *Top Hat*) and having its law firm prepare a letter stating that there had been no breach. This evidently placated the dancer because he chose not to pursue the matter. In March a new deal was finally concluded giving Astaire a substantial salary increase, a larger percentage of the profits of his films, and the right to choose his female costar in at least one picture each year.[10] Catastrophe had been averted; Fred Astaire would continue to perform in pictures exclusively for RKO, at least for a few more years.

The Katharine Hepburn situation was altogether different. While Astaire was still riding the crest of national popularity, Hepburn's reputation nosedived in 1936. The principal reason was *Sylvia Scarlett*.

The making of *Sylvia Scarlett* could provide ample ammunition to those who believe in autocratic studio control. George Cukor, whose last RKO film had been the triumphant *Little Women*, was borrowed from MGM and given a free hand to film the Compton Mackenzie novel without studio interference. Hepburn also adored the property and, coming off the success of *Alice Adams*, was in a stronger position to assert herself than usual. Together, they made the picture their way while the RKO executives, including Pan Berman, who produced, sat back and hoped that the *Little Women* magic would once again operate. Cukor felt it had; after filming was completed, he believed they had created "something really fine."[11]

What a shock it must have been to all when the film had its initial preview in Huntington Park. Both Cukor and Hepburn have similarly described the audience's brutal rejection of the picture and the unrestrained anger of Pandro Berman toward them after the screening.[12] There was

Figure 13. *Sylvia Scarlett* (1936). Filming Cary Grant in the ocean. Grant was one of the few participants whose reputation was enhanced, rather than damaged, by this production. (Courtesy of the University of Southern California Cinematic Arts Library)

even talk of scrapping *Sylvia Scarlett* entirely, but the production cost too much ($641,000) to bury in some film vault. It was released early in the year, prompting a flood of bad reviews, irate letters from exhibitors and movie patrons throughout the country, and anemic box-office receipts. The only individual who emerged unscathed from this disaster was Cary Grant, whose comic performance was singled out for praise by numerous reviewers.

In February, Ned Depinet wrote B. B. Kahane about the film's pathetic performance.[13] Kahane replied: "It [*Sylvia Scarlett*] is just a bad picture, and it has undoubtedly hurt Hepburn. No one, of course, could have foreseen that a combination like Berman, Cukor, Hepburn, Cary Grant and Brian Ahearne [*sic*] could produce such a 'flop.' Our only hope is that 'Mary of Scotland' . . . will turn out to be an outstanding production and enable Hepburn to retrieve some prestige."[14]

Without question, *Sylvia Scarlett* was one of the most offbeat, atypical, uncommercial motion pictures ever produced during the studio system era. Its picaresque story about a group of incompetent con artists in Victorian England required Hepburn to masquerade as a boy throughout much of the narrative, even though the reason for her disguise disappeared near the beginning. It is difficult to imagine this picture being made by MGM, Twentieth Century–Fox, or any of the other companies. Only at RKO, where hits were few and far between and production philosophies in constant flux, would a gamble like this have been taken. In this instance, the company was badly burned: the film lost $363,000 and quickly eradicated the good will Katharine Hepburn had earned from *Alice Adams*. The press took considerable delight in the *Sylvia Scarlett* wreckage because, unlike most stars, Hepburn had not been accommodating to its membership for years.

The studio executives responded by starring Hepburn in *Mary of Scotland* and by pleading with her to grant more interviews and be more gracious to her interviewers. B. B. Kahane described the situation in a letter to Ned Depinet:

> Here we are about to spend around $800,000. to $900,000. on "Mary of Scotland" in the hope of bringing Hepburn back—giving her Frederick [sic] March to support her, John Ford to direct, and not stinting in any way on the production. We certainly ought to be entitled to her co-operation in combating the ill effects of "Sylvia Scarlett" and the bad publicity resulting from her attitude towards the Press. Any one but Hepburn would see readily that she has reached a point in her career when she needs all the help possible to stay up where she is, but Katharine is just one of those peculiar girls who is not logical or normal in her viewpoints and attitude.[15]

Hepburn did open up somewhat with reporters, but otherwise, she continued to be stubborn and less than rational. At least, this was the opinion held by the men running the studio. While *Mary of Scotland* was in production, she began to make new demands through Leland Hayward. She asked for more money, a larger profit participation in her pictures, and the right to approve her scripts. The last request struck special terror in the hearts of her employers. Hepburn had had unofficial script approval on all her pictures. As Sam Briskin informed Leo Spitz in a telegram, the only film she had been forced to make against her will was *Break of Hearts*.[16] In fact, she had insisted on the production of the two pictures that damaged her most: *Spitfire* and *Sylvia Scarlett*. This fact alone indicated to Briskin that "her judgment [is] of no value." He further suggested the ruinous position in which the studio might find itself if Hepburn's request were accepted: "Know of no one in business who has script approval and you can obviously see that this would result in huge cost in preparing script plus commitments to director, actors, etc. that might be wasted if, at last minute, she refused approve script."

Part of Katharine Hepburn's disgruntlement related to RKO's decision not to bid on Margaret Mitchell's *Gone With the Wind*, then on the auction block, and star her as Scarlett O'Hara. In the same telegram to Spitz, Briskin conveyed the studio's position regarding this popular novel: "This very dangerous picture to make from commercial viewpoint as great similarity to *So Red the Rose* and subject matter has always proven unsuccessful. Berman advances additional reason which very good, namely Hepburn must have extremely sympathetic role as she basically unsympathetic on screen and, if make *Gone With the Wind* with her which is very unsympathetic role, picture will be unsuccessful and, in addition, do great damage to Hepburn's career."

In retrospect, it may seem that RKO blundered outrageously by passing up the property that redefined the meaning of the term "blockbuster." But Briskin and Berman were correct in their reservations. Had RKO made *Gone With the Wind*, it would not have been the lavish spectacular fashioned by David Selznick and would not have had Clark Gable as Rhett Butler (imagine Richard Dix in the part), and Hepburn might very well have overpowered the role of Scarlett to the point of audience antipathy. This is, admittedly, meaningless conjecture; perhaps we should simply say that RKO was not in a position—either financially or in terms of available talent—to make *Gone With the Wind* properly. Katharine Hepburn, however, found this difficult to accept.

Refused script approval by the studio, Hepburn tested her bosses by calling her next project, *A Woman Rebels*, "mediocre" and remaining in New York as the start date drew closer and closer. Finally, Pandro Berman was forced to send her a strongly worded wire in which he surveyed the actress's career, reminded her of her own considerable errors in story selection, and emphasized his own perceptivity: "I think you are making big mistake in this whole matter. . . . If you will recall, there has never been a picture you have made about which I have been honestly enthusiastic from my own opinion that has turned out badly. I have strongly advocated production of *Morning Glory, Little Minister, Alice Adams* and *Mary of Scotland* from wholehearted enthusiasm for these subjects." Arguing from the position that his instincts had, so far, proved unerring (*Mary of Scotland* was not yet in release), Berman proceeded to lavish praise on *A Woman Rebels*. He called it "box office," "sympathetic in character," and "different from anything you have done."[17] In closing, the producer urged his star to leave immediately and set to work on the picture as soon as she arrived. He expressed confidence that she would thank him within six months. His arguments were convincing; Hepburn reevaluated her position and headed for Hollywood.

Lost amid the turbulence created by Fred Astaire and Katharine Hepburn was the departure of a highly talented studio employee: Max Steiner. Steiner was one of the pioneers of motion picture music, a genius whose scores for *King Kong, The Informer, Gone With the Wind, Casablanca, The Searchers,* and other films are now considered classics. If his creations sometimes sounded repetitive and occasionally tended to overwhelm a movie's narrative elements, it should be remembered that he was among the studio's hardest workers. He had written music for an astounding sixty-seven RKO pictures released in 1933 and 1934. The wonder is that so much of his scoring sounded fresh and inventive. One of Steiner's gifts was an ability to interweave well-known songs and classic material with his own original compositions.

But Max Steiner felt underpaid and underappreciated at RKO. He had signed a contract in 1934 in order to secure enough money to help his mother out of a difficult political situation involving the Nazis in Vienna.[18] Now he revealed to B. B. Kahane that he was "very unhappy" with the contract and would never have signed it if he had not been faced with his "mother's financial troubles."[19] The unhappiness festered, manifesting itself in emotional outbursts and unpredictable behavior. Although he signed another agreement with the studio late in 1935, Steiner began to seem more trouble than he was worth. In May 1936 the RKO executives agreed to cancel the contract, thereby freeing Steiner to take a job with Warner Bros. Another of Hollywood's creative geniuses slipped away.

B. B. Kahane also cleaned out his office during the year. Now that Odlum's lieutenants had taken over, Kahane knew he was expendable. When Columbia Pictures offered him a newly created vice-presidency in August, Kahane quickly accepted the job.[20] It must have been an emotional decision for the former president of RKO Pictures who had worked for the corporation since its inception. Kahane was not a dynamic leader, but he was well liked and a good company man. Indeed, his record compares favorably with those of RKO's other executives. After moving to Hollywood from New York, he had acted in several different capacities for the studio and handled them efficiently and sensibly. Perhaps Kahane's greatest achievement was the superior 1935 production year—the only full year he functioned as head of the studio's filmmaking operations. But the time had come to get out and Ben Kahane knew it; he would remain with Columbia for more than twenty years.

Kahane's stalwart partner in 1934 and 1935, J.R. McDonough, receded into the background, accepting a vague studio position and lying low. In April, Briskin wrote Spitz that Mac was ducking him: "If he wants to sit in a room and mope there is nothing I can do or intend to do about it but let him sit and mope to his heart's satisfaction. It all seems so mysterious to me that I can't quite figure it out. Perhaps he is studying for a part in the Invisible Man."[21]

Other personnel matters of note included the end of Ann Harding's RKO employment and the signing of George and Ira Gershwin, Edward Small, Jesse Lasky, and Howard Hawks. Harding had been with RKO since the Pathe merger, but her drawing power had declined considerably. Prior regimes had considered the actress overpaid; in 1936, when her contract ran out, she was simply let go.

Regarding the Gershwins, it came down to a choice between them and Vincent Youmans, who had written the score for *Flying Down to Rio*. Since Youmans's music had helped to launch the Astaire-Rogers team, the studio owed him a great deal. But he had become undependable, with health problems compounded by a fondness for the bottle. In a letter to Leo Spitz, Pandro Berman argued persuasively that the Gershwins were "definitely responsible, high-class people" who would probably do a better job than Youmans, even if he worked at peak efficiency.[22] Thus, one of the great names of twentieth-century American music—Gershwin—became associated with RKO in 1936.[23]

To shore up its producing ranks, Briskin recruited Small, Lasky, and Hawks. Edward Small, whose Reliance Pictures had previously been distributed by United Artists, brought a number of properties with him, including the rights to Rudyard Kipling's famous poem "Gunga Din." Jesse Lasky was a respected name in the motion picture industry, having played a significant role in the development of Paramount. But he was now entering the twilight of his career, and the announcement of his new "long-term contract" with RKO would soon be cause for regret.[24] Producer-director Howard Hawks had made *The Criminal Code* (1931) and *Twentieth Century* (1934) for Columbia while Briskin was employed by that company. He would be expected to complete two or three pictures a year for RKO.

The one important executive who joined RKO in 1936 was Sid Rogell. Rogell had been studio manager of RKO Pathe before that organization was

Figure 14.   *Shall We Dance* (1937). Director Mark Sandrich and composer George Gershwin on the set. Gershwin, one of the giants of American music, died not long after this photograph was taken. (Courtesy of the Academy of Motion Picture Arts and Sciences)

completely absorbed by RKO in 1933. He had also worked as a production manager on a number of pictures, had produced a series of John Wayne Westerns for Warner Bros. release, and was working as an associate producer at Columbia when he accepted the RKO job. Rogell became RKO's studio manager, meaning he would take charge of scheduling, budgeting, coordinating the work of the technical departments, and handling other logistical details. His tenure with the company would last (except for a brief period in 1942) until 1950.

Without question, Sam Briskin's most lasting contribution to RKO was his signing of Walt Disney to a distribution contract in 1936. Disney's foresight regarding television proved a prime factor in his decision to link up with RKO. For the previous five years, his award-winning cartoons had been distributed by United Artists. His contract was up for renewal, and negotiations were proceeding agreeably when they suddenly came to a halt over one small detail. Disney indicated he might wish to retain the television rights during the distribution period for his

Figure 15. Samuel Briskin in his office during the period when he was head of production at RKO. (Courtesy of the Academy of Motion Picture Arts and Sciences)

pictures, and the United Artists board of directors, particularly Sam Goldwyn and Mary Pickford, refused to give in on the matter. As Tino Balio reported in his history of UA, this "foolish quibble over a minor detail" gave RKO an opportunity to propose an even better deal to Disney which he accepted.[25]

Sam Briskin had worked with Walt and Roy Disney around 1930 when the brothers were using Columbia as a distribution outlet. Briskin made the initial contact and wooed them with an arrangement wherein RKO would advance $43,500 for the production of each cartoon and split the profits fifty-fifty with Disney after the production cost was recouped.[26] A separate arrangement was made for distribution of Disney's first animated feature, *Snow White and the Seven Dwarfs*, then in production. For once, RKO's close ties with radio and RCA's sponsorship of television development proved helpful. Although the specific contract provisions regarding video rights were vague, television was definitely on Walt Disney's mind. He issued the following statement when the deal was announced: "In looking to the future, and that includes television, we believe our association with RKO offers greater opportunities for the broader and more expansive fields of development."[27] An ecstatic Merlin Aylesworth praised Disney for his vision: "Disney, as others, is looking forward to future television and is wondering what is going to happen. That is the extent of his interest right now. Being primarily an artist, he is considering the possibilities of a new medium for his art. He is not alone among film producers who have shown interest. Irving Thalberg likes to talk about television for hours."[28]

It is fascinating to reflect on Disney's prescience. In 1936, he was already thinking about the possibilities of an unknown medium which he would eventually mobilize more completely and successfully than any other "film person."

Almost lost amid the tumult regarding RKO's Disney coup was the fact that the studio already had a deal with the Van Beuren Corporation to distribute its Rainbow Parade series of animated short subjects. This turned out not to be a problem. Disney still owed United Artists fifteen cartoons and could not begin delivering under the RKO contract until January 1937.[29] Thus, there would be time to phase out the Van Beuren efforts.

Back in New York, the executives and lawyers continued trying to solve the receivership dilemma. During the initial months of the year, a series of postponements in the hearings were necessitated by the inability of N. Peter Rathvon and others to formulate a suitable plan. The chief impediment was Rockefeller Center's huge claim against the company, as the *Motion Picture Herald* explained:

> The claim is based on a 20-year lease made by RKO with Rockefeller Center in 1931, which provides for an annual rental of $950,000. Under articles of the lease RKO was also held liable for the unamortized construction costs of the Music Hall and Center Theatre. The claim was filed for $12,185,000 and, after hearings last year, was reduced to approximately $9,150,000. As the claim now stands Rockefeller Center

is the largest unsecured creditor of RKO and as such would be a power in the reorganization of the company. The status of the huge claim has been the principal obstacle to the development of a plan of reorganization for RKO and it is apparent that until the claim is disposed of little or no progress on a plan can be made.[30]

Nevertheless, Leo Spitz told RKO's June sales convention that the reorganization would be effected by January 1937.[31]

The process dragged on into the fall when, suddenly, significant pressure was brought to bear on the situation. RKO's earnings had improved, and its stock was rising: "The rapidly increasing earnings of RKO, which are being reflected in the market value of its stock, were said to be a factor in the current demand for an immediate presentation of a plan. A sharp rise in the market value of the stock would complicate the provisions for treatment of the stockholders. . . . The same consideration applies in lesser degree to any creditors who are designated to receive common stock of the new RKO company in settlement of their claims."[32]

The news that RKO was doing better financially was indeed welcome. But a close look at the numbers disclosed reasons for concern. More than half of the profits from the 1936 releases were generated by two pictures: *Follow the Fleet* and *Swing Time.* The former brought in $945,000, and the latter $830,000. Both of these Astaire-Rogers pictures opened at the Radio City Music Hall, where they played to capacity crowds. They also did strong business throughout the country, but a decline in attendance for *Swing Time* came sooner than expected. Fred Astaire stated in his autobiography that he believed all along that *Swing Time* was not the best of the team's pictures and interpreted the slight diminution in profits as an indication that "the cycle was running out its course."[33] Despite the fact that *Swing Time* cost more than any previous Astaire-Rogers musical ($886,000) and made less than either *Top Hat* or *Follow the Fleet*, the RKO executives were still overjoyed. But Astaire was right: the numbers would continue to trend downward.

There was a giant falloff between the two musicals and the studio's other hits. *The Ex–Mrs. Bradford,* a comedy-mystery performed very nicely, earning a profit of $350,000, but it featured two performers under contract to other studios, William Powell from MGM and Jean Arthur from Columbia. Thus, it would be difficult to build upon its success. And the only other films that spawned six-figure results were *The Bride Walks Out,* starring Barbara Stanwyck ($164,000), and two films featuring Gene Raymond and Ann Sothern: *Walking on Air* ($106,000) and *The Smartest Girl in Town* ($101,000).

Among the losers, the most worrisome were the Hepburn pictures. Following the *Sylvia Scarlett* debacle, Pandro Berman put Academy Award–winners Dudley Nichols and John Ford to work on Maxwell Anderson's play *Mary of Scotland*. RKO was determined to shoot the works on the historical drama and spared no expense. The final budget amounted to $864,000; of the films produced in 1936, only *Swing Time* cost more.

When shooting was completed, word-of-mouth around the studio indicated RKO had a hit. A large advertising campaign was designed, and the preview reaction was totally encouraging, as Berman indicated to Spitz in the following wire: "Very happy report had wonderful preview *Mary* Santa Barbara last night. . . . Had spontaneous applause during picture and enormous round of applause at finish which did not expect account sadness of execution. Definitely a sock with audiences of all types. Not necessary have highbrow gang to appreciate it. Couldn't be more pleased."[34]

The company decided to experiment by releasing the film in late July, traditionally a taboo period for expensive pictures because the stifling summer heat tended to keep people away from movie houses. The theory was that since other companies were tossing only low-level product into theaters at this time, *Mary of Scotland* would stand out in bas-relief. The concept seemed to work at first; initial box-office returns were very good. However, the film soon began to falter, and it rapidly became apparent that *Mary of Scotland* was going to flop. It did—to the tune of a $165,000 loss.

Pandro Berman's next Hepburn project was a novel by Netta Syrett entitled *Portrait of a Rebel*. As mentioned earlier, Hepburn found the material "mediocre," while Berman believed in it strongly. The central character, Pamela Thistlewaite, seemed a perfect Hepburn heroine. A nonconformist in strict Victorian society, Pamela asserted herself on such subjects as a woman's right to work, to choose her own husband, to live alone, and to read whatever she pleased.

Its title changed to *A Woman Rebels*, the final product confirmed the actress's worst suspicions. The public demonstrated its aversion to the character and the picture by assiduously avoiding theaters that presented it. *A Woman Rebels* cost only $574,000, a modest amount for a Hepburn vehicle, but lost $222,000—even more than *Mary of Scotland*. Following her ingratiating performance in *Alice Adams*, Katharine Hepburn had starred in three successive pictures that hurt her career. Rather like Helen Gahagan bathed in the flame at the end of *She*, RKO's most important actress was withering away rapidly. Sam Briskin, Pan Berman, and the other RKO executives appeared unable to do anything to reverse her diminishing appeal.

Figure 16. *Mary of Scotland* (1936). Victor McLaglen visits the set and chats with Katharine Hepburn and director John Ford. McLaglen had recently captured the Best Actor Academy Award for his work in *The Informer,* which Ford directed. (Courtesy of the Academy of Motion Picture Arts and Sciences)

Pandro Berman's campaign for more prestige pictures ended with *Winterset,* another play by Maxwell Anderson. Berman believed this thinly disguised rumination on the Sacco and Vanzetti case could become another *Informer.* Anthony Veiller, now considered one of RKO's best writers, went to work on the adaptation. His biggest challenges were the elimination of most of Anderson's blank verse dialogue and the substitution of a happy ending for the original tragic denouement. When Veiller's script was finished, playwright Anderson lavished praise on it:

> The Veiller version of *Winterset* is extraordinarily ingenious in construction, and keeps the atmosphere so well that I begin to believe it may turn into one of the best pictures ever made. It has the weird power of *The Informer,* with the addition of an attractive love motive. The picture technique is an actual advantage in telling the story, especially in the early scenes. . . . Some of this is only skeletonized, and could be given more flesh and blood with a word or two here and there, but in the main I like it and I'm sure it will be effective.[35]

This must be one of the few extant examples of an artist actually complimenting someone for tinkering with his work.

Released at the end of 1936, *Winterset* impressed most of the critics. However, unlike *The Informer,* it won no major awards and fared less well with audiences. Although it almost broke even (with a $2,000 loss), its indifferent box office, along with the Hepburn failures, convinced Leo Spitz that high-minded, sophisticated productions were not the ticket to RKO success. Soon, his thinking would favor the opposite type of movie.

Sam Briskin must have been pleased when he learned he had been allocated $13 million to complete forty-one pictures (another seven releases would be provided by independents) for the 1936–1937 season.[36] It would be his first complete program and represented the largest appropriation given a studio head in RKO's history. Yet he was still having problems in the fall of 1936. The major difficulty involved locating and purchasing acceptable story material. If good material existed, RKO was not having much success acquiring it. A September letter from Spitz to Briskin indicated that the studio expected nineteen A pictures during the season, to be made for an average expenditure of $510,000 each.[37] From the beginning of the program in September until December, however, only one A picture, *Swing Time,* was released by RKO. The studio, under Sam Briskin's stewardship, was not living up to its obligations.

Even so, the receivership problem was beginning to seem solvable. In November the Rockefellers agreed to accept 500,000 shares of common stock in a reorganized Radio-Keith-Orpheum as payment for their claim, thus clearing the way for the long-awaited reorganization plan. The plan called for $33 million in new capitalization, corporate simplification through the merger of several subsidiary companies (RKO Studios, Inc., the RKO Distributing Corporation, the RKO Pathe Studios Corporation, Ltd., and three others) into RKO Radio Pictures, Incorporated, and the issuance of new common stock.[38] Shareholders would receive one-half new share for each share of the old RKO common they held. The company's other creditors (in addition to Rockefeller Center) would also receive stock equal in value to the amount of their claims.

In addition to canceling the $9,100,000 debt, the Rockefeller Center arrangement was supposed, once again, to give RKO a participation in the operation and profits of the two Radio City theaters. A new rental rate of $2 per square foot (reduced from $2.75) was also agreed upon for the office space RKO occupied in Radio City.[39] The agreement between RKO and the Rockefellers was set to last for twelve years.

According to the *Motion Picture Herald*, "the reorganization plan should not meet with any serious opposition and may have the court's approval by March 1."[40] This prediction was overly optimistic. Several problems soon became apparent, problems that would delay the company's emergence from receivership. Nevertheless, one important fact was now apparent. No matter what happened, the Rockefellers would play a significant role in the future of RKO.

While all this activity was taking place, RKO's board chairman, Merlin Aylesworth, remained above the fray. Early in 1936, Aylesworth resigned as president of the National Broadcasting Company, though he continued to serve as vice-chairman and a director of the radio network. He severed all ties with NBC in October.[41] Finally, after almost four years as a high official of the movie concern, he would be able to give his undivided service to RKO. But this was truly odd because there was not very much for him to do, or very much he *could* do. The company's direction was now being plotted by Floyd Odlum's men—Leo Spitz and Sam Briskin—and Aylesworth represented something of an excrescence on the corporate body.

Aylesworth's stated reason for parting company with NBC was a desire to devote more time to RKO in his position as chairman of its board. That would actually translate to devoting himself to an old pastime—preaching the gospel of radio-film harmony. He once again began to advocate more radio-movie cooperation in July. Calling radio the "best friend" of motion pictures, he proposed a new working arrangement to aid both industries.[42] Aylesworth was in a better position to make his plea than ever before. Many motion picture stars were now appearing regularly on radio, despite the grumblings of exhibitors. Joan Crawford, Shirley Temple, Clark Gable, and Marion Davies were only a few of the performers realizing munificent salaries (up to $25,000 per week) for their broadcasting efforts.[43] RKO's biggest name, Fred Astaire, signed an agreement with the Packard Motor Car Company in 1936 for a series of NBC radio shows, thanks to a personal request from Pandro Berman, acting on behalf of Aylesworth.[44]

In addition to denying that radio "de-glamorized" Hollywood stars, Deac Aylesworth continued to challenge the contention that broadcasts cut into box-office receipts: "The motion picture is grossly mistaken when it says that the radio keeps people in their houses, thereby cutting off potential theatre patronage. . . . Except in the summertime, Saturday and Sunday evenings are still the best days for the box office grosses. Yet there are more good radio programs broadcast on those evenings than any other night."[45] Aylesworth's prescription for mutual cooperation was simple:

more utilization of radio to exploit pictures, more freedom of access for radio use of film personalities, more technical assistance from film companies in the development of commercial television.

Now that Aylesworth was solely allied with RKO rather than both the movie company and NBC, one movie executive began to claim that the studios had a "double agent" in their midst. Jack Cohn, vice-president of Columbia, became a spokesman for the anti-radio faction. In August he answered Aylesworth, calling his mutual cooperation philosophy "ridiculous" and charging "treason within the ranks." Cohn debunked the contention that radio "plugging" helped to sell pictures and urged "drastic steps to force producers to bar their stars from the air." He also spoke sympathetically of exhibitors whose business had supposedly been damaged by radio cooperation. Cohn concluded: "Radio is competition for the motion picture, and no arrangement can be worked out for an amicable arrangement under which both will benefit. We have met the competition in the past and we will continue to meet it in the future. And we will do it when and if television becomes a commercial reality. But we are treading on dangerous ground, selling ammunition to the enemy, when we lend our stars for the enhancing of competing programs."[46]

Jack Cohn's bluster was disingenuous. Columbia had few stars to exploit—on radio or otherwise. Thus, Cohn was clearly attempting to ingratiate his company with theater owners since Columbia had nothing of consequence to gain from a radio partnership. In fact, Aylesworth's (and Sarnoff's) position now had the upper hand. Movie personalities were appearing on national broadcasts every evening, and most of the studios had come to understand the advantages of this exposure.

In addition, RCA's sound recording and theatrical sound business now held approximately equal sway with that of Western Electric. The company's annual report for 1936 revealed that "contracts covering the use of RCA Photophone recording equipment in picture production were consummated with Columbia Pictures, Warner Bros., 20th Century-Fox, RKO Radio-Pictures, Pathe News, and Walt Disney Pictures, and other contracts are being negotiated. In theatre equipment and service, RCA enjoys a substantial share of the business."[47] Thus, the principal goals that had drawn David Sarnoff into the motion picture business back in 1928 had been accomplished. No wonder he had decided to peddle RCA's controlling interest in RKO to Floyd Odlum.

RKO sailed into 1937 on the strength of its best showing since the early years of the company. On the whole, movie corporations had enjoyed a remarkable year in 1936. Reports by United Press and other reliable sources indicated that industry grosses were $250 million greater than the previous year and that estimated weekly theater attendance had increased to 81 million, up 10 million from the 1935 weekly average.[48] The Depression had moderated throughout America with most of the studios reaping remarkable benefits:

> Motion picture shares on the New York Stock Exchange gained $162,636,250 in market value during 1936 on a wave of prosperity that swept the industry and the country and promised further advance in the new year.
> With film earnings definitely "in the black" for the first time since the late depression, the market value of listed picture stocks increased for the fourth consecutive year, totaling $825,456,250, as of the close on December 28. This compared with $666,820,000 at the end of 1935 and $402,973,125 at the close of 1934.[49]

The improving business climate enabled RKO to report a net profit of $2,514,734 for 1936. Significantly, theater operation showed the biggest gain in profits—$1,414,886 in 1936 as compared to $87,063 in 1935. RKO Radio Pictures, Inc., the production entity, reported a profit of $1,088,384.[50]

The corporate logo, announcing the commencement of each of its films, now proudly proclaimed "RKO Radio Pictures Presents," instead of just "Radio Pictures Presents." This was in line with the consolidation of various subsidiaries into the producing concern, but it also suggested a change in corporate identity. Now known principally as "RKO," rather than "Radio," the studio could assert an independence from broadcasting and a full commitment to film that had been questioned in the past.

The symbolic detachment from radio was further augmented in February 1937 when Merlin Aylesworth quit the company to join the executive staff of the Scripps-Howard chain of daily newspapers.[51] The move was not unexpected; though chairman of the RKO board, Aylesworth had not had much input into the running of the organization since Odlum's men had taken power. The board of directors voted that he should receive a parting gift of $25,000 "in consideration of his services to this Corporation."[52]

It was ironic that Merlin Aylesworth chose this particular moment to desert the world of motion pictures. A week before his departure, the *Motion Picture Herald* indicated that his efforts to make allies out of radio and the movies had borne fruit: "Increasing attention is being given by producing and distributing companies, large and small, to organized use of radio facilities as an outlet for publicity, either institutional or for a particular picture. The home office publicity forces have geared their machinery to manufacture ideas and material designed to turn the air outlet to best advantage and in many cases the radio release bureau has become one of the most important cogs in the department." The story proceeded to outline the various uses of radio by all the studios (even Columbia).[53] Merlin Aylesworth had finally won; his ideas had been vindicated. The victory must have seemed rather hollow, however, for now he had to forget about show business and turn his attention to the prosaic world of print journalism. Replacing him as chairman of the RKO board would be Leo Spitz.

Strangely, considering the concerns about A film production that existed at the end of 1936, Sam Briskin began fussing with the Bs in early 1937. He called a meeting of his producers, which included Leo Spitz, Ned Depinet, and other high company officials, where he outlined a new policy regarding B films. In essence, the Bs were to be broken down into two categories: "intermediates" costing between $300,000 and $400,000, which would generally serve as vehicles for potential stars and unusual stories; and "programmers," designed to cost no more than $115,000 each and enable the company to fulfill is product obligations. When news of the meeting was communicated to the trade papers, no mention of the cheap productions was included. Instead, Briskin was quoted as saying that budgets for the B pictures "are to be increased from 25 to 30 percent in the effort to elevate films in this classification to the point where they can play first run and single feature houses with success."[54]

Briskin omitted the information, however, that for most B productions his producers had been instructed not to expect musical scores, "extravagant" titles, crane and dolly shots, or even retakes.[55] The producers were also being told to keep the footage down to 5,200 feet, because no more "money is grossed on a picture with a footage of 6,200 ft . . . and on the shorter script we can save a day or two on the schedule and it means nothing to the gross on this type of picture."[56]

By May, Sam Briskin and Leo Spitz had grown even more unhappy with the inexpensive films. The quality of *Behind the Headlines, Too Many Wives,* and others was so low that audiences were actually razzing the films throughout the country. Briskin pointed this out to Lee Marcus, the head of the B production group: "Personally, I have been very disturbed in the past few months . . . about the quality we were getting in some of these pictures and at the cost of them. I have never had any illusions about making great or outstanding pictures in the 'B' group and I am sure no one in New York expects us to win the Academy Award with any of these pictures. However, they are entitled to a quality that is at least fairly good."[57] Briskin proceeded to criticize Marcus for allowing the budgets on these films to average between $120,000 and $130,000, instead of the $115,000 figure that had been stipulated.

Marcus responded with a profit analysis of the previous nineteen films made under his supervision. He had little to say about quality, preferring to concentrate on box-office performance instead. Using this as a barometer, Marcus argued that the key to B pictures' success was not budget, but "names." Films that included at least one known performer—such as Lee Tracy or Sally Eilers or Robert Armstrong or Zasu Pitts—made money; those films without established players inevitably ended in the red. The only exception to the rule was *Yellow Dust*, a Richard Dix film that, according to Marcus, "shows a loss, not due to cast, but due to excessive negative cost."[58] Marcus defended himself well; for a time, the B unit was left alone and Marcus was encouraged to work more "names" into his films.

Why was Sam Briskin fixated on B pictures when his company needed more As? Because he could not do much about the A problem. RKO was able to turn out only a limited number of A films because of its small group of bona fide stars: Astaire, Rogers, Irene Dunne. Katharine Hepburn had faded and now occupied a kind of limbo between A and B status, although company management still insisted each Hepburn picture was an A. Joining Hepburn in the A-B limbo were such performers as Barbara Stanwyck, Jack Oakie, Lily Pons, and Miriam Hopkins. The team of Bert Wheeler and Robert Woolsey had long been relegated to B status; they completed their last comedy, *High Flyers*, for the company in 1937 and were dismissed. And Briskin's roundup of new talent had been woefully unproductive. Several radio comedians, including Joe Penner, Milton Berle, and "Parkyakarkus," were put under contract but none clicked with moviegoers. By September, Leo Spitz was forced to write Briskin suggesting ways in which the studio's investment in these individuals might be "salvaged."[59] Joan Fontaine was also under contract, but no one seemed to know what to do with her. The same was true of Lucille Ball.

The lion's share of the blame for the failure of RKO to develop a solid stock company during this period must lie with its production chief. The studio had always been weak in this area, and Briskin failed not only to upgrade the talent but, in fact, to maintain the level of star power he inherited when he took over the job. Still, Sam Briskin was not wholly at fault. Ned Depinet illustrated the myopia affecting the entire group of officials running the company at the time when he wired Leo Spitz concerning a performer who had been appearing in B cowboy movies since the early 1930s: "Jules [Levy], myself believe would be mistake distribute

John Wayne Westerns. He is in same category as dozen others with disadvantage having been sold cheaply and our opinion little prospect of gaining popularity. . . . He is one of the poorest of so called western stars, seems miscast and his pictures doing little at Universal. We believe would be better to go ahead with George Shelley who has not been identified with cheap western pictures and with whom we would have chance building . . . worthwhile singing western star like Autry."[60] And, of course, we all remember George Shelley.

The producer situation was also aggravating. In 1937 Briskin had Edward Small, Edward Kaufman, Howard Hawks, Cliff Reid, Jesse Lasky, Robert Sisk, Joseph Sistrom, Maury Cohen, and P. G. Wolfson, plus Pandro Berman supervising pictures. Reid, Sisk, Sistrom, and Cohen mainly handled B releases under the administrative control of Lee Marcus.

Among the A producers, Jesse Lasky had been a disappointment and the studio was biding its time, waiting for his contract to expire.[61] Pinky Wolfson, after a brief shot at producing, returned to screenwriting, a less remunerative occupation he had momentarily transcended. Edward Small had not contributed any significant work as yet, but management was still deliberating his fate, as it was that of Edward Kaufman. Kaufman had guided *The Ex–Mrs. Bradford* but also some misfires. Berman remained the company's indisputable top man, regardless of several slips during the past two years. This left Howard Hawks, a filmmaker of unquestionable talent but questionable value to RKO.

Hawks worked for almost a year, drawing a salary of $2,500 per week, before he put his first RKO picture into production.[62] The film had special importance to the studio because *Bringing Up Baby* was designed to introduce a new Katharine Hepburn persona—the screwball comedienne—and to reinvigorate her flagging box-office appeal. To have some chance of making a profit, however, the picture's budget had to be reasonable. Indications were that no Katharine Hepburn vehicle could make money, during this juncture in her career, if it cost much more than a half-million dollars.

Hawks was well aware of this, but maneuvered and finagled until the budget of *Baby* topped $1 million. Sam Briskin simply was not strong enough to keep the director in line. The following memo, written by Briskin's assistant Lou Lusty as shooting was about to commence, both confirms the basic auteur contentions about Hawks and shows why someone like Howard Hawks could have a devastating impact on a studio like RKO:

> I know, because the gentleman has said so in so many words, that he's only concerned with making a picture that will be a personal credit to

Mr. Hawks regardless of its cost—and your [Briskin's] telling him the other day that it would be suicidal to make a Hepburn picture for seven or eight hundred thousand dollars I know made no impression on him at all. . . . Hawks is determined in his own quiet, reserved, soft-spoken manner to have his way about the making of this picture. . . . With the salary he's been getting he's almost indifferent to anything that might come to him on a percentage deal—that's why he doesn't give a damn about how much the picture will cost to make— and you know so well that you couldn't even break even if a Hepburn show cost eight hundred grand. All the directors in Hollywood are developing producer-director complexes and Hawks is going to be particularly difficult.[63]

The picture (released in 1938 and discussed in the following chapter) is now considered a preeminent example of the comedy genre and one of the finest films ever produced by RKO. But in its time *Bringing Up Baby* was nothing but trouble for the company—and for Sam Briskin.

Meanwhile, Briskin's concerns about the B productions continued to increase. In August he suggested to Leo Spitz that he (Briskin) might take over Marcus's job, utilizing two producers (probably Reid and Sisk) to help him oversee the B pictures. Spitz vetoed the idea. The company president was a supporter of Marcus and, quite rightly, explained to Briskin that supervising the B films could be a time-consuming burden that would hamper Briskin's overall performance.[64]

Spitz believed the B-unit producers were the problem. He believed RKO was employing too many of them, and not one had an impressive record. Something had to be done, but about the only definite idea was to get rid of Joe Sistrom, an impossibility since he had ten months left on his contract.[65] RKO was stuck. As Lou Lusty opined, "If it wasn't for the continued guidance and help from the front office, some of the gentlemen on the lot would never be able to finish a script—much less put it into production."[66]

Very little information about B releases had been forthcoming back in June when the company held its sales convention at the Ambassador Hotel in Hollywood. In the announcement of fifty-six features for the 1937–1938 season, the emphasis was, as always, on the most important coming attractions.[67] But Sam Briskin did make an interesting statement regarding A and B production: "As to the gradation of pictures in terms of alphabet, we have had it definitely proven to us that public opinion is the conclusive marker. Our classification of a picture before it is put into production, either through budgeting its cast or by studding its cast with star names, has little bearing so long as it clicks at the box office."[68]

This was a rather clumsy verbal smokescreen, manufactured by Briskin to conceal the fact that RKO planned to produce fewer A films than in the past. Briskin was attempting to sidestep the question of just how many of RKO's 1937–1938 releases would actually be topnotch productions. In fact, only about fifteen were targeted for the A category.[69]

Briskin's ploy evidently didn't work, because later that summer an ominous state of affairs became apparent to RKO executives. Exhibitors were refusing to sign contracts for the 1937–1938 program. Many of them were fed up with the company's inability to complete films in time to meet promised release dates. Ned Depinet wrote Briskin bemoaning the fact that "we have had to change our release schedule time and time and time again during the past year."[70] The larger issue was the quality of the product when it did arrive. According to Leo Spitz, theater owners were spurning the entreaties of RKO salesmen, "due, of course, to our record of performance and although we are all certain that we are going to show a tremendous improvement, the exhibitors want to be shown first."[71]

Part of the problem related to a decision to begin asking for better terms in RKO contracts. But then, the other studios were also demanding a larger cut of the box-office take. As Spitz suggested, the real difficulty was the substandard quality of recent RKO productions. RKO was depending on *Stage Door,* a hotly anticipated film that would launch the new season, to woo exhibitors into buying its product. The letter from Spitz to Briskin containing the sobering information about exhibitor resistance also stated, openly and frankly, what RKO expected from its production chief: "I believe you are satisfied now that the only thing all of us are interested in—and that includes Trustees, lawyers, bankers, committees, etc.—is box-office pictures. Nobody cares who makes them or how they are gotten out—the final result is the only thing that counts."[72] The implication was clear. If Briskin did not start producing moneymaking films pretty soon, someone else would be given the opportunity.

In September, Sam Briskin's problems became unmanageable. The "intermediate" pictures had turned into a plague. These films, mentioned prominently at the beginning of the year as a nurturing ground for new talent and a perfect venue for treating unusual story material, were losing money. Sam Briskin wrote Spitz blaming the situation on rising costs that he claimed were largely the result of militant labor activity in Hollywood: "It seems that every day there is a new organization formed and every day we are giving them something. You are familiar, of course, with the labor deal and the strike situation we had which resulted in giving the painters a fifteen percent increase. . . . We are now dealing with the office workers, the film editors, and the assistant directors."[73]

Related directly to picture budgets, this meant that intermediate films that cost $250,000 to $350,000 in 1935 now ranged between $300,000 and $500,000. The chances of turning a profit at these figures were virtually nonexistent because the pictures remained, in essence, B releases. Briskin suggested the idea of holding down A films to "six or eight," striving to make those few truly "great" and eliminating the intermediates as much as possible.[74] This was the Columbia Pictures philosophy that Briskin had helped to implement in his former position. Leo Spitz evidently did not give the idea any credence; he made no mention of it in his reply to Briskin.[75]

Sam Briskin's struggles in Hollywood were paralleled by the efforts to resolve the receivership situation in New York. Financial experts had predicted that the reorganization plan submitted by Atlas Corporation would be approved early in 1937. Instead, involved parties bombarded the court with objections. This mass of litigation so swamped Judge Bondy, tying up the proceedings completely, that the judge was forced to appoint a "Special Master" to impose order on this quagmire of stockholder and creditor complaints. The unenviable job went to George W. Alger. He was instructed to "divide creditors and stockholders into classes according to the nature of their claims" and then evaluate the "fairness and feasibility of the proposed [reorganization] plan in light of the various objections."[76]

Most of the complaints were related to the proposal to turn over 500,000 shares of new RKO stock to Rockefeller Center in settlement of the latter's $9,150,000 claim against RKO. Creditors argued that the Rockefellers were being given preferential treatment, that RKO had no business continuing its financial arrangement with the giant theaters, and that they (the creditors) had been offered a much less generous settlement. Stockholders also expressed concern that the Rockefeller family would control "one-fourth or one-fifth of the entire stock equity" in RKO if the plan gained acceptance.[77] H. C. Rickaby, attorney for Atlas Corporation, attacked the malcontents, calling them an "insignificant minority." He also defended the Rockefeller Center agreement in his summation before Special Master Alger: "He pointed out that all creditors accepted the settlement and that rejection of the settlement might require a new plan to be written. Mr. Rickaby said that few New York first run houses earned large profits but that the Music Hall's value to RKO was 'a national advertisement.' The plan was characterized as fair, equitable and feasible. . . . He added that he regarded rejection of the plan and continuation of the trusteeship as 'inconceivable.' "[78] Settlement of the Rockefeller claim, though the major source of contention, was not the only one. Conversion privileges for holders of the proposed new debentures and preferred stock and the lack of a physical appraisal of the company's assets were also hot-button issues.[79]

The hearings foundered for months. An amusing incident transpired in the midst of the inquiry. Special Master Alger decided that since he was becoming an authority on the motion picture business, he ought to begin offering advice about RKO's story selection. Alger contacted Odlum representative Peter Rathvon and suggested that Sam Briskin and his staff consider two properties: *Young April,* a novel by Edgerton Castle, and *Hell and High Water,* a story published in *Argosy* magazine. Rathvon mentioned the two items to Briskin and concluded: "It might be useful for the record if you would write me a note that you are much obliged to Mr. Alger for these suggestions and that you will have someone in your story department check them up immediately. Later we will face the problem of what to do when you find they are no good."[80]

Sam Briskin obliged, dispatching his "grateful" note on August 9.[81] On August 21 he sent a second letter to Rathvon with the story department evaluations. They were, of course, negative. Briskin ended his letter by instructing Rathvon to "please tell Judge Alger that although these two stories did not fit the studio program, should he have any further suggestions to make, we would be very happy to receive them."[82] One can imagine what the acerbic Briskin would have said to Alger about his "helpfulness" if the studio head could have spoken frankly.

Indeed, the last thing Briskin wanted to deal with at this time was some "civilian" offering story recommendations. He knew the RKO board was debating whether he should be offered a new three-year contract, and he probably also knew that certain RKO representatives had had preliminary discussions with Samuel Goldwyn about replacing him.[83] While the Odlum faction was initially in favor of keeping Briskin in his position, other board members and the trustee had reservations.[84]

Those reservations increased as the summer months ended and the new release year began. Besides the difficulties with exhibitors and the bad news flowing out of the studio, earnings were trending downward; two of Briskin's most expensive pictures, *New Faces of 1937* and *The Toast of New York,* had opened and were performing poorly; and company officials were aware that *Bringing Up Baby* was about to go into production despite its inflated budget. All support for Sam Briskin quickly disappeared, and he was forced to resign in October.[85]

No reasons were announced for Briskin's departure. A number of factors lay hidden beneath the surface and all contributed to the production chief's undoing:

1. Briskin had had difficulty finishing films in time to meet promised release dates.

2. Leo Spitz had become more and more involved in production decisions, and he and Briskin disagreed on certain significant matters.

3. Briskin had hired a number of producers, most of whom turned out to be undependable. He also demonstrated an inability to control certain profligate producers, such as Howard Hawks.

4. He had failed, during almost two years at the helm, to develop a talent pool of any consequence.

5. The films made by Briskin's regime had been largely second-rate, and too many had been unprofitable.

Paramount in this list was number 5. Ultimately, the performance of any studio head is measured by his releases. During Sam Briskin's stewardship, RKO moviemaking stumbled and fell backwards, with the 1937 pictures being less satisfactory than those released in 1936, which had been considerably less impressive than the 1935 releases. The motion picture industry had entered another favorable period; everyone was making profits, even RKO. But the one component of the RKO machine that had fallen down and was minimizing the corporation's income was production. Sam Briskin could not be blamed for all the problems, but production remained his responsibility and he had to answer for the profusion of misfires. Evidently a good deal of pressure was put on him to resign because a "golden handshake" was agreed upon that paid Briskin $84,000 spread out over twenty-one weeks after he left the company.[86]

First reports indicated that Leo Spitz might assume control of Hollywood studio operations.[87] Spitz, however, did not wish to devote his energies to production, though he intended to be heavily involved; instead, RKO was going to call upon an old standby to run filmmaking: Pandro Berman. Berman accepted the job reluctantly as a favor to Spitz. Although he had headed the studio before, during Merian Cooper's two separate convalescence periods and for a short time after Cooper resigned, Berman had always preferred to concentrate on his own production unit. Uncertainty generated by Berman's expressed partiality is evident in this ambivalent letter, sent to the new production head by New York story editor

Lillie Messinger: "I am in a quandary. . . . I don't know whether to congratulate you or not. Maybe I'm psychic, but I feel you did not really want to take over so much production. You've been working so hard that it seems to me just a burden you are taking over out of necessity. So I'll reserve my congratulations until I see you and know whether you do want it. All I can say is that it's swell for me . . . AND FOR RKO."[88]

Just how "swell" the new production setup would be remained a question mark. No one doubted Berman's ability; he was one of Hollywood's proven picture makers. But would he be content spreading his energies over an entire program of films, rather than concentrating on a few? Over and above this consideration was the obvious problem that, fewer than two years after Spitz and Briskin had taken charge, RKO was entering a new phase. The change would necessitate an obligatory grinding of gears during which, if history was any indicator, the studio could anticipate more discord and uncertainty. Almost ten years had elapsed since its birth, yet the "Titan" was still groping for a guiding philosophy and continuity of management.

With the Briskin matter resolved, attention switched back to the receivership quandary. In mid-November, Special Master Alger issued a preliminary report on the RKO reorganization plan. The only major change was a recommendation that Rockefeller Center's claim be reduced from $9,150,000 to $5,100,000 and that the Rockefeller interests receive 38,250 shares of new RKO preferred stock and 76,500 shares of new common stock, in place of the 500,000 shares of new common that the plan originally proposed.[89] Obviously, the revision was designed to placate those disgruntled creditors and stockholders who felt the Rockefellers were receiving special treatment. Alger's recommendations were tentative—they did not constitute an official or accepted revised draft of the proposal. Now Judge Bondy would take over once again, and attorneys would begin preparing arguments for and against Alger's ideas in Bondy's federal court.

The "final" hearings rejected Alger's Rockefeller solution. The claim of $9,150,000 was upheld, though the stock the center was to receive was reduced from 500,000 shares to 460,000.[90] Nevertheless, sources suggested that approval of the plan appeared imminent. Objections remained, especially among small stockholder groups, but none of the major creditors filed fresh complaints.[91]

One unforeseen problem surfaced at the end of the year. The Atlas Corporation had been expected to take full control of RKO's affairs in December 1937 by exercising its option to purchase RCA's remaining stock in the company. This purchase would have short-circuited any power struggles among different factions concerning the functioning of the corporation. Floyd Odlum, however, had begun to question the wisdom of his RKO investment. Instead of exercising the option, thereby smoothing the way for approval of his own reorganization plan, Odlum backed off and negotiated a one-year extension.[92] Atlas now had until December 31, 1938, to pay RCA approximately $6 million for its still-considerable holdings in RKO, and the receivership situation, which had already lasted more than four years, would persist even longer.

Odlum's reluctance was based on a number of factors, chief among them the declining performance of the company's pictures. Nearly all of RKO's recent A pictures had bombed: *The Toast of New York* lost $530,000; *Music for Madame* $375,000; *The Woman I Love* $266,000; *New Faces of 1937* $258,000; *Quality Street* (Hepburn) $248,000. The only exception was *Shall We Dance*, the single Astaire-Rogers musical released in 1937. However, its profit of $413,000 showed a substantial decline from previous efforts, and the duo dropped from third to seventh in the exhibitors' poll of top stars.[93]

Compounding the uneasiness, Astaire began once again to lobby for a dismantling of the Astaire-Rogers combination. After working sans Rogers in *A Damsel in Distress*, Astaire feared "all that 'well they're back together again' talk" that would surely arise if he made his next film with Ginger.[94] RKO, however, could not afford to grant Astaire's wish. His pairing with Joan Fontaine in *Damsel* resulted in the first loss ($65,000) posted by any Astaire film. So it would be back to basics—and Ginger Rogers was the basics.

The most baffling release of 1937 was unquestionably *Stage Door*. The original Edna Ferber–George S. Kaufman play about a group of young actresses waiting and hoping for their big break had opened on Broadway in 1936. The comedy-drama contained a strong anti-Hollywood bias at its core, but Pandro Berman immediately recognized cinematic potential in the material and convinced Leo Spitz to buy it. From the beginning, *Stage Door* was envisioned as a costarring vehicle for Ginger Rogers and Katharine Hepburn.

Morrie Ryskind and Anthony Veiller were assigned to transform the play into a screen story, removing the nasty comments about Hollywood in the process. Then Gregory La Cava, who had managed *My Man Godfrey* and several other successes since leaving RKO years before, was signed to direct. La Cava rewrote much of the story and dialogue as he filmed, making the final picture quite different from the Ferber-Kaufman prototype.

The movie had special importance for Katharine Hepburn. After several flops in a row, she had become persona non grata to many exhibitors.

Figure 17.   *A Damsel in Distress* (1937). Director George Stevens (white shoes) and crew film the "fun house" number. The actors are Fred Astaire, Gracie Allen, and George Burns. (Courtesy of the Academy of Motion Picture Arts and Sciences)

Witness what Harry Brandt, president of the Independent Theatre Owners Association, telegrammed to Sam Briskin in early 1937: "Understand you are considering Katharine Hepburn in STAGE DOOR. Consider this collossal [*sic*] mistake. Believe you have very valuable piece of property in this play. Us [*sic*] exhibitor with contracts in over sixty theatres with your company and interested in output of your company am advising strongly against Hepburn in this picture. Theatre owners of New York join me in voicing this protest to you."[95] This was the prelude to a war against Hepburn (and other performers) that would take on an ugly complexion in 1938. With respect to *Stage Door*, the message was clear: Hepburn better not fail this time. Her role indeed seemed molded comfortably to her talents. In a story that bore a marked resemblance to *Morning Glory*, she would play an idealistic character very much like Eva Lovelace, the part that had won her an Academy Award.

When the film was completed, Pandro Berman's spirits were buoyant. He called *Stage Door* "the best picture in RKO's history and I am including them all."[96] Berman was so excited, he tried to twist some arms to get either a cover story in *Time* magazine or a *March of Time* segment produced about the picture. He was unsuccessful, but the entire RKO publicity apparatus worked overtime in preparing for its release. Since *Stage Door* represented one of the first pictures of the 1937–1938 season, there was hope it would melt exhibitor opposition to booking blocks of RKO product.

Even before the opening of *Stage Door,* the quality of Hepburn's performance ensured that the company was not going to give up on her, as had been contemplated. Berman wired the actress after the first preview: "A star was reborn last night which is going Gaynor one better. Seriously you came off tremendously and picture looks like smash."[97] Hepburn had indeed delivered a strong performance, fitting in beautifully with the ensemble cast and displaying none of the annoying mannerisms that had perturbed audiences of her recent productions. RKO renewed her option soon after *Stage Door* opened.

Ned Depinet, after seeing it, predicted the film would gross $1.5 million in the United States alone.[98] It opened big in the East, then slumped a bit in the Midwest and South. When final figures were tallied, the domestic gross was $1,250,000, and the final profit only $81,000. Of course, this still meant the picture had done a lot of business, because its production cost had been $952,000. Nevertheless, Pan Berman and Leo Spitz were disconcerted; their surefire blockbuster had turned out to be a modestly successful picture. Why this excellent film failed to earn more substantial profits and did not put Hepburn back on top will forever remain a mystery. At least the Hollywood establishment recognized its achievement— *Stage Door* garnered four Academy Award nominations: Best Picture, Best Director, Best Screenplay, Best Supporting Actress (Andrea Leeds).

Concerns about RKO production were underscored by an exchange that took place near the end of 1937. A. H. McCausland from Irving Trust wrote Leo Spitz suggesting he sell *Gunga Din,* one of the few exciting unproduced properties the company owned.[99] MGM had made a firm offer that RKO had rejected, even though the studio was having difficulty casting the picture. Another negative factor was that the now infamous Howard Hawks was scheduled to direct. When Spitz expressed a disinclination to part with *Gunga Din,* McCausland reminded the RKO president of the current state of the company's filmmaking business: "With respect to *Gunga Din,* the question of whether or not this picture should be made ties in with the question of the picture company finances which, as you appreciate, are in a very bad condition. We have been requested to loan additional money to the picture company to see it through to the end of the year, even in the face of the loan they received from the Bank of America."[100]

This did not mean that RKO's other large divisions, distribution and exhibition, were faltering. It did, however, not bode well for the future. Once again, as in the early 1930s, studio operations could not pay for themselves. No wonder Floyd Odlum backed away at this time and a-dopted a wait-and-see attitude, rather than investing several more millions in RKO Radio Pictures.

At least the final release of the year cheered everyone up. Walt Disney's first feature, *Snow White and the Seven Dwarfs,* had been eagerly awaited, but no one quite expected the avalanche of critical and audience approval that greeted its arrival. William R. Weaver of the *Motion Picture Herald* called its December 1937 baptism at Hollywood's Carthay Circle Theater "the most extraordinary world premiere in cinema history."[101]

Statistics released by RKO indicated that the film had taken three years to complete at a cost of $1,500,000. A total of 570 artists worked on the production, and some 250,000 drawings came together to create the finished product.[102] All the painstaking effort, however, was overshadowed by the extraordinary media blitzkrieg that accompanied the opening. There were features on *Snow White* (several of them cover stores) in *Life, Time, McCall's, Collier's, Popular Science, Town and Country, Better Homes and Gardens, Popular Mechanics,* and practically every important newspaper in the country. National radio broadcasts joined the parade, bombarding listeners with the eight hit songs from the picture. Snow White dolls, toys, books, and novelties soon popped up throughout America, all bringing substantial royalties into Disney's coffers (but not RKO's).[103] RKO's distribution arm was not complaining; in five weeks an estimated 800,000 people paid to see this triumph of animation art at Radio City Music Hall, meaning that almost half of the cost of production had been grossed at this one site.[104]

Throughout 1938 the Hollywood trade papers continued to run stories about the incredible performance of *Snow White.* By July it appeared the film would post the highest domestic gross in the history of the business.[105] Although financial records from the silent era were incomplete and notoriously unreliable, *Snow White* was sure to surpass such earlier successes as Warner Bros.' *The Singing Fool,* Paramount's *The Covered Wagon,* and Metro's *The Four Horsemen of the Apocalypse.* These pictures had each accumulated known revenues of $4.5 million or more.[106] When the smoke finally cleared, *Snow White* was on top, having piled up $7,846,000 in film rentals.

RKO's profit was only $380,000.[107] The company had offered Disney very favorable terms in its distribution contract, meaning it would never earn large profits on his releases. The trade-off was that the Disney name and prestige would help sell the studio's blocks of product and make exhibitors more favorably inclined toward RKO. Sam Briskin had certainly pulled off a major coup when he enticed Walt Disney to join forces with the studio. Briskin, however, was not around to receive the well-deserved hurrahs.

The tenure of *Snow White* atop the list of all-time box-office successes would be short-lived. By 1940 *Gone With the Wind* had eclipsed the former champion. But Walt Disney would not be outclassed by any of his Hollywood competition. Having established himself as a major filmmaker with his first feature, his name would continue to penetrate every facet of American life for years to come. Perhaps the fundamental reason for Disney's success is contained in a memorandum written by one of his employees in 1938: "May I add that Walt built this institution up to what it is today by concentrating on one idea—that of giving quality entertainment no matter what the cost, and, as you know, in spite of many protests from the bookkeepers and financial departments, he has, up to this time always, without exception, been right."[108] RKO's executives should have paid closer attention to their new partner's approach.

Numbers don't lie . . . except when they do. Judged purely on the basis of financial reports, RKO appeared to make impressive strides after Floyd Odlum gained the upper hand in the company's affairs. Odlum's hand-picked Spitz-Briskin regime once again came through with a net profit for 1937: $1,821,165.[109] Although this was about $600,000 less than the year before, the figure still seemed encouraging, especially when compared to the disastrous 1932–1934 period. But 1937 was a bountiful year for the entire film business: MGM made a profit of $14.3 million, followed by Twentieth Century–Fox with $8.6 million, Paramount with $6 million, and Warner Bros. with $5.9 million. Placed in this context, the RKO yield was less than spectacular. In addition, the receivership situation was still unsettled. Roy Chartier of *Variety* called the RKO reorganization "something that's been reported around the corner for so long it must be an awfully long corner."[110] Indeed, Odlum's men had not, as promised, brought a speedy conclusion to the situation, and no end was yet in sight.

The performance of Odlum's appointees also left much to be desired. Leo Spitz had so far displayed no special abilities or strengths in steering the entire organization. And Sam Briskin's departure from RKO in October was a clear indication that he had failed to deliver. In addition to the many obvious signs of deterioration at the studio, the film unit reported a net loss of $236,909 for 1937.[111]

Briskin was not stupid, as the deal with Disney demonstrated, nor did he lack an understanding of the inner workings of Hollywood. But turning over production to him, a man who had never functioned in a purely creative capacity before and who had no prior service with RKO, and thus did not perceive its special demands, was a mistake. Sam Briskin never straightened out the disordered state of affairs he inherited when he took over his position. Like other past and future RKO executive producers, he lost his job before he fully understood it.

Looking ahead, there was reason for hope. Thanks mainly to theater operations, RKO was still in decent financial shape, and a few winning pictures could bring studio operations back into the plus column. The naming of Pandro Berman as production head also conjured positive vibrations. Berman had taste, talent, and years of service to the company. Although he did not savor the prospect of supervising a large number of films, it is hard to imagine anyone in Hollywood who could have been more right for the job. Pan Berman knew the strengths and weaknesses of the studio and its personnel. The era of uncertainty would continue, but at least Berman offered qualities some of his predecessors lacked: knowledge, experience, creativity, achievement, continuity.

7. "Plaything of industry"

The Spitz-Berman Regime (1938)

RKO celebrated its tenth birthday in 1938. During its lifespan, the organization had experienced six major shake-ups in leadership. This was not the case with its competitors. At MGM, Nicholas Schenck and Louis B. Mayer had directed their company throughout the same period; so had Harry and Jack Warner at Warner Bros. and Harry and Jack Cohn at Columbia. Upper management at Paramount, Fox (Twentieth Century–Fox), and Universal was less settled during the same time frame, but these companies now employed trustworthy executives who would offer positive guidance through the war years and, with the exception of Universal, beyond. Only RKO remained an uncertain, confused operation.

Consequently, the corporation's trustee, the Irving Trust Company, decided to take a more active role in management. Irving Trust was, in fact, said to have forced Sam Briskin's resignation.[1] This situation caused rumors to reverberate concerning RKO's executive alignment. Reports circulated, for example, that Merlin Aylesworth would be returning to replace Leo Spitz as corporate president. Full charge of production might go to J. R. McDonough or even Ned Depinet, although Pandro Berman, who held the position, was a leading candidate to continue. The chairmanship of RKO was likely to be assumed by N. Peter Rathvon.[2] Rathvon, an Odlum man, had been laboring on the receivership predicament for more than two years.

Pandro Berman became so frustrated that he wired Leo Spitz denying the rumors that a meeting had been held in Hollywood to discuss what would happen to RKO if Spitz stepped down. Berman told his boss he was having a tough time keeping studio employees working "with full morale and top speed in view of daily editorials and stories tossing company to and fro like rubber ball. Hope they someday establish this organization on businesslike basis so it is not plaything of industry."[3]

149

The disorder calmed down in late February. Both Leo Spitz and Pandro Berman were officially confirmed in their respective positions. Spitz, not Rathvon, would continue as chairman of the RKO board. The only addition was the naming of McDonough as a vice-president and board member to oversee financial matters at the studio.[4] Irving Trust, during a series of conferences held in Hollywood and New York, had recommended that this operational group be given full control of the company's future.

The most interesting aspect of this announcement was the return of J. R. McDonough to prominence. Formerly president of the production arm of RKO, McDonough had faded to virtual invisibility after Floyd Odlum took control of the corporation. Now he regained a position of importance at the studio, where he would once again focus his meticulous eye on expenditures. His appointment also suggested renewed interest by David Sarnoff in RKO's affairs. McDonough had joined RKO originally at Sarnoff's behest; since the company had not thrived after Odlum's handpicked management took over, and since Odlum himself had postponed his decision regarding acquisition of RCA's remaining RKO stock, it was understandable that Sarnoff would resurface, if only to protect RCA's substantial investment in the movie company.

The RKO receivership, always a complex state of affairs, became even more exasperating in 1938. The various interested parties had never come to an agreement on the reorganization plan submitted in 1937. The early months of 1938 were filled with delays in the proceedings, necessitated by uncertainty over the corporation's executives, controlling interests, and financial status. Federal judge William Bondy became irked: "RKO has been reorganizing for five years now. In that time, creditors of the company have died, stockholders have changed and, I suppose something has happened to the lawyers, too. It seems to me that this reorganization ought to be disposed of soon."[5]

Although the judge had a point, nothing would happen right away. The 1937 plan was already out of date and needed amending. It had been based on company earnings in 1935, 1936, and the first half of 1937 and presupposed that the RKO performance would continue at the same rate of improvement.[6] But profits had decreased during the final months of 1937, and this trend continued in 1938. Thus, the process would begin again; a new, "amended" plan had to be drawn up before any positive action could be taken.

Judge Bondy attempted to stimulate the proceedings by threatening in court that "unless a plan of reorganization [is] formed, the company [will] have to be liquidated."[7] Printed in various newspapers, this remark caused repercussions at the Hollywood studio. The Disney organization expressed special anxiety. Disney representative Gunther Lessing forthrightly explained his concerns to J.R. McDonough, who then wrote A.H. McCausland: "He is doing business with a company which apparently is unable to get itself reorganized, a company that has no stability of organization or management; while he is pleased with the job that RKO is doing for the Disney product now, he is still concerned as to whether the company is a permanent factor with which to continue doing business."[8]

The situation was also damaging the studio's relations with its contract players. As McDonough told McCausland in May, Fred Astaire's future association with the company was a question mark. Astaire was "unwilling to commit himself . . . with any company whose management may be subject to change and whose financial set-up is indeterminate."[9]

The revised reorganization plan was finally submitted to Judge Bondy in late May. It called for holders of the old common stock to receive one-sixth of a share of new RKO common for each share currently held, "plus a warrant to buy one share of new common at $15 a share for a period of ten years, or at the option of the holder to buy one-half share of new common at a price of $10 per full share for a period of five years." General creditors were to collect ten shares of new common stock for each $100 in claims. Rockefeller Center, whose claim had been reduced, would still be granted 464,000 shares.[10] The Atlas Corporation promised to provide $1,500,000 in new cash to the company and to underwrite a sufficient amount of new common stock. Rather than dealing with the plan himself, Judge Bondy referred it to Special Master George Alger who, for a second time, was charged with determining its fairness.

Alger suggested four minor amendments, called the plan "fair, feasible and equitable," and returned it to Bondy in late July.[11] Nathan Rosenberg, an attorney for a group of independent debenture holders, indicated that he would oppose it in Judge Bondy's court, but otherwise there seemed to be no organized resistance from either shareholders or creditors. It finally looked as if RKO might be wrenched free of receivership within the next few months. However, about the time the amended plan was due to be filed, Floyd Odlum made an announcement that further muddied the waters. Odlum had decided to drop his option to purchase RCA's remaining holdings in RKO. He gave as his reason the renegotiated $5,500,000 price, which he considered "too high." This meant that the movie concern was not going to achieve the single-minded leadership of one individual or group. Odlum remained the principal stockholder, but RCA held almost as much stock as Atlas, and the Rockefellers also owned a substantial block and stood to acquire another huge chunk through the reorganization. Even before Odlum declined the stock, RCA officials had indicated that they would want participation on the board of directors and "management authority" in the reorganized RKO, if they remained involved.[12] A potential battle was shaping up among the three principal owners of RKO: the Rockefellers, David Sarnoff of RCA, and Floyd Odlum of Atlas. No one could say what would come of this, but the likely tug of war did not augur well for RKO's future.

In Hollywood, Katharine Hepburn's association with RKO came to a conclusion. Early in 1938 the actress was loaned to Columbia to make *Holiday*, a George Cukor–directed picture costarring Cary Grant. It was the first time studio management had ever rented Hepburn out, always having felt she was too valuable. Harry Cohn of Columbia paid RKO $50,000 for her services, as well as picking up her salary for the duration of the picture's shooting.[13]

When Hepburn returned in the spring, her status had fallen to an all-time low. *Bringing Up Baby*, primarily because of its excessive production cost, had been released and was a giant loser. In addition, various exhibitor groups around the country were voicing their distaste for Kate. Perhaps believing that a role in an old-fashioned saccharine story like *Little Women* would increase her appeal, RKO assigned Hepburn to *Mother Carey's Chickens*, a film that had been in preparation for several months. There is some evidence that this move was a ploy on the part of the executives to effect cancelation of Hepburn's contract. If this is true, the strategy worked. The actress refused to appear in *Mother Carey*, thus giving them cause to suspend her and begin negotiating the termination of her agreement.[14] Negotiations were completed in early May, prompting the following telegram from Pandro Berman to Hepburn:

> It is with great regret that I find a termination of your contract has been decided upon definitely. It is not easy to turn aside from an association of years as pleasant as ours has been and while I am of the opinion that you will probably be better off with the choice of material and collaboration of all the industry instead of just our studio, I deeply regret the fact that this had to happen. I hope you will be very happy in whatever association you make and that some day we may work together again.[15]

May 3, 1938, the day the above telegram was sent, must have been severely trying for Katharine Hepburn. On that date, a paid announcement appeared in the *Hollywood Reporter* headlined, "WAKE UP! Hollywood Producers." It began:

Practically all of the major studios are burdened with stars—whose public appeal is negligible—receiving tremendous salaries necessitated by contractual obligations. Having these stars under contract, and paying these sizable sums weekly, the studios find themselves in the unhappy position of having to put these box office deterrents in expensive pictures in the hope that some return on the investment might be had.

This condition is not only burdensome to the studios and its [sic] stockholders but is likewise no boon to exhibitors who, in the final analysis, suffer by the non-drawing power of these players. Among the players, whose dramatic ability is unquestioned but whose box office draw is nil, can be numbered Mae West, Edward Arnold, Garbo, Joan Crawford, Katharine Hepburn and many, many others. Garbo, for instance, is a tremendous draw in Europe, which does not help theatre owners in the United States. Hepburn turned in excellent performances in "Stage Door" and "Bringing Up Baby" but both pictures died.[16]

The Independent Theatre Owners Association sponsored the attack. It marked the opening volley in the famous "box-office poison" campaign against a number of Hollywood performers. For a time it appeared Hepburn might be the biggest loser; no studio signed her after she left RKO, and she made no films released in 1939. But the RKO distribution executives, who, according to Leo Spitz, had been "greatly relieved" when Hepburn refused to appear in *Mother Carey's Chickens*, would ultimately regret the precipitancy of their celebration.[17] Hepburn returned to Hollywood prominence in the 1940s, earning a good deal of money for MGM in the process.

Kate Hepburn's sparring partner in *Stage Door*, Ginger Rogers, also caused some anguish during the year. Rogers had always been a loyal employee, willing to go out of her way for the studio's benefit. In appreciation of her efforts, Leo Spitz and Pandro Berman decided to present her with a bonus of $10,000. Spitz wrote Rogers on April 14, enclosing the check. The last paragraph of his letter read: "I hope our relationship in the future will always remain as pleasant as it has been in the past. I am certain that nothing will ever occur to disturb it."[18] Mr. Spitz would be eating his words within two weeks.

The next Astaire-Rogers picture, *Carefree*, was supposed to begin dance rehearsals on April 18. Ginger Rogers had other notions, however, and informed J. R. McDonough she would not report. She had several grievances against RKO: a promise made by Berman that Mark Sandrich would never again direct any of her films (Sandrich had been assigned to direct *Carefree*); failure to deliver a script of the new film for her scrutiny; and the studio's refusal to renegotiate her contract.[19] The conflict with San-drich stemmed from statements the director had made to Rogers and about her. For example, he had told Ginger's mother, Lela Rogers, that "if Ginger [does] not learn to improve her singing and dancing she [will] at some fu-ture date find herself in great difficulties in the picture business." In addi-tion, Sandrich's behavior caused the actress to feel she was decidedly less important to the team than Fred Astaire.[20] These, and a variety of other aggravations, soured Rogers on Mark Sandrich. The script problem was easily taken care of. Although she did not have script approval, a script of *Carefree* was sent to her as soon as one became available. As always, money was the major hurdle. In this, the RKO executives refused to budge.

When Rogers failed to appear on April 18, J. R. McDonough instructed company lawyers to begin preparing documents necessary to sue her for breach of contract. Marathon negotiations involving Berman, McDonough, the lawyers, and Rogers's agent, Leland Hayward, continued for days. They finally ended on April 21, when Ginger Rogers agreed to do the picture.[21] She actually received few concessions: a promise to *discuss* amending her contract with RKO in September or October; six weeks' vacation follow-ing *Carefree;* and delivery of her scripts in advance of the start date of each picture. No mention of Sandrich was made in the final settlement, but Berman dispatched a letter to the director that very day, pointing out the ways he had antagonized Ginger and firmly suggesting that Sandrich be more careful in the future.[22] The director would be released by RKO after finishing the picture.

This was actually a close call. Ginger Rogers had become the queen of the studio, its biggest female star. Because she had spent so many years in pictures, because she had labored in Astaire's shadow for a significant por-tion of her RKO career, and because she was not as luminous as Hepburn or many of Hollywood's other "celestial" females, it is doubtful that either RKO or Ginger realized how popular she had become. During the next few years, however, her appeal would climb even higher, and her films would dominate the company's list of box-office winners. If RKO had lost Ginger Rogers at this point, the financial impact would have been sizable.

A mass exodus of producers, in the works for many months, finally took place in 1938. One of the first to go was Howard Hawks. At a meeting on March 17, J. R. McDonough informed William Hawks, Howard's brother and agent, that it would be best if RKO and the producer-director severed relations.[23] Although McDonough would not say so specifically, the studio's dissatisfaction with Hawks was based primarily on the budget overrun on

Bringing Up Baby. Also, Hawks was scheduled to direct *Gunga Din,* a challenging and extremely important picture, and there was no room for a profligate on that production. Howard Hawks was upset by this turn of events—not so much because he was leaving RKO and his $2,500 weekly salary as because he would not be able to direct *Gunga Din.* The film was precisely the type of male adventure saga that he loved best, and he had helped to shape its story. Nevertheless, the deal was canceled upon payment of $40,000 to Hawks.[24] This severance money was $20,000 less than the studio would have paid him if he had been kept on for the duration of his contract.

Also departing the studio in 1938 were Edward Kaufman, Jesse Lasky, and Edward Small. Kaufman's 1936 productions had done well, but his last three films, *The Life of the Party, Breakfast for Two,* and *Wise Girl,* had all flopped. Lasky had joined RKO to produce six films over two years. He had made only two, *Music for Madame* and *Hitting a New High,* and both had been harsh disappointments.[25] Small guided six pictures—some hits, most misses. His doom was sealed by *The Toast of New York,* a crushing fiscal calamity for the company. Small did leave behind one gem: the Gunga Din property.

To replace these gentlemen, Pandro Berman and Leo Spitz instituted an aggressive campaign to lure new producers and directors to the organization. The campaign produced notable results and one surprising rejection. Ernst Lubitsch expressed a strong desire to join RKO in order to work with Fred Astaire, but was passed up by Leo Spitz.[26] No one questioned the German director's genius or achievements, but Lubitsch was now regarded as an extravagant and difficult individual whose record at Paramount had been declining during the past few years. Lubitsch signed with MGM instead, where he made the delightful *Ninotchka* with Greta Garbo as his first production.

RKO did manage to work out deals with two "hot" producer-directors. Leo McCarey, fresh from his *Awful Truth* success at Columbia, and Gregory La Cava, the *Stage Door* director, both joined the talent pool. Their contracts gave them considerable freedom regarding selection of story material and casting, which no doubt appealed to these veterans of the Hollywood wars. In addition, George Stevens was promoted to producer-director status and chosen to replace Hawks on *Gunga Din.* The picture would be his biggest undertaking so far. P. G. Wolfson once again emerged from the stable of studio writers to attain coveted producer-writer status. Finally, a young man who had been working for Sam Goldwyn managed to free himself from his contract and sign with RKO, where he would be given an opportunity that Goldwyn had refused him—to direct pictures. His first—*A Man to Remember*—indicated that RKO had stumbled upon a major new talent in Garson Kanin. All in all, 1938 was a felicitous year for producer and director acquisitions.

A different story was written in the acting department. Besides the loss of Katharine Hepburn, the studio also watched helplessly as Fred Astaire's reputation declined. Astaire was listed by Harry Brandt of the Independent Theatre Owners Association as being among the "box-office poison" contingent. The story was picked up by *Time* and *Newsweek*, much to the dismay of Astaire and RKO.[27] Actually, the charge was ridiculous. Only one of Astaire's films (*A Damsel in Distress*) had ever lost money. Despite the studio's attempts to secure retractions from the Independent Theatre Owners and *Time*, none was forthcoming. And by the end of the year, Fred Astaire and Ginger Rogers had disappeared from the upper echelon of Hollywood's box-office champions.[28]

The studio foolishly gave up on Joan Fontaine in 1938. Jules Levy of the New York office, noting that Fontaine had been chosen to appear in *Gunga Din*, sent a strongly worded protest to Leo Spitz. After reporting that many of RKO's field men believed the actress had "little promise" and should be dropped from the studio roster, Levy added that he found Fontaine "a very colorless personality [who] certainly should not be cast in as important a picture as GUNGA DIN."[29]

Spitz then wrote Pandro Berman, suggesting that an unknown female replace Fontaine in the picture and remarking that he doubted the actress would ever make the grade.[30] He and Levy were badly mistaken. RKO had never had much patience for "grooming" its talent; if a performer failed to "click" immediately with audiences, he or she was usually looking for work shortly thereafter. Often these actors came back to haunt the studio later, and such would be the case with Fontaine. She did play the role in *Gunga Din*, but it was an abbreviated and thankless part. Soon after that assignment concluded, she was released.

In his new position, Pandro Berman achieved one goal that the studio had been working toward. He almost completely eliminated the "intermediate" pictures, concentrating on films that were truly B grade (less than $275,000 in production cost) or A grade (more than $700,000 in budget). Of the year's releases, only *Wise Girl*, *Mother Carey's Chickens*, and *The Mad Miss Manton* would fit into the mid-range that had been generally unprofitable in the past. Although the production year again proved disappointing, this was a sound fiscal strategy and helped the studio move toward a more positive record in 1939.

Berman naturally devoted most of his attention to the studio's top productions and continued to personally produce a small number of A pictures. The B films rested in the hands of Lee Marcus. In May, Leo Spitz became uneasy about the B unit; he wrote Berman asking him at least to assume responsibility for approving the major ingredients of the B films. "I am fearful of your having to devote too much time to 'B' production, but I think that you should, without loss in efficiency in your more important problems, be able to give enough time to 'B' product to be sure that stories, casting and direction meet with your approval."[31] Pandro Berman enjoyed a good working relationship with the corporate president, but this idea did not appeal to him. He simply ignored the request, preferring to keep one eye on all the As while devoting the other to his own special projects, such as *Carefree* and *Room Service.*

In fact, it was Leo Spitz rather than Berman who paid special attention to the Bs. At the beginning of the year, Spitz advocated that Lee Marcus's unit focus on melodramatic action pictures, which, the president felt, would generate the best results of all "cheap" budget features.[32] Marcus responded with a group of crime and prison pictures that were mostly above average, considering their minimal budgets.

By June, however, there were rumblings that the Hays office or the Legion of Decency, or both, might crack down on crime pictures, a staple of the studios for years but now considered "overabundant." Spitz wrote Marcus about the potential danger. He did not recommend abandoning crime subjects altogether but cautioned Marcus to "watch your step in this direction."[33] J. R. McDonough and Lee Marcus then discussed the possible problem and came up with a list of nineteen future B productions, only six of which could be considered crime oriented.[34] Of these six, four were stories for the new "Saint" series.

At this time, a new kind of film entered the studio's field of vision, the "exploitation" film. Again, Leo Spitz provided the impetus for this special type of picture, though he would ultimately lack the courage to move forward aggressively in the area. Exploitation films dealt with subject matter of a topical and sensational nature, stories that might prove especially titillating to the audiences of the day. *Smashing the Rackets,* about a crusading district attorney who uncovers all manner of corruption, was the first of this type, scheduled for an August release. Suggested to follow were pictures about spies, fake evangelists, air piracy, and the "beauty" racket.[35] Working overtime, Lee Marcus came up with two more exploitation ideas in August. After discussing them with Berman, he wrote Ned Depinet for a reaction:

The first is to make a picture titled "CLIP JOINT." I know this title was disliked by Mr. Spitz previously, but nevertheless, we feel that it is definitely box office and exploitable. This picture would show all of the workings and ramifications and flim-flamming that takes place in a typical clip joint in a large city, such as rolling drunks, slipping knockout drops to customers, and then throwing them out when they squawk, showing the connection that taxi drivers have with these places, and doing a story which would be as close to sensatioal as the limits of censorship would permit.

The second idea is to make a picture called "STRIP TEASE." This title certainly is provocative and is box office. The story would have to do with the life of burlesque girls, the heroine probably being a very nice girl, the heavy girl being a tough tease artist, using as a basis for authenticity the article that Fortune ran on Minsky's and strip tease some time ago.[36]

No one suggested that such ideas had any artistic value or social significance; they were blatant sensationalism, designed to siphon dollars directly into the company's coffers. Even though Leo Spitz had stated in no uncertain terms that profits were his only interest, he backed away from *Clip Joint* and *Strip Tease*. Perhaps concerned about the company's image or the likely difficulties that such projects would raise with the censors, he refused to give the green light to either project. The exploitation pictures that RKO did produce were rather bland and poorly advertised and distributed. Lee Marcus recalled in 1940 that when Spitz finally got his wish, in the form of *Smashing the Rackets*, he and the sales force "didn't know what the hell to do with it."[37] If Spitz had displayed more courage, Marcus suggested, the studio's financial status might have improved dramatically.

No company sales convention was held in 1938, so the announcement of the 1938–1939 program came later than usual. Deciding to make sure his pictures were "on celluloid and not on paper," Pandro Berman waited until August to release a full description of the year's coming entertainments.[38] RKO had "more notable attractions in production and actually on film for early fall release than at any time in the company's history," according to Berman, who named *Room Service, Gunga Din*, Leo McCarey's *Love Match* (final title: *Love Affair*), and a new Astaire-Rogers musical as the top offerings soon to be available.[39] Fifty other features were also promised.

Berman's public disclosure masked the fact that his production operation was wrestling with its own set of problems. *Gunga Din* had begun shooting without a finished script and looked as if it would far exceed its budget. Likewise, the McCarey picture had run into unforeseen difficulties and would go before the cameras without much of a script at all. And, because of their elevated costs, the Astaire-Rogers films were no longer sure box-office winners. Still, Pandro Berman had been on the job for less than a year, and prospects for the future were already looking brighter than they ever had during the Briskin period.

Back in New York, a skirmish between financial titans was drawing to a conclusion. From the very beginning, the Rockefeller family had been unhappy with the entry of Floyd Odlum and his Atlas cronies into the RKO equation. They were particularly upset by the efforts of Peter Rathvon to convince the courts to reduce the Rockefeller Center claim against RKO in the receivership deliberations. They were also offended by the way that Spitz and Briskin had been placed in charge without any input from them or David Sarnoff. And they became more disgruntled as RKO's fortunes sank under the leadership of the Odlum men. Their board members had supported the ouster of Sam Briskin; by late summer, they had Leo Spitz in their crosshairs.

At this point, a new and rather surprising individual enters RKO's melodramatic narrative: W. G. Van Schmus. Van, as the Rockefellers called him, had been managing director of Radio City Music Hall since they wrested control of the theaters from RKO in 1934. He was well liked and respected by his employers, especially Nelson Rockefeller, who had emerged as the family member most involved in RKO business. On June 2, 1938, Van Schmus wrote Nelson, recommending George J. Schaefer for an executive position at RKO. At the time, Schaefer was in charge of distribution at United Artists. The Music Hall had presented nineteen weeks of UA films in 1937, and Van Schmus expected it would show even more in 1938, thanks to the cordial relationship that had developed between the two men. Van Schmus described Schaefer as being "very friendly and cooperative."[40] Two weeks later, Schaefer had lunch with Van and Nelson, who took an instant liking to him. Nelson wrote Sidney Kent, an executive with Twentieth Century–Fox: "I was very much impressed with Mr. Schaeffer [*sic*] and feel more strongly than ever that he is the man for the job."[41]

Floyd Odlum also knew and respected Schaefer and had talked to him about possibly joining RKO. But Odlum had some lesser executive position in mind, whereas Van Schmus and Nelson Rockefeller envisioned Schaefer replacing Leo Spitz as corporate president. The situation was complicated by the desire of UA management to retain Schaefer—he would soon have to make up his mind whether to sign a new contract with the company.

In September the stew pot really began to boil. By then, it had been pretty well decided that Leo Spitz had to go. Odlum seemed resigned to this outcome but preferred that his man, Peter Rathvon, succeed Spitz.

Merlin Aylesworth reemerged at this juncture and began attempting to broker a deal in which George Schaefer would become corporate president and Ned Depinet president of the picture company, with Aylesworth possibly taking up his old position as chairman of the RKO board. Van Schmus continued to press for George Schaefer to become RKO's leader, and Nelson Rockefeller became fully committed to the idea.[42] The different parties needed to reach a consensus soon because United Artists was leaning on Schaefer to re-up.

By the end of the month, David Sarnoff had been persuaded that Schaefer should be RKO's corporate president, and Floyd Odlum had given in. But he was not happy about it. Still unconvinced that Leo Spitz had done an inadequate job and should be replaced, he insisted that Spitz's exit be handled tactfully.[43] He also drafted a press release indicating that "Mr. Shaeffer [sic] was nominated for the position by the Rockefeller interests."[44] Since he was being blamed for RKO's decline during the past couple of years, Odlum wanted to make sure that the Rockefellers would bear responsibility for the George Schaefer administration.

Nelson Rockefeller was furious. He put together his own "material for the basis of a press release in connection with the RKO situation." After asserting that the Rockefellers had "done everything in our power to cooperate with the Atlas Corporation in working out a reorganized plan [for RKO]," he alluded to the problems of agreeing on "sound management" and then stated that his family was giving up: "we feel there is nothing further to be gained by our participating in these discussions and that we can take no further responsibility in connection with the management of the reorganized company."[45]

Cooler heads prevailed, and neither press release was ever made public. By midmonth, George Schaefer had been announced as the new president of the corporation.[46] Odlum made sure, however, that word leaked out concerning which ownership group had backed Schaefer for the job.

Leo Spitz negotiated a graceful, and lucrative, exit. Journalists reported that Spitz had not been fired, but allowed to return to his legal practice. For several months, they claimed, he had been voicing a desire to shed the RKO job. Company publicists obviously did a good job of helping Spitz save face. He had worked hard for RKO, and he continued to address himself to the company's needs until the very end.

For example, just before departing RKO, Spitz began encouraging his producers to consider making a different type of film. After heaping praise on Garson Kanin's first picture, *A Man to Remember*, Spitz continued:

The more recent pictures that seem to be doing the best business throughout the country are BOYS TOWN, YOU CAN'T TAKE IT WITH YOU and FOUR DAUGHTERS. It is noteworthy that all of them are down-to-earth simple stories. It seems that the public, in seeking refuge from the complex problems of life today, confused as they are by the unrest and disturbances prevalent throughout the world, find escape for at least a couple of hours in a make-believe world, in which the way of life is simple and which they understand. This type of picture is apparently serving that purpose.[47]

Spitz did not demand more pictures like *A Man to Remember* or *Mother Carey's Chickens*, but the implication was clear. Leo Spitz's recommendations in 1938 had run the gamut from melodramatic action films through exploitation pictures to down-to-earth, sentimental entertainments.

Spitz's principal bequest to RKO was the continuing series. Although other studios had been profiting from inexpensive pictures that presented the same actors playing the same roles in picture after picture, RKO had dawdled in this area. The studio did make the Hildegarde Withers mysteries—first starring Edna Mae Oliver and then Helen Broderick—but these had expired in the mid-1930s. While RKO had neglected the category, Paramount had sponsored the adventures of Bulldog Drummond; Twentieth Century–Fox, Charlie Chan; Warner Bros., Perry Mason; Columbia, Nero Wolfe; and MGM topped everyone with the "Thin Man" and Andy Hardy family pictures.

It was a sensible, if not exactly original, move for Spitz to insist RKO initiate some series pictures in 1938. Two resulted: the Saint and Annabel. The Saint series, based on novels written by Leslie Charteris, featured a suave private detective who solves homicides with the same self-possession and style that he displays while selecting the correct wine. Louis Hayward played the role in the original, *The Saint in New York*, which proved a definite triumph ($180,000 profit on a production cost of only $128,000), thus ensuring the continuation of the series. Hayward, however, would not play the role again; George Sanders replaced him in the remaining RKO pictures.

Lucille Ball was chosen to portray Annabel, a Hollywood actress whose press agent (Jack Oakie) decides she must live her parts before she plays them. Thus, in the first effort, *The Affairs of Annabel,* Annabel spends a month in prison before tackling a prison picture. *The Affairs of Annabel* was also a minor success, meaning there would be, at the very least, a second installment. RKO had been tardy in climbing on the series bandwagon, but it would make up for that during the next few years.

Pandro Berman was allowed to continue as production head in the Schaefer administration, even though his first year on the job had been less than scintillating. Still, most of the true clunkers had been prepared under Sam Briskin. They included *Hitting a New High* (loss: $431,000); *Joy of Living* (loss: $314,000); *Radio City Revels* (loss: $300,000). And *Bringing Up Baby* (loss: $365,000).

Howard Hawks's production of *Bringing Up Baby* is one of those touchstone films that RKO is remembered for. Its germination began in the spring of 1937 when story editor Bob Sparks introduced Sam Briskin to a witty tale that Hagar Wilde had published in *Collier's* magazine.[48] Briskin felt the story would cost too much to translate to the screen but expressed an interest in hiring writer Wilde.[49] Howard Hawks was then casting about for a property and, liking the story immensely, talked Briskin into letting him tackle it. Wilde joined the RKO staff shortly thereafter to work with Dudley Nichols on the screenplay. From early on, the picture was designed to star Katharine Hepburn and Cary Grant.

Despite Briskin's warnings that the film would have to be made on a moderate budget because of Hepburn's feeble drawing power, Hawks encouraged his writers to give full rein to their comic inventiveness. The first estimating script came in at 242 pages, the revised draft at 194 pages, and the final shooting script at 202. Given a certain amount of overwriting, this still represented a mammoth amount of material. By the time the picture was ready to begin production in September 1937, the budget had been set at $767,000 for a fifty-one-day shooting schedule.[50]

This was way too much from Briskin's point of view, but the studio head had little choice in the matter. If he stopped Hawks at this stage, RKO would have to write off the substantial costs already accrued, plus pay its commitments to Hepburn, Grant, and others. *Bringing Up Baby* started shooting and the situation soon evolved into a full-fledged nightmare. Hawks, working slowly and painstakingly, fell far behind schedule. Associate producer Cliff Reid's job was to keep nudging the director in the right direction, but he proved totally ineffectual in his efforts to speed things along. Sam Briskin also failed to inspire the imperturbable Hawks; he was forced to quit the studio while the film was still in production. The original fifty-one-day schedule eventually ballooned to ninety-three days, with completion finally attained on January 8, 1938.[51] The final budget amounted to a ruinous $1,073,000. It should not have surprised Howard Hawks very much that, shortly thereafter, J. R. McDonough began negotiations to sever the relationship between RKO and the director.

Figure 18. *Bringing Up Baby* (1938). A publicity still taken on the studio lot with Cary Grant, "Baby" (the leopard), and Katharine Hepburn. This renowned screwball comedy would be Hepburn's last picture for RKO. (Courtesy of the Academy of Motion Picture Arts and Sciences)

The film turned out to be a brilliant comedy, one of the best of the 1930s. RKO officials, however, winced instead of laughing. Even the excellence of the production could not overcome Hepburn's stigma and the inflated negative cost. *Bringing Up Baby* was a resounding flop, hastening the departures of both Hawks and Hepburn from the ranks of RKO contract talent.

Pandro Berman also suffered a pair of serious disappointments. His personally produced *Carefree* became the first Astaire-Rogers film to lose money ($68,000). The musical still attracted $1,731,000 in film rentals, but its negative cost ($1,253,000) was $250,000 more than that of *Shall We Dance* and practically guaranteed it would end up in the minus column. This undoubtedly upset Berman, but the outcome of *Room Service* troubled him even more.

This farcical play about a hotel that serves as a haven for three crazy and thoroughly unscrupulous theatrical producers became a big hit on Broadway in May 1937. A furious bidding war ensued among the studios. Lillie Messinger, Robert Sparks, and Leo Spitz all were sold on the potential of *Room Service,* and RKO eventually won the auction, paying an unprecedented $255,000 to authors John Murray and Allan Boretz.[52]

The notoriously weak RKO male-talent roster caused problems in casting. After considering and rejecting Joe Penner, Parkyakarkus, Jack Oakie, Burgess Meredith, and others for the major roles, Sam Briskin decided to go outside and offer the Marx Brothers a shot at the picture. There was considerable resistance to the idea. Robert Sparks, producer Edward Kaufman, and even Leo Spitz attempted to change Briskin's mind. Briskin himself felt unsure about putting Groucho, Harpo, and Chico in *Room Service,* but he believed this solution could provide some box-office insurance. As he wrote Leo Spitz:

> For many reasons I would . . . like to see them [the Marx Brothers] in ROOM SERVICE. The primary reason is, of course, the question of cost. It is my opinion that it will cost somewhere around $800,000 to make ROOM SERVICE with ordinary name actors. . . . In spite of the fact that I know ROOM SERVICE will get plenty of road playing time and will be an important playing property by the time we make the picture, I am wondering if we can afford to make an $800,000 picture without any names. On the other hand, I think the picture with the Marx Brothers in it will cost about $1,100,000. From a purely business point of view I think it is safer, when we are spending this kind of money, to have names in it.[53]

Sam Briskin's arguments won out; the manic comics were cast in the three primary roles.

With William Seiter directing and Berman personally supervising, the production phase went beautifully. Before shooting began, the estimated budget was reduced to $950,000, and Seiter actually brought it in for $884,000. For once, an RKO picture had been made for considerably less than anyone expected. The high spirits and prospects continued when a print was screened for the New York executives. Ned Depinet wired Berman: "Feeling mighty good today and still laughing over ROOM SERVICE which we saw this morning. Our crowd roared at many funny situations and thoroughly enjoyed themselves from start to finish. You have done a fine job with this show. Please tell Bill Seiter, Marx Brothers and those responsible how happy we are over this riotous entertainment."[54]

Regrettably, audiences did not find the film riotous. The Marx Brothers represented part of the problem. Their brand of surrealistic humor was uniquely their own, and all of their scripts had been carefully fashioned to

Figure 19. *Room Service* (1938). Chico Marx, Harpo Marx, director William Seiter, producer–production head Pandro Berman, and Groucho Marx pose on the set. The play, whose rights RKO purchased for the princely sum of $255,000, did not yield a successful movie. (Courtesy of the Academy of Motion Picture Arts and Sciences)

showcase the well-established personalities of the threesome. With *Room Service*, the big question was whether to alter the personae of the Marxes to fit the play, or to remold *Room Service* to accommodate the expected Marx characters. The latter path was chosen, thus compromising a property that the studio had paid a huge sum to purchase. Instead of a fresh new comedy, *Room Service* emerged as just another Marx Brothers picture. The only obvious omission was the usually obligatory musical performances by Harpo and Chico.

The most expensive property ever purchased by RKO, made on a respectable budget, nevertheless resulted in a loss of $340,000. Pandro Berman was not totally to blame, since Sam Briskin had signed up Groucho, Chico, and Harpo. But Berman was now both production chief and the film's producer, so it was ultimately his show. And a poor one at that.

Pandro Berman's teaming with Leo Spitz, lasting less than one year, became the shortest regime in company history—thus far. This was certainly not Berman's fault, and it wasn't really Spitz's fault either. His fate had been determined by the results of his earlier partnership with Sam Briskin. Since the company's financial fortunes did not perform a quick about-face after Briskin left, Spitz soon became RKO's latest dead man walking.[55]

Leo Spitz was handing over RKO to George Schaefer at yet another disadvantageous moment. The corporation barely managed to eke out a profit of $173,578 in 1938. The "Roosevelt recession," the president's ill-considered decision to cut back (or cut off) funding for many New Deal initiatives, was causing trouble for many industries including the movies.[56] Box-office receipts had slumped during the spring and summer months.[57] Certainly there was not as much cause for alarm as there had been in the dark days of the early 1930s, but profits would definitely be harder earned from now on than they had been during 1936 and 1937.

The totalitarian influence and burgeoning war clouds in Europe also represented matters of concern. European film receipts had been declining for some time, principally because of the growing intransigence of the governments in Germany and Italy. Thanks to the Nazis, Austria and Czechoslovakia were eliminated as markets for American movies during the year. In addition, a new Films Act was passed in Britain in April 1938, adding significant restrictions on American operations in that country.[58] Closer to home, the big news was a lawsuit filed by the U.S. government in July aimed at forcing the major companies to divorce their theater holdings from their production and distribution concerns and ending the distribution practice of block booking. A formal statement that accompanied the filing of charges against the major studios read, in part: "It is the belief of the Department of Justice that certain rearrangements must be made in the moving picture industry in order to maintain competitive conditions in the future. Those rearrangements require a more constructive effort than mere prosecution for past practices. The aim of the civil suit which is now instituted is to accomplish those arrangements under the guidance of the court. In the opinion of the Department, this can only be done by proceedings before a judicial tribunal."[59]

The action was taken at the behest of independent theater owners who had long complained that the distribution practices of the major studios were monopolistic and unfair to their businesses. Although nothing concrete had been determined when the year came to an end, the future operations of RKO, as well as those of MGM, Paramount, Warner Bros., Twentieth Century–Fox, and the other companies, were uncertain.

Then there was the receivership imbroglio, which, like the man who came to dinner, seemed determined never to depart. After the leadership issue was resolved in October, it was predicted that the latest reorganization plan submitted to the court was truly *the one*.[60] By year's end, however, final arrangements were still incomplete; various postponements, technical details, and objections had again bogged down the hearings.

On the bright side, box-office business in general made an upward move at the close of 1938, and Pandro Berman had some attractive-looking pictures ready for release early in the new year.

The biggest question mark was George J. Schaefer. How long would it take the new RKO president to analyze his company and formulate an enlightened program for the future? How would he approach the job in comparison to his predecessors, particularly Aylesworth and Spitz? How would he get along with such seasoned executives as Depinet, McDonough, and Berman? And what would Schaefer's relationship be to the three powerful groups whose interest in RKO remained keen: Atlas (Odlum), RCA (Sarnoff), and the Rockefellers?

8.   "The company's best interest"

The Schaefer-Berman Regime (1939)

Unlike all of RKO's previous corporate presidents, fifty-one-year-old George J. Schaefer was a tempered industry veteran. He had spent more than a quarter century in the distribution end of the business, beginning as a salesman for the old World Film Company. Later he worked as a booker, branch manager, district manager, general sales manager, and vice-president of Paramount before accepting the position of vice-president and general manager of United Artists.[1]

Given his background, it could be expected that Schaefer would work closely with Ned Depinet on the promotion and marketing of RKO films, leaving the creative decisions in the hands of Pandro Berman and his West Coast staff. But the new RKO president had different ideas. He intended to involve himself in every aspect of the corporation—especially production strategies and decision making. Approaching his job with a passion never previously demonstrated by any RKO corporate head, George Schaefer completely revamped the RKO filmmaking emphases and image within one year. In the process, he implemented a number of policies that would contribute both to the everlasting fame of RKO and to its near-ruination.

Schaefer must have felt blessed that *Gunga Din,* one of the most exciting productions in RKO history, would be among the first releases of his new regime. As previously mentioned, rights to the famous poem had been purchased from the Kipling estate by Edward Small's Reliance Pictures in 1936. The cost, 4,700 pounds plus 100 pounds for the rights to a song entitled "Gunga Din" written by Rudyard Kipling and Gerard Cobb, were assumed by RKO as part of its production deal with Small.[2] After some preliminary script work by William Faulkner, Howard Hawks was given the directorial assignment. Hawks interested two of the industry's foremost writers, Ben Hecht and Charles MacArthur, in the project, arranging to meet them in New York in fall 1936 to work on the screenplay. The three cloistered themselves at the Waldorf Astoria Hotel, but made little progress for the first six weeks. Sam Briskin, production head at the time, was becoming desperate when he received the following telegram from the threesome: "Have finally figured out tale involving two sacrifices, one for love, the other for England, which neither resembles BENGAL LANCERS nor CHARGE OF THE LIGHT BRIGADE and contains something like two thousand deaths, thirty elephants and a peck of maharajas. We have this now in a cocktail shaker and have poured out some thirty five pages of glittering prose."[3]

Briskin's reply, wired the same day, revealed a notable absence of humor: "Can't understand your going so far wrong as to write story which does not resemble BENGAL LANCERS and CHARGE OF LIGHT BRIGADE. Are you boys slipping? Besides, when I want something out of a cocktail shaker I don't want prose."[4]

While the writing continued, Briskin began attempting to line up a suitable cast in hopes that shooting could begin before the end of 1936. Predictably, the major challenge would be securing virile male stars to play the three leads. RKO had no one suitable under contract, so it had to negotiate borrowing arrangements with other studios or independent producers. For a time, it appeared Ronald Colman might head the cast, but the script was not finished in time and Colman proceeded to other commitments.[5]

When the Hecht-MacArthur screenplay was finally ready (April 1937), casting difficulties made it impossible to go forward. Briskin tried to convince Louis B. Mayer of MGM to loan to RKO Clark Gable, Spencer Tracy, and Franchot Tone in exchange for an old RKO property that Mayer wished to remake, *Rio Rita*. Mayer agreed to Tone and Tracy, but absolutely refused to lend out Gable.[6] So *Gunga Din* was placed on the shelf while Hawks directed *Bringing Up Baby* and the studio executives attempted to find a way to cast the adventure film properly.

After the *Bringing Up Baby* debacle, Howard Hawks was fired and George Stevens inherited the project. A good deal of rewriting had taken place in the interim, with Anthony Veiller, Dudley Nichols, Joel Sayre, Fred Guiol, and others taking a crack at the original Hecht-MacArthur work. Believing that the picture had enormous box-office potential, Pandro Berman consented to Stevens's request to shoot some of it on location and to spare no expense in making *Gunga Din* an epic spectacular. The cast was finalized just before the June starting date. For the three appealing leads, Cary Grant, whose popularity had skyrocketed in the past two years, was joined by Victor McLaglen and Douglas Fairbanks, Jr. Sam Jaffe accepted the role of the eponymous hero.

The sets were readied at Lone Pine, California, where the Sierra Nevada mountains would provide a majestic backdrop for the action. RKO also had to construct a small city nearby capable of housing, feeding, and entertaining the six hundred workers who would be contributing to the production. The initial shooting took place in the studio, however. Because commitments were piling up, Berman decided to begin the picture as scheduled on June 24 even though Stevens still did not have a script that satisfied him. It was suicidal to start a picture of this magnitude without a final script (and thus, without a reliable budget), but production chief Berman had faith in George Stevens, a man whose record exemplified reliability as well as quality.

Even though the writing was still only a few days ahead of daily shooting on July 6, a tentative budget of $1,332,000 was determined, based on a sixty-four-day shooting schedule. As J. R. McDonough wrote Leo Spitz, there appeared to be room for further cutting, and Stevens believed he could bring in *Gunga Din* for a $1.2 million final cost.[7]

Everything changed when the company actually went on location. Suddenly, Stevens became slower and more painstaking than Howard Hawks had ever been. In the words of Pandro Berman: "We sent him [Stevens] up to Lone Pine, Cal., to photograph the mountains up there where we built the temples and so on to represent Indian backgrounds. And we sent him up for ten days with a big crowd of extras and a big camp and a big catering operation. That ten days was very expensive. Well, it wasn't ten days. It was thirty."[8]

Before Berman finally blew the whistle and demanded that Stevens return to the studio, the production was far behind schedule and the budget had bloated to a disastrous level. On September 1, J. R. McDonough placed the new estimate at $1,750,000 with at least thirty days of work left.[9] McDonough's prognostication again proved conservative; shooting finally culminated in mid-October. Instead of the originally planned 64 days of production, 104 were necessary to complete the movie. And the final cost was a staggering $1,915,000, making *Gunga Din* the most expensive picture RKO had ever produced. When it was over, Pan Berman felt sure the undertaking would bankrupt the studio.[10]

George Schaefer was not so pessimistic. A month after assuming the RKO presidency, Schaefer attended a preview and wired Ned Depinet: "Tremendously enthusiastic over screening of GUNGA DIN last night and very happy . . . with audience reaction. Picture played just about as fine as one could expect and I'm really and truly very enthusiastic about it. Great suspense, action, and Grant, Fairbanks and McLaglen each give finest jobs I have seen on the screen. . . . It is so important that we do the right kind of job both domestic and abroad and give [GUNGA DIN] every piece of exploitation and advertising possible."[11]

The sales staff followed Schaefer's instructions. Before and after the world premiere on January 24, 1939, at the Pantages Theater in Hollywood, RKO proclaimed the achievements of *Gunga Din* from coast to coast and around the world. It did superlative business every place but India, where the censorship board banned the picture because of imperialist overtones and objectionable plot elements, such as the intention of the three sergeants to loot a sacred temple. However, the prohibitive cost made it impossible for *Gunga Din* to show a profit. After the initial release, the picture was a $193,000 loser, though subsequent rereleases would bring it firmly into the black. *Gunga Din* launched 1939 for Schaefer and RKO with a bang, but there would be other cinematic triumphs during the year as well.

In January, George Schaefer and Ned Depinet traveled to California. After studying studio operations for a time, the two executives left Hollywood for a few days to discuss RKO production strategy for the coming year with Pandro Berman. They chose La Quinta, a quiet desert community near Palm Springs, for their meetings.

The deliberations produced the following tentative plans. The 1939–1940 program would cost $14,844,000, including both features and short subjects. Twelve "big" pictures, to be made for a total expenditure of $10 million, would headline the releases. In addition, there would be six "in-between" films, budgeted at $200,000 each; twenty B pictures ($125,000 average cost); and six George O'Brien Westerns, to be made for $85,000 each.[12] The scheme reflected a healthy distrust, developed in earlier years, of the true "in-between" or "borderline" picture—a film in the $300,000 to $700,000 range. None would be produced.

As George Schaefer indicated to Andrew Christensen of Irving Trust later in January, the most immediate necessity was to acquire suitable story material for the expensive pictures: "Other than the one property, THE HUNCHBACK OF NOTRE DAME, which we are purchasing, there is no material ahead of us, either in story or original script form and we, therefore, have to start from scratch. We are proceeding to try to line up from ten to twelve worthwhile productions."[13] Schaefer then decided to pursue independent production deals in hopes of acquiring "important" properties for his company to release.

Figure 20.   George Schaefer, photographed while he was
serving as RKO corporate president. Schaefer decided to
transform the company's image and filmmaking practices
during his time at the helm. (Courtesy of the University of
Southern California, on behalf of USC Special Collections)

He moved quickly. One of the first independents signed was a team of
Broadway theatrical impresarios, Max Gordon and Harry Goetz. Their
company, Max Gordon Plays and Pictures, would provide RKO with the
services of the two men as producers and give the studio an inside position
on the plays they produced.[14] Schaefer was especially anxious to secure
the rights to *The American Way*, a patriotic drama Gordon and Goetz
controlled. The deal enabled RKO to acquire the play (for a fee of $250,000),
plus *Abe Lincoln in Illinois*, another coveted theatrical property.

Also joining RKO would be the screenwriting team of Gene Towne and
Graham Baker. They had penned the scripts for *You Only Live Once* (1937),

the Fritz Lang–directed film about the plight of ex-convicts in America, and for the RKO disappointment *Joy of Living*; now they intended to produce films based on classic literary works through a company called The Play's The Thing Productions. *Swiss Family Robinson* would be their initial undertaking. In addition, former silent comedy star Harold Lloyd agreed to oversee movies for RKO release. And a new American-British producing concern, Imperator-Radio Pictures, was formed between Herbert Wilcox and RKO.[15] Wilcox had decided to relocate his operations from London to Hollywood, where his first film would be *Nurse Edith Cavell*, directed by Wilcox and starring Anna Neagle.

In late February, George Schaefer wrote Pandro Berman disclosing his plans "to release possibly eight (8) or ten (10) quality pictures, independently financed but produced on our lot." Schaefer listed *Ivanhoe*, two George Stevens productions, two Leo McCarey productions, one Gregory La Cava production, and *The First Rebel* (later produced and released under the title *Allegheny Uprising*) as constituting the bulk of the company's own forthcoming A releases. Berman was instructed to give his "undivided attention" to this group of "special" offerings, leaving the "program" pictures securely in the hands of Lee Marcus. Marcus was to receive $4 million to produce twenty-eight pictures, and he was to decide the budget of each film in consultation with J. R. McDonough. The last paragraph of Schaefer's letter to Berman is of special interest: "In connection with the approval of this budget, it is important to note that I am working on the principle, with which the Board concur, that having approved the budget for the number of pictures indicated, thereafter the selection of material, stories, plays et cetera, and the producing of pictures is left entirely to the management."[16]

George Schaefer's performance already belied his words. As the year unfolded, he would become more and more involved in production decisions—from story selection to creative assignments to casting. Predictably, conflict between Schaefer and Berman soon took root, grew, and flowered very quickly. Schaefer's constant interference, as well as his cavalier decisions regarding the hiring of independents, disturbed the production chief intensely.

On March 1, 1939, Berman announced to Schaefer:

I will not bore you by going into the detail of how long I have been attempting to accomplish this deed, and for what various reasons of loyalty and friendship I have restrained myself, but I simply want to state that regardless of any circumstances whatsoever I do not wish to continue my employment in the motion picture business as of the

expiration of my present contract in March, 1940. I am going to take
off a considerable amount of time and travel around the world for my
health, which my doctors have advised me will not stand many more
years of the strain and responsibilities that I have been going through
for the past ten years. . . . I know the only way to get peace of mind
will be by severing all connections with the industry until I am in a
position to return.[17]

Continuing, Berman informed his boss that he was happy with the company and with Schaefer as president and that there were no ulterior motives
in back of his decision. There was more politeness than veracity to Berman's
words. In truth, Pandro Berman was distinctly upset with George Schaefer's
leadership.

Naturally, Berman resented Schaefer's meddling in the studio chief's
job and his insistence that final say in production decisions (even involving B pictures) belonged to him. Another sore point was Schaefer's head-
long rush to sign up independent units. Pandro Berman was not antagonistic to the unit concept, but he was offended that George Schaefer
negotiated agreements without consulting him about the potential producers. As Berman later told Mike Steen: "I was always resentful of the
fact that he [Schaefer] did not discuss any of his deals with me. . . . I felt I
had a lot to tell about an awful lot of people he was hiring whom I wouldn't
have hired. . . . So, this really started me on my way out of RKO. I began
to get burned up about it, and I resigned as a result."[18] George Schaefer did
not try to change Berman's mind, nor did he shed any tears at the prospect
of the RKO veteran's departure. Soon enough he would be in full control
of all aspects of the corporation, which is precisely what he wanted.

Pandro Berman took no credit for one of the company's best 1939 productions, *Love Affair*, though he deserved praise for backing producer-
director Leo McCarey despite some very long odds. Like *Gunga Din*, the
McCarey picture went before the cameras without benefit of a completed
script. The original story was called *Love Match*. It concerned a tragic affair between a French ambassador and an American woman in the mid-
1800s. Irene Dunne, who had worked with McCarey in *The Awful Truth*,
and Charles Boyer were cast in the major roles. Shortly before production
was to begin, however, the French government launched a formal protest
against the project, which it felt might disturb Franco-American relations
at a time when war was becoming a certainty. RKO decided to abandon
Love Match, but to allow McCarey to go ahead with a new film, working
"off the cuff," as Mac McDonough called it.[19] A number of writers toiled
on the picture, though Mildred Cram and Delmer Daves concocted most

of it. McCarey also encouraged his actors to improvise a good deal. With a lesser director at the helm, the results would likely have been calamitous.

Leo McCarey was no miracle worker. The film did go over schedule and over budget, though these overages hardly compare to the ones run up by *Gunga Din*. Approximately ten days into shooting in October, McDonough guessed the film would cost about $800,000.[20] Without a script to estimate from, this figure was purely hypothetical, but when the picture wrapped in late December, its final cost was only $60,000 more than McDonough had figured.

The biggest surprise of all came when the film was assembled for preview. Magically, it appeared to be one of the most carefully constructed and skillfully executed love stories in the history of the cinema. Sensitive, poignant, heartbreaking, and heartening at the same time, *Love Affair* certainly did not look like an "off the cuff" job. The film earned a respectable profit of $221,000—not stunning, but still amazing considering the circumstances that surrounded its production. It also garnered Academy Award nominations for Best Picture, Best Actress (Irene Dunne), Best Supporting Actress (Maria Ouspenskaya), Best Original Story (Mildred Cram and Leo McCarey), Best Art Direction (Van Nest Polglase and Al Herman), and Best Song (Buddy DeSylva for "Wishing").

Two weeks after *Love Affair* opened, the last of RKO's Astaire-Rogers pictures was released. As if Pandro Berman's problems with George Schaefer were not vexatious enough, the troubled production history of *The Story of Vernon and Irene Castle* might have convinced any studio head to take an extended vacation.

The idea for the film had come from Irving Berlin, who in 1934 suggested to Berman that the story of the Castles would make a good vehicle for Fred and Ginger.[21] The Castles had been precursors to Astaire-Rogers, a charismatic husband-wife team who danced their way to fame during the early years of the twentieth century. Just when their talent and renown reached its peak, Vernon died tragically, thus making their story a natural for a Hollywood biopic.

Pandro Berman pursued Berlin's suggestion for some time without success. Finally, he reached a tentative agreement in early 1937 with Irene Castle McLaughlin (she had remarried), who believed that only Fred Astaire was capable of portraying her dead husband. Astaire was anxious to do the role and agreed with Mrs. McLaughlin on one other crucial detail: Ginger Rogers should not be cast as Irene.[22] The studio not only promised the widow that a wide-ranging search would be launched to find the perfect leading lady; it also gave Mrs. McLaughlin story approval, agreed to hire her as technical advisor during the shooting, and acceded to her demand that she design all of the leading actress's costumes.[23] Obviously, RKO wanted to make this picture in the worst way.

Mrs. McLaughlin worked with Oscar Hammerstein on the treatment, which she happily approved toward the end of 1937. George Stevens was set to direct, but a delay in production was necessitated by the difficulty in casting a leading lady. It appears that from the beginning, Berman wanted Ginger Rogers for the part, but he went through the motions of attempting to find someone else for months. Finally, he convinced Astaire and Irene McLaughlin that the picture would never be made unless they accepted Ginger. They reluctantly agreed and it was scheduled for production in the fall of 1938. By that time Stevens was fully occupied with *Gunga Din*, so RKO borrowed H. C. Potter from Sam Goldwyn to direct. George Haight was hired to produce since Berman was too busy overseeing the entire program to give it his full attention.

It is not difficult to understand why RKO gave Irene Castle McLaughlin so much influence over the making of the film. Evidently, Pan Berman and other company officials believed she would be valuable to the creative process or, at worst, prove a minor annoyance. Little did they realize that McLaughlin would become a raging virago, disrupting the production work from beginning to end. One can sympathize with her to a point. RKO was filming the story of her life, and naturally she wished it to be as accurate and affecting as possible. But her demands and complaints were nitpicky at best, outrageous at worst, and based to a certain extent on her own desire to squeeze some extra income out of the biopic.

The battles between McLaughlin and practically the entire production staff could fill a small book, so what follows is only a compact summary. One major subject of dispute involved the costumes. Ginger Rogers, who had no great fondness for the woman she was portraying, disliked most of Irene McLaughlin's designs and asked Walter Plunkett to modify them. This brought an immediate protest, and threat, from McLaughlin: "I cannot let any other designer collaborate on the designing or share in the credits on these particular clothes. Having designed most of the clothes I wore during our successful career, you [Berman] may feel sure I am up to the job. . . . If someone else makes them up or 'modifies' them, and I did not see them until the test was run, and then did not like them—it would perhaps mean a serious delay to you."[24]

As shooting continued, the crew soon became weary of Mrs. McLaughlin's continual demands. Hoping she would get the message, they proceeded to make the picture as best they could and to ignore her as much as possible. McLaughlin, however, was stiff-necked to a fault. In a December memo to Pandro Berman concerning an objectionable coat, she fulminated:

> My contract, naturally, you are familiar with, so I will refrain from going into the authority it gives me on the dressing of the Mrs. Castle role, except to say that should I find, at any future date (even after the picture is released) that the coat, I had rejected, was being worn or depicted on the screen in "The Castles" picture, I will be forced to exact retribution. It seems necessary to take this type of stand as, time and time again, things have been slipped over on me and used in spite of my insistance [*sic*] that they were not acceptable to me.[25]

Later, the filmmakers discovered why Mrs. McLaughlin was so adamant about the costumes. With the assistance of her business manager, George Enzinger, she planned to release a line of clothes based on the costumes when the film was finally in circulation. Thus, the picture was to tie in with her own merchandising scheme, and so all the gowns, dresses, hats, and miscellaneous apparel worn by Ginger had to be her creations.[26] Mrs. McLaughlin was concerned with authenticity, but potential profits also appear to have been a major consideration.[27]

Among Mrs. McLaughlin's other grievances, which she proclaimed loudly to anyone who would listen, were Ginger's refusal to cut her hair, Ginger's "inability" to perform the dances precisely as she had done them, H. C. Potter's "insubordination," the shooting script, which McLaughlin insisted deviated from the original story she had approved, the portrayal of the scene in which she learns that her husband has died, the film's title (she also had approval rights on that), and literally hundreds of other details. Arlene Croce's study of the Astaire-Rogers series of films states that, toward the end, McLaughlin "went roaring" into the California antivivisection campaign and left the company "to finish the film in peace."[28] This is inaccurate, for she continued to harangue the studio throughout production and afterward. In late February 1939, her lawyers sent RKO a letter demanding damages for the many violations of her contract and warning that legal proceedings would be instituted unless an agreeable settlement could be reached.[29] In addition to paying her $5,000, RKO managed to negotiate a settlement by appealing to her vanity. Her name was to be included in the credits of the film no less than three times.[30] All in all, RKO had expended $40,000 on McLaughlin: $20,000 for the story, $15,000 for her services as advisor and costume designer, and $5,000 to settle the contract dispute.[31] Still, the money seemed insignificant compared to the turmoil she had caused.

The final scene of *The Story of Vernon and Irene Castle* practically cries out for allegorical interpretation. After Vernon dies in an airplane accident, Irene receives the news while waiting for her husband in a local hotel. She looks out into the garden where Vernon has hired a band to recapitulate all the important songs of their lives together. Superimposed over the scene we see the two of them, dancing immortally. The death of Vernon (Fred) also represents the death of Astaire and Rogers as the foremost dance team in the world and the conclusion of RKO's most famous and satisfying series of films. And the ghostly imagery suggests that the two dancers (Fred and Ginger) have entered the realm of myth—they will symbolize, forever, the epitome of style and beauty in the musical form.

Another Astaire-Rogers picture was contemplated in 1940, but it was wise to end the series here. The two stars both wished to move in new directions, and this production was their second straight financial failure (a $58,000 deficit). The careers of Fred Astaire and Ginger Rogers were far from over, even if their RKO collaboration had come to a close. They would dance together one more time—for MGM rather than RKO—in *The Barkleys of Broadway* (1949).

The 1939 sales convention took place in June at the Westchester Country Club in Rye, New York. There, George Schaefer unveiled the most audacious production program in company history, promising to spend "a minimum of $21,000,000 on '39–'40 product."[32] The $14,844,000 January estimate had obviously proven inadequate. The enumeration of coming attractions suggested that the studio and its affiliated independents had been busy acquiring well-known literary properties. *The Hunchback of Notre Dame, Ivanhoe, The American Way, Abe Lincoln in Illinois, Swiss Family Robinson, Tom Brown's School Days,* and *Anne of Windy Poplars* (from a novel by the author of *Anne of Green Gables*) were all scheduled for production.[33] Several of the new unit arrangements were revealed at the convention, including the ones with Towne and Baker and Gordon and Goetz. Schaefer had also signed some impressive actors who would be appearing in future RKO productions, including Charles Laughton, Raymond Massey, Carole Lombard, John Wayne, and Claire Trevor. None of these individuals had inked exclusive contracts with RKO, but the lineup surely sounded more promising than Joe Penner, Parkyakarkus, and Lily Pons. One month after the convention ended, Schaefer made an announcement that overshadowed all of his previous ones: Orson Welles and his Mercury Productions Company were about to join RKO on an *exclusive* basis.

Welles had been on the RKO radar screen since late 1937. His Broadway production of Shakespeare's *Julius Caesar* electrified story editor Lillie

Messinger, who raved about it to Leo Spitz. She concluded, "There must be some place in a Studio for this kind of talent."[34] Spitz was not interested in Welles at that time, but George Schaefer began to court him in May of 1939. By then, Welles had become a national celebrity, largely because of his "War of the Worlds" radio broadcast on Halloween night 1938, which petrified many inhabitants of the Eastern Seaboard.

George Schaefer finally signed Welles and Mercury Productions on July 22, 1939. The agreement was for two pictures that Welles would write, produce, direct, and act in. Many sources have called this deal a unique, carte blanche contract. It was certainly unique, but did not give Welles as much freedom as has been supposed. For example, RKO had the right to approve the basic story and the budget, which was not to exceed $500,000. Otherwise, control of the productions, including the editing, would rest wholly with Welles.[35] Unless the new director departed radically from the story or exceeded a half-million dollars in expenditures, RKO could not interfere in the making of either film. This was definitely unprecedented; a neophyte filmmaker had been granted a contract with a Hollywood studio guaranteeing he would be able to work in total freedom.

The addition of Welles and his Mercury Productions group was a coup for Schaefer, but it was also perfectly in sync with his new unit-production strategy. Welles—like Goetz and Gordon, Towne and Baker, Wilcox, and others who would join the company in the next couple of years—would be expected to create innovative, artistic motion pictures that energized the RKO brand, making George Schaefer's company stand out. Without an understanding of this context, the Welles saga at RKO might seem an aberration. It was, instead, simply part of George Schaefer's master plan.

There was room to question the wisdom of the plan itself. The individuals signed by Schaefer were not industry veterans. Some, like Welles, Wilcox, and Goetz and Gordon, had no Hollywood experience at all. The ability of others, such as Towne and Baker and Harold Lloyd, to produce successful films was suspect. It is little wonder that Pandro Berman was shocked and angered by many of George Schaefer's decisions. Schaefer, during his initial year in office, took several sizable gambles. If they paid off, he would soon be elevated to full "mogul" status in Hollywood. But if they did not . . .

By the time of the Orson Welles announcement, relations between Pandro Berman and George Schaefer had reached such an impasse that the two men were hardly communicating with each other. Berman retained his title, though Schaefer had essentially usurped his authority as RKO production leader. J. R. McDonough was now the intermediary, conveying all the important studio information to Schaefer in New York. A supplemental agreement was worked out in September that allowed Berman to terminate his obligations to RKO four months early.[36] This agreement was later amended, so that Berman could continue working on two pictures—*The Hunchback of Notre Dame* and *Vigil in the Night*—until they were completed.

Schaefer did not recognize it, but he was losing a very valuable man, as the production history of the Ginger Rogers comedy *Bachelor Mother* illustrates. The movie was based on *Kleine Mutti* (*Little Mother*), a picture produced by a subsidiary of Universal in Hungary.[37] G. B. (Buddy) DeSylva had first purchased the rights from Universal, then sold the property, along with his services as producer, to RKO in August 1938. Norman Krasna took on the script assignment and, working in concert with prospective director Garson Kanin, completed the screenplay in late February 1939. The studio announced an early March start date for the production.

Ginger Rogers, however, had acute reservations about the project, based principally on her distaste for the script. Two days before the film was to begin shooting, she wrote Berman:

> I have just read [the script of "Little Mother"] again and am writing you merely to go on record as having said: "The characters affect the story instead of the story affecting them. Instead of working laughs out of natural situations—we do it differently—we build our situations around a laugh. Why, I don't know. There is no love between these two people and a story that has a boy and girl as its leading characters is expected to be a love story. The thing that is wrong with "Little Mother" is that it leaves too much to the imagination as far as their love is concerned.
>
> . . . .
>
> If we were to meet these two people in our drawing rooms we would say that they were bores—so why do we make a picture about them? Just because it would be cute to say, "Ginger Rogers picked up a baby and tried to convince her intimate friends that it wasn't hers?" Even the landlady isn't surprised that she has a baby! God! WHAT ARE WE COMING TO!

Continuing, Ginger expressed genuine fear about the damage the film might do to her career:

> I cannot live on past performances. In this picture "Little Mother" I am Ginger Rogers. And it seems to me that you are relying on me as a personality—instead of an actress with a personality . . . the same as in "Having a Wonderful Time." This story is just as sketchy as

"Wonderful Time" and I'm afraid that if this story isn't worked on it will end up with the same rank odor.

. . . .

After all, Pan, people in the industry know—perhaps. I say perhaps, because when anyone's name is on the screen as having written, directed, or produced a vehicle—those are naturally the people who are rightfully blamed for it. But the public blames me! They don't know it's an R.K.O. picture—nor do they care. They know they don't like it—and that I am in it. If you think that this is serious to you, then you know how serious it is to me.[38]

Pandro Berman's reply was a combination of tact, salesmanship, and toughness. It also revealed a much more perceptive grasp of the material than the actress had:

I am terribly sorry that you feel as you do about this picture, and I want you to know that quite contrary to some statements in your letter this picture was purchased because we honestly believed it had a sincere and fine underlying story which would serve as a good vehicle for you, and that our efforts in writing this script have been of fine entertainment quality, and that I for one am proud of the script rather than apologetic about it, and that I think it is better than 90 per cent of the scripts that are made in Hollywood every day, and that I think if you never get a worse one you will be extremely fortunate because this is a difficult business and one that is dependent upon creative talent, and scripts as good as this are hard to create. . . . I am extremely sympathetic to every point of view you could ever express, because I know how sincere and earnest and helpful you are, [but] I do think that there are times when the judgment of an actor or actress with regard to the entertainment value of a script is colored by their personal and professional ambitions, which compels [sic] them to look at it from an inverted point of view of what constitutes audience values.

Berman's further remarks may seem self-serving, but they were pretty accurate. Up to this point, Ginger Rogers' career had been skillfully managed by RKO:

I am anxious to impress upon you the fact which I am sure you do not quite understand, which is namely that I never deliberately put you into anything I do not have the utmost faith in, and that you are wrong in assuming that RKO or myself is willing to bandy you about in inconsequential material. Your career to date has been handled more judiciously and more carefully than any woman's in pictures. I do not know an actress today, and I include the Garbos, Shearers, Crawfords, and even Bette Davis who rates at the top of her profession, who has been handled with such a succession of box-office successes and

Figure 21.   *Bachelor Mother* (1939). Producer and production chief Pandro
Berman visits Ginger Rogers and director Garson Kanin on the set. Rogers's
expression suggests that she was not very happy during the making of this film,
but it turned out to be one of the biggest hits of her career. (Courtesy of the
Academy of Motion Picture Arts and Sciences)

characters beloved by audiences, as you have. . . . I am prouder of my
record with you than I am of any record that has been established over
a period of years in the industry by anyone with any particular
personality, and I am willing to stand on that record in this matter
which in my best considered judgment appears to me to be a picture
that cannot in any way harm you and may do you good, because I
believe in it.[39]

Pandro Berman's persuasive powers did not work; he was forced to suspend Rogers without pay when she refused to make the picture. After a
short time, the actress grudgingly reported for duty and completed the
film without further protest. The outcome must have shocked her and
made Berman feel like the proverbial soothsayer.

George Schaefer viewed the picture in mid-May and immediately pronounced it "a real smash."[40] He was right. When the retitled *Bachelor
Mother* opened in June, it immediately blasted off and did not come back

to earth for months thereafter. Since it was considered a solo effort (costar David Niven had not yet gained significant box-office standing), *Bachelor Mother* boosted Rogers's status more dramatically than any picture since the early musicals with Astaire. Before long, the film became the studio's champion sleeper of the 1930s, earning a profit of $827,000.

The reputation of RKO's product grew steadily throughout 1939, but neither President Schaefer nor Pandro Berman were allowed sufficient time to enjoy their company's increasing status. In September, World War II began in Europe, provoking upheaval at RKO corporate headquarters. The warring nations of England, France, and Poland represented an estimated 30 percent of the worldwide revenue of American film distributors, and about 60 percent of their total foreign revenue.[41] The closing of all theaters in these countries signaled the most immediate problem. While the situation was not expected to last, it seemed probable that film programs would be curtailed due to the vulnerability of cinemas to air raids. Another serious anticipated effect involved restrictions that would be placed on the transfer of funds earned by U.S. companies. France immediately halted the outflow of money, and all the Hollywood companies remembered vividly that they had suffered from transfer restrictions during both the Spanish Civil War and the undeclared Sino-Japanese war.[42] The potential loss was infinitely greater this time because of the magnitude of the conflict.

George Schaefer postponed a scheduled visit to the West Coast in order to study the developments. He examined the situation for a week, then dispatched telegrams to several important RKO employees. After describing the bleak conditions to Berman, the RKO president came to the point:

> All this . . . puts us in position where we must watch every dollar and for that matter every nickel. . . . Indications at present are that there will be curtailment of imports into England and possibly monetary restrictions and it is certain for some time to come we are going to be solely dependent upon returns from the Americas. . . . Show wire to Marcus and urge him do likewise on all his product. Present indications are that we will cut from eight to ten pictures out of his program. You can better appreciate the need of this when I let you know that we would have lost money on every important picture in the past five years had we eliminated revenue from Great Britain, France, Poland.[43]

Berman was at that time producing one of the most demanding and expensive films ever undertaken by RKO, *The Hunchback of Notre Dame*. The problems, as outlined by Schaefer, appeared so severe that he began to believe *Hunchback* would be one of the last of the large-scale, costly pictures.

It now appeared financially suicidal to make big-budget films when prospects for foreign revenue were so slender. Years later, Berman reflected on his belief: "I was quite wrong because there were plenty [of expensive spectaculars] made after that. In any case, it seemed to me like the end of an era while we were shooting it [*Hunchback*]."[44]

Actually, Schaefer was wrong as well. His facts and figures were accurate, but he had failed to consider the possibility that an increase in domestic attendance might offset any decline in foreign revenue. As the *Motion Picture Herald* reported: "Box office receipts always go up in wartime. The situation may result in cutting out some of the costly mistakes made at the top and in cutting down costs of some of the million dollar pictures that ought not to cost that much anyway. And it may give some new talent a break."[45] Indeed, the war years proved to be the most profitable period in the history of the American motion picture industry, though top earnings came after the United States entered the conflict as a combatant.

Of course, George Schaefer could not foresee the coming halcyon days. He looked at the deteriorating conditions across the Atlantic and saw nothing but problems for his business. His initial response was to revive a strategy employed during the Depression: salary cuts. On September 25, 1939, this announcement was sent to all RKO employees: "RKO has devised a broad program of intensified effort and curtailment of costs to meet the grave situation confronting our company due to serious loss of revenue from abroad caused by the war in Europe. Temporary reductions in pay are unavoidable, but such reductions will be confined to employees in the higher brackets. No employee receiving $4,500 per year or less will be affected. From this point upward a graduated scale will apply, so that the largest salaries will receive the largest percentage cuts."[46] Employees earning in excess of $75,000 took the most substantial hits—a reduction of 50 percent. This approach generated significant anger among those affected, mainly because several of the other studios did not resort to the same remedy.

Schaefer believed the problem could not be solved by salary cuts alone. RKO earnings from abroad would, inevitably, be reduced, and this loss of income would have an impact on all aspects of the corporation's functioning. Schaefer also wrote J. J. Nolan, the man in charge of studio commitments who had recently been designated Schaefer's Hollywood adjutant: "We must be careful of all our commitments and it is quite possible that there may be drastic revisions on our entire budget and program due to the international situation, therefore, proceed slowly as to final commitments. However, keep uppermost in mind that we must drive through but be ready to halt and pull in our reins at a moment's notice."[47]

Schaefer's immediate feeling was that "we cannot from this point on make pictures that cost more than $500,000, if the revenue is to be curtailed in Europe."[48] This meant a radical revision of the studio's production plans. Nothing could be done about large-budget pictures, such as *The Hunchback of Notre Dame* and *Abe Lincoln in Illinois*, already before the cameras. But savings could be effected elsewhere. For example, *The American Way*, a stage play by George S. Kaufman and Moss Hart that Schaefer acquired in the Gordon-Goetz deal, was put on the shelf. The play had an "Americanism" theme, highly topical at the time, but its estimated production cost was more than $1 million. Even though the studio had invested $250,000 for the rights, Schaefer believed the high budget requirement made it too risky to proceed.

Orson Welles's first scheduled picture, *Heart of Darkness*, was postponed for the same reason. Welles was working on his script, an adaptation of the famous Joseph Conrad short novel, when the war broke out. Like Berman, he received a pessimistic wire from Schaefer urging him to make every effort to trim the budget of the picture to a bare minimum. Welles's reply to Schaefer read in part: "You have my word that because of conditions as you explained every cent will be counted twice in HEART OF DARKNESS. No single luxury will be indulged, only absolute essentials to effectiveness and potency of story. Because you have entrusted me with full authority in this, I will be the more vigiland [*sic*] and painstaking about costs."[49]

Nevertheless, the preliminary budget figures on *Heart of Darkness* amounted to a staggering $1,057,761.[50] This was not only more than twice as much as Schaefer reckoned RKO could afford to spend on a film, but was also double the amount Welles's contract allowed him to spend. George Schaefer did not order immediate cancelation of the project, however. He wanted to keep Welles happy, and he wanted to get some pictures from his young Faustian talent. Negotiations were conducted that resulted in the following plan: *Heart of Darkness* would be kept on the company's schedule while efforts were made to chop at least $250,000 off the budget. Meanwhile, Welles would prepare another film, which he would write, direct, and star in for *nothing*. Thus, the package of two pictures could probably be made for a reasonable figure since the second film would certainly cost much less than $500,000.[51] The proposed title of this second film was *The Smiler With a Knife*. Near the end of the year, the ongoing revision of *Heart of Darkness* had reduced the budget by $73,000 with more eliminations expected, and Welles was working feverishly to finish his *Smiler* script.[52] It looked as if RKO would be producing two Orson Welles pictures for release in 1940.

The concern for economy manifested itself in other ways. The first eight months of 1939 had been a period of prodigality, of unparalleled expenditure on studio operations. But after the war erupted, the kinds of worries that had plagued RKO during the Depression returned. President Schaefer, for example, began to fret about the total footage of pictures and the amount of eliminated material between first and final cut. Schaefer sent J. J. Nolan a memo listing five films completed after January 1, 1939, that showed a 20 to 37 percent elimination between rough cut and final cut. Noting that such eliminations add "that much more expense to the cost of production," Schaefer asked Nolan to suggest ways of preventing the waste.[53] Once again, studio executives were pinching pennies, worrying about details and mechanical problems rather than the overriding necessity of producing good pictures.

At least the end of the agonizing receivership process became assured in 1939. The actual emergence of the company from 77B did not take place during the year, though it should have. As in the past, petitions, objections, delays, last-minute changes, and other complications interfered with the final reorganization.

An indication that the long battle was drawing to a close came in January 1939 when Judge William Bondy approved the Atlas-sponsored reorganization plan.[54] One of the provisions of the plan allowed stockholders who had already consented to its contents to withdraw their support within three weeks after the approval. This caused an initial delay that was prolonged when additional hearings proved necessary to determine if Irving Trust Company had to notify 20,000 stockholders of objections to the plan filed by Ernest W. Stirn, a holder of class A stock.[55]

Summer arrived, but still nothing concrete had been accomplished. Judge Bondy was spending time weighing the makeup of the new board of directors while three more objectors to the plan filed suits against it in a New York circuit court of appeal.[56] The proponents of the reorganization plan were vindicated in July when the appeals court unanimously affirmed Judge Bondy's original approval.[57] Bondy also approved a thirteen-member board, leaving only one matter to be disposed of: the capitalization plan for the new RKO.

The Atlas proposal called for the issuance of 2,230,000 shares of new common stock that would be given to RKO creditors in settlement of their claims, and 4,367,554 shares, some of which would be reserved for options warrants and the rest sold to raise working capital. This stock would have an initial market value of approximately $4 per share. Also part of the capitalization was $13,000,000 in 6 percent cumulative convertible first preferred stock with a par value of $100.[58] Atlas promised to underwrite $1,500,000 of the new stock if the federal court accepted the offer by August 29. The date came and went with proceedings still snarled, prompting Atlas to withdraw its offer.[59] Once again, the reorganization had descended into limbo.

Judge Bondy grew angry in October. Calling the proceedings "interminable," he insisted that immediate progress be made.[60] Seemingly in answer to Bondy's request, Floyd Odlum revealed that Atlas had not abandoned RKO but needed more time to formulate a new capitalization proposal. The outbreak of war in Europe had considerably altered the future prospects of motion picture companies, and Odlum wanted his staff to evaluate the situation before presenting a second offer to underwrite the RKO stock.

In mid-December, Atlas submitted its new offer to underwrite 500,000 shares of RKO common at $3 per share. There was actually very little difference between this offer and the original one. Only the $3 price (down from $4) was different; according to Floyd Odlum, "changing world conditions" had necessitated a lower price than Atlas had proffered in August.[61] The procedure contained the following ground rules: "An offer of shares must be submitted by December 31st to holders of unsecured claims and to Rockefeller Center, Inc. These creditors will be allowed 20 days to exercise their option to buy the stock. Within two days of the expiration date of the option to creditors, RKO must notify Atlas of the number of unsubscribed shares remaining. Atlas binds itself to purchase and pay for all unsubscribed stock at the $3 price within two to seven days after the notice from RKO."[62]

And so, finally, the long, debilitating process was drawing to a conclusion. All indicators pointed to the emergence of a revitalized, self-directed RKO early in 1940.

Pandro Berman, who had enjoyed many triumphs and suffered many disappointments while RKO was in receivership, would not be an RKO employee when it finally ended. On December 28, 1939, Harry Edington, a former agent with limited production experience, was named to succeed Berman "in charge of all the important pictures to be made on the RKO lot."[63] Pan Berman abandoned his world travel plans, signing a contract to produce pictures for MGM.

Berman's parting gift to RKO was *The Hunchback of Notre Dame*. Victor Hugo's famous novel was in the public domain, yet RKO was forced to buy the rights to the story from MGM. Metro had acquired those rights from Universal, which had made a famous silent version starring Lon Chaney. Such interstudio arrangements imposed order on the wild scramble for good story material, even taking precedence over copyright laws.

The cost to RKO was $125,000, a figure partially offset by the sale (for $85,000) of *Rio Rita* to MGM.[64] In essence, the two properties had been traded, with RKO sweetening the deal by $40,000.

Pandro Berman decided to personally supervise *Hunchback*. Since this would be his last major production for RKO, he vowed to make it a proper finale to his career at the studio. George Schaefer encouraged Berman because the undertaking supported his own belief in prestigious productions. Academy Award winner Charles Laughton was signed to play Quasimodo, William Dieterle was borrowed from Warner Bros. to direct, and the production staff began the most ambitious (and costly) set construction in the history of RKO. By the time they finished building the Cathedral Square, the Court of Miracles, and the Palace of Justice at the studio ranch in the San Fernando Valley, the outlay for this facet of the production alone was approximately $250,000.[65] The original $2 million budget estimate was reduced to $1,833,866 by casting a pair of unknowns in important roles: Maureen O'Hara as Esmeralda and Edmond O'Brien as Gringoire, the poet.[66] Still, it is a testament to the talents of Berman and Dieterle that they were able to complete the picture within the budget allowance. That fact alone makes *Hunchback* an impressive technical and logistical achievement.

The Hunchback of Notre Dame was rushed through postproduction so that it could open during the Christmas holidays at Radio City Music Hall. At the eleventh hour, an incident transpired that brought a number of personal tensions into focus. It seems a relatively minor disagreement, yet it reveals how obsessed Pan Berman had become with the production, how bitter the rift had grown between him and George Schaefer, and how determined Schaefer was to exercise final authority regarding all production decisions.

Alfred Newman's musical score sparked the controversy. At the urging of Charles Laughton, Schaefer decided to eliminate the musical background to three scenes: the pillory sequence after the whipping of Quasimodo, the poignant scene between Quasimodo and Esmeralda in the bell tower, and the climactic flight-chase sequence involving Lord High Justice Frollo (Cedric Hardwicke) and Quasimodo. Schaefer and Laughton believed these scenes would play more successfully without musical underscoring.

When Pandro Berman learned what the New York office had in mind, he exploded. The following telegram was sent to Schaefer on December 15: "Am so shocked by information your instructions to studio regarding THE HUNCHBACK that hardly know how to speak. I wouldn't treat a dog the way you have treated me in this situation by your extreme lack of courtesy in even discussing it after I have spent one year nursing this terrific endeavor for screen masterpiece. Know that you will live to regret actions such as these and can only hope they will not weigh too heavily on your conscience in the future."[67]

George Schaefer replied on the same day: "Your wire is so typical . . . that I am again going to refrain from making any comment. However, since in the last analysis it is the company's investment and since many important people who have seen it here agree that the particular scenes would play better without music and especially since Laughton advised me that both you and Dieterle promised him not to put any music behind those scenes, I felt it most important to do what I thought was for the company's best interest and am terribly sorry you don't agree."[68]

A few days later, Schaefer changed his mind and decided to leave the music under the pillory scene, eliminating it in the other two sections.[69] The picture opened, as scheduled, in late December. It performed quite well, earning $100,000, despite its huge production cost, and bringing in more than $3 million in gross film income. This seems even more extraordinary when one recalls that its chief competition was *Gone With the Wind*, which opened around the same time.

For RKO, it was not only the end of a decade, it was the end of an era—the Pandro Berman era. He had been a fixture on the lot since the FBO days and had endured the many ups and downs and executive shuffling that took place during the thirties. Without question, he was the company's most respected employee when he departed. And his final year at the studio's helm became a personal testament: one of the most memorable release years in RKO history.[70] It is important not to inflate Berman's achievements or abilities. He made mistakes during his RKO tenure, and his batting average as a production head does not rival those of Irving Thalberg at MGM, Hal Wallis at Warner Bros., or Darryl Zanuck at Twentieth Century–Fox. Still, these men had their share of disappointments, and they were not appreciably superior to Pan Berman. Certainly no producer or executive at RKO during the last half of the 1930s could compare to him, and thus, his loss represented a tremendous blow to the company.[71] George Schaefer, however, seemed blithely unfazed.

At the end of 1939, RKO was a very different company than it had been one year before. During Schaefer's first full year as president of RKO, the studio underwent a radical transformation. After a period of producing nearly all of its own pictures, it suddenly became the home of a number of independents that would be responsible for a significant percentage of future RKO releases. Turning away from an era of Depression-forced neglect,

RKO began competing for the most expensive literary properties. In 1939 alone, Schaefer's company invested $550,000 in the acquisition of plays and books. This was some $260,000 more than MGM, $290,000 more than Paramount, and $355,000 more than Warner Bros. (the nearest competitors).[72] With *The Hunchback of Notre Dame* setting the tone, it became clear that George Schaefer intended to turn RKO into a "quality" studio—one known for serious, ambitious, bravura productions rather than the escapist musicals, run-of-the-mill melodramas, and erratic comedies that had characterized its past. Orson Welles's *Heart of Darkness*, still in preparation at the end of the year, was part of the Schaefer program for glory.

The U.S. government lawsuit regarding theater ownership and block booking, unresolved in 1939, carried over into 1940. This, plus the European conflict and growing concerns about America's possible entrance into the war, troubled all of RKO's workers and investors. In addition, the industry's economic rebound had been reversed; despite arguably the greatest release year in Hollywood history, every studio except Universal and United Artists made less money in 1939 that it had in 1938. Notwithstanding all these uncertainties, there was one indubitable fact that engendered hope: RKO finally had a vigorous and experienced president, a man determined to involve himself in all important decisions and to run the company his way. The future of RKO rested firmly in the hands of one person: George J. Schaefer.

9. "Quality pictures are the lifeblood of this business"

The Schaefer-Edington Regime (1940–1941)

George Schaefer's determination to make RKO the preeminent company in the industry might have been motivated by a desire to please Nelson Rockefeller. Besides being Schaefer's major supporter, Rockefeller was an art collector and, along with his mother, Abby Aldrich Rockefeller, one of the most active patrons of the Museum of Modern Art in New York. Given that MOMA was the first museum in the United States to recognize motion pictures as an art form and to begin to amass a film collection, Rockefeller undoubtedly would have been pleased to see RKO become a leader in the artistic development of the medium.[1] But Nelson Rockefeller was also a businessman who expected his family's investment in RKO to be a success, and there is no evidence that he ever prodded George Schaefer in the direction he chose.

Rather, it seems more likely that Schaefer's vision for RKO took shape during his time with United Artists. That company existed to distribute films made by independent producers, and its major suppliers while Schaefer worked there were David Selznick and Sam Goldwyn, both of whom favored prestigious pictures based on eminent works of literature. Thus, it was not surprising that RKO's new president immediately began recruiting independents who he believed could supply his company with similar product. Later, in a July 1940 report to the RKO board, he stated that he had decided on this course of action because of his belief that "quality pictures are the lifeblood of this business, since they affect both theatre and picture company earnings." To upgrade RKO's substandard releases in the shortest possible time, Schaefer continued, "the only conservative answer . . . was to secure the best independent producers *available* to strengthen the company's product with a minimum of financial risk."[2]

But Schaefer's rationalization is hard to swallow, because significant risk did exist. Unlike most of the UA arrangements, a number of the deals he set up were not straight distribution agreements. Each one was different, but some offered total financing by RKO (the Welles–Mercury Theatre operation, for example), while others required bank loans that would have to be repaid by RKO if the pictures did not perform well at the box office (Gordon-Goetz). United Artists also employed a very different business model; it did not own a studio or theaters and thus had much lower overhead costs than RKO. But George Schaefer believed he could combine the best elements of the UA approach with the advantages of a vertically integrated company in his master plan for RKO.

In spite of concerns about the world war, President Schaefer's confidence level was high early in the new decade. On Friday, January 26, 1940, at 2:30 P.M., RKO officially emerged from receivership.[3] The actual return of assets from Irving Trust into the hands of RKO took place when representatives from each company sat around a table and exchanged papers until the transaction was completed. The date itself was significant—it was exactly seven years, less one day, from the time the company filed its bankruptcy petition in federal court. According to *Variety*, this case held the record for longevity of receivership proceedings.[4]

The final stumbling block to reorganization had been cleared when the Supreme Court denied a writ of certiorari to two companies that held stock and securities in RKO, both of which had opposed the plan for some time. The new stock offer went forward smoothly, with Rockefeller Center subscribing to 163,629 shares and Atlas taking up some 249,280 unsubscribed shares, as it had promised.[5] The event represented a strangely tranquil culmination to a process that had almost always been agonizing. The company now appeared to be on solid ground. During the seven years administered by the trustee, RKO and its subsidiaries had reduced their fixed debt by more than $11 million, and gross income had grown from $44 million in 1933 to $52 million in 1939. The new company was starting fresh, with "no outstanding indebtedness" and working capital of "more than $8,000,000," an amount almost twice as large as its liabilities.[6]

The end of receivership was not as simple as it seemed. Atlas Corporation and a battery of lawyers bombarded Judge William Bondy with requests for reimbursements of expenditures generated in the reorganization proceedings and payments of fees for services rendered. These pleas continued throughout most of 1940, with the funds for their payment expected to come from purchases of new common stock. Atlas alone was asking for $875,037 plus 100,000 shares of RKO common.[7] Total claims amounted to

$3.1 million.[8] George Schaefer urged Bondy to reduce the claims drastically. RKO's president invoked the perilous conditions brought on by war in his affidavit to the judge. "In my opinion," Schaefer said, "the motion picture industry is now confronted with the most serious crisis in its history. Recent statements by various leaders of the industry give evidence that major and drastic readjustments are inevitable if the industry is to survive."[9] Bondy was sympathetic. His final decree slashed the original request to $638,073. Atlas, naturally, received the largest amount: 120,000 new common shares, $170,000 for legal fees incurred, and $20,517 for disbursements.[10] Still, this was far below the amount originally requested.

All of this must have felt anticlimactic. The important thing, though, was that RKO had thrown off its economic shackles. In fact, the company had not actually been in danger of collapse for years; nevertheless, there was a stigma attached to receivership, and company officials greeted its removal with equal measures of relief and optimism. Stories like the following circulated to alert the industry that RKO's executives were bullish about their company's future: "Strengthening of manpower in all branches with a view to making the company second to none in the business, including in that step various promotions from the ranks as well as some possible shaking up of personnel and solidifying of policies, is reported to be in the cards for RKO following the long period of receivership from which the company recently emerged. The wheels are already in motion and various changes are likely to come."[11] Indeed, RKO would make a number of forceful moves shortly after reorganization was complete, despite the worsening world situation. George Schaefer wanted to demonstrate that RKO was a revitalized company.

The first of President Schaefer's "appointments from within the ranks" named J. J. Nolan "vice-president in charge of the RKO studios."[12] Nolan, who had worked for RKO since its early days, represented an important conduit of information for the president. Nolan's new title was, however, misleading. He did not supersede J. R. McDonough, who still administered the filmmaking plant. Nor did he take over as the new production chief; he would have some input into production decisions, but most would be made by Schaefer in consort with Harry Edington and Lee Marcus. In truth, Nolan's principal activities would remain as before: contacts with agents, commitments, and negotiations for artistic talent. RKO desperately needed to shore up its acting talent, and Schaefer must have believed that Nolan's new title would help the company compete for the most attractive individuals.

In February the studio continued its aggressive campaign of acquiring high-profile literary properties, spending $390,000 in a seven-day period.

The extraordinary outlay of cash bought RKO rights to *Too Many Girls* ($100,000 price), a Broadway musical hit to be produced and directed by George Abbott; *Two on an Island* ($50,000) by Elmer Rice; *Mr. and Mrs.* ($60,000), an original story by Norman Krasna, who had written *Bachelor Mother*; *Benjamin Franklin* ($50,000), the Carl Van Doren biography in which Schaefer hoped to star Charles Laughton; *Sister Carrie* ($40,000) by Theodore Dreiser, a novel no one else had dared touch because of censorship concerns; *Half Rogue* ($40,000) by Garrett Fort, another Laughton project; *The Unbreakable Miss Doll* ($25,000) by Grace Perkins, bought with Carole Lombard in mind; *Sanda Mala* ($15,000) by Maurice Collis; and A. P. Herbert's *Water Gypsies* ($10,000).[13] George Schaefer's belief in critically acclaimed plays and novels as the key to prestige and box-office rewards, as well as his determination to elevate RKO to a more important position among the major companies, fueled this amazing buying spree.

Schaefer also implemented some fresh, unusual strategies. Chief among them was his hiring of Dr. George Gallup, head of the Institute of Public Opinion in Princeton, New Jersey, to conduct "a scientific study of the motion picture public and the tastes, habits and interests of picture patrons." The function of Gallup's new organization, called the Audience Research Institute, would be to "scientifically assist and guide the studio in its selection of stories, cast and titles."[14] The notion of scientific public opinion "pretesting" to determine audience interest was bold and forward-thinking, but whether it would actually work remained an open question.

George Schaefer became one of the most visible executives in the film business during 1940. In addition to the long hours he spent running his own company, Schaefer campaigned vociferously against the government's continuing attempt to end block booking and force the Big Five to sell their theaters. When final hearings were held on the Neely bill, which contained a provision that would have prevented the selling of movies in blocks, Schaefer became the industry's point man in Washington. He told the politicians that RKO did not "force" all of its product upon exhibitors, stating that 67 percent of the company's contracts for the past season "called for the exhibition of less than the number of pictures we had to offer." Schaefer added that the bill was untimely because "it would add vastly to the burdens of an industry gravely affected by the war."[15] Spokesman Schaefer must have made an impact because the bill never became law. Instead, a compromise consent decree that included new rules concerning block booking was negotiated later in the year.

Schaefer also assumed the chairmanship of the motion picture industry's Coordinating Committee on National Defense. This group was formed to further the contributions of the film business to the national defense effort. Schaefer clarified his committee's mission in November 1940: "It is to be emphasized that the voluntary organization being developed by the industry is not intended in any way to limit the initiative, contribution, or service which any elements within it may apply to the problems of national defense. The intention is to provide a clearing house for such plans as may best serve our national needs, insofar as the screen is properly concerned."[16]

In addition, Schaefer presided at a ceremony in which RKO turned over Pathe news footage, shot between 1910 and 1930, to Nelson Rockefeller's favorite repository, the Museum of Modern Art.[17] Clearly, the RKO president enjoyed the roles of industry spokesman, leader of Hollywood's national defense effort, and preserver of America's film heritage. Schaefer took his position very seriously and seemingly intended to become the most "public" executive in RKO history.

One wonders how Schaefer ever found time to sleep, considering that in addition to all his other activities, he was still riding herd on studio production. His new production chief, Harry Edington, had worked in Hollywood since the silent days as an agent or manager (or both) for Erich Von Stroheim, Greta Garbo, Marlene Dietrich, Douglas Fairbanks, Jr., Nelson Eddy, Ann Harding, Cary Grant, Joel McCrea, and others. His production experience, however, consisted of only one film, *Green Hell,* which Universal released shortly after Edington took up his position with RKO. So why did Schaefer choose him to head filmmaking at 780 Gower Street? It's not possible to say for certain, but it seems plausible the RKO leader viewed Edington's lack of experience as a plus. Schaefer expected Edington to carry out his instructions without complaint (unlike Pandro Berman). And that appears to be precisely what happened; if Harry Edington ever initiated any film projects at RKO, there is no evidence of it. He was production chief "in name only," to borrow a title from one of the company's 1939 releases.

Schaefer and Edington paid close attention to what was happening in Europe. The surprising success of the Nazi war machine brought gloom to much of America during 1940. In sync with the general industry trend, Schaefer decided to steer clear of any stories based on contemporary realities. Fearing isolationist factions and believing American audiences desired cheerful, diverting material that would take their minds off the European hostilities, Schaefer frowned on any story of a potentially controversial nature.

In March, for example, Schaefer decided to eliminate *Man Without a World,* a picture that Lee Marcus wished to make. In a letter to J. J. Nolan,

Schaefer explained that his decision was based on the fact that *Man Without a World* dealt "with Dictatorships and the foreign situation and I want to be so careful that we do not make something that is apt to either cause us trouble or be outmoded by some sudden turn in world events."[18] Schaefer's feelings were reinforced by Harry Edington. In April, Edington wrote New York story editor Leda Bauer concerning the company's needs:

> I went over this with Mr. Schaefer . . . and I believe he was quite in accord, especially with the idea that a good portion of our program should be made up of romance, romantic comedies, and romantic dramas. I think this is especially true for the following year. Nobody can tell how much more the world is going to become entangled in this war situation and it is my opinion that, more than ever in the past ten year history of the business, we should strive for nothing more than "entertainment." I dont [*sic*] think we should allow ourselves to take sides or carry a torch for either side or even get involved in anything that has to do with the so-called present day moral problems having to do with world affairs.[19]

Thus, even though the conflict was wreaking havoc on RKO's business, the prevailing production philosophy would be to pretend World War II did not exist. Other studio executives were also reticent, though a few anti-Nazi films did appear in 1940 following the success of *Confessions of a Nazi Spy*, which Warner Bros. released in May 1939.

Getting a head start on its competitors, RKO announced in late March that it would release between sixty-one and sixty-six pictures during the 1940–1941 season.[20] The announcement was remarkable for two reasons. First, this represented the largest number of features the company had ever promised in a single season. Second, it came at a time when most studios were cutting their production schedule due to the loss of foreign revenue. According to a story in the *Motion Picture Herald*, the gross budget for the films would be $29 million, with twenty of the new features to be made by independents, twenty to be "top budget" studio productions, twenty to come from Lee Marcus's "program" unit, and six to be inexpensive Westerns.[21]

In fact, this bold proclamation was pure propaganda. Actual plans for 1940–1941 fell well short of sixty productions. Earlier in March, Schaefer, Depinet, Edington, Nolan, and other company executives met at La Quinta, where they outlined the following plans for the coming season:

12 "A" Specials
  6 Outside Specials to be independently produced
  6 Specials—Marcus unit

12 Program pictures—Marcus unit

  6 O'Brien Westerns

  6 Pictures, independently produced in which we have no interest except making available our releasing facilities.[22]

This totaled forty-eight pictures, not sixty.

One can only speculate concerning why RKO's publicity department purposely circulated erroneous information of this kind. In all probability, it was part and parcel of the hype surrounding the "new RKO" campaign, the buildup that had been under way since emergence from receivership and included announcements concerning the story purchases and the continuing addition of more independents.

According to the actual blueprint, RKO looked to release twelve A specials, made for an average cost of approximately $670,000 each. This represented a total expenditure of about $8 million. The biggest change concerned the low-budget unit, where Lee Marcus was promised $1,400,000 to make six "specials," pictures costing about twice as much as the normal B offerings. Marcus would also be responsible for twelve "program" releases to be made for $1,500,000 and six George O'Brien Westerns costing $480,000.[23] Despite its grandiose announcements, the "new RKO" remained conservative. There would be no big-budget extravaganzas, and the total expected budget for the new season was well below that of the previous year. The unknown factor in these plans was the independent product. Schaefer had set up so many different deals, and the financing of these deals was so variable, that it was hard to guess how much the new season's expenditures would actually be.

One sour note in this regard was sounded by the release of *Abe Lincoln in Illinois* early in the year. In February 1939 George Schaefer was about to finalize the deal with Max Gordon and Harry Goetz when he received word that Twentieth Century–Fox planned to make a film about Abraham Lincoln starring Henry Fonda. The news was especially disturbing because a major element of Schaefer's arrangement with Gordon and his partner involved the rights to Robert Sherwood's play *Abe Lincoln in Illinois*. Since Fox's Lincoln film would be finished and into theaters before RKO could release its picture, this jeopardized the entire arrangement.

Schaefer nevertheless went forward with Gordon-Goetz, giving RKO *The American Way* as well as *Abe Lincoln*. *The American Way* was never made because of its large projected costs, but the Lincoln film was placed on the schedule, perhaps because it received the Pulitzer Prize in May 1939 and embodied a patriotic hymn to Americanism that Schaefer thought would appeal to audiences of the time. Preliminary estimates indicated that the picture's budget would be more than $1 million.

Since this was before the outbreak of the World War and its disruption of foreign revenue, Schaefer gave it a green light. Shooting began in August 1939 with John Cromwell directing and Raymond Massey portraying Lincoln, as he had in the stage production. In an attempt to "open up" the drama, the picture was filmed largely on location in Oregon. This caused problems. Rainy weather and days of poor light brought on by forest fires in the Klamath Falls area caused the company to fall nine days behind schedule.[24] By the time they finished in October, the company had lost three more days, but Cromwell managed to bring the picture in under the budget estimate. Still, at a price of $1,004,000, the film was an expensive undertaking by RKO standards.

Even though *Abe Lincoln in Illinois* was considered an independent deal, the financing came from bank loans guaranteed by RKO—whether the picture made money or not. The only cash advanced by the producers was half the cost of the screenplay ($112,500).[25] In effect, RKO had invested almost $900,000 in the picture. If the film did well, both RKO and Max Gordon Plays and Pictures Corporation would profit. But if it fared poorly, RKO would bear the brunt of the losses.

RKO hoped to release *Abe Lincoln in Illinois* for the Thanksgiving holiday, but it proved difficult to cut, score, and dub, so it was held for a January 1940 release. Schaefer saw a rough cut in late October, then dispatched the following telegram to Max Gordon:

> Even twenty-four hours after seeing the "Abe Lincoln" production, I still think it is a great motion picture. It makes one proud that he is in the picture business, proud that he is an American, and for my part, I am proud that we in some small measure participated in its production with Gordon and Goetz. It is not sensational but sentimental, packed with human interest, and stays with you days after you have seen it. Everything that you said about it during the course of production was corroborated by the screening. . . . I think you have every right to feel assured of a very fine public reception. Kind regards and congratulations.[26]

Schaefer was so overjoyed by *Abe Lincoln in Illinois* that he personally devised a unique release pattern. He wanted the picture to open at a gala premiere in Washington, then have special showings with proper ceremonies in several Illinois towns, and subsequently move into Cincinnati, Los Angeles, Boston, San Francisco, and other major cities—all showings at special increased admission prices.[27] The Washington premiere must have been the highlight of the film's chronology. Max Gordon dictated the following to Schaefer's secretary: "We had dinner with President Sunday night and saw picture. President and Mrs. Roosevelt were very enthusiastic and kept repeating 'Great. Great' about picture. Last night's audience tremendously enthusiastic. Spoke to Justice Douglas, Henry Morganthau [*sic*], Alice Longworth and people of their kind and they were all tremendously enthusiastic."[28]

The enthusiasm continued as critics from around the nation hailed the achievement of *Abe Lincoln in Illinois*. Frank S. Nugent's encomium in the *New York Times* was typical:

> It's a grand picture they've made from Robert Sherwood's Pulitzer Prize play of two seasons back; a grand picture and a memorable biography of the greatest American of them all. . . . There isn't by jingo, a trace of jingo in [the] drama. There isn't a touch of national complacency, of patronage or boastful pride. But Lincoln, and the film they have made about him, is a grave and sincere and moving and eloquent tribute to these United States and to what they stand for, and must stand for, in these and future times. It is a grand thing when the life of a man can come down through the years as a fingerboard pointing a nation's direction; it's almost as grand a thing when the life of a man can be told as beautifully as this one has been told.[29]

The ultimate critics—the American audience—were not impressed by the enthusiastic reviews, or the awards garnered by the drama. They found the film sorely wanting and did not support it. The company's attempts to charge increased admission prices for *Abe Lincoln* were quickly abandoned, yet the film still failed to draw. Hunting for reasons, the studio blamed the failure on the John Ford–directed *Young Mr. Lincoln,* released by Twentieth Century–Fox six months earlier, which supposedly took the edge off the RKO production. The casting of Raymond Massey, an actor relatively unknown to motion picture enthusiasts at the time, was also believed to have damaged its box-office potency. When the dust settled, two things were certain: RKO had a financial catastrophe on its hands (final loss to the studio: $740,000), and the team of Max Gordon and Harry Goetz no longer possessed an independent production deal with the company.

Ultimately, the pitiful commercial performance of *Abe Lincoln in Illinois* must have been devastating to George Schaefer. It called into question his unit-production philosophy, his preference for "important" literary properties, and his own ability to predict what the public wished to see, even after he had seen it.

Nonetheless, Schaefer never wavered in his game plan for RKO success. Even the departure of two of the company's major talents did not seem to bother him. First to leave was Fred Astaire. His contract had expired in 1939, but negotiations continued into the new year for future pictures on a non-exclusive basis. Astaire even indicated he would be willing to make another musical with Ginger Rogers, but he and the RKO management could never get together on salary. Astaire, through agent Leland Hayward, asked for $150,000 per picture, but George Schaefer decided that $75,000 was as high as RKO would go. Before the negotiations with Astaire commenced, he had completed *Broadway Melody of 1940*, costarring Eleanor Powell, for MGM. The picture lost money, confirming Schaefer's belief that Fred needed Ginger more than she needed him: "Astaire on his own was not a success either in the picture in which he was starred recently [*A Damsel in Distress*] or in the Astaire-Powell picture. Certainly we should not pay him the price he is asking in view of the fact that we contribute 50% of the asset that makes it possible for him to be a success."[30]

Schaefer did have a point. Astaire without Rogers had not yet demonstrated the ability to carry a picture successfully. But Schaefer should also have considered that Astaire was more than just a performer; many of the brilliant dance routines in the Astaire-Rogers series had been created and choreographed by him and his associate Hermes Pan. As several critics of the musical genre have pointed out, Astaire is an example of the actor as auteur—an individual whose talents shaped the films he appeared in. RKO was losing a superstar in Fred Astaire; his subsequent career proved conclusively that there were reasons for his preeminence besides Ginger Rogers.

Another longtime member of the studio family, director George Stevens, ended his RKO employment in 1940. A rift between Stevens and the company had been widening for some time. It began with the development of slow, perfectionist characteristics in his handling of *Gunga Din*. The film's skyrocketing budget did not endear him to management, despite its quality and respectable box-office performance. After the completion of *Gunga Din*, Stevens took what was supposed to be a four-week vacation. Without permission, however, he stretched the vacation into eight weeks. When he finally returned to the studio, he claimed to have spent the extra time in New York working on potential properties with Pandro Berman's permission.[31] Berman, however, denied giving such permission and took Stevens off the payroll. Negotiations between Stevens's agent, Charles Feldman, and the RKO officials commenced regarding this salary, to which the director felt he was entitled. Apparently, Stevens was also put off by George Schaefer, who refused to allow him to make *The Mortal Storm* or *Address Unknown*, both properties about fascism and its effects. As Pan Berman told Stevens in a telegram, Schaefer was "afraid [to] commit us to any picture that is propaganda against anything."[32] Schaefer, for his part, was growing more and more peeved with Stevens. He wrote Berman during the wage controversy: "I am very much disturbed about the whole George Stevens situation. I think he is acting up very badly, bearing in mind all the considerations that were given him, especially in view of his personal affairs. I think you and the company have been very lenient and considerate and it is about time Stevens was made to realize this."[33]

An agreement was finally hammered out in April 1939, paying Stevens more than half of the disputed $15,000 back pay.[34] George Stevens's performance through the rest of the year did not return him to the company's good graces, however. It took him altogether too long to get his next project, *Vigil in the Night*, under way, and the eventual results proved quite discouraging (a $327,000 loss). When the director's contract came up for renewal on April 2, 1940, George Schaefer did not pick up the option.[35] Both parties were apparently pleased by the termination, but Schaefer was kidding himself if he thought the loss of George Stevens would not leave a gaping hole in his directorial ranks, just as the loss of Fred Astaire had left a void in RKO's male talent and Pandro Berman's loss invited serious trouble in the production domain.

George Schaefer continued to believe that his additions would more than compensate for the subtractions. Shortly after the end of receivership, the "Rambling Reporter" column in the *Hollywood Reporter* contained this humorous blurb: "Most of the major plants are being confronted with the agent's answer: 'Sorry, we just signed with RKO.' And the same goes for story properties. Which prompted one exec to send a wire to George Schaefer reading: 'Read that you were signing so many people that I came out of retirement. My salary's cut to a bone a day. What about it?' The wire was signed by Rin-Tin-Tin. . . . But, kidding aside, there's more activity in that plant than there has been since the sheriffs walked in."[36] Indeed, the number of independent deals alone must have amazed industry vets. United Producers Corporation (William Hawks, president), Voco Productions (Jack Votion, president), Pyramid Pictures Corporations (Jerrold T. Brandt, president), Vogue Pictures, Ltd. (Lou Ostrow, president and producer), Franklin-Blank Productions (former RKO executive Harold B. Franklin, president), and Frank Ross–Norman Krasna Productions (Frank Ross, producer) all signed to have pictures distributed by RKO.[37] And previous independent arrangements, such as the ones with Towne and Baker, Herbert Wilcox, Walt Disney, and Harold Lloyd, still remained in effect.

The studio also secured the services of actors Charles Boyer, Jean Arthur, and Cary Grant. Although the advertising department referred to these individuals as "RKO stars," this was misleading. All had signed at least one picture deal with the studio, but were not under long-term or exclusive obligations. In reality, the RKO stock company was in woeful shape. Except for Ginger Rogers (whose contract would expire in 1941), the company had no box-office personalities on call and was constantly forced to borrow from other studios—even for supporting players. Dan Winkler, an assistant to J. J. Nolan, pointed out the problem to his boss:

> In general there is the matter of adopting a policy of whether or not we intend to have a so called stock company. If we intend having one, we should go about setting it up and we should then use the players that we sign in the pictures that we make. If we do not intend having a stock company then we should make up our mind that we are going to be in the same position next year and the year after that we are in now,—that is, to borrow stock players from other studios and put them . . . in our important pictures.[38]

Winkler concluded by listing a number of individuals who had been dropped by RKO and were presently making good at other studios or getting large salaries whenever RKO borrowed them. The names included Joan Fontaine, Laraine Day, John Shelton, Joel McCrea, Linda Darnell, James Ellison, and Ann Sheridan.[39] Over the years, talent development had always been one of the company's weakest areas; now, this flaw was beginning to exact a heavy toll.

Schaefer did hire Erich Pommer, producer extraordinaire from the famous German studio UFA, to handle three to four films per year. The decision to engage Pommer was based largely on his work with Charles Laughton in England before the outbreak of war. There, Pommer had produced *Jamaica Inn*, *Sidewalks of London*, and *The Beachcomber*, all starring Laughton. They would be teamed again at RKO.

Pommer's efforts, however, would be reduced by a steady diminishment in the company's production plans during the remainder of the year. In early April the RKO board of directors approved a $12,000,000 budget for the 1940–1941 program, with the stipulation that no single picture would cost more than $900,000.[40] By May, however, the gloomy European situation and the lackadaisical performance of RKO pictures in the United States forced George Schaefer to establish $700,000 as the maximum budget for any one picture.[41]

This information was not conveyed to the participants at the ninth annual sales convention of the company, held at New York's Waldorf-Astoria in late May. RKO at that time reduced its promised offerings for 1940–1941 to fifty-three pictures, although it had no intention of releasing even that many.[42] Schaefer did give the salesmen a short pep talk. After describing the European war in gloomy terms but emphasizing "THE SHOW MUST GO ON," he declared, "And let no one forget that this isn't to fiddle while Rome burns. The surcease, the recreation, the inspiration that entertainment brings, are as vital in this emergency as bread and meat and other necessities of life. It is not merely the stomach but the spirit that must be fed in these days of trial."[43]

In July, further production cuts were ordered. Schaefer decided to eliminate *Sister Carrie* from the program because of its estimated $700,000 production cost, and also to reduce the number of program pictures from twelve to eight, thus saving $480,000 more. A series of Westerns featuring Tim Holt would be substituted for the announced George O'Brien vehicles, saving an additional $60,000. Producers now understood that $600,000 was the top budget for any picture, making for an estimated reduction of $1.5 million from the original 1940–1941 budget.[44] A revived budget summary issued by George Schaefer at the end of July included *Citizen Kane*, thus bringing the total figure for A pictures back up to $8 million.[45] Still, the corrected plan for 1940–1941 showed a total expenditure of only $10,920,000. This was a rather feeble amount when one considered that a company like MGM could be expected to spend nearly three times that figure on its production operations.[46] But then, RKO seemed to be suffering more than its competitors, primarily because it had, once again, been turning out a group of underperforming pictures. Besides *Abe Lincoln in Illinois* and *Vigil in the Night*, other disappointments in the 1939–1940 program included *Dance, Girl, Dance* ($400,000 loss), *Allegheny Uprising* ($230,000), *Swiss Family Robinson* ($180,000), *Anne of Windy Poplars* ($173,000), *Tom Brown's School Days* ($110,000), and the remake of *A Bill of Divorcement* ($104,000). There were some bright spots: *My Favorite Wife* earned a profit of $505,000; *Irene*, starring Anna Neagle, made $367,000; the Kay Kyser musical comedy *That's Right, You're Wrong*, $219,000; and *Lucky Partners* with Ginger Rogers, $200,000. But when all the figures were totaled, the picture company had fallen back into the red with a $480,000 loss.

Part of the reason for this may be traced to an old bugaboo—final production authority, a source of conflict that had begun to generate morale problems at the studio. Throughout 1940 George Schaefer continued to dictate answers to all production questions. Harry Edington did not seem perturbed by this; he was willing to go along with anything his boss decided about A pictures even though he was supposed to be in charge of them. However, Lee Marcus, the potentate of the B realm, had held his position longer and was used to making this own decisions. He did not take Schaefer's interference lightly. Marcus was both angered and stupefied by it. In March, Schaefer canceled two of his pet projects, *The Peter B. Kyne Story* and the aforementioned *Man Without a World*. The incensed executive fired off the following memo to J. J. Nolan:

> I wish to state at this time that I am in complete disagreement with this decision, that I think it dangerous and unsatisfactory. . . . This unit has functioned with reasonable success for the past three years, and during that entire time has selected, developed and produced its pictures without submitting scripts to New York. I feel quite certain that if this procedure had been followed in the past we would not have made a good many pictures which have turned out successful, such as: A MAN TO REMEMBER, GIRL FROM MEXICO, SKY GIANT, FIVE CAME BACK, TWO THOROUGHBREDS, FLIGHT FROM GLORY, WITHOUT ORDERS, CONDEMNED WOMEN, LAW OF THE UNDERWORLD.
>
> I state this because none of these scripts in first drafts were as good as the two which have just been turned down by Mr. Schaefer. In every instance, the subject matter was similar to previous pictures that have been made. I think it is a dangerous thing to have one man's viewpoint control program pictures.[47]

Marcus was also offended by Schaefer's insinuation that the B pictures did not contain enough "showmanship." Marcus spelled out his feelings on the matter:

> Showmanship in pictures is not enough to make them successful at the box office. We have made some pictures replete with showmanship, but no advantage has been taken by the company of these pictures, and by this I mean, they have woefully failed to advertise, publicize and exploit them. . . .
>
> There is a certain amount of futility in making pictures with showmanship ideas if nothing is done with them after they are finished. While this is no excuse for not making them, these ideas are very hard to find, and the best idea we have had along these lines in the studio was killed by Mr. Schaefer, namely, the WARSAW INCIDENT picture, which we could have gotten out and which would have capitalized [on] the whole Polish incident.[48]

Relations between Marcus and Schaefer continued on a lukewarm basis throughout the rest of the year. Schaefer would not surrender the reins as far as final decisions were concerned, however. He was the RKO leader, and he did not believe in true delegation of authority. Lee Marcus must have boiled inside when he received the following letter from his boss, late in 1940:

> Returning herewith copy of story, PRETTY PENNY and here is my reaction.
>
> While it is interesting, it seems to me to be just another picture. No doubt you could make a very interesting one but it seems to serve no particular purpose and, in particular, has no unusual showmanship. Think, in our approach to some of the more important pictures you are going to make, we should definitely have the showmanship idea in mind—the type of pictures Warner Bros. have been making which, quite frequently, turn out to be sleepers.[49]

One person that Schaefer treated more gingerly was Orson Welles. Early 1940 found Welles working on *Heart of Darkness* and *Smiler With a Knife*. The plan was to film and release both by the end of the year. However, in late spring the projects were canceled. The reasons were varied and complicated. Budget was the major problem with *Heart of Darkness*. Despite a series of long, arduous cost-cutting sessions, the final projection could never be reduced to less than $1 million. The script itself may also have figured prominently in the shelving of the project. Eight years later, RKO story editor William Fadiman read Welles's screenplay (much of it to be conveyed through subjective camera) and wrote the following memo to Edgar Peterson, who was looking for unproduced properties of value:

> I read HEART OF DARKNESS Saturday afternoon—all 174 pages of it. . . . I think it is postured, mannered, unreal, overwritten, possessing a plot reminiscent of TARZAN combined with KING KONG, cumbersome in its symbolism, repetitious in its sequences, murky in its thought, expansive in its potential cost (we already have $116,000 in charges against it), likely to turn into a mystical melodrama reminiscent of M.G.M.'s ill-fated ADVENTURE, potentially capable of arousing laughter instead of tension, frequently grisly and unpleasant in its horror sequence—I bet you've guessed by now that I don't like it.[50]

This is just one man's opinion, but there is nothing in the RKO files to indicate that any of the executives were ever enthusiastic about the project.

Smiler With a Knife was canceled for a different reason. A mystery thriller about a plot to overthrow the U.S. government, the film would have centered on a bridal couple who discover a secret subversive organization and unmask its playboy leader, thus averting disaster. Since the story had strong political overtones, one might suspect that George Schaefer quashed it because of his disinclination to mount anything controversial. Actually, Welles and Schaefer together decided against production. The problem related to expectations—the expectations of the public, the industry, and the critics regarding Welles's initial motion picture.

Orson Welles had joined RKO with tremendous fanfare. His unprecedented contract, his much ballyhooed belief that he could handle four major areas on a picture (acting, producing, directing, writing), and his reputation as a theatrical and radio "genius" generated both a surplus of publicity and an abundance of ill will. In Hollywood, many were offended by the audacity of Welles and the foolishness of Schaefer in giving an untested filmmaker such an outrageous contract. Welles had not "paid his dues," and there were many who expected, indeed hoped, he would fall flat on his face, taking RKO to the canvas with him.

As the months unfolded, months in which Welles tried and failed to make *Heart of Darkness*, Orson Welles jokes became a staple in Hollywood. Gossip columns were filled with sarcastic stories about "Little Orson Annie," the boy wonder determined to revolutionize moviemaking in America.[51] The pressure mounted as his first anniversary as an RKO employee approached—a year without verifiable progress toward filming anything. Both Welles and Schaefer realized that the first Mercury Theatre production would have to be sensational in order to silence the many carping voices. Thus, *Smiler With a Knife* was dropped because it was little more than a routine thriller. Even if it were a good thriller, the subject matter precluded its being taken seriously. No doubt Welles could imagine the critical reaction: Is this the best he can do? Is this what we have been waiting eighteen months for? Orson Welles's first motion picture had to be special—original, innovative, a production that would galvanize film audiences and strike his critics dumb.

In May, RKO asked the Audience Research Institute to conduct a poll regarding the story that audiences would most like to see Welles tackle. The winner, by a wide margin, was "Invasion from Mars," a picture based on *War of the Worlds*—and Welles's famous radio broadcast of it.[52] Both *Heart of Darkness* and *Smiler With a Knife* elicited much less public curiosity than the science fiction tale. Welles, however, had no desire to make "Invasion from Mars," at least not as his first production. This prompted production chief Harry Edington to write George Schaefer about the big mistake he felt Welles was making:

It seems to me that the whole mental attitude of everybody in the United States during the last two weeks has completely changed. . . . Everybody is talking about war and the underfeeling seems to be a terrific dread of what this great machine of Germany is doing. . . . This all to me seems to point exactly in the right direction to warrant terrific excitement in what might be Welles' interpretation on the screen of this sort of thing and if ever the time was right for it to be done at all, I cant [*sic*] but think that time is now.

There is no doubt that the publicity that has surrounded Welles, and the curiosity concerning what he is going to do, is a terrific backwash of something that could be capitalized on with very little additional exploitation and might be built into a public curiosity campaign quite comparable to what went on in the public mind prior to the making and distribution of "GONE WITH THE WIND."[53]

Edington's idea to transform the H.G. Wells's novel into a cinematic allegory about the present war was intriguing. Schaefer agreed with his thinking, but also pointed out why Welles was adamant in his refusal to film *War of the Worlds:* "The only way I was able to secure Orson originally, was because of my sympathy with his viewpoint,—that he did not want to go out and be tagged and catalogued as 'the horror man' by appearing in a picture such as the HUNCHBACK or immediately go into the production of a picture such as THE MEN FROM MARS. He was anxious to do something first, before Hollywood typed him. This has been uppermost in his mind and I know it would be difficult to change."[54]

It would have been impossible to change Orson Welles's mind at that point, for he finally had a project nearly ready to go before the cameras. The film was, of course, *Citizen Kane*, and its preproduction was veiled in secrecy. Once again, the immediate problems were budgetary. The initial estimate, based on a sixty-eight-page treatment outline, was $1,083,000.[55] Evidently, Welles had not learned a great deal from the *Heart of Darkness* experience. Herman Mankiewicz and Welles's first screenplay for the project ran 214 pages, prompting J. R. McDonough to wire George Schaefer: "We have told Welles that his shooting script is about fifty to sixty pages longer than the longest script we have ever shot in this studio and in our opinion the result in final negative will be far longer than the one hour and thirty-five minutes he is aiming at. We will time the script. I told him as far as I knew the cost we were aiming at is in the neighborhood of six hundred thousand dollars. Welles says he is figuring on a minimum of seven hundred thousand dollars."[56]

This time, the negotiations between Welles and the RKO bean counters did result in a substantial reduction of the budget. By July everyone knew that Orson Welles was finally making a picture. *Citizen Kane* and the altercation with William Randolph Hearst concerning its release are discussed later in this chapter.

Let us turn our attention now to *They Knew What They Wanted*, a ripe example of the bungling that was beginning to characterize RKO film production. Sidney Howard's Pulitzer Prize–winning play, first presented in 1924, had been filmed twice before. The initial production, a silent made by Paramount in 1928, was called *The Secret Hour* and starred Pola Negri. MGM acquired the rights and released a talkie version entitled *A Lady to Love* in 1930. On February 19, 1940, Don Gordon and Ardel Wray, readers on Lillie Messinger's staff, both submitted negative reports on the property.[57] Disregarding their advice, Schaefer acquired the screen rights in early March for $50,000.[58] From the beginning, the story was viewed as a Charles Laughton–Carole Lombard vehicle to be produced by Erich Pommer and directed by Garson Kanin.

Both studio readers had indicated there would certainly be censorship problems with *They Knew What They Wanted*, an adulterous drama about a waitress who agrees to marry an Italian grape grower in the Napa Valley and is then seduced by the farmer's hired man. Someone forgot to check with the Production Code Administration before the purchase, however, prompting the following letter from chief Hollywood censor Joseph Breen to Mac McDonough:

> As I think you know, this property for many years has been listed on the, so-called, "banned list" of the industry. Inquiry from Mr. Hays in New York brings back the information that *if* a screen play, based upon this story, (which is so thoroughly unacceptable in its original form) can be made acceptable under the provisions of the Production Code, the picture made from this new and revised story may be approved, providing it is agreed by your studio that (a) the original title will not be used, or referred to in connection with this revised story; and (b) no reference whatever is to be made at anytime, either in the advertising or in the publicity, that the new and revised story is based upon the play, THEY KNEW WHAT THEY WANTED.[59]

At that very moment, RKO was paying for trade-paper advertisements announcing its plans to make *They Knew What They Wanted*. Schaefer decided he had better pacify Breen quickly, so he sent him the following repentant letter:

> Am terribly sorry we made the mistake of buying THEY KNEW WHAT THEY WANTED without having checked with you. It has

been on the "banned list" so long that none of our boys knew, and I assure you that I did not know, it was not acceptable. I am hastening to send not only my apologies and that of the company, but to assure you that we have put into effect an operating policy whereby no stories will be purchased in the future without first having checked with you, securing your approval. . . .

   With regard to the production of the above picture, I am assured that it will be handled in such a way so as to meet all the provisions of the Production Code and, although an announcement has already been made to the effect that we have bought it and we have announced it in the tradepapers [sic] through an ad, nothing from this point on will appear to the effect that we are producing it and the title will definitely be changed.[60]

So RKO had paid a handsome price for a property that would, of necessity, be gutted in its scripting, with its title changed to throw audiences and critics off track and Sidney Howard's original efforts completely disavowed. *The Other Man* became the working title.[61]

The filmmakers, particularly Garson Kanin, Erich Pommer, and screenwriter Robert Ardrey, were outraged by RKO's cringing attitude toward the Production Code Administration. They began an exhaustive battle to force Breen to accept the title of the play and its basic story. After persistent appeals based on the recently deceased playwright's reputation and the "classic" stature of the play, Breen and his boss, Will H. Hays, finally acceded to the use of the title and the essential plot, so long as the latter conformed to Production Code requirements.

Meanwhile, even before production commenced, George Gallup's Audience Research Institute tested the "audience acceptance value" of the property. Using a short synopsis and including the information that Lombard and Laughton would star, Gallup's researchers determined that audience enthusiasm for the project was low.[62] J. R. McDonough decided to keep this information from the individuals making the picture—for obvious reasons.

A second survey was conducted between July 27 and August 2 using *They Knew What They Wanted* as the announced title. Once again, public interest remained lukewarm at best. According to Gallup, the reasons seemed not to lie in "the marquee values of Laughton and Lombard," but in "the basic elements of the story, which does not find favor with a large number of theatre-goers."[63] Movie patrons were evidently less impressed by prestigious properties than George Schaefer was. Gallup, incidentally, did not pretend his system was foolproof: "It may be, of course, that the

Figure 22. *They Knew What They Wanted* (1940). Director Garson Kanin and writer Robert Ardrey discuss censorship problems with the head of the Production Code Administration, Joseph Breen. One year later, Breen would be running production at RKO. (Courtesy of the Academy of Motion Picture Arts and Sciences)

picture will do better business than we predict. In 1939 we underestimated the box-office performance of NINOTCHKA, by failing to make sufficient allowance for the Lubitsch touch. Perhaps the Kanin touch will succeed in raising THEY KNEW WHAT THEY WANTED above 100%; that is the kind of rare element which cannot easily be evaluated in advance."[64]

Notwithstanding the gloomy forecast, George Schaefer dispatched one of his customary ecstatic telegrams to Harry Edington after viewing the finished film. Schaefer called *They Knew What They Wanted* "one of the finest pictures we ever received" and praised Lombard ("she has never done a better job") and Laughton ("absolute perfection").[65] When it opened in October, however, the response was even less enthusiastic than Gallup had predicted. Schaefer immediately tried a new advertising approach with no discernible effect. On Halloween, Ned Depinet regretfully informed his boss: "I dislike very much to report that the receipts generally from around the country where THEY KNEW WHAT THEY WANTED has opened are poor and exhibitors are beginning to holler. We have not had any engagement that we could point to with pride."[66] The eventual loss was $291,000.

Even though George Schaefer's productions were not performing as he had hoped, his spirits must have been boosted by the outcome of the government's anti-trust suit against the major studios. The signing of a consent decree on November 20, 1940, revealed that the Big Five companies would not have to jettison their theater chains, at least not in the following three years. It did, however, mandate significant changes to be implemented in the future distribution of motion pictures. Tino Balio has admirably summarized these modifications "Blind selling was prevented by requiring trade shows of films; block booking was limited to five pictures; the forced purchase of shorts was abolished; and the use of unreasonable clearance was proscribed."[67]

RKO executives began to consider the ramifications of a new sales landscape, beginning the following fall, in which each picture would be shown to exhibitors before it could be booked. The era of blind selling was over. This would certainly affect the production staff; they would be required to complete five different films and have them ready for trade-showing on a certain date, and these five represented the largest block the studio could sell at one time. Without question, the new regulations were going to impact company cash flow as well.

But if the consent decree was vexing to RKO and the other movie suppliers, it was an outrage to exhibitor groups that had expected more profound changes. According to the *Motion Picture Herald*, every independent exhibitor in the country had opposed this particular solution.[68]

The war in Europe went badly in 1940. Denmark, Norway, Holland, and Belgium all fell to the Germans, and heavy aerial bombardment closed many theaters in Great Britain.[69] The situation hit painfully close to home in the fall when New York headquarters learned that Ralph Hanbury, managing director of RKO's English distribution operation, had been killed by a Luftwaffe bomb.[70] Just two days before his death, Hanbury had written Schaefer assuring him that he was doing everything he could to "further the Company's business," but also informing him that "owing to the severe bombing of London the business in the London cinemas is just non existent [*sic*] these days."[71]

Perhaps the greatest shock of all was the fall of France. In December, George Schaefer received the disheartening news that three of RKO's Paris representatives had been arrested by German military authorities and the company's records had been confiscated along with half a million francs.[72] While Secretary of State Cordell Hull was aware of the situation, there appeared to be little the U.S. government could do about it. The ban on American films in all the countries under German control and monetary restrictions placed on British earnings meant that salary cuts remained in place for many RKO employees, and careful scrutiny of the Latin American market as a possible source of additional revenue would continue.

At least 1940 ended on one of the high points of the Schaefer era. RKO's holiday release, *Kitty Foyle,* not only brought the studio its first major Oscar in many years (to Ginger Rogers for her performance) but also became a gold mine, earning profits of $869,000.

The studio had first begun to consider the purchase of Christopher Morley's novel in September 1939. Two of the readers in Lillie Messinger's department evaluated it, and both recommended against its acquisition. Don Gordon's remarks are indicative of Ardel Wray's feelings as well as his own:

> This is a slow, dull long-drawn-out account of a girl's life. It hasn't any
> point that I can see. Her romance is about as trite as one can be. It is
> also a futile romance which fizzles out over the old problem about the
> girl from the wrong side of the railroad tracks and the young man of a
> wealthy family. As to the struggles of the white collar girls, which fill
> one part of the story—there is absolutely nothing new in the treat-
> ment of that material. There have been scores of pictures dealing with
> the problems of stenographers; and it is more repetition here. Alto-
> gether, I am unable to see any screen value in this story.[73]

Gordon's taste did not mirror that of the general public, which readily embraced Morley's novel. One of the staff members of the *Saturday Review of Literature,* Morley had written a tale that particularly appealed to American women. The property soon had a presold audience.

In spite of his readers' negative feelings, George Schaefer went ahead and pursued the rights. Among his reasons were the need for vehicles for the company's female performers and David Hempstead's desire to produce the picture. The deal was closed on December 20 at a final cost of $50,000.[74] Although Hempstead had Ginger Rogers in mind from the beginning, Schaefer believed that Carole Lombard, or perhaps Maureen O'Hara, would be better suited to the part.[75] Hempstead convinced Schaefer, then began to sell Rogers, who was skeptical at first. She eventually agreed, and Sam Wood, formerly a contract director at MGM, was hired to take charge of the filming.

While the picture was in production, J. R. McDonough asked the Audience Research Institute to run some tests concerning its potential popularity. The results were disappointing. They indicated that *Kitty Foyle* would be "popular with female theatre-goers" but not popular enough to compensate for its almost complete "lack of appeal for male theatre-goers." While predicting that the film would probably do only average business, Gallup's organization made two important suggestions. First, recalling that *Rebecca* had been "serialized in twenty-six mass circulation newspapers immediately prior to the picture's release," the institute suggested that RKO arrange a similar tie-in with *Kitty Foyle*. This would surely contribute to the box-office performance of the film. Second, since a number of respondents to the poll had reacted favorably to the story's "picture of everyday life," the publicity department was encouraged to play up this angle in the advertising.[76]

Both of these ideas were mobilized. The company obtained the serialization rights to *Kitty Foyle* and arranged syndication in key newspapers throughout the country. Advertising for the picture emphasized that Ginger was playing an everyday working girl and had even changed her hair color from blonde to brunette to "de-glamorize" her image. These two strategies, plus the fact that Rogers won her Oscar not long after the film premiered, surely contributed to the extraordinary success of *Kitty Foyle*.

The *Kitty Foyle* euphoria unfortunately did not last long. At 5:40 P.M. on January 9, 1941, Louella Parsons telephoned George Schaefer's office. The gossip columnist for the Hearst newspaper chain was enraged. She had just viewed Orson Welles's *Citizen Kane* and demanded to speak to the RKO president, who had already departed for the day.[77] "How dare Mr. Schaefer ever do a thing like that," she said indignantly, referring to *Kane*, which she viewed as a libelous biography of her boss, William Randolph Hearst. Speaking to Schaefer's secretary, Parsons promised that Hearst would "bring a terrific amount of pressure on the Motion Picture Industry" and that RKO would be hit with one of the "the most beautiful lawsuits" in history if the movie were ever released. After demanding to know Schaefer's home phone number, the columnist emphasized that the situation was "a matter of life and death to RKO" and hung up.

This verbal assault marked the beginning of the nastiest controversy that had ever affected the company: W. R. Hearst versus RKO and Orson Welles. The escalating squabble is discussed in detail later in this chapter. At this point, it is sufficient to say that the Hearst problem simply provided the prologue to a year and a half of sound and fury, one of the most tumultuous periods in RKO's history.

As might be expected, the root cause of growing trouble was financial. Now that RKO had pulled out of receivership, it was expected to make profits. But in its first year (1940) the "new" RKO lost $988,191.[78] George Schaefer blamed the deficit on a long list of expenses derived from the reorganization process, but these expenses were only part of the problem. Anyone could look at the inferior 1940 releases and understand why RKO was falling further behind its competitors. All of them made profits in 1940 except Twentieth Century–Fox, which had a rare off year (with a $500,000 deficit).

Schaefer in effect acknowledged that the company's films were the problem when he announced he would be moving his office to Hollywood and taking over production early in 1941.[79] Only industry insiders realized that this was not at all a bombshell. George Schaefer had been running production since he had become president of RKO. While it was unusual for a corporate head to set up shop in Hollywood, the move itself would not fundamentally alter matters. The public announcement did, however, throw the jobs of all the other studio executives into limbo. What would Harry Edington's position be from now on? His contract still had one year to run. What about J. J. Nolan and J. R. McDonough? Would their jobs and titles remain the same? Would Lee Marcus continue to supervise B pictures in the new alignment? Rumors concerning another big RKO shake-up began to spread.

Initial confirmation of the scuttlebutt came in February when J. R. McDonough took charge of the B unit, relieving Lee Marcus of his former duties. Schaefer announced that Marcus would continue to work as an associate producer in the unit, but this subterfuge dissolved in April when Marcus quit RKO.[80] Marcus had been head of the low-budget unit for several years, but he and Schaefer had never seen eye to eye.[81] Now J. R. McDonough would face the challenge of producing commercial pictures on middling budgets.

Shortly after Schaefer moved his principal office to Hollywood, he announced that the pay cuts imposed on company personnel when World War II began would be restored.[82] Then, suddenly, the *Citizen Kane* controversy began to take up much of his time.[83] It appears he was surprised by Louella Parsons's livid reaction to the picture in January and blindsided by the subsequent attack that her employer, William Randolph Hearst, launched against him, Welles, and RKO. Back in September 1940, the following item had appeared in the "Miscellany" section of *Newsweek:* "The script of Orson Welles' first movie, 'Citizen Kane,' was sent to William Randolph Hearst for perusal after columnists had hinted it dealt with his life. Hearst approved it without comment."[84] Thus, Schaefer did not anticipate any difficulties from the newspaper baron. But evidently, Hearst never read the script.

Kane was in production when the *Newsweek* blurb appeared. Shooting continued throughout much of the fall, and word began to leak out that Welles was creating something special. J. J. Nolan viewed 7,000 feet of the picture in September and pronounced it "great."[85] The RKO executives planned a major advertising blitz to coincide with the release, set for February 1941. Trade papers carried ads for the picture well in advance of its opening date, and excitement built through the early part of the new year.

Hearst, however, took Louella Parsons's assessment very seriously. Without screening a print to see if the film actually was an unflattering biography of him, Hearst began to exert pressure on RKO. He had his agents deliver an ultimatum that the picture be shelved and, to prove he meant business, ordered his papers to withhold mention of RKO and its productions. The financial effects of a wide-ranging newspaper boycott were indeed sobering, but George Schaefer refused to be intimidated—at first. In his initial response Schaefer stated that the company was giving "no serious consideration" to the idea of withholding *Citizen Kane*.[86] Meanwhile, Welles maintained the film was not about Hearst.

In February, however, a conflict developed among the members of the RKO board of directors. One faction, headed by Schaefer, insisted that the picture should be released, while another group believed strongly that it should be suppressed.[87] For Schaefer, *Citizen Kane* meant more than a potential box-office success. It was a personal vindication—the film that would prove that his questionable policies, including the hiring of an unproven Orson Welles, had paid off. To assure that he would receive the credit he was due, Schaefer began to show the picture to industry professionals, who were awestruck by what they saw. The following telegram from Schaefer to Welles describes the result of one of these screenings:

> Know you will be happy that never in my experience in the business have I screened a picture before such a tough and professional audience as I did last night and received such wonderful reaction. Present at the screening were directors Vidor, Dieterle, Bob Stevenson, Garson Kanin and producers Hempstead, Hawks, Edington, and agents Stein and Wasserman of MCA and Leland Hayward and actors Kay Kyser and Sir Cedric Hardwicke. At the conclusion, picture not only received a wonderful round of applause, but each and every one most enthusiastic as one of the great motion pictures that had ever come out of Hollywood. Most every one was so impressed that they were virtually speechless and some came back the second and third time after the picture was concluded and told me how much they were impressed.[88]

Finally, one of George Schaefer's protégés had fashioned an unquestionable masterpiece; yet the RKO president was having to fight just to place the film before the public.

W. R. Hearst showed no signs of backing down. A minor lawsuit against RKO won by Joseph Ermolieff, producer of *The Soldier and the Lady* (1937), that cost the company $7,000 was used as a pretext for a coast-to-coast vilification of RKO and Schaefer on the front pages of the Hearst newspapers.[89] War had broken out and Hearst owned the heavy artillery.

February came and went without the release of *Citizen Kane;* prospects for the film began to appear dicey. Schaefer, who had given Welles assurances all along, suddenly started to act evasive and indefinite and was difficult to reach. Welles became desperate. After an unsatisfying telephone conversation with Schaefer on March 7, he sent the RKO president a long telegram. In part, it stated:

> I managed to say very little of what I want to on the phone. Your answers to my questions were themselves unanswerable even if they weren't good answers. Here's what I mean. When I ask you when the picture will be released, you say you hope to be able to tell me Monday or Tuesday. I ask you to tell me more about it and you simply repeat answer number one. The picture was supplied [*sic*] to open the fourteenth and the[n] on the twenty-eighth. No real reasons were offered for either postponement. When this trouble first descended upon us, we spoke almost twice daily by phone. Now I have to sit up until four o'clock in the morning trying to get in touch with you and failing to do so. When I finally reach you, the only satisfaction you can give me is expressed in the merest of generalities. . . . Don't tell me to get a good night's rest and keep my chin up. Don't bother to communicate if that's all you have to say. There's no more rest for me until I know something concrete, and as for my chin, I've been leading with it for more than a year and a half. Finally, never think I'm insensible to the great gift of your own loyalty. It is that very loyalty that has spoiled me. Always remember that I well know you're the best man I'll ever work for, but do try to realize that you owe both us something better than what I now receive.[90]

Schaefer replied: "Have been trying to get you on the telephone all day, it seems that you are 'ducking me.' Now laugh that off. Seriously speaking you probably have just cause to complain but please be assured you have nothing to worry about."[91]

The events of the following week undercut Schaefer's words. A press preview of the film was canceled at the last minute, and the RKO legal staff began scrutinizing its contracts with Welles and Mercury Productions to discover the company's possible liability if it decided not to release *Kane*.[92] Furious about the quashing of the preview, Orson Welles called a press conference and announced he would sue RKO. His formal statement included the following:

> I believe that the public is entitled to see "Citizen Kane." For me to stand by while this picture was being suppressed would constitute a breach of faith with the public on my part as a producer. I have at this moment sufficient financial backing to buy "Citizen Kane" from RKO and to release it myself. Under my contract with RKO I have the right to demand that the picture be released and to bring legal action to force its release. RKO must release "Citizen Kane." If it does not do so immediately, I have instructed my attorney to commence proceedings.[93]

The "financial backing" that Welles mentioned probably came from Henry Luce, publisher of *Life, Time,* and *Fortune* and no lover of Hearst. According to one report, the film had so impressed Luce that he was willing to put up $1 million for it.[94] Welles was also correct about another matter. Pursuant to his contract, RKO was obligated to begin distribution of the film within three months after delivery of the finished print.[95] Thus, Welles was on firm legal ground in his threat to sue.

It is not possible to say what was going on behind the scenes at this time. Certainly, Hearst was still pressuring, and some members of the RKO board were withering under the pressure. They were concerned because Hearst had banned advertising for some RKO films in his papers and because other industry executives had told Schaefer they would not play the film in their theaters.[96] One popular story is that Louis B. Mayer, in an attempt to pacify Hearst, offered Schaefer $800,000 to destroy the negative of *Citizen Kane* and all the prints.[97] This may have happened, though nothing in the RKO records indicates that it did. Mayer might have made such an offer for his own self-protection; among other things, Hearst was threatening to expose all the dirty laundry in Hollywood, turning his muckraking journalists loose on the movie capital with a vengeance if *Citizen Kane* ever opened.

Most likely, the crucial event in this narrative took place in a small screening room at Radio City Music Hall where the heads of the major film companies and their lawyers viewed a print of *Citizen Kane*. Editor Robert Wise was there and so was Welles. Wise later described the speech Welles delivered before the screening as "one of the best performances I've ever seen."[98] Evidently Welles's oratory and the film itself swayed them, because Wise was required only to make a few trims and have actors dub in a few different lines of dialogue before the movie was approved for release.

In early April, RKO presented *Citizen Kane* to four hundred members of the press at the Broadway Theater in New York.[99] Welles's legal position, the tremendous enthusiasm generated by people who had seen it, the OK from the industry leaders, and the humiliation that would have been RKO's had it destroyed the picture all contributed to the decision to distribute. No doubt, hopes for huge financial rewards must also have played a part in the decision to defy Hearst. The controversy had made *Kane* the most anticipated picture since *Gone With the Wind*. George Schaefer received numerous letters commending him for his bravery and also applauding the gamble he had taken on Orson Welles. The following reply, written to one of the people who congratulated the president, suggests that Schaefer felt rather proud of himself:

> Thank you for your letter. . . . Letters such as this have amply repaid me for the heartaches and the "predicted" failure of the proposed "Welles picture."
>
> They were making bets out here that Welles would never even get started, and then again, bets to the effect that after he had been shooting ten days he would fold up.
>
> Every important producer and director personality in Hollywood has now seen the picture, and they are unanimous in their praise. They all say it is one of the finest things that has ever been done, not excepting the most important pictures that have been released in recent years. Understand, I am only passing on to you what others have said, which corroborates your own judgment.[100]

Schaefer was finally getting a chance to thumb his nose at all the naysayers who disputed his wisdom.

"It's Terrific" proclaimed the ads for *Citizen Kane*, and, for once, the boast was not an overstatement. The film opened to general audiences in New York in early May. Critical response ranged from positive to rapturous, except for the Hearst *Daily Mirror* and *Journal-American*, which refused to review it and closed their advertising columns to its notices. Initial business was also very gratifying.[101] Subsequent openings in Chicago and Los Angeles, however, indicated the film would not be a smash, and when it reached the smaller towns of America, the picture died.[102] Evidently, the complex structure and visual and aural bravura of the film were confusing, rather than exciting, to many moviegoers; they reacted apathetically, despite the feud that had kept the film in the public's eye for months before its release. *Citizen Kane* ended up losing $160,000.

That feud continued for some time thereafter. Hearst papers were full of stories accusing Welles of being a Communist and a draft dodger, but maintained a stony silence about anything pertaining to RKO. In July, Welles drafted a reply to Hearst designed to be run as a paid advertisement by RKO in various newspapers:

> William Randolph Hearst is conducting a series of brutal attacks upon me in his newspapers. It seems he doesn't like my picture "Citizen Kane." I understand he hasn't seen it. I am sure he hasn't. If he had, I think he would agree with me that those who have advised him that "Kane" is Hearst have done us both an injustice.
>
> I have stood silently by in the hope that this vicious attack against me would be spent in the passing of a few weeks. I had hoped that I would not continue to be the target of patriotic organizations who are accepting false statements and condemning me without knowing the facts.
>
> But I can't remain silent any longer.
>
> The Hearst papers have repeatedly described me as a Communist. I am not a Communist. I am grateful for our constitutional form of government, and I rejoice in our great tradition of democracy. Needless to say, it is not necessarily unpatriotic to disagree with Mr. Hearst. On the contrary, it is a privilege guaranteed me as an American citizen by the Bill of Rights.
>
> . . . .
>
> I want to say that I am proud of my American citizenship. As a citizen, I cherish my rights and I am not fearful of asserting them. I ask only that I be judged by what I am and what I do.[103]

As time went on, the agitation subsided. By early 1942, perhaps pleased by the commercial failure of *Citizen Kane*, William Randolph Hearst had called off the dogs. The efforts to "get" Welles and injure RKO faded away, and Hearst never made good on his threat to dig up all the dirt in Hollywood and present it to the world at large. Perhaps his own extramarital relationship with fading star Marion Davies had something to do with that.

George Schaefer overlooked the box-office disappointment of *Kane*, content to bask in the luminescence created by its critical acclaim. Schaefer signed Welles and Mercury to a new three-picture contract during the year. He also managed to attend most of the ceremonies where the film was honored—including those of the National Board of Review and the New York Film Critics.[104] Both groups selected *Citizen Kane* best picture of 1941. The Academy of Motion Picture Arts and Sciences, however, largely ignored its accomplishment, probably because of all the disagreeable publicity. The picture did receive nine nominations but landed only one Oscar—for best original screenplay (shared by Welles and Herman Mankiewicz).

From the perspective of film history, the story of the near-destruction of *Citizen Kane* is mortifying. It is still considered by many to be the greatest film ever made. George Schaefer deserves special commendation for backing the film and fighting for it. But it is quite possible that the ultimate decision to release *Kane* was made by one of the powerful figures in the RKO shadows—Floyd Odlum or perhaps Nelson Rockefeller. Unfortunately, the full story of the behind-the-scenes wrangling will probably never be known.

Because of the *Citizen Kane* situation, George Schaefer spent more time in New York than he had planned in spring 1940. Still, he had not forgotten that his studio needed revamping. In April, J.J. Nolan, vice-president in charge of the RKO studio, lost his title and became an assistant secretary of the corporation. According to Schaefer, Nolan's salary and status would "remain the same," and he would continue to be Schaefer's "liaison man in the studio."[105] During the same week, William Mallard resigned as general counsel and secretary of the corporation, and Frank R. Donovan stepped down as operating head of RKO Pathe News. As the unsettledness continued, little was said about nominal production head Harry Edington, who was actually now functioning as a straight producer.

Schaefer also had to cope with a personnel crisis. Ginger Rogers was RKO's last remaining star, the only actor under exclusive contract to the studio whose presence meant both A-level recognition and probable box-office success. Rogers's seven-year contract was scheduled to expire in May 1941, so Schaefer took it upon himself to convince Ginger to remain with the studio. He failed, at least in his principal goal. Negotiations between Schaefer and Rogers's agent, Leland Hayward, began in March and continued for the next several months. Schaefer naturally wanted to retain the actress's services exclusively and offered her $390,000 per year on a three-year basis.[106] Rogers, however, was determined to make pictures for other studios and held firm for that option. When the bargaining finally ended, Ginger Rogers had agreed to make three pictures for RKO within the next three years.[107] Otherwise, she would be free to act in films for whomever she pleased. By the end of 1941, she had signed to make three pictures for Twentieth Century–Fox, and no new Rogers RKO production was on the schedule.[108]

Late in April, George Schaefer, perhaps exhausted by the Rogers negotiations and the *Citizen Kane* imbroglio, let it be known that he could not continue to oversee production and function as corporate president. According to journalists' accounts, Schaefer offered the job of filmmaking chief to Sol Lesser, the independent producer who had provided the Bobby

Breen musicals such as *Rainbow on the River* (1936) to RKO for release, as well as numerous pictures to other companies. Lesser wanted to accept but was prevented from taking the position by a contract he had signed with United Artists.[109] The stories in the trade papers confirmed that RKO was shopping for someone to take charge.

In reality, the shopping had begun earlier in the year, and Lesser had been offered a slot overseeing A pictures, not steering all RKO production. A lunch meeting back in February at Floyd Odlum's River House apartment in New York had included Odlum, Ed Weisl (who was Odlum's attorney), George Schaefer, and Joseph Breen.[110] While the meeting had been arranged to try to heal a serious rift that had developed between Odlum and Schaefer, Breen had been included so Odlum could become better acquainted with the head of the Production Code Administration. Everyone knew Breen because of his position as industry censor, but Breen was tiring of the job and Schaefer had begun to think Breen might be a valuable addition to the RKO organization. The meeting dispelled any immediate thoughts that Floyd Odlum might sack Schaefer and, evidently, made Odlum positively disposed toward Breen.

Not present at the luncheon was the man who had kick-started this set of wheels in motion. W. G. Van Schmus of Radio City Music Hall was now a member of the RKO board of directors representing the Rockefeller interests, and thus had been paying close attention to the company's fortunes since the reorganization. Joe Breen happened to be one of Van Schmus's closest Hollywood friends. Breen generally viewed films before anyone else except studio insiders, and he alerted Van Schmus whenever he felt a new movie might be a good choice for booking in the Music Hall.[111] Van Schmus repaid Breen by recommending him to George Schaefer.

By late April, Schaefer had become convinced that Breen was the right person to take over the studio. Van Schmus was ecstatic. In a letter to Nelson Rockefeller, he called Breen "the best possible man for the job" and his selection "a decided victory" for Schaefer.[112] In May it was formally announced that Joseph I. Breen had signed a contract with RKO.[113]

It is doubtful that RKO's Hollywood employees were as pleased as W. G. Van Schmus by the news. Breen had been directing the Code Office since 1934, a job he approached with fervor and reasonable tact. He definitely knew what could *not* go into pictures, but there was no assurance he understood what made them work (i.e., what elements comprised good *and* commercial cinema). Joseph Breen's creative abilities were both unknown and untested. He had never developed a property or produced a picture, much less superintended the entire output of a studio. Thus, to many who made their livings in the movie colony, George Schaefer's decision bordered on the outlandish.

One thing was certain—Breen's honeymoon period would be very short. RKO needed moneymaking pictures and it needed them right away. Besides *Citizen Kane*, other box-office failures released in the first half of 1941 included *They Met in Argentina* ($270,000 loss), *Little Men* ($214,000 loss), and *Too Many Girls* ($170,000 loss). The Kay Kyser film *You'll Find Out* topped the winners with a profit of $167,000, but the only other releases that brought home more than $100,000 in profits were *The Devil and Miss Jones* and reissues of *Vivacious Lady* and *Bringing Up Baby*. Despite George Schaefer's efforts, there really was not much new about the "new RKO." It was still churning out lots of movies that its customers had no burning desire to see.

10.   "Crossing Wires"

The Schaefer-Breen Regime
(1941–1942)

By midyear 1941, RKO had been revamped once again. In addition to the arrival of Joe Breen, Charles Koerner, former West Coast division manager for RKO exhibition, was now in charge of the entire network of theaters.[1] Koerner succeeded John J. O'Connor, who handed Schaefer his resignation in May. Like J. J. Nolan before him, J. R. McDonough was forced to surrender his title as vice-president of the company. The following memo from McDonough to Schaefer explains the reason for this and clearly indicates McDonough's feelings about the matter:

> I attach, as requested by you, my letter resigning the office of Vice President of this company. I have already told you that it was not only a surprise but a shock to me that I should be asked to relinquish this title. You have told me that you believe that proper organization of the studio calls for only one man to have such a title in order to avoid any possibility of a question of his authority. Since I have always been a man who gave loyalty to an organization rather than to a title I am naturally following your wishes, though I had hoped to persuade you otherwise.[2]

The only man at the studio holding the title of vice-president would be Joseph Breen. Schaefer, perhaps concerned about Breen's lack of production experience, went ahead and hired Sol Lesser as executive producer in charge of "the studio's A product."[3] Lesser by that time had managed to obtain his release from the United Artists commitment. Within the new power structure, Breen would have overall responsibility for RKO film production with Sol Lesser supervising the high-budget films and Mac McDonough running the B unit.[4] George Schaefer was moving back to New York, leaving the studio in the care of his handpicked subordinates.

The biggest unanswered question concerned final production authority. Schaefer had always insisted on making the important decisions, whether his office was in New York or at the studio. Many were aware of this, and most believed Schaefer's micromanagement had played a role in RKO's problems. Even W. G. Van Schmus, one of Schaefer's biggest supporters, felt that way. Shortly after the hiring of Joe Breen, Van Schmus sent "my dear George" a letter congratulating him "on achieving the objective" and gently suggesting that he should allow Breen to do his job without interference.[5] After observing that Schaefer's friends were "all very much concerned about the way you have been driving yourself in the past two years," Van Schmus continued:

> I have read so many proverbs about the greatness of the man who delegates, that it has been second nature to me to delegate. Here, for the first time, you have an opportunity with 100% backing to carry out the only sane way of conducting any business, and especially one with the ramifications of a great organization like RKO.
>
> I hope you will not mind my sending you this thought, but I know that in the final analysis you and Joe [Breen] will be happier because of it.[6]

Schaefer replied to Van Schmus five days later:

> Really feel that a load has been lifted off my back. If I did not have complete and absolute confidence in the appointment [of Breen] with the realization that I could delegate complete authority, I would not have made it. I doubt very much if I could have stood the strain of carrying on as we have for the past two years. The selection of the right man has been the all-important thing in everyone's mind and, at long last I think we have that man.[7]

After taking some time to familiarize himself with the studio and its personnel, Joseph Breen began speaking to the press. His initial public remarks proved unsettling: "A studio-wise shuffle in actors, producers and directors is necessary for the studio to turn out good product." Emphasizing that the only thing wrong with the business was "too many bad pictures," Breen promised not to make "that kind."[8] Breen's comments contributed to the angst that pervaded the RKO lot. In half a year there had been a record number of comings and goings, and now more were promised. A few days later, J. J. Nolan resigned, and reports indicated that the studio was trying to "wash up" Harry Edington's contract and get rid of him as soon as possible.[9]

Instead of providing fresh leadership and inspiration, the new studio team fostered acrimony and distrust. In his zeal to succeed, Sol Lesser managed to alienate most of the production staff. Within a month, Breen found himself having to mediate between Lesser and such producers as David Butler, Tay Garnett, and David Hempstead, all of whom had been pushed to the point of mutiny by Lesser's brutal attempts to whip things into shape. Apparently, Schaefer had instructed Lesser to "put pictures into production . . . no matter how ruthless [you have] to be," but Lesser's approach brought rebellion rather than results.[10]

The storm calmed somewhat in the next few months, although Lesser's reputation was tarnished by the events. Rumors began to spread that he was next in line for excommunication. Lesser committed another small blunder in September that is worthy of mention because it clarifies Schaefer's concept of the chain of command. Lesser wrote Ned Depinet directly to ask his opinion of a proposed property, *Hunky*. Schaefer sent Lesser a telegram expressing his disaffection for *Hunky*, then laid down the law to Joe Breen:

> Think it is a mistake for any executive producer to communicate direct with the sales organization as to the advisability of making certain pictures. All such matters should clear from the executive producers through you. You, in turn, can take it up direct with me. In this way, we will eliminate unnecessary delays, confusion and misunderstandings. Mr. Depinet may, on the one hand, think favorably of it and, on the other hand, I may have an opposite opinion. The first thing you know, we will be crossing wires.[11]

Thus, despite all the changes, nothing had changed. Notwithstanding the top man's assurances to W. G. Van Schmus, final word regarding production matters still flowed from the mouth of President Schaefer. The new heads of the two basic units, as well as Joseph Breen, were to function as screening agents and recommending bodies, not decision makers. Two and a half years at the RKO helm had failed to teach George Schaefer the folly of this modus operandi. New York interference in studio affairs had cost RKO David Selznick and Pandro Berman, and it remained a leading cause of RKO's difficulties.

Despite the instability on Gower Street, RKO kept turning out product. The consent decree of 1940 was a major factor. According to the provisions of the decree, RKO and the four other vertically integrated companies were required to begin offering their films to exhibitors in blocks of five around August 1, 1941. Thus, there was heavy pressure to finish pictures as quickly as possible, building up a backlog of movies that would make each company competitively strong when the bidding began. Since releases would generally commence four to twelve weeks after the trade screenings, the new system meant that all the studios were unusually busy. On August 23, 1941, RKO had seventeen pictures finished and ready for presentation.[12] This meant that the spring and summer were an unusually busy period at the studio.

In June, George Schaefer had announced that RKO planned forty to forty-five features for the 1941–1942 season. This information was released at the annual sales convention held in New York, where most of the conversation concerned new strategies for selling the smaller blocks.

Shortly after the convention, Joseph Breen expressed his feelings about future RKO production. Not surprisingly, they echoed the preferences of his boss. Breen emphasized that "escapist" pictures were "what the public wants." He pledged that his administration would adopt a policy of "pictures for entertainment only." He added, "In my considered judgment, when you put preachment, religion or politics on the screen you get into controversy with your audience."[13] In addition, Breen mentioned the need for RKO to acquire new talent and the importance of good stories that might turn some of the young RKO actors into stars. Joseph Breen clearly favored safe and reliable productions and intended to steer clear of any subject matter that could be upsetting to anyone. Just like George Schaefer.

Schaefer's enthusiasm for independent deals did not lessen, despite the disappointing outcome of his arrangements with Max Gordon and Harry Goetz and Gene Towne and Graham Baker. Every one of the Towne-Baker literature-based productions (*Swiss Family Robinson, Tom Brown's School Days, Little Men*) had tanked. Like Gordon and Goetz, Towne and Baker had been expelled from the RKO roster. Taking their place would be Gabriel Pascal, a Hungarian producer-director who controlled the film rights to George Bernard Shaw's plays; Broadway producer Jed Harris; documentary filmmaker Pare Lorentz (*The River, The Plow That Broke the Plains, The Fight for Life*); and William Dieterle. Dieterle, who had become one of the top directors at Warner Bros. in the 1930s and made *The Hunchback of Notre Dame* for RKO, was the only name on the list with Hollywood experience. In these choices, Schaefer remained true to his reputation for intrepid deal making that might be expected to contribute, at least, to RKO's artistic reputation.

The biggest business transaction of 1941 was the signing of Samuel Goldwyn, whose brand reeked of prestige. Goldwyn, almost a major studio unto himself, had been embroiled in a bitter legal dispute with United Artists since 1939.[14] A settlement was reached on March 11, 1941, freeing him to contract with RKO for the release of his independently produced and financed pictures. The original agreement entitled RKO to only two films: *The Little Foxes* and *Ball of Fire*. After that, Goldwyn could go elsewhere if he felt unsatisfied. In December, however, Sam Goldwyn expressed the opinion that Ned Depinet was "a fine guy" and that the RKO organization was "doing a swell job" handling his productions.[15]

He should have been pleased; to entice Goldwyn to affiliate with RKO, Schaefer had granted him a distribution fee (17.5 percent) lower than he could have negotiated with any other Hollywood entity. The fee was, in fact, so low that RKO would lose money on every film it handled for Goldwyn. Schaefer's rationale: the Goldwyn pictures would not only upgrade RKO's standing in the industry but would also make it easier to sell the studio's other releases to theater owners, just as the Disney pictures had. Nevertheless, Goldwyn's deal soon became the talk of Hollywood and would remain a divisive subject among RKO executives for years to come.[16]

RKO lost two producers and one special director during the year. The director was Garson Kanin, by now the leading light of the contract staff. Kanin was drafted into the army shortly after completing *Tom, Dick and Harry* with Ginger Rogers. Twenty-four other RKO employees also entered the service during the year, but the departure of the entire group was less traumatic to the organization than the loss of this one individual.

The two producers—Robert Sisk and Erich Pommer—left under different circumstances. Sisk, formerly the director of advertising and publicity, quit around the time that Lee Marcus exited the studio.[17] Bob Sisk had been a B producer for several years, guiding a number of successful films. Like several others, though, he resented George Schaefer's intrusions into his domain. In February 1940 he wrote Schaefer protesting the president's assigning of an actress to one of his pictures without even informing him. His letter contained the following warning: "I have good respect for you—I think you know that—but I can't have any self-respect and be a stooge producer. I'd rather leave here, George, than begin going through routines again."[18] Fourteen months later, Sisk made good his threat and departed.[19]

The Pommer situation was more unpleasant. On April 16 the esteemed producer suffered a heart attack. The studio closed him off the payroll on April 19 and began to look for a way to terminate his contract.[20] The reasons were self-evident. Pommer was receiving a high salary, but both of his films (*Dance, Girl, Dance* and *They Knew What They Wanted*) had been financial disappointments. The illness provided a convenient excuse to get rid of him. Naturally, Pommer protested, taking his case to California superior court in June.[21] Before a verdict was reached, however, Pommer and the attorney representing RKO, Mendel Silberberg, agreed on an out-of-court settlement. The producer would return to the studio and produce at least one more film before his contract expired in December.[22]

Pommer was assigned a property entitled *Passage from Bordeaux.* Various stalling tactics ensued, however, and it became clear in November that RKO had no intention of allowing him to make the film. Pommer received nothing but evasions from Sol Lesser and found it impossible to gain access to Joseph Breen, who had entrusted him with the project in the first place. The producer wrote anguished letters to Breen, insisting that RKO fulfill its promises. Breen did speak to Henry Herzbrun, Pommer's agent, but refused to discuss the situation with the producer directly.[23] The only concession that Breen would offer involved giving Pommer credit on *Passage from Bourdeaux* when it was finally filmed, even though the picture would be supervised by someone else. This was an insult to a man of Pommer's stature. On December 15 RKO terminated Erich Pommer. He had been duped by Joseph Breen and Sol Lesser, who reneged on the pledge they made him.

Breen and President Schaefer seemed to get along nicely throughout the last half of 1941. If there were conflicts between the two men, no evidence exists to confirm them. A major quarrel did develop between Schaefer and J. R. McDonough, however. It commenced shortly after McDonough took control of the B unit. Believing that the new block-of-five selling system would demand higher-quality program pictures, Schaefer instructed McDonough to make ten "special" films for an average of $250,000 each as part of the 1941–1942 schedule.[24] McDonough was also responsible for seven other routine "programmers," made for a little over $100,000 each, and six Tim Holt Westerns, costing about $50,000 apiece.[25]

At this point, it is interesting to recall J. R. McDonough's early days with RKO. Reputed to be the tough, no-nonsense type, Mac's first responsibilities in Hollywood included riding herd on spendthrift producers, making sure budget estimates were within proper boundaries and were adhered to scrupulously. His position in the executive hierarchy changed several times over the years, but his major duties generally remained the same. During that time, McDonough mellowed as he came to appreciate the mercurial interplay between finances and the creative process. However, he was never considered a pushover by producers hoping to squeeze out a few extra dollars for their pictures.

McDonough was now on the other side of the table. Assigned the task of supervising a substantial group of films, he quickly discovered that holding down costs was no easy task. In March, George Schaefer became concerned when he learned that five of Mac's proposed productions (including *Parachute Battalion, Father Takes a Wife,* and *The Mayor of 44th Street*) all had estimated budgets of $300,000 or more. In a letter to McDonough, Schaefer demanded that the figures be "cut down or . . . justified by the submission to me of the cast to be used and other good reasons."[26] Otherwise, such spending would cause RKO to exceed its total production budget by a considerable amount.

McDonough failed to comply with Schaefer's ultimatum. He estimated that by fall his ten specials would cost some $470,000 more than Schafer desired. In a long memo to Joseph Breen, McDonough attempted to explain the situation and justify his actions.[27] He blamed commitments made on *Parachute Battalion* and *Father Takes a Wife* before he took them over for the excess of $211,000 on the two productions. Among other excuses offered was the necessity to replace the directors of two films (*Call Out the Marines* and *Sing Your Worries Away*) after they had each been shooting for more than a week. Nevertheless, it seemed to McDonough that the extra expenditures would definitely pay off in the long run: "Based on all information given to me, I believe our pictures are being made with a quality comparable with and a cost equivalent to that in the other big studios in town. In every instance where the appropriation of $250,000 has been exceeded there has been an adequate reason for it,—either because of production difficulties or because of the submission of better cast names than afforded us by our contract players."

McDonough's last argument suggested that $250,000 was an insufficient budget for these specials anyway, thereby challenging George Schaefer's conception of the pictures: "My impression is,—confirmed by experience,—that we have a better chance to make this class of picture for an average of $300,000 than we have for $250,000,—particularly if we want to get quality,—and we can only get quality in them by employing the class of director I have mentioned and the type of cast I have given."

Joseph Breen wired the contents of McDonough's memo to President Schaefer, who responded with a livid telegram. Schaefer stated that he believed it was "simply impossible for this company to make money on pictures of that quality based on such cost" and emphasized that, all other matters aside, McDonough had been told to make ten pictures averaging $250,000 each and was going to "far exceed" the established target.[28] Schaefer ordered Breen to put a vise grip on McDonough: "It is my suggestion that you instruct McDonough to make no further commitments in any respect to any of remaining pictures without consulting you, having in mind these pictures must be brought through at $250,000 budget. We cannot permit him to go overboard on commitments which affects [*sic*] budget limitations we have established. Other studios are making showmanship pictures and are keeping their cost within $250,000." As for McDonough's remark that he needed $300,000 budgets to produce the quality pictures Schaefer wanted: "That opinion is not shared here in New York and wish you would please inform McDonough that we will lay out policy and will expect him to adhere to it; that everyone here is greatly concerned with quality we have received so far and at the cost they have come through. In conclusion, repeat my suggestion that McDonough consult with you before any commitments are made on balance of pictures so that we may have full control of his costs."

By the end of the year, Schaefer had given up on McDonough completely and was preparing to dismiss him. Not only had he failed to keep costs down, but his pictures were disappointing. J. R. McDonough had not developed the creative abilities demonstrated by Lee Marcus. Through the years, Marcus had made many poor pictures, but his overall record as "king of the RKO Bs" was respectable. Of course, George Schaefer had been responsible for Marcus's departure from the studio, just as he had driven Berman and others away. The tribulations of Marcus's successor therefore represented an addition to the growing list of Schaefer's executive errors.

Above and beyond the personalities involved, one has to question the new B-unit philosophy. Over the years, a strong belief had developed that "in-between" films were an economic liability. B pictures costing more than $150,000 had shown a clear record of losses, which had convinced the executives to abandon them in the late 1930s. This policy continued during Schaefer's first year as well, but then he suddenly decided to start making "specials." As mentioned, Schaefer thought he had to upgrade the quality of the Bs because of the new sales requirements. Still, the idea disregarded the lessons of the past, lessons learned by RKO the hard way.

Neither Schaefer nor Breen nor Lesser nor McDonough was able to boost the quality or box-office performance of RKO pictures during the remainder of 1941. Films like *Father Takes a Wife, Unexpected Uncle*, and *Weekend for Three* all lost more than $100,000 each, and even when the company managed a surprise hit, such as *Look Who's Laughing*, starring Lucille Ball and some popular radio comedians, it was dismissed by the critics. The one exception that made sizable money and impressed the full spectrum of movie enthusiasts was *Suspicion.*

Back in 1935, RKO had paid $5,000 for the rights to an unusual novel entitled *Before the Fact.*[29] Written by British author Anthony Berkeley Cox under the pseudonym Francis Iles, the book told the story of Lina McLaidlaw, a woman so in love, and obsessed, with her husband that she allows him to plot and perpetrate her own murder. For various reasons, RKO could never get the picture off the ground. In 1938, an unsuccessful attempt was made to sell the property. Upon reading a synopsis in January 1940, George Schaefer wrote: "I really do not think 'BEFORE THE FACT' is important enough for an outstanding personality. It seems very ordinary,— certainly, nothing unusual and, as a matter of fact, just another motion picture. I think when you make an important picture now-a-days, you must get away from anything trite and commonplace. It would be a good 'B' picture and not a specialty picture."[30]

For a time, the story was planned as a B production with George Sanders and Anne Shirley earmarked for the main roles. But then Alfred Hitchcock expressed a desire to make a film based on the novel, thereby changing everything. With a director of Hitchcock's caliber, the project immediately became viable and gained A status. J. R. McDonough described Hitchcock's conception for the film in a June 3, 1940, memo to Harry Edington: "In a conversation that Danny Winkler and I had with Hitchcock last night he said he would shoot 'BEFORE THE FACT' in seven weeks. He also told us that he would follow the novel as to story, persons, locale, and sets, except-ing only that he would tell the story through the eyes of the woman and have her husband be villainous in her imagination only."[31]

The original plan for the picture included Laurence Olivier and Frances Dee as the principals and called for a total budget of $680,000.[32] George Schaefer, however, thought the film should cost no more than $550,000 and postponed it while Hitchcock directed his only screwball comedy, *Mr. and Mrs. Smith.* In the meantime, the script was prepared by Samson Raphaelson, along with Hitchcock's wife, Alma Reville, and his former secretary Joan Harrison. When a new preproduction budget was prepared in January 1941, the estimate had climbed to $845,423.[33] A healthy per-centage of the additional budget came from the casting of Cary Grant and Joan Fontaine as the two leads. Fontaine—like Hitchcock, borrowed from David Selznick—would cost RKO $44,750 more than Frances Dee. Ironi-cally, RKO had discharged Fontaine two years before when she was earning a small fraction of the money she now commanded. The RKO executives

Figure 23. *Suspicion* (1941). Director Alfred Hitchcock and star Joan Fontaine examine costume sketches for her character. The film would earn Fontaine an Oscar for Best Actress. (Courtesy of the Academy of Motion Picture Arts and Sciences)

had been blind to her acting ability and star quality, attributes subsequently made manifest by George Cukor in *The Women* and Hitchcock in *Rebecca*.

George Schaefer believed $845,423 to be "more money than I think we should spend" and asked J. R. McDonough to pare the budget of the film to $800,000 or less.[34] There was no question of postponing or canceling the picture now, however. Commitments to Grant, Fontaine, Hitchcock, and others had already been made, and shooting commenced shortly thereafter. Instead of cutting costs, however, McDonough and Harry Edington, the actual producer of the picture, watched helplessly as the budget mounted. Illnesses affecting Grant, Fontaine, and Hitchcock put the company behind schedule. By April 18 the picture was already $80,000 over the estimate.[35]

After shooting was completed, retakes were deemed necessary. They pushed the final cost to $1,103,000, making it the most expensive RKO picture since *The Hunchback of Notre Dame.* Thus, there was considerable trepidation about the economic impact the film might have on RKO. Although scant evidence exists to support this view, it appears that George Schaefer blamed the excesses on Hitchcock and Edington. The files contain cryptic remarks about Hitchcock shooting things not in the script and not giving the picture his full attention, and Schafer refused to allow Edington a producer credit when it was released.[36]

Throughout the filming and after, the question of a title plagued the individuals involved. *Before the Fact* was felt to be stuffy and incapable of arousing any curiosity. Hitchcock's suggestion was *Fright,* a title that George Schaefer believed would "frighten people away." Schaefer's preferences were *Suspicion, That Suspicious Lady,* or *On Suspicion.*[37] Other suggestions included *Here Is a Man* and *Riches and Sin,* neither of which was close to satisfactory. It was decided to use *Before the Fact.* In August, however, the Audience Research Institute conducted a poll and discovered that *Before the Fact* was "seriously lacking in audience appeal." Not only that, but it created the impression that the film was another Cary Grant comedy. The associate director of the institute, David Ogilvy, informed George Schaefer: "We have also tested the title SUSPICION. It outpulls BEFORE THE FACT by no less than three to one. The customers think SUSPICION would be a mystery. It arouses a lot of curiosity. It goes a long way towards killing the expectation of comedy implicit in Grant's name."[38] And so the studio chose *Suspicion* as the release title.

It was a wise decision, for the film earned $440,000 despite its high cost. Part of the profits no doubt came as a result of Joan Fontaine winning the Academy Award for her performance. Clearly the financial value of an Oscar had increased enormously since the early thirties when a film like *Cimarron* could cop the major prize and still post a startling loss for its company.

Joan Fontaine's performance was an able job, though many of her votes were probably cast because she had been passed over for her work in

Rebecca the previous year. At any rate, RKO films had now won Best Actress Oscars in two consecutive years—Ginger Rogers for *Kitty Foyle* and Fontaine for *Suspicion*—and their films had helped the RKO bottom line considerably. Unfortunately, both actresses, as well as director Hitchcock, were working elsewhere by the end of the year.

Around the time *Suspicion* went into wide release, the Japanese bombed Pearl Harbor, and America became an official participant in World War II. Since the film industry had been feeling the effects of war for more than two years, the immediate impact on the studios was not dramatic. Everyone in Hollywood pledged his or her support for the war effort, and defense precautions were inaugurated at the various plants. RKO, for instance, issued instructions that no more visitors would be allowed, any packages brought on the lot would be subject to careful inspection, and an air raid siren would alert employees to danger.[39] Evacuation procedures were disseminated to all employees. Shooting schedules also had to be rearranged to avoid night work, thus saving electricity and gas and enabling workers to get to their homes without traveling in the dark.

Most of the companies stepped up their preparations to make pictures with war themes. RKO announced that the starting date for *Bombardier* would be advanced from January 15 to December 15.[40] One of the most worrisome aspects of the crisis was the loss of many talented members of the industry who enlisted in the military shortly after Pearl Harbor. John Ford, Frank Capra, and William Wyler led the directorial contingent. RKO came out all right in this regard, principally because it had few major figures under contract.

Around this time, George Schaefer began to deal with another fiscal crisis at his company; RKO's cash position had been deteriorating steadily for weeks. The block-of-five selling meant the distribution department had to hold valuable merchandise on the shelf much longer than had been the case in the past, and this factor, combined with the mediocre earnings of most of the films when they did reach the marketplace, was endangering the repayment of RKO's revolving bank loans.[41] Floyd Odlum was well aware of the problem and had been growing more and more disenchanted with Schaefer's performance for some time. Indeed, rumors had floated around Hollywood for several months that Schaefer would be sacked. And, at the very moment when the RKO board was poised to begin considering a new contract for Schaefer, his number-one fan, W.G. Van Schmus, had taken ill and been hospitalized.[42] Van Schmus would die in early 1942. Meanwhile, Nelson Rockefeller was ensconced in Washington, having accepted the invitation of President Roosevelt to become coordinator of inter-American affairs, and did not have time to devote to the travails of Schaefer or RKO. And David Sarnoff continued to remain preoccupied and aloof.

Another ominous note was sounded in mid-December when Floyd Odlum had one of his personal favorites, N. Peter Rathvon, elected an RKO vice-president.[43] Although Rathvon devoted some of his energies to other Atlas interests, including Madison Square Garden and Bonwit Teller's Department Store, he had spent most of his time on RKO business during the past six years. He badgered the Rockefellers to reduce their claims against RKO throughout the receivership proceedings, which did not endear him to Schaefer's principal allies. George Schaefer was also well aware that Odlum had backed Rathvon for the corporate presidency before Nelson Rockefeller and David Sarnoff secured the position for him. Subsequently, he had often locked horns with Rathvon regarding company policy. Therefore, Schaefer had good reason to feel uneasy about the appointment. Odlum was also able to get another of his associates, Garrett Van Wagner, named comptroller of the parent organization. Should RKO continue to falter, Floyd Odlum was well positioned to assert himself and protect his investment.

Just before Christmas, Schaefer received a memo from the new head of his theater company. Charles Koerner, who followed box-office trends closely, recommended his boss consider making some low-budget horror pictures:

> It is interesting to note the successes of several pictures of the horror type at the present time.
>
> Fox's SWAMP WATER is doing exceptionally good business in the so-called B or exploitation houses. The horror and gruesome angle is stressed very strongly in this picture.
>
> While we have not had as many bookings on Universal's WOLF MAN the first indications are that this will also prove an uncommonly good grosser.[44]

Schaefer, uninterested in horror films and coping with much bigger issues, disregarded Koerner's suggestion. Charles Koerner would, however, find himself in a position to act on this idea sooner than he could have known.

President George Schaefer predicted that 1942 would be "a great year for RKO" because the studio had "more holdover pictures in theaters and more important plays in production than at any other time in the studio's history."[45] In reality, the organization was a tottery mess at the beginning of the new year. Besides Odlum's determination to become more involved, there was much conjecture about new policies and personnel changes. Among the possibilities mentioned were dissolution of the executive committee of the board of directors, reduction of the number of members on the board, and changes in the studio's executive personnel. Since Joseph Breen was "expected to remain in charge of production," the implication was that either Sol Lesser or J. R. McDonough (or both) might be going the way of Harry Edington in the near future.[46] Edington had been persona non grata throughout 1941. Because of the executive producer's contract, Schaefer could not get rid of him, so he assigned Edington to work on pictures while refusing to give him producer credit. Although Edington remained on salary until January 1942, he stopped reporting for work in early November.[47] It is not possible to say if Harry Edington was as big a bust as he appeared to be, or simply a scapegoat for the president's own blunders.

The departure of Ginger Rogers dealt a crucial blow to RKO's withered stock company. *Variety* assessed the situation in its last issue of the year:

> RKO, as result of all reorganization and management turmoil, was weakest of all companies for permanent star listing. It's [*sic*] best bet, Ginger Rogers, flitted out to free-lance, and company which has been making its product through individual picture deals with outstanding stars, had to take its chances on the open market for its top talent.
>
> . . . .
>
> RKO is figured the problem child of Hollywood, and a frequent query is, "When are they going to get some players, or develop some that mean box office." Joe Breen and Sol Lesser . . . have been scouting around, but nothing has happened as yet. Studio had its talent scouts . . . but their percentage of new faces for the outfit has been nil. May be better luck in 1942.[48]

The mood at RKO headquarters in Manhattan and at the studio in Hollywood turned very gloomy in early 1942. Since the beginning of tradeshow selling in August 1941, the production arm of the corporation had lost money every month. November and December were especially devastating, producing losses of $243,109 and $305,804, respectively.[49] Much of the problem was blamed on the necessity to complete pictures far in advance of their actual releases, thus requiring the investment of funds without hope of recovery for many months thereafter. But the other studios adjusted to the new requirements imposed by the consent decree without major strain. Indeed, Twentieth Century–Fox had bounced back from its small loss in 1940 with a corporate profit of $4.9 million in 1941, and MGM, Paramount, and Warner Bros. each performed better financially than Fox.

The root cause of RKO's difficulties was simple and obvious: despite considerable outlays of cash, the studio had not produced a requisite number of commercial films since George Schaefer had assumed the presidency. A special loan of $3 million had to be secured from the Bankers Trust Company in mid-1941 to keep the cameras turning.[50] That money was rapidly disappearing. Unless a swift uptick in the performance of RKO pictures occurred, it appeared the studio might run out of cash, thereby causing the corporation to collapse once again into receivership or perhaps quit the business altogether. Of course, the possibility of fresh financing always existed. But considering the company's history and recent performance, the prospects for more funding were not encouraging.

New corporate vice-president N. Peter Rathvon went to work analyzing the picture company's financial needs, while George Schaefer began looking for ways to reduce studio overhead. One positive factor was that by mid-January, only four pictures were left to finish off the entire 1941–1942 program.[51] Thus, the company could coast for a while, planning the 1942–1943 season without expending too much cash. Around January 20, studio manager Sid Rogell was fired, sparking renewed rumors of another shake-up in personnel.[52]

The Hollywood trade press picked up on the disarray at 780 Gower Street and began publishing speculative stories about studio upheaval. This infuriated George Schaefer, who blamed head of publicity Perry Lieber for allowing the insider information and gossip to leak out.[53] Lieber replied to Joe Breen that he realized it was important "to keep bad and false material out of print," but that there was little he could do about embittered former employees who were feeding the material to trade paper writers.[54] He suspected Sid Rogell, Harry Edington, and Erich Pommer were the sources of most of the stories.

Perry Lieber had his hands full because, soon enough, many of the rumors became facts. In early February Sol Lesser and J. R. McDonough both quit, along with a number of other employees. Needing desperately to reduce the salary requirements of running the studio and believing that Lesser's contributions had been indifferent at best, George Schaefer asked him to "disassociate himself" from the position of "Executive in Charge of 'A' Production." Instead, Schaefer requested that Lesser assume a vague job in which he would be concerned with "certain of the business, financial and administrative phases of our problem, and not have any responsibility for the actual production of pictures."[55] In addition, a 50 percent reduction in salary was solicited. After considering Schaefer's proposal for a week, Lesser submitted his resignation to Joseph Breen.[56] Lesser had decided that Schaefer's real goal was to get rid of him: "I have been thinking over the accumulating situation not only as it affects me, but as it affects the studio as well. You [Breen] know how troubled I have been because I have spoken of it to you each time we have met since your return. I know that George Schaefer and you must be fully aware of this as I am, and from every indication I must in all frankness say that my feeling is that George does not want me to continue at the studio."[57]

Lesser's departure was reasonably amicable, but the windup of McDonough's RKO career was not. Relations between McDonough and Schaefer had been blustery since Mac had taken charge of the low-budget unit. Following the forced resignation, Schaefer refused McDonough's request for severance pay, a request based on some nine years' service to the company. McDonough was outraged. He set to work compiling a report of studio conditions under Schaefer's regime. The picture he painted would not be rosy.[58]

Other radical changes were occurring at 780 Gower Street. In mid-February, Charles Koerner, head of the theater department, moved to Hollywood to take over production "temporarily" while Joseph Breen recovered from an unspecified illness. On March 2, 1942, Schaefer reported to the RKO board that he believed Breen should "divorce himself from a number of studio details and be relieved of the burden of operating the studio"; he and the board also agreed Koerner should assume permanent production responsibility.[59] Joe Breen had been another mistake, a man incapable of piloting the complex production machinery. He was also—it should be emphasized—the latest in a growing list of Schaefer appointees who had failed to come through for RKO. The story released by the publicity department to the trade journals was deliberately misleading. *Variety* reported that Koerner would be replacing Breen for six weeks while the studio head vacationed in Mexico.[60] Upon Breen's return, Koerner was supposed to go back to his theater job in New York, and Breen was supposed to again rule the studio. This was not at all what RKO had in mind.

The strategy George Schaefer and the RKO board contemplated was suggested by recent developments at Universal. There, Nate Blumberg and Cliff Work, who had been hired away from the RKO distribution-exhibition ranks in 1938, had taken on the responsibility of shaping production policies.[61] Drawing on their knowledge of theater patrons and the pictures that appealed to them most, the twosome managed to turn out movies that boosted Universal's bottom line. Following seven consecutive losing years, the company brought in profits of $1 million in 1939, $2.2 million in 1940, and $2.3 million in 1941. Koerner had toiled in exhibition since the 1920s. The RKO leaders hoped that, given the opportunity, he would also coax forth films that the public wanted to see.

Unlike his predecessors, Koerner would have a free hand to shape RKO production. George Schaefer no longer required all important matters to be cleared through him. Having seen many of his pet projects turn to ashes, Schaefer may finally have decided to abdicate responsibility in favor of someone else. Perhaps he had more faith in Koerner than he had in Berman, Edington, Lesser, McDonough, or Breen. Or perhaps the board of directors insisted that Koerner be given free rein. Whatever the reason, Charles Koerner enjoyed an attractive bonus that went along with an otherwise unenviable job—freedom from New York interference.

While Koerner was setting up shop in Hollywood, George Schaefer was laboring to keep his company from unraveling completely. His efforts were hampered by an unending stream of bad news, much of it related to Orson Welles.

Welles's second RKO picture, *The Magnificent Ambersons*, had gone into production in the fall of 1941. The first budget calculation amounted to $987,024, prompting a letter from Schaefer to Welles: "Momentarily I was flabbergasted when I looked at the pre-budget estimate of THE MAGNIFICENT AMBERSONS totalling $987,024 but I came to immediately when I saw the words 'pre-budget.' Am, of course, taking it for granted that that is just the wildest kind of guess and, when the final budget comes through, it will be less than $600,000."[62] Even before Schaefer wrote that letter, Jack Moss, Welles's business partner, had promised the budget would be reduced, though probably not below $750,000.[63] The final budget, however, came to $853,950. This presented a problem. The estimate exceeded not only the $600,000 now established as a maximum in Welles's new contract, but also the $750,000 figure RKO had promised would be the ceiling for a single feature in its bank loan arrangements.[64] As had been the case with *Bringing Up Baby, Suspicion*, and other past productions, the executives were in a hopeless predicament. Sets had been built and commitments signed, and so Orson Welles was allowed to proceed. George Schaefer, Joseph Breen, and the other executives could only wait with fingers crossed, hoping that Welles would bring the film in for less than the projected figure. They should have known better. Welles's dedication to his

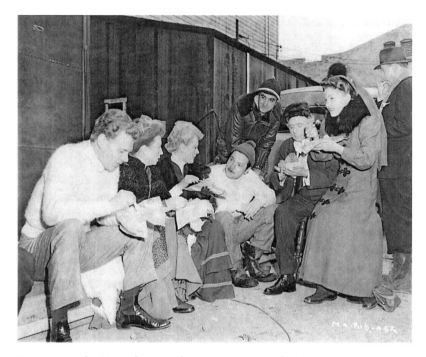

Figure 24. *The Magnificent Ambersons* (1942). Joseph Cotten, Agnes Moorehead, Dolores Costello, Orson Welles, Ray Collins, Anne Baxter, and others eat
lunch outside an ice house where winter scenes were filmed. (Courtesy of the
Academy of Motion Picture Arts and Sciences)

art, plus a spate of illnesses among cast members and the deliberate working habits of cinematographer Stanley Cortez, boosted the amount expended. When the production finally came to a conclusion, it had cost over
$1 million.

Even so, high hopes for the finished product abounded. In early December, George Schaefer saw approximately one hour of the footage and felt
very enthusiastic. He wired Welles: "Even though I have seen only a part
of it, there is every indication that it is chock full of heartthrobs, heart-
aches and human interest. From a technical standpoint it is startling and I
should not forget to mention especially that Agnes Moorehead does one of
the finest pieces of work I have ever seen on the screen. Although I saw
only part of the picture her work in particular made a tremendous impression on me. Again I am very happy and proud of our association."[65] Joe Breen
was equally thrilled. "I have not been so impressed in years," he wrote
Welles. "The material we saw was really excellent, and although you know

me to be a chronic kicker, in this instance I have nothing but praise—from my heart."[66]

The final editing could not be supervised by Welles, who left for Brazil in February to make *It's All True.* Studio cutter Robert Wise had to assemble the footage with Welles cabling instructions and calling Wise to discuss problems. RKO fully expected the film to be a success and, needing a big winner, scheduled its release for Easter week. The great distance between Welles and Wise made the editing difficult, and the studio contemplated sending Wise to Rio de Janeiro in early March so that Welles could put the final touches on the picture.[67] Wartime travel restrictions prevented this, however.

Meanwhile, the distribution department formalized its campaign for *The Magnificent Ambersons*, placing advertisements in *Life, Time, Look, Good Housekeeping, The New Yorker,* and other magazines.[68] The ads would run in late March and throughout April.

In mid-March, the initial preview was held in Pomona, California. George Schaefer attended. He described the evening in an airmail, special-delivery letter to Welles marked "Personal—Confidential":

> I did not want to cable you with respect to THE MAGNIFICENT AMBERSONS as indicated in your cable of the 18th, only because I wanted to write you under confidential cover.
>
> Of course, when you ask me for my reaction I know you want it straight, and though it is difficult to write you this way, you should hear from me.
>
> Never in all my experience in the industry have I taken so much punishment or suffered as I did at the Pomona preview. In my 28 years in the business, I have never been present in a theatre where the audience acted in such a manner. They laughed at the wrong places, talked at the picture, kidded it, and did everything you can possibly imagine.
>
> I don't have to tell you how I suffered, especially in the realization that we have over $1,000,000 tied up. It was just like getting one sock in the jaw after another for over two hours.
>
> The picture was too slow, heavy, and topped off with somber music, never did register. It started off well, but just went to pieces.[69]

After describing preview card comments that decried the "artiness" of the film, Schaefer chastised Welles for his extravagance and his failure to establish contact with the movie audience:

> In all our initial discussions, you stressed low costs, making pictures at $300,000 to $500,000, and on our first two pictures, we have an investment of $2,000,000. We will not make a dollar on CITIZEN

KANE and present indications are that we will not break even. The final results on AMBERSONS is [sic] still to be told, but it looks "red."

All of which again reminds me of only one thing—that we must have a "heart to heart" talk. Orson Welles has got to do something commercial. We have got to get away from "arty" pictures and get back to earth. Educating the people is expensive, and your next picture must be made for the box-office.

God knows you have all the talent and the ability for writing, producing, directing—everything in CITIZEN KANE and AMBERSONS confirm that. We should apply all that talent and effort in the right direction and make a picture on which "we can get well."

That's the story, Orson, and I feel very miserable to have to write you this.[70]

Schaefer was not being fair to Welles. After all, the RKO president had hired the wunderkind and his Mercury Theatre group to upgrade the studio's prestige—which, it could be argued, is exactly what Welles had accomplished with *Citizen Kane*. Also, Schaefer had allowed Welles to go forward with films even though he had contractual authority to stop them because of their excessive budgets. One can, however, certainly understand Schaefer's miserable feelings. He had fought for Welles throughout the *Citizen Kane* brouhaha, thereby alienating some members of the RKO board of directors. The critical esteem accorded *Kane* had been a momentary vindication for Schaefer, but its box-office failure and now the prospects of an *Ambersons* catastrophe provided ample ammunition to Schaefer's detractors. On top of this were the simple economic facts of life. At a time when the company desperately needed income, the release of *Ambersons* would have to be postponed while further cuts were made.[71]

The development of Welles's next project, *It's All True*, began in the summer of 1941. The director had in mind an omnibus film composed of at least four separate stories. A portion of the shooting of one of these stories, tentatively entitled "Bonito the Bull," was done in Mexico while *The Magnificent Ambersons* was in production. Welles, in fact, had little to do with this section; being preoccupied with *Ambersons,* he surrendered the directorial reins to Norman Foster. In December the plan for *It's All True* changed. Originally, the stories were to be set in North America, but the Office of Inter-American Affairs became involved, and before long, the project acquired a Brazilian background.

As previously noted, Nelson Rockefeller headed up this new government office, ostensibly created to foster good relations between the United States and countries in Latin America. His primary duty, however, was to make sure none of America's southern neighbors drifted into the enemy camp. The Roosevelt administration was concerned that the Nazis might attempt to persuade the leaders of Argentina, Brazil, Chile, and other countries to side with the Axis in the global conflict and wanted to pre-empt any action of this kind.[72]

It is not possible to determine if Orson Welles approached the government office with the idea of making *It's All True* in Brazil, or if Rockefeller approached him. John Hay Whitney, a good friend of Nelson's and by then a Hollywood fixture, thanks to his investments in Technicolor, Pioneer Pictures, Selznick International, and *Gone With the Wind*, had been placed in charge of the agency's motion picture division. A wire from Whitney to Welles dated December 20, 1941, does establish the position of the office clearly: "We understand you are willing and may be able to undertake a trip to Brazil where you would produce motion pictures in cooperation with Brazilian government. If this can be arranged it will be enormously helpful to the program of this office and energetically supported by it. Personally believe you would make great contribution to hemisphere solidarity with this project."[73]

Since Nelson Rockefeller was an important behind-the-scenes power in RKO and had been the main supporter of George Schaefer in the first place, he may have used his leverage to "encourage" this particular project into being. At any rate, by early January it was settled: Welles would soon be headed for Rio de Janeiro to make a multistory film, at least one section of which would revolve around the famous Rio Carnaval in February.[74] "Bonito the Bull" would probably still be part of *It's All True*, but the other contemplated sections, including one about the history of jazz and another about a San Francisco fisherman, were abandoned. Welles was going to Rio without a script; presumably, the atmosphere would inspire him and he would come up with suitable stories.

The logistics involved should have been enough to make Schaefer wary. It would be necessary to ship nearly all the equipment down, as well as the personnel necessary to operate it. Part of the film was to be shot in color, thus complicating the production further. And to top that off, America was at war, and there were travel and shipping restrictions to cope with. The Inter-American Affairs Office promised to help facilitate matters. It also offered a financial incentive, which definitely made the venture more attractive to George Schaefer. The government would not actually invest in the picture, but if *It's All True* showed a loss after its release, the office promised to make good the loss up to $300,000.[75] Schaefer expected Welles to spend no more than $600,000 on the production; thus, it appeared RKO could contribute to the needs of the government without any serious risk to its own financial well-being. The arrangement made sense, on paper.

The first production contingent arrived in late January. Welles's personal assistant Richard Wilson, unit production manager Lynn Shores, and several technicians were members of this group. They had some, but not all, of the necessary equipment with them. Welles flew down during the second week of February. Phil Reisman, vice-president in charge of RKO's foreign sales, accompanied Welles and dispatched the following jubilant telegram to Schaefer shortly after they debarked:

> Reception of Orson Welles Rio not only equal to but surpassed Disney's success here. Orson can qualify for my money as a great ambassador. Know that it is no surprise to you that his outlook and understanding are intelligant [sic] and comprehensive and that he has complete grasp of the importance of this job. Despite the handicap of lack of equipment, it is my honest opinion that we are going to get great and unusual picture out of here. His enthusiasm is boundless. This is reciprocated by the reception of the Brazilian officials who are cooperating to an unbelievable extent. The press has been uniform in telling the Brazilian public what I'm now telling you.[76]

Welles also gushed enthusiasm. After two weeks in Rio, he wrote Schaefer:

> We're working too hard down here for good letter writing, or even one good long letter. Since you are my most understanding friend, I won't even attempt to explain my silence or alibi the brevity of this.
> . . . .
> The new radio series emanating from here should start in a week or two, which means that the picture will receive the most potent exploitation imaginable. The public interest should be aroused to a really wonderful extent by the time we're ready to release. I have great hopes for the film itself. Quite apart from its importance as a documentary, its entertainment values promise to be very great. Every day it grows on us. The Carnaval sequence alone—as a colorful and picturesque finale to the entire film—is going to mark a totally new departure in musicals. Indeed, every aspect of this picture is as fresh as even you could ask for.
> This is a big job and a tough one, and I am truly and deeply grateful for the opportunity. I do think our rewards will be great. This is real pioneering and—after all—pioneering is what we like best.[77]

If one were dependent only on the reports of Reisman and Welles, the story of *It's All True* would seem a stirring, glorious adventure. But the studio was also receiving weekly reports from another source, a man who portrayed the activities quite differently. Lynn Shores was the company production manager. His duties entailed dispensing the funds, keeping the books on the picture, and taking care of the many problems that cropped up. From the very beginning, Shores's reports were disturbing. Over a period of weeks, their tone changed from concern to outrage. Early on, Shores revealed that the hot weather, the bad food, and the impossibility of operating in an efficient Hollywood manner were contributing to a morale crisis among the members of the crew. Even more upsetting was the communication gap between Welles and the people working on his movie. While the crew established its headquarters at the Palace Hotel in downtown Rio, Welles, Richard Wilson, and the Welles inner circle took rooms at the Copa Cabana Hotel on the beach. According to Shores, shooting was proceeding in a completely "off the cuff" manner. Welles had no script, assigned things to be shot arbitrarily, and frequently did not show up for the filming. On many occasions, Shores or Wilson handled the actual direction. On February 24, Shores reported:

> I will not go into the details of my various attempts at trying to pin Welles down as to future plans. In a vague way he has given me to understand that we are to travel over most of South America with Mercury Players, various units of Technicolor and black and white, radio set-ups, good-will speeches and general messing around the next two or three months. . . .
>
> It has been a horrible nightmare to me personally. I am carrying not only the working but the personal problems of 27 individuals, each one with an axe to grind and a grievance of some sort at every hour of the day.[78]

In early March, Welles and Schaefer had their first major disagreement. From the beginning, the use of Technicolor was supposed to be restricted to the Carnaval footage. It was deemed too expensive to make the entire film in color. Welles decided, however, that he had to make a section of the film about the exploits of four Brazilian fishermen in color, as well. He claimed it would be "part" of the Carnaval story. He planned to recreate an actual incident in which four men from Fortaleza in northern Brazil had sailed their primitive raft (*jangada*) two thousand miles to Rio, where they handed a petition to the Brazilian president calling his attention to the plight of the starving people in their region. Welles's notion was to juggle history just a bit, having the local heroes (he planned to use the actual fishermen rather than actors) sail in at the height of Carnaval. Schaefer, however, absolutely forbade Welles to use color for this sequence. He explained why:

Orson, I want you to believe me that I am personally on the hook for
the whole South American venture. My board were not enthusiastic
even with government help. Thought I was taking too much risk.
Nevertheless, I pushed it through and prevailed upon them to be
guided by my judgment. Further, we receive help from government
only up to a certain extent and that was also clearly outlined to my
board. That certain extent does not permit us to shoot FOUR MEN [in]
Technicolor. It would cause your Man Friday tremendous amount of
personal embarrassment and everyone in particular taking a keen
delight pointing out you had not lived up to what I expected and what I
had stated would be done. Most anxious bring this through at least
possible cost. Urge you do so for me. Even though photography black
and white, can still blend in to Technicolor Rio carnival.[79]

The RKO board was debating Schaefer's new contract at this point, so he
desperately needed positive news from Rio.

Welles continuously reassured Schaefer that he intended to keep expenses down and emphasized he was getting "ten times more" for the
money than would be possible in Hollywood.[80] However, the letters from
Shores kept arriving like clockwork, each one more hair-raising than the
last. Welles was portrayed as dissipating his energies on "research," on travels throughout South America as part of his "cultural ambassador" role, on
preparation of his radio program. *It's All True* was being shot haphazardly
with Welles showing up only sporadically, having sets built, then changing his mind and never using them, and ordering miles of film to be shot
without an established plan. As far as expenses were concerned, the cost of
Welles's telephone calls and cables alone was running close to $1,000 per
week.[81] Back in California, some of the Brazilian footage began to arrive.
It did not look promising.

The disappointment with the film mirrored the general mood at the
studio, which must have seemed like a besieged medieval township at this
time. The departures of Rogell, Lesser, McDonough, and others were only
the first salvo in a wide-ranging wave of dismissals and eliminations that
swept over the lot during the first four months of 1942. Because of the financial crunch, RKO had to cut its expenditures to the marrow. Only
workers deemed essential were retained.

Around the time J.R. McDonough and Sol Lesser were handing in
their resignations, Cliff Reid and Howard Benedict both departed.[82] Reid
had functioned primarily as a B producer since 1934 with a number of hits,
but many flops, on his record. His pictures had performed poorly of late,
so he was a logical candidate for a pink slip. Howard Benedict also had

logged considerable service with the organization. For five years, he had been the studio's publicity director before becoming a B producer in 1940. Fortunately, Benedict had a job waiting for him at Universal.[83] Frank Woodruff, a B film director, and Reeves Espy, a producer, were also removed from the staff around the same time.

Probably the most vulnerable group during the "great purge" was the independents. One by one, it seemed, nearly every independent association was expunged. Gabriel Pascal, for example, wound up his RKO tenure before it actually began. Pascal began preparing Shaw's *Arms and the Man*, to star Cary Grant and Ginger Rogers, but became so exasperated with RKO's volatile production environment that he quit and went back to United Artists, where he had been putting together projects before becoming involved with the studio. Pascal gave "interference by studio executives" as his reason for pulling out.[84]

Close behind Pascal was Broadway veteran Jed Harris, whose wartime comedy project failed to spark any enthusiasm among the RKO executives. William Hawks also checked out without producing a film, mentioning "differences" with the production staff as the problem.[85] There were also dismissals of actors and actresses, but since RKO had no big names left under exclusive contract, none was very dramatic or saved the company significant money. Certain individuals were added to the company's payrolls, mostly at the suggestion of Charles Koerner, who needed help if the studio intended to continue in the filmmaking business. Lou Ostrow, previously a producer at MGM and Twentieth Century–Fox, took over the low-budget unit. Frank Ross signed on as a producer, following the success of *The Devil and Miss Jones*, and Leo McCarey returned to fill the noticeable gap in A production. His first film (as a director) since *Love Affair* would be *Once Upon a Honeymoon* starring Ginger Rogers and Cary Grant. Koerner also hired Val Lewton, a literate protégé of David Selznick, to produce a series of inexpensive horror films. And J. J. Nolan returned to his old office. He would again take charge of contract negotiations and commitments.[86] Obligations of all kinds, however, were being kept to an absolute minimum. There was no other choice; the picture company was running out of money.

Sometime in March, J. R. McDonough's forty-two-page report, which was not complimentary of George Schaefer's stewardship of RKO, landed on David Sarnoff's desk. Sarnoff had not paid close attention to RKO for several years, but RCA still owned considerable stock in the corporation and had representation on its board of directors. Sarnoff had originally dispatched McDonough to RKO, and the RCA leader was fond of his former employee. Thus, Sarnoff's reaction to the treatment of McDonough by Schaefer and to the contents of McDonough's document was predictably swift and heated. He issued a statement detailing his "complete dissatisfaction with conditions at RKO" and asking for a full accounting and a new executive setup. Sarnoff also promised to take legal action, if necessary, to block the signing of Schaefer to a new, long-term contract. These events transpired in late March, at a time when even Floyd Odlum was reportedly inclined to support a five-year pact for Schaefer (with six-month option clauses).[87]

Meanwhile, George Schaefer's blood pressure spiked each time a fresh report on *It's All True* arrived from Brazil. After Welles announced that he planned to spend $25,000 to "remodel" a Rio nightclub (the Urca Casino) for a sequence that would be part of the Carnaval story, Schaefer tried desperately to reach the director by telephone. Four days later he gave up, believing that Welles was ducking him. At one point the hotel operator even reported she had heard Welles's voice on the line, but still Schaefer was told he was unavailable.[88] Finally, the RKO boss cabled Welles. The last portion of the message read:

> Sure you can appreciate my worry and concern when I hear commitments have been made to augment show and practically reconstruct Urca Casino at cost $25,000. At that rate we will have another AMBERSONS situation on our hands. This latter picture as you know well over one million. It is very painful to send this cable because I know what stickler you are for quality but on other hand I am rapidly coming to conclusion you have no realization of money you spend and how difficult it is to recoup cost.[89]

Welles's reply seemed designed to pacify Schaefer, but it also contained a veiled threat:

> Prices for this [the Urca sequence] were quoted to Hollywood before I had chance to cut them down. Twenty five thousand dollars is more than I intend to spend. However that money buys the basis for carnaval production. It would cost one hundred fifty thousand dollars Hollywood and any studio would be happy to pay for it when they saw what they were getting. . . . When I finish this picture you will see what I mean. Must however be allowed to finish it as I wish to. I have added nothing to original project. We are working night and day to bring closed [*sic*] production as soon as possible [at] greatest possible saving. Our problems here have been tremendous but unless I can finish film as it must be finished for entertainment value the entire expenditure of time and effort and money will be total loss.[90]

Schaefer fired back another cable, which also contained a not-so-veiled warning:

> Your cable received and have full appreciation production difficulties so far away from home but on other hand I must take firm position and cannot permit moneys to be expended to finish. You have been away now for three months and surely we expected you back long before this. On top of that records indicate over $33,000 in March, 1st week in April $10,500 and budget calls for $15,000 weekly for next four weeks. This is all out of proportion to what we ever estimated and we cannot go along on that basis even if we have to close down show and ask you to return. That is how serious situation is with respect to my own apprehension.[91]

Schaefer's words apparently had little effect on Welles. As described by Lynn Shores, the following week's filming seems almost like a scene from a Fellini picture:

> I cannot say much for this week's work because I do not feel any progress whatsoever has been made toward getting out of here. After working day and night to build three sets on the stage, Welles decided to shoot a building . . . called the Rio Tennis Club. This was supposed to be one night's shooting but . . . it went on and on through the week and to the best of my knowledge it seems that these sets are not finished yet. These particular scenes were mostly young girls and boys making love in various odd corners . . . with a background of 50 or 60 extras and continual calls every day for more beautiful girls. As far as I can judge there [*sic*] seems to have no bearing whatsoever on what we are trying to do in connection with shooting carnival.[92]

Shores's letter, plus mounting requests from crew members wishing to be replaced, forced George Schaefer to take action. He decided to send Phil Reisman, who had returned to the States after spending the first month with Welles, back to Rio with authority to close the picture down. On April 27 an enlightening telephone conversation took place between Reisman in New York and Reg Armour at the Hollywood studio. Armour, an executive who had spent years working for RKO distribution in various foreign countries, had relocated to Hollywood in 1941 at Schaefer's behest. Their phone call places the *It's All True* saga squarely within the context of RKO's and George Schaefer's mounting difficulties:

MR. ARMOUR: When are you leaving, Phil?

MR. REISMAN: In about ten days.
He's a tough baby—he [Welles] has done a magnificent job of selling himself to Nelson Rockefeller.

MR. ARMOUR: From what we have seen from here, the best thing you can do is to send him back—the crew do not feel any loyalty to him. We have received 60,000 feet here and there is no picture in it. If we can get 800 or 1000 feet out of it we will be doing well. We have roughly $60,000 in film stock in Technicolor.

MR. REISMAN: Maybe we could make a couple of shorts out of it.

MR. ARMOUR: I don't think so. George [Schaefer] will lose his job out of this.

MR. REISMAN: George wrote Orson a strong letter which I am to deliver. After he has read the letter he will either come back as George says—or quit.

MR. ARMOUR: I think Orson wants to stay out of the country. He wants to duck military service.

MR. REISMAN: I think I could get the authorities to take him off our hands.

MR. ARMOUR: This picture will put us back in 77B.

MR. REISMAN: Do you really think so?

MR. ARMOUR: Yes, I do, Phil.[93]

Setting aside Armour's gossipy speculation about Welles attempting to avoid military service and Reisman's mean-spirited remark about getting the government to induct him, the most significant portions of the conversation are Armour's predictions that the making of *It's All True* would cost Schaefer his job and throw RKO back into receivership. Clearly, the pressure on George Schaefer was increasing daily.

Evidence of this pressure is apparent in Schaefer's long letter to Welles, which Reisman delivered in May. The author is clearly a beleaguered man:

Here I am in New York endeavoring against all odds to maintain the same confidence in you as I have had in the past. Facts and developments come so fast and are so overwhelming that it is no longer possible for me to sustain that frame of mind. The facts and developments recall our early discussions wherein you were so enthusiastic with respect to picture-making and your repeated assertions that pictures could be made costing no more than $400,000 to $500,000. These assertions and discussions are corroborated by our written contract which states that the pictures are to cost a maximum of $500,000. I mention this only as an indication of what we originally planned and discussed and I am prompted to point only to the results because of the crisis which has risen in my relationship with my company and my relationship with you.

After detailing the expenditures on the film, pointing out the near-rebellion of the crew, and reminding Welles of his responsibility to RKO, which should have taken precedence over his role as "Ambassador of Good Will," Schaefer continued:

> I am now again put in the painful position where I have to write you a letter which I never, in God's world, thought I would have to write wherein I am begging you to fulfil in an honorable way your obligation and not put such a terrific load on my shoulders. In respect to the latter, I think I have carried that load a long time.
>
> As stated in the opening part of this letter, we agreed to make pictures at a cost of about $500,000. CITIZEN KANE cost nearly $900,000 and, because of all the controversy that arose in connection with it, it is doubtful that we will ever come out whole. Let's forget about the cost as to dollars. What it cost this organization, and me, personally, never can be measured in dollars. All of that, however, I accepted willingly so far as you are concerned. You made a production of which I was proud but which was severely condemned by all my associates and my friends of long standing in the motion picture industry.
>
> The abuse that was heaped upon myself and the company will never be forgotten. I was about as punch-drunk as a man ever was. I made my decision to stand by you and I saw it through. I have never asked anything in return but in common decency I should expect that I would at least have your loyalty and gratitude. To the extent I have received it with respect to the Brazilian enterprise up to the present time, I would say it has been merely lip service.[94]

The final portion of the letter informed Welles that Reisman was empowered to shut the picture down if he deemed it necessary.

In mid-May, Schaefer received more discouraging news. The studio budget department forwarded a report showing that $526,867 had already been expended on *It's All True* and estimated that $595,804 more would be needed to complete it. That placed the total budget in the neighborhood of $1,120,000.[95] Shortly thereafter, Schaefer cabled Reisman:

> After careful thought and considering all circumstances have decided best thing to do discontinue all work and arrange Welles and troupe return. Would much prefer do best we can with film so far received and write off our loss than continue. Be assured this comes only after most careful deliberation and with full recognition of our responsibility to

company and stockholders. . . . Under certain conditions I would be
willing let Welles continue, namely that he deliver to you immediately
complete story outline covering material to date and his plans from
this point on including shooting FOUR MEN RAFT delivering at same
time schedule of shooting days and permitting him finish within a
maximum cost of $30,000.[96]

Additional bad luck struck on the day after this cable was sent. Manuel
Olimpio Meira, one of the four fishermen and a national hero of sorts
known as Jacare, drowned in an accident that occurred while the fisherman's raft was being towed to a filming location. There was no negligence
on RKO's part, but the tragedy did not endear the company, or Welles, to
the local inhabitants.

After further negotiations, Schaefer agreed to allow Welles and the
crew to continue filming until June 8. At that time, the technical crew and
most of the equipment would be shipped back to Hollywood. Since Reisman's arrival, Welles had been working very hard, perhaps because the RKO
executive was constantly looking over his shoulder.[97] Following the departure of the studio contingent (except for Lynn Shores, who would have to
stay behind tying up loose ends and arranging for the shipping of equipment and film), Welles, Wilson, and a small group of his associates would
be allowed to go to Fortaleza for about a month to shoot material for the
section about the four fishermen. Despite the tragic death of Meira, Welles
did not intend to abandon this section of the story. He planned to find
someone to double for the deceased *jangadeiro*.

RKO still hoped to get a picture out of the *It's All True* fiasco.[98] It would
not matter to George Schaefer, however. The film, among other things,
had broken him—just as Reg Armour predicted. Schaefer's tenure as RKO
president was rapidly drawing to a close.

In first position among those other things was the embarrassing prod-
uct. Of the pictures released in the first five months of 1942, only *Joan of
Paris* made a six-figure profit ($105,000). Nearly all of the other A pictures
were hammered by critics and lost money: *Four Jacks and a Jill* ($113,000),
Obliging Young Lady ($118,000), *Valley of the Sun* ($158,000), *Sing Your
Worries Away* ($255,000), *The Tuttles of Tahiti* ($170,000), *Syncopation*
($87,000).

Schaefer shared the blame for the poor pictures with Joseph Breen, the
man who headed up the studio when they were produced. Breen returned
from his Mexican vacation in early May. As rumored, he took up his former post as director of the Production Code Administration instead of
going back to RKO. Geoffrey Shurlock had functioned as acting head of

the censorship board after Breen's departure, but some Hollywood moguls were apparently not pleased with Shurlock's performance.[99] They banded together and lobbied RKO to allow Breen to return to his old job. The studio was more than happy to oblige. By mid-May, Joseph Breen was the chief censor of the industry once again, and Charles Koerner had the "acting" removed from his title as general manager in charge of RKO production.[100] Edward Alperson succeeded Koerner as head of the RKO theater circuit. Koerner had the full support of the RKO board of directors; although he had no production experience, the men at the top seemed convinced that he possessed the right instincts and would give RKO what it needed most—box-office winners.[101]

Shortly after Koerner's official appointment, it began to look as if the new studio chief might never have an opportunity to prove himself. Financial projections indicated that around the middle of June, the company would not have enough cash to meet the studio payroll. Unless more capital could be raised quickly, there appeared to be only two possibilities—the studio would either be closed or plummet once again into receivership. The chances of new funding were not good, because the major ownership groups (Atlas, RCA, the Rockefellers) "could not agree upon any method of getting new money into the company."[102]

George Schaefer was finally held accountable. In late April two board members who represented minority interests, Raymond Bill and Lawrence Green, returned from a fact-finding trip to Hollywood, "where they went all over the RKO production unit with the officers." According to a letter from Burton Turnbull to Nelson Rockefeller, they came back "very much disappointed with the management and very critical of Schaefer—so much so that it is reported they would vote against renewing Schaefer's contract at this time."[103] Two days later, Nelson replied: "I must say there seems to be a growing lack of confidence in our friend."[104] One can almost hear him sigh.

Schaefer had no one left to blame the problems on; no one left to fire. He had ruled RKO like a potentate for more than three years and now had to take responsibility for the organization's dire condition. The numerous box-office failures, the independent deals that had miscarried, the multitude of expensive stories bought but never produced—all had contributed to the current state of affairs. The RKO board was even unhappy about the Sam Goldwyn arrangement. They second-guessed Schaefer's decision to allow Goldwyn such a small distribution fee that RKO would lose money every time it released one of his pictures.[105] *The Little Foxes* and *Ball of Fire*, each brought in more gross film income than any of the 1941–1942 releases except *Suspicion*. Yet the first two Goldwyn RKO releases were carried on company ledgers as $140,000 and $147,000 losers, respectively. And then there was Orson Welles, hanging like the proverbial albatross around Schaefer's neck. He knew he could not hold on much longer.

But George Schaefer refused to give up. In late May he and Malcolm Kingsberg, vice-president of the RKO theaters, attempted to convince several powerful financial groups to invest in the company. Floyd Odlum had made it known that he would be willing to sell his interest in RKO for $7.8 million. If a new financial connection could be made, one willing to bankroll RKO through the uncertain days ahead and absorb Odlum's considerable stock holdings, Schaefer would have a second chance. Several groups with Wall Street and show business connections were mentioned as possibilities, but nothing came of Schaefer's quest.[106]

Having failed with potential investors, George Schaefer tried another eleventh-hour gambit. For some years, the major film companies had maintained a united front with respect to frozen monies in Great Britain. In sympathy with the war effort, the companies had been content to allow their profits to accumulate in the British Isles, asking only for a small percentage of the funds to be disbursed to them each year. At the time, RKO was owed approximately $3 million in frozen English funds. Realizing that this money could avert disaster at least for a time, and perhaps save his job, Schaefer went to Washington and requested that the Treasury Department intercede on RKO's behalf.[107] The plea was to "unfreeze" $2.8 million of RKO's money.[108]

The U.S. government did not receive Schaefer with a deaf ear. A major corporation was in danger of collapse, so an agreement was made to negotiate with British authorities. However, delicate matters of this type always take time, and Schaefer's had run out. With no immediate assurance of funding and RKO approaching collapse, Schaefer tendered his resignation.[109] One day after his meeting at the Treasury Department, he wrote Nelson Rockefeller, informing him of his decision and telling him that it "was physically and mentally impossible to bear up any longer." He added: "I am mostly sorry because of my personal relationship and regard for you."[110]

George J. Schaefer was one of the most iron-willed and vigorous leaders in RKO's history. But today he is remembered, if at all, primarily because of a 1999 HBO film about the *Citizen Kane* controversy, *RKO 281*. Like much of the film's content, its portrayal of Schaefer contains many inaccuracies. As played by Roy Scheider, Schaefer is a spineless "suit" who offers no resistance against Louis B. Mayer and the other studio heads who wish to placate Hearst and destroy Welles's film. In the film's fabricated climax, *Citizen Kane* is saved because of Hearst's massive financial difficulties!

Published opinions of George Schaefer vary widely. On the one hand, John Cromwell, who directed *Abe Lincoln in Illinois,* characterized him as a figurehead "controlled by the financial people."[111] On the other, Orson Welles biographer Roy Alexander Fowler described the RKO president as "at the time the most enlightened and progressive man to be head of a major Hollywood studio."[112] In fact, neither of these descriptions fits.

Although the Rockefeller influence may have affected Schaefer's preference for "quality" production, it is impossible to believe he was the family's puppet. The Rockefellers never became actively involved in the functioning of the studio, and Schaefer was too engaged, too determined to have things his way, to be anyone's puppet. Nor was George Schaefer the "most enlightened" of the various studio heads. Sadly, he was one of the most inept.

Schaefer deserves praise for his attempts to make quality product, to be innovative, and to give special filmmakers more freedom than was generally available throughout Hollywood. But he went about it the wrong way. Making blind deals with untested producers was foolhardy. Had Orson Welles and his cohorts not created *Citizen Kane,* this experiment would be viewed as a total fiasco. Schaefer certainly deserves commendation for fighting to save *Kane.* But it was ultimately a Pyrrhic victory because of the immense toll the battle took on him and on the organization.

Schaefer's intentions were always admirable. He wanted to raise RKO's reputation as well as make it a successful business enterprise. But he failed to accomplish his goals in almost every way. Schaefer demanded the final say in production decisions, yet proved manifestly incapable of nurturing a significant number of films that were either distinctive or profitable. After driving off one of the best production minds in the business, Pandro Berman, Schaefer hired a number of "experts" unable to do much of anything—either because he interfered in their work or because they were ill-suited to their jobs. Harry Edington, J. R. McDonough, Sol Lesser, and Joseph Breen must have considered their production experience at RKO during this period an absolute nightmare.

Some of George Schaefer's other shortcomings are obvious. He allowed the RKO stock company to dwindle to the point that the studio had no stars left under exclusive contract. He spent large sums of money purchasing literary properties that presented significant challenges in their adaptability to the screen. Most were never made, and those that were (such as *Abe Lincoln in Illinois* and *They Knew What They Wanted*) turned out poorly. Schaefer's efforts to cope with the loss of foreign revenue caused by war in Europe and the cash-flow problems necessitated by the consent decree also left much to be desired. All these liabilities contributed to the devastating financial predicament that cost him his presidency. George Schaefer will always deserve a place in some cinematic Hall of Fame for his encouragement of Orson Welles and his defense of *Citizen Kane.* But Schaefer's egocentric approach to corporate management nearly destroyed the "Titan" studio.[113]

APPENDIX

"The whole equation of pictures"
RKO and the Studio System

While many of the pioneering motion picture companies still exist today (unfortunately, RKO is not among them), they now operate very differently than they did in the 1920s through the 1950s. Thus, it should prove valuable to those unfamiliar with the workings of the "old" studio system, and augment the knowledge of individuals who understand the ins and outs of the system, to read this primer on RKO operations. It describes the corporation's general business practices and organizational structure.

RKO's business model was based on a prototype developed by other movie companies, and it functioned in a way that mirrored the operations of its competitors. Each studio, however, had its own organizational quirks and special policies.

Like most of its competitors, RKO was bicoastal with its business head-quarters in New York and its filmmaking plant in Los Angeles. Five of the organizations—MGM, Paramount, Warner Bros., Fox (later Twenti-eth Century–Fox), and RKO—were vertically integrated. They operated a studio to produce their product, a worldwide distribution arm to market it, and a chain of theaters where the films almost always played. Columbia and Universal were also considered major studios, though they did not own theaters, and United Artists rounded out the "Eight Majors" even though UA was purely a distribution enterprise releasing independently made films. In addition, a number of smaller, "poverty row" movie concerns existed during RKO's lifespan. Mascot, Monogram, Republic, Majestic, Grand National, Producers Releasing Corporation (PRC), and a few others turned out, almost exclusively, cheap genre pictures that did not challenge the oligopoly enjoyed by the majors.

MANAGEMENT

RKO's *corporate president* resided at the top of the company's administrative pyramid. He was responsible for the overall performance of the organization and for hiring the other major executives. Though RKO's structure included a large number of subsidiary companies (most set up to handle distribution in specific countries or regions of the world), the pivotal executives were the ones with primary responsibility for *production, distribution,* and *exhibition.* The latter two were based in New York along with the corporate president, while the head of production worked in Hollywood.

Each of the principal components of the corporation was expected to run in an efficient and profitable manner, but everyone knew the most important of the three was production. Success in the movie business depended on the creation of feature films that would attract enough paying customers to generate profits after all the attendant costs had been subtracted. Thus, the *head of production* at the studio was arguably the most critical company employee. In addition to understanding story, personnel, and budget, a superior head of production needed to combine the best qualities of a drill sergeant, a high-stakes poker player, a cheerleader, a psychiatrist, and a soothsayer. It was one of the toughest jobs imaginable, not just in the movie business but in any business. F. Scott Fitzgerald recognized this when he wrote, "Not half a dozen men have ever been able to keep the whole equation of pictures in their heads."[1]

The production chief along with his staff had to develop, oversee, and complete forty or more feature productions a year. One of the overriding issues of RKO's history was "final production authority," the ability to make all-important decisions about which stories would be made and how they would be staffed and cast. At most companies, final decisions of this kind were unquestionably the responsibility of the head of production. But this was not always the case at RKO, where the function was sometimes usurped by the corporate president or another powerful executive. Serious problems always resulted from this managerial rupture.

Industry personnel understood that the movies released by a company like RKO fell into two basic categories: *A pictures* and *B pictures.* The A films were also known as "important productions." They showcased a studio's top talent (actors, producers, directors, writers, technical talent) and were accorded the most fulsome budgets and longest-running times (generally seventy-five minutes or longer). Most important, they were leased to theaters for a percentage of the box-office intake.

B films, which usually ran about an hour, were made for much less money than the A pictures. From top to bottom, they featured individuals who were not considered capable of generating any special excitement among theatergoers. At a time when many theatrical programs included two features, the B film settled comfortably into the bottom half of the double bill. Still, these pictures enjoyed an importance that transcended their economical origins. They (along with the shorts that studios also produced) offered a platform to try out new talent. Some of RKO's most successful writers, directors, and actors cut their teeth on B pictures before graduating to the big leagues. B pictures also provided a reliable source of income to the company. Leased to theaters for a flat fee, most brought in a small profit.

In the mid-1930s, RKO management determined that superintending a full slate of feature releases was too demanding for one individual. After that, the studio added an *executive producer for B films* who worked closely with the production chief but freed him to concentrate on the A pictures. Both men had considerable resources at their disposal. For most of its history, RKO controlled two studios: the main lot at Gower Street and Melrose Avenue in Hollywood and the RKO Pathe lot on Washington Boulevard in Culver City. In addition, the company owned a ranch in Encino where outdoor pictures (mostly Westerns) were shot and large standing sets (such as the cathedral square for *The Hunchback of Notre Dame*) were erected.

Within the studio walls worked hundreds of individuals whose jobs were to help the company make the very best movies. Many of them signed exclusive contracts with RKO and, thus, could be counted on to contribute for a number of years. They were organized by department.

DEPARTMENTS

Acting. A studio's most prominent employees were its contract actors. Spectators loved stars, and the studios whose films featured the most popular performers, such as MGM, were consistently successful. In RKO's early days, the *acting department* included Richard Dix, Irene Dunne, Bert Wheeler and Robert Woolsey, Constance Bennett, Katharine Hepburn, Fred Astaire and Ginger Rogers, as well as an impressive group of character actors including Edna May Oliver, Lee Tracy, Anne Shirley, Eric Blore, Erik Rhodes, and Helen Broderick. For some years beginning in the mid-1930s, the studio maintained an acting workshop where young contract performers received training. Ginger Rogers's mother, Lela, was placed in charge of the budding talent. Lucille Ball studied with Lela and appeared in "Fly Away Home," the first play produced and directed by Rogers at "RKO Radio's Little Theatre on the Lot" in January 1936. The general public was invited to attend, with tickets priced at twenty-five cents.

Writing. The *writing department* brought together experts on adaptation, construction, character, dialogue, and the other skills required to produce quality screenplays in a timely fashion. It included Jane Murfin, Howard Estabrook, Dorothy Yost, Edward Kaufman, Allan Scott, Dudley Nichols, and John Twist.

Directors. The *directors department* listed Luther Reed, Wesley Ruggles, George Cukor, John Cromwell, Mark Sandrich, and George Stevens among its ranks. Most of the men who directed for RKO had to guide several movies a year; they were expected to bring the principal photography of each to a budget-conscious and successful conclusion.

Producers. The *producers department* was particularly important to the studio because its members often initiated projects and worked on even more of them than the directors, closely monitoring their productions from the writing stage through postproduction. Some of RKO's staff producers in the 1930s were Louis Sarecky, Pandro Berman, Kenneth Macgowan, Lou Brock, Cliff Reid, P. J. Wolfson, David Hempstead, and Robert Sisk.

The aforementioned groups were considered the studio elite and, generally speaking, represented the highest-paid members of its staff. But other studio departments also proved crucial to the enterprise. The following departments, listed in alphabetical order so as not to suggest any hierarchy of importance, all did their part to make RKO successful. Without them, the production process would not have been efficient or competitive.

Art Direction. The *art department* (*art direction and set design*) was responsible for designing the environments in which screen action was presented. Headed by Van Nest Polglase throughout the 1930s, it was composed of unit art directors (assigned to individual pictures), sketch artists, draftsmen, and a matte artist (who also worked with the camera effects department). RKO became famous for its sparkling art deco style in the 1930s (especially in the Astaire-Rogers pictures), thanks to the efforts of Polglase, Carroll Clark, and others. Perry Ferguson, who designed the *Citizen Kane* sets, was also an important unit art director.

Camera.   Crews in the *camera department* comprised three to five people each depending on the number of cameras being used in filming. The basic crew included a director of photography, operating cameraman, and an assistant (loader, clapper). Bill Eglington, the head of the department, assigned crews to films (in consultation with the production chief, producer, and studio manager). The department also took care of maintenance, repair and inventory of equipment, and the purchase or building of new devices such as cranes, dollies, lens mounts, and blimps. Camera employees also worked closely with the laboratory that processed the studio's exposed film and made work prints. Since RKO did not operate its own lab, most of its processing and printing was handled by Consolidated Film Industries (CFI). Among the outstanding cinematographers who shot films for RKO were Edward Cronjager, David Abel, J. Roy Hunt, Joseph August, and Nicholas Musuraca. The *still department* was considered part of camera. It employed still photographers to shoot set stills, publicity stills, portraits of the stars, and the like, and maintained a lab for processing and printing those stills. Ernest Bachrach headed this department for many years.

Camera FX.   Process work, miniatures, matte shots and inserts, and optical printer work (such as lap dissolves, wipes, and double exposures) fell to the *camera FX department,* closely allied to the camera department. Its workers usually handled the actual shooting of process backgrounds, second-unit work, and chase sequences. The primary goal was to save money, though camera FX was also responsible for the extraordinary visual effects in *King Kong* and other films. Vernon Walker ran the department, and throughout most of RKO's life, Linwood Dunn worked there as the optical printer specialist. Many industry professionals considered it the best department of its kind in the business.

Casting.   The *casting department* primarily filled secondary roles. Major casting decisions were made by the production head and producer and sometimes the director.

Construction.   The *construction department* employed a small army of carpenters, machinists, plasterers, joiners, laborers, and so forth. They erected the sets based on the plans from the art department. Often their activities took place at night because of the noise factor and the need to have sets ready when the company arrived to shoot each morning. Its members also tore down sets when shooting was finished and stored the ones that were deemed worth saving. They did not build major additions to the studio itself—this work was contracted out. Harold Barry was in charge.

Costume. The *costume department* designed the *new* clothing worn by leading actors in RKO films. Edward Stevenson, head of costume from 1936 to 1950, created the clothing for many of the studio's expensive movies. He also assigned other designers to specific pictures and oversaw the tailor shop and sewing room where the garments were actually produced.

Editing. Jim Wilkinson, the head of the *editorial department* throughout most of the company's lifespan, maintained a good-sized staff including full editors (called cutters), their assistants, negative cutters, stock footage librarians, and technicians to maintain the equipment. Each film had a full editor and at least one assistant assigned to it. The editing process began after the first day of shooting and was ongoing throughout principal photography. Consequently, most editors had a fairly tight rough-cut ready soon after the end of shooting, which would be shown to the producers and the person who was going to score the picture. From this point on, the process was mainly fine-tuning with the editor working closely with the producer, composer, and sound department. Most films were then taken out for preview and brought back to editorial for any last-minute changes. After these were completed, the negative would be cut and shipped to New York, where in most cases the release prints were manufactured. The process was quite efficient, enabling many films to arrive in theaters a few months after shooting began. William Hamilton was considered RKO's most skillful editor, with Ted Cheesman, George Hively, and Henry Berman also often assigned to the company's premier pictures. Several RKO editors eventually moved on to directing, such as George Nicholls, Jr., Edward Dmytryk, Robert Wise, Mark Robson, and John Sturges.

Electrical. Overseen by William Johnson and later Earl Miller, this department maintained and repaired all of the studio's electrical equipment, except that which fell directly under the aegis of the camera, camera FX, editing, and sound departments. Its workers also took charge of the upkeep of wiring, lighting, and telephone lines at the studio. It was involved directly in production in two ways:

1. It assigned gaffers and best boys to pictures. They were experts in the safe handling of a production's electrical needs, including

high-voltage connections for portable generators when a crew was on location.

2. After 1936 the *special effects department,* which included fog, rain, lightning, and snow effects and the handling of explosives, fire, and wind machines, became part of the electrical department.

Makeup and Hair Stylists. The people who worked in this department were among the first to arrive at the studio in the morning. Their job was to make the actors look good and feel *right*—for the roles they were playing. Mel Berns was in charge.

Music. Another substantial department, music was headed up in the early years by one of the greatest composers in film history, Max Steiner. He wrote scores for most of the A pictures and supervised secondary composers, conductors, music librarians, and about fifteen contract musicians. He often had to hire freelance performers to supplement the studio musicians when a score (like that for *King Kong*) required full orchestral treatment. Steiner also assumed responsibility for acquiring the rights to any outside music (old standards, recent popular songs) that a producer wished to use in a picture. For its big musicals, RKO imported several of the leading composers and lyricists of the day (Irving Berlin, Jerome Kern, Cole Porter, the Gershwins, and others). They worked with the music department, but more closely with the production team—especially the producer, director, and Fred Astaire.

Production. This was the domain of the studio manager, a very important position held by Sid Rogell for many years. The department assigned production (or unit) managers, assistant directors, script supervisors, grips, drivers, and other personnel to pictures. It also prepared budgets, received and analyzed production reports (which conveyed what had been accomplished each day and whether the company was ahead or behind schedule and over or under budget). Finally, Rogell and staff assumed responsibility for the scheduling of sound stages and other studio space, which was often at a premium.

Property. The head of this department (Darrell Silvera for most of RKO's history) assigned a prop man or head set dresser to each picture. This person's job was to make sure all props were there on time for shooting and did not "disappear" afterwards. *Greens* (plants, trees, shrubbery) also fell under this department. And *drapery*—which included interior decorators and experts on the upholstering of furniture—also reported to the head of property, though these people would generally work closely with the art department as well. Silvera's biggest challenge was control, maintenance, and inventory of the company's props. RKO had upwards of 300,000 items—furniture, rugs, fixtures, knickknacks. For each picture, new props were usually purchased and others rented (often from the other studios, which exchanged information with one another about their holdings). Individual prop men often had to be detectives to find the necessary items. The department maintained a list of tinsmiths, silversmiths, wood carvers, taxidermists, boat builders, toy makers, portrait artists, and other outside specialists who could be hired as needed for individual pictures.

Sound.   This was one of the largest departments directly involved in the production process. It included sound recorders and mixers, sound effects specialists, rerecording experts, sound effects librarians, sound effects cutters, and a sizable group of technicians for maintenance and repair of all sound and projection equipment. John Aalberg ran this department for years. He would assign sound crews to the pictures—usually a first recorder, second recorder (boom man), and assistant (for microphone placement and the like). Projectionists also fell under the sound department; they were parceled out to different projection rooms from 9 A.M. to midnight to run film for a variety of purposes—dailies, dubbing, music recording, process projection, and the showing of finished films.

Wardrobe.   This department, run by Claire Cramer, worked in collaboration with the costume department. Analogous to the prop department, it maintained an inventory of costumes from earlier films in the hope they could be used again in future pictures (with proper alterations). Eventually, wardrobe ran out of on-site space, so RKO began to store some of its clothing at Western Costume, a rental company close to the Gower Street lot.

Most of the aforementioned departments were expected to do some research and development in addition to their other responsibilities. This was particularly true of the camera, camera FX, and sound departments, where efforts to invent new pieces of equipment that would improve the production process were ongoing. This was also true of the costume and makeup areas, which were constantly experimenting with new fabrics and new makeup compounds that would photograph better. The people who worked in these departments were creative individuals, and they were challenged to develop advancements that could keep the studio on the cutting edge. From early in its history, the Academy of Motion Picture Arts and Sciences became a clearinghouse for these improvements. It began giving awards for the most important breakthroughs in 1931.

All of the above departments participated directly in the filmmaking process. But a number of other departments existed that operated at some remove from filmmaking operations. These were, nonetheless, equally important to the company's mission. They included the following.

Accounting.　This large, bicoastal department assumed responsibility for payroll, timekeeping, insurance matters, tax matters, typing and duplication of all production budgets and the preparation of a number of reports—some daily, some weekly, some monthly, some yearly. One of the most important functions of the Hollywood accountants—from the viewpoint of the production personnel—was computation of overhead, the amount of money it was costing to run the studio. These costs would be figured as a percentage of the actual production outlays for each picture and added to the final budget. As such, overhead charges were a matter of special concern to studio heads, producers, and individuals with profit participations in their films.[2] William H. Clark, C. F. Woit, G. B. Howe, and Garrett Van Wagner were some of the leading executives.

Commitments.　A small staff monitored the studio's contractual commitments to its many employees and alerted executives of any problems. They were especially careful to inform company leaders well in advance of the time when they needed to exercise an option or begin negotiations for renewal of an actor's, writer's, producer's, or director's contract. J. J. Nolan took charge of this department.

Legal.　This sizable department drew up contracts, rendered legal opinions about scripts (especially those containing potentially libelous or defamatory content), and provided the first line of defense with respect to lawsuits filed against RKO. The company also placed prestigious law firms in both Los Angeles and New York on retainer to handle more complicated lawsuits, as well as problems dealing with corporate matters and the functioning of the individual companies. Daniel T. O'Shea ran the legal department for a time in the early 1930s. He would return as RKO president near the end of the corporation's lifespan.

Publicity.　The company maintained a large publicity staff in New York and one in Los Angeles as well. Their job: to make the public aware of, and excited about, RKO films and RKO personalities. Each movie had a unit publicist who constantly sought ways to get positive notices about the production and its actors in all the available communications media. Jobs in publicity also involved developing strong relationships with the chief gossip columnists of the era (Louella Parsons, Hedda Hopper, Jimmy Fidler, Walter Winchell, Sheilah Graham) and pitching or planting stories in trade papers, newspapers, motion picture fan magazines, and other national magazines. In addition, the staff was expected to arrange public and radio appearances for stars and cook up a wide variety of exploitation ideas to promote the films. Perry Lieber supervised publicity in Hollywood for many years.

Research.   A special sort of library, this department answered questions that came primarily from the art, costume, property and writing departments. The studio did care about authenticity in its productions, so the small research staff was expected to provide information about architecture, clothing, furniture, and thousands of other details—everything from the dates of the Ming Dynasty (1368–1644) to whether women wore veils while inside a harem (they did not). The department also worked closely with company lawyers in an effort to head off potential lawsuits. It maintained telephone directories of major cities to make certain the phone numbers of actual people weren't used, particularly when the number belonged to a criminal or other dubious character in the story. If a script contained scenes that took place in the Black Cat Club in Chicago, research would find out if one actually existed and suggest a name change if it did—to avoid legal problems. The department maintained a large number of reference books and clippings files and, if necessary, conducted research at local libraries. It also maintained a list of experts on various subjects who could be hired as consultants if the need arose. Elizabeth (Bessie) McGaffey headed up this department.

Story.   There were two of these as well. The New York story department was more important than the one in Los Angeles because New York was the locus of the publishing and theatrical worlds. Most A pictures were based on material from another medium—novels, plays, nonfiction books, short stories. Thus, the employees, called readers, in the New York office were supposed to maintain good relations with publishing executives who would sometimes give them an advance peek at material. They also had to attend the openings of all the new Broadway plays. They would "cover" each new piece of material, synopsizing it and adding a short critique that either recommended or did not recommend its acquisition by the company. A good reader kept one eye on the potential of the story and the other on the studio's needs and strengths. A similar process took place at the studio, though readers in Hollywood evaluated more original scripts and treatments than published material. The story departments would circulate a "story bulletin" every Friday; producers were supposed to study it and be prepared to discuss the purchase possibilities with the head of production during a meeting the following Tuesday. By that time, however, one of the top executives might already have bought the rights to a property rather than risk losing it to a competitor. Quick response was crucial when the best material became available. The RKO story departments were run by a number of different people through the years. Among the most prominent heads were Katharine Brown, Lillie Messinger, and Collier Young.

Talent.   This bicoastal department hired talent scouts whose job was to discover potential new stars, as well as individuals who might be groomed as producers, writers, or directors. Talent and story were combined for several years in New York, but they eventually split into different departments. The New York staff made screen tests of such individuals as Katharine Hepburn and Fred Astaire. These were sent to the Hollywood studio, where the head of production would decide whether to offer them contracts. While the Hollywood talent department, whose leader was Ben Piazza, spent most of its time evaluating the hordes of neophytes who flocked to the movie capital, its staff members, as well as those from the New York office, were also required to spend some time on the road. Their travels took them to beauty contests, nightclubs, amateur plays, musical performances, and vaudeville theaters in search of the one commodity that separated the most powerful studios from the rest: STARS.

DISTRIBUTION

The lord of RKO's *distribution division* was Ned Depinet. From his office in Rockefeller Center, he and his staff planned the release strategies for hundreds of feature films. Their goal was to convince as many theater owners as possible to book RKO's product. Even though the corporation did own a considerable number of theaters, it could not exist solely on the revenues generated by these houses. It needed independent theater owners, both in the United States and overseas, to make a commitment to RKO. This was not an easy sales job; for much of the company's existence, the RKO merchandise was considered inferior to that of the other vertically integrated studios.

Nevertheless, Depinet and his staff never stopped beating the drum for RKO movies. The first members of their audience were the company's domestic salesmen who worked out of offices geographically situated throughout the country.[3] RKO maintained distribution exchanges (or branches) in Boston, New York, Philadelphia, Charlotte, Atlanta, Cleveland, Detroit, Chicago, Minneapolis, St. Louis, Dallas, Kansas City, Denver, Salt Lake City, Los Angeles, San Francisco, Portland, Seattle, and some fifteen other U.S. cities. It also set up Canadian offices in Montreal, Toronto, Vancouver, and three other cities. The salesmen in each exchange were expected to convince independent theater owners in their region to buy a "block" of RKO pictures. Thus, Depinet and friends needed first off to sell their own employees on the quality of the coming season's movies.

The season lasted from September to the following August and, during a time when theater owners were not allowed to book one film at a time, a block ranged from a full year's worth of product (including shorts and the company newsreel) to about a dozen features. To ramp up excitement about the coming films, the New York office would organize a yearly *sales convention*, usually in late spring or early summer. Chicago was the most popular site because of its central location, but New York and Hollywood occasionally played host. Invited to the convention would be the branch managers and top salesmen; they listened to a preview of the forthcoming films, received hyperbolic promotional material about the product, and then were wined and dined and offered a variety of extracurricular diversions. If it were possible, Depinet loved to include the head of production and a few of the company stars in the festivities. Paul N. Lazarus has offered this colorful description of a typical sales convention: "In the halcyon days, attending a national meeting combined the best features of a revival meeting, a six-day bike race, a saturnalia and a college reunion. The all-day sessions alternated between being inspirational and somnolent; the all-night activities gave you a simple choice of booze, broads or table-stakes poker."[4]

Thus, when they returned to their offices, the conventioneers were primed to sell, sell, sell. Their potential customers, however, were not usually too receptive. Theater owners based their decisions on the recent performance of RKO films, not the free-flowing promises made by a hyped-up supplier. In addition, many were unhappy with the system itself, which they believed was heavily stacked in favor of the major distributors (not just RKO) and placed them in an untenable business position. Besides block booking, they disliked the fact that they were buying blind (no chance to view the movies before they committed to play them), as well as the many examples of obvious collusion among the majors. These "competitors" played each other's films in their theaters, fixed admission prices, and set up a system of zoning and clearance periods that meant the independents were rarely able to show movies when they were still relatively fresh. In the late 1930s, the U.S. government would heed their complaints and bring suit against the majors for monopolistic practices.

The leaders of the foreign sales force would also attend each convention. Their jobs were considerably more taxing than those of the domestic salesmen. In addition to different laws, languages, censorship rules, and business practices, they had to navigate idiosyncratic governmental regulations and cultural sensitivities that Hollywood moviemakers never considered when they produced product with American audience members in mind. Nevertheless, RKO had offices or subdistributors in almost all major countries and realized approximately one-third of its gross income from overseas sales. As previously mentioned, many of the smaller companies incorporated under the RKO corporate umbrella existed to facilitate distribution in Great Britain, India, Australia, France, Spain, Mexico, and other lands.

The distribution office in New York also devised the advertising campaigns for each film, preparing billboards, posters, lobby cards, still photographs, and press books that were sold inexpensively to theater owners. Its workers developed ad slicks as well. These would be used in local newspapers and would form the basis for advertisements in national magazines. Distribution employed a local lab to manufacture release prints, then shipped them to the exchanges that circulated the prints to theaters in their geographical area. The company generally struck around two hundred prints for domestic distribution.

Depinet and staff were always anxious to have a big picture kick off each new release year in September. This, they felt, could really help sell large blocks of product, because theater proprietors would be anxious to secure a run of the special production. The opening of *Top Hat* over the Labor Day weekend in 1935 made them particularly happy. It would soon become the company's most successful film of the decade. The distribution people also believed that the best time to release prime A productions was just before other holiday weekends and encouraged the studio to plan accordingly. The only exception was Independence Day. Because of the summer heat (most theaters were not air conditioned in the 1930s) and because many movie fans went on vacation around that time, July 4 was not considered a favorable time to release a major picture.

THEATERS

The RKO *theater division,* originally comprising some 175 houses, was whittled down to about 125 during the Depression. It was the smallest chain operated by any of the vertically integrated companies. Paramount could count on more than a thousand affiliated houses, Fox and Warner Bros. each had more than five hundred, and MGM (Loew's) controlled about 150. RKO's particular strength existed in the New York City area, where it ran more than thirty-five theaters. It also had a solid presence in the rest of New York State and New Jersey, plus a number of midwestern cities including Chicago, Detroit, Cleveland, Columbus, Cincinnati, Minneapolis, Dayton, Des Moines, and Kansas City. Its weak areas were the southern and western United States, although it did operate houses in Los Angeles and San Francisco.

Similar to foreign distribution, the RKO theater empire included a number of secondary divisions and small companies set up for the operation of theaters where RKO shared ownership with another entity. The Pantages Theater on Hollywood Boulevard in Los Angeles, for example, was a cooperative venture between the Pantages organization and RKO.

Nearly all the RKO theaters were "picture palaces" with more than one thousand seats. Some were quite large. In the New York metropolitan area, for example, the Coliseum, the Center, the 58th Street, the 86th Street, the Brooklyn Albee, the Brooklyn Kenmore, and Keith's in White Plains all boasted more than three thousand seats. So did the Boston in Boston, Keith's Palace in Cleveland, the Palace in Columbus, the Albee in Cincinnati, and the Mainstreet in Kansas City.

As with most of RKO's executive positions except the head of distribution, leadership of the theater division was a revolving-door proposition. Harold B. Franklin and Major L. E. Thompson were the major figures leading RKO's theater arm during the first half of its history, though Nate Blumberg, J. J. O'Connor, Malcolm Kingsberg, Charles Koerner, and Edward L. Alperson also functioned at or near the top at certain times.

Occasionally, friction developed between the theater executives and both production and distribution personnel. Though often referred to as the distribution department's "best customer," RKO theaters did not present RKO films exclusively; they also showcased features and short films produced by other studios. This was acceptable during the times when the company did not have an A picture to release. The theater division was supposed to run in a flexible, efficient fashion and make a profit—everyone knew that. But once in a while some RKO theaters would jump ranks and book a competitor's movie for a date when one of the company's own important films was due to open. The theater men believed they would make more money from the non-RKO release than from the company's own production and made a business decision to boost revenue. But this ignored the importance of launching company product in the very best venues and elicited howls of protest from Hollywood as well as from Ned Depinet's shop. These situations would generally require the intervention of the corporate president to calm the waters.

The studio system was not a monolithic enterprise. It constantly evolved during the 1930s, forties, and fifties as world events, government intervention, and other factors affected its business model. On one level, the history of RKO Radio Pictures is the history of its leaders' efforts to respond to all the forces that impacted the movie industry and to develop an approach and assemble personnel that could make the enterprise a success.

Notes

INTRODUCTION

1. Richard B. Jewell, with Vernon Harbin, *The RKO Story* (London: Octopus Books, 1982).

2. For more information related to this ledger and the data contained within it, see my article, "RKO Film Grosses, 1929–51: The C.J. Tevlin Ledger," *Historical Journal of Film, Radio and Television*, Vol. 14, No. 1 (1994), pp. 37–49.

3. Cari Beauchamp, *Joseph P. Kennedy Presents: His Hollywood Years* (New York: Knopf, 2009).

4. Terry Ramsaye, "Terry Ramsaye Says . . . ," *Motion Picture Herald*, 20 December 1952, p. 14.

CHAPTER 1

1. Perry Lieber, "History of RKO Radio Pictures," 27 May 1946. All references that do not indicate a source are from the RKO archival materials I photocopied in the 1970s and '80s. See the Introduction.

2. Ibid.

3. Cari Beauchamp, *Joseph P. Kennedy Presents: His Hollywood Years* (New York: Knopf, 2009), pp. 36–37.

4. Ibid., p. 13.

5. Ibid., p. 39.

6. Ibid., p. 73.

7. Ibid., p. 82.

8. *Motion Picture News*, 14 July 1928, p. 347.

9. "Radio Corp. and General Electric Acquire Interest in FBO," *Motion Picture News*, 7 January 1928, p. 17.

10. Ibid.

11. Tino Balio, *United Artists: The Company Built by the Stars* (Madison: University of Wisconsin Press, 1976), p. 77.

12. "Radio Corp. and General Electric Acquire Interest in FBO."

13. "Joseph P. Kennedy with Pathe as Advisor; Merger Denied," *Motion Picture News*, 18 February 1928, p. 501.

14. Ibid.

15. "K-A-O Buys FBO Interest," *Motion Picture News*, 3 March 1928, p. 735.

16. Ibid.

17. Edwin Schallert, "Kennedy Urges Conservatism," *Motion Picture News*, 4 August 1928, p. 347.

18. "William Le Baron Again Sounds Warning to Go Slow," *Motion Picture News*, 25 August 1928, p. 612.

19. "R.C.A. Claims Complete Interchangeability; Western Electric Silent," *Motion Picture News*, 11 August 1928, p. 457.

20. "Rivoli Booking Sheds Further Light on Interchangeability Issue," *Motion Picture News*, 18 August 1928, p. 537.

21. "Kennedy Signs Five Year Contract with First National," *Motion Picture News*, 18 August 1928, p. 529.

22. "Kennedy Withdraws from First National," *Motion Picture News*, 25 August 1928, p. 607. See also the description of Kennedy's dealings with the First National board in Beauchamp, *Joseph P. Kennedy Presents*, pp. 201–207.

23. According to Cari Beauchamp, Sarnoff paid too much for FBO, some $7.5 million in a stock swap deal. This was seven and a half times more than Kennedy and his partner Guy Currier had paid only two and half years earlier. See Beauchamp, *Joseph P. Kennedy Presents*, p. 219.

24. "RCA Getting Control of KAO and FBO in 300 Million Deal," *Exhibitors Herald and Moving Picture World*, 13 October 1928, p. 23.

25. Ibid.

26. "Radio-Keith-FBO Deal Closed with Sarnoff as Board Head," *Exhibitors Herald and Moving Picture World*, 27 October 1928, p. 21.

27. Ibid.

28. "Kennedy on RKO Directorate; Sarnoff Silent on Presidency," *Exhibitors Herald and Moving Picture World*, 10 November 1928, p. 25.

29. "Hiram S. Brown Enters Film Industry as RKO President," *Exhibitors Herald and Moving Picture World*, 8 December 1928, p. 27.

30. Martin Quigley, "A New Executive," *Exhibitors Herald and Moving Picture World*, 8 December 1928, p. 20.

31. "Brown Has Full Control at RKO," *Motion Picture Herald*, 27 February 1932, p. 11.

32. Balio, *United Artists*, p. 83.

33. Beauchamp, *Joseph P. Kennedy Presents*, p. 231.

34. "Warners Acquire Stanley Co. in $100,000,000 Deal," *Motion Picture News*, 15 September 1928, p. 843.

CHAPTER 2

1. "RKO Productions Is New FBO Title," *Exhibitors Herald-World*, 19 January 1929, p. 23.

2. "Radio Pictures Advertisement," *Exhibitors Herald-World*, 9 February 1929, pp. 7–10.

3. Ibid., p. 9.

4. "Radio Pictures Is Trade Name Selected for RKO Productions," *Exhibitors Herald-World*, 9 February 1929, p. 39.

5. Martin Quigley, " 'Radio' Pictures," *Exhibitors Herald-World*, 9 February 1929, p. 34.

6. "Radio Pictures," *Exhibitors Herald-World*, 18 January 1930, p. 28.

7. " 'Broadway Melody' Opens in Cleveland at Stillman, March," *Exhibitors Herald-World*, 23 February 1929, p. 28.

8. Bosley Crowther, *The Lion's Share* (New York: E. P. Dutton, 1957), p. 151.

9. "RKO's Production Program Points to Big Sales Year, Says Schnitzer," *Exhibitors Herald-World*, 23 February 1929, p. 28.

10. "LeBaron Outlines RKO $10,000,000 Production Plans," *Exhibitors Herald-World*, 23 February 1929, p. 39.

11. "Soundproof Stages at RKO in $250,000 Program," *Exhibitors Herald-World*, 2 February 1929, p. 42.

12. Douglas Hodges, "RKO Adds $3,000,000 to Its Budget; Expansion Is Planned," *Exhibitors Herald-World*, 17 August 1929, p. 51.

13. "RKO Organization Is in Business to Stay, Says Hiram S. Brown Denying Merger," *Exhibitors Herald-World*, 23 February 1929, p. 25.

14. "Kahane Denies RKO and Paramount Plan Similar Deal in U.S.," *Exhibitors Herald-World*, 8 June 1929, p. 31.

15. "Purchase of Proctor Circuit Welds RKO Theatre Holdings," *Exhibitors Herald-World*, 8 June 1929, p. 21.

16. "Publix Lead Fox by Only 100 in Race for Theatre Control," *Exhibitors Herald-World*, 16 November 1929, p. 21.

17. "RKO's Production Program Points to Big Sales Year, Says Schnitzer."

18. *Upper World*, based on Hecht's story, would eventually be produced by Warner Bros., starring Warren William and Mary Astor and released in 1934.

19. "Most Popular Stars of the Era," *Exhibitors Herald-World*, 9 March 1929, p. 63.

20. RKO Starts Year September 7 with Coast to Coast Campaign," *Exhibitors Herald-World*, 7 September 1929, p. 33.

21. "Le Baron's Contract with RKO Is Renewed for Three Year Term," *Exhibitors Herald-World*, 26 October 1929, p. 26.

22. "Hecht and MacArthur Signed to Write Originals for FBO," *Exhibitors Herald-World*, 12 January 1929, p. 41.

23. Ligon Johnson, letter to RKO Radio Pictures, Inc., 9 November 1937.

24. J. I. Schnitzer, telegram to V. Baravalle, 7 October 1929.

25. Douglas Hodges, "'Rio Rita' a Triumph in Many Ways for Many People," *Exhibitors Herald-World*, 30 November 1929, p. 36.

26. Laurence Stern, "Buying Concentrated in Stocks Assured of 1930 Profits," *Exhibitors Herald-World*, 8 February 1930, p. 26.

27. "RKO Gets Rights to Spoor-Berggren Wide Film Process; Plans Building Sets," *Exhibitors Herald-World*, 25 November 1929, p. 25.

28. "RKO Votes $1,000,000 for Use of Spoor Stereoscopic Process," *Exhibitors Herald-World*, 6 July 1929, p. 63.

29. Each studio's preferred widescreen process employed different-width film and was incompatible with the others. See John Belton, *Widescreen Cinema* (Cambridge: Harvard University Press, 1992), p. 54.

30. "Warner Operetta Begins; RKO Is Using Wide Film Cameras," *Exhibitors Herald-World*, 8 February 1930, p. 35.

31. "RKO Silent on Dropping Spoor Wide Film Process," *Exhibitors Herald-World*, 15 March 1930, p. 21.

32. "Wide Film Finally Passed Up by Public and Producer," *Variety*, 26 November 1930, p. 5.

33. "Irene Dunne Signs with RKO for Singing Roles; Was Hit in Ziegfeld Show," *Exhibitors Herald-World*, 26 April 1930, p. 24.

34. "Leading Film Names, 1930," *Variety*, 31 December 1930, pp. 54–55.

35. "Amos-Andy Not for 2nd Talker," *Variety*, 18 February 1931, p. 2.

36. "Leading Film Names, 1930," p. 55.

37. "Vaudeville as Aid to R-K-O," *Variety*, 1 October 1930, p. 23.

38. "Think Schnitzer West to Stay on Production," *Variety*, 17 December 1930, p. 5.

39. Daniel Okrent, *Great Fortune: The Epic of Rockefeller Center* (New York: Viking, 2003), p. 142.

40. "Big Rockefeller Project Gives Electric Group Strongest Hold," *Exhibitors Herald-World*, 21 June 1930, p. 43.

41. "Radio Corporation of America Annual Report 1930," 10 March 1931, pp. 3, 21.

42. Eugene Lyons, *David Sarnoff* (New York: Harper & Row, 1966), p. 144.

43. "Big Rockefeller Project Gives Electric Group Strongest Hold," p. 44.

44. Beauchamp, *Joseph P. Kennedy Presents*, p. 229.

45. "Definite Denial of Merger Between RKO and Pathe Is Issued by E. B. Derr," *Exhibitors Herald-World*, 22 February 1930, p. 21.

46. Beauchamp, *Joseph P. Kennedy Presents*, p. 300.

47. Benjamin B. Hampton, *History of the American Film Industry* (New York: Dover, 1970), p. 126.

48. Donald Crafton suggests that RKO also needed a source of additional product because in "July 1930, Paramount stopped playing its films in RKO houses." See Crafton, *The Talkies: American Cinema's Transition to Sound, 1926–1931* (Berkeley: University of California Press, 1999), p. 208.

49. "Individual Company Analyses," *Motion Picture Herald*, 3 January 1931, p. 58.

50. "Pathe Only the Nucleus of a Broader Plan," *Motion Picture Herald*, 21 February 1931, p. 18.

51. Ibid.

52. "$10,000,000 Budget in New Season for RKO-Pathe," *Motion Picture Herald*, 7 February 1931, p. 9.

53. "N.Y. Critics All Go for 'Cimarron'; Ad Campaign Set," *Motion Picture Herald*, 31 January 1931, p. 35.

54. FDR quoted in Leon J. Bamberger to RKO Managers, Salesmen, Bookers, 16 July 1934.

55. "Big Royalties for Big Picture Writers," *Motion Picture Herald*, 3 January 1931, p. 62.

56. Charles R. Rogers to Lee Marcus, 1 May 1931.

57. "Brown Borrows Six Millions for RKO Pathe," *Motion Picture Herald*, 20 June 1931, p. 9.

58. Ibid.

59. "Reductions of Admission Price Adopted in Most Large Cities," *Motion Picture Herald*, 24 October 1931, p. 9.

60. "Pathe-Radio May Save $2,000,000 to RKO by Merge," *Variety*, 10 November 1931, p. 4.

61. David O. Selznick, *Memo from David O. Selznick*, ed. Rudy Behlmer (New York: Viking Press, 1972), p. 42.

62. Harry Joe Brown, memorandum to All Department Heads, 2 November 1931.

63. Ibid.

64. Rogers continued to work in the industry for almost twenty years, primarily as a producer. In 1936 he became head of production for Universal, but retained the position only until 1938.

65. "The Best Money Film Stars," *Variety*, 5 January 1932, p. 38.

66. "Radio Comes to Screenland and Adventures Enroute," *Motion Picture Herald*, 16 April 1932, p. 13.

67. "Depinet Becomes Pathe G.M.," *Motion Picture Herald*, 28 February 1931, p. 18.

68. "RKO in Dilemma over Refinancing," *Motion Picture Herald*, 21 November 1931, p. 24.

69. "RKO Primer," *Time*, 7 December 1931, p. 75.

70. "Hiram Brown Unusually Frank Telling Legmen All about RKO," *Variety*, 8 December 1931, p. 7.

71. "RKO Theatres' Big Net," *Variety*, 8 December 1931, p. 27.

72. "RKO Gets Its New Money Jan. 2," *Variety*, 29 December 1931, p. 1.

73. "RKO Primer."

74. "Radio and Pathe to Deliver '31–'32 Films," *Motion Picture Herald*, 21 November 1931, p. 25. By "negative quality," Marcus meant the quality of the

final negative, that is, the conformed negative of the production from which release prints were then struck for distribution.

75. Thomas Schatz, *The Genius of the System* (New York: Metropolitan Books, 1996), p. 87.

76. "RKO Reports a Net Loss but Gains in Theatre Operation," *Motion Picture Herald*, 12 March 1932, p. 28.

CHAPTER 3

1. "New Chief of Theatre Operation Expected as Next Move in RKO," *Motion Picture Herald*, 9 January 1932, p. 10.

2. "Brown Has Full Control at RKO," *Motion Picture Herald*, 27 February 1932, p. 11.

3. His career as a producer would not be memorable; later, he became co-owner of Western Costume, the leading costume rental house in Hollywood.

4. "Aylesworth Made RKO President; Brown in an Advisory Capacity," *Motion Picture Herald*, 16 April 1932, p. 13.

5. Ibid.

6. David Selznick, memorandum to B. B. Kahane, 9 May 1932.

7. LeBaron would enjoy better fortune at Paramount, where he produced *She Done Him Wrong*, starring Mae West, and *It's a Gift*, one of W. C. Fields's funniest movies. In 1938 he took over as the studio's production chief, but his tenure in the position was short-lived. In the early 1940s, he began producing for Twentieth Century–Fox. There he guided such pictures as *The Gang's All Here* and *Pin-Up Girl*.

8. "Notes on Interview with Merlin H. Aylesworth," RKO Publicity Department, 14 April 1932.

9. "Rough Notes of Luncheon Address Presented to the Academy by M. H. Aylesworth," 13 June 1932.

10. Ibid.

11. Martin Quigley, "Mr. Aylesworth's Bad News," *Motion Picture Herald*, 18 June 1932, p. 7.

12. "Aylesworth Sees Theatre Revival," *Motion Picture Herald*, 25 June 1932, p. 22. For more information on the developing relationship between the movies and radio, see my article, "Hollywood and Radio: Competition and Partnership in the 1930s," *Historical Journal of Film, Radio and Television*, Vol. 4, No. 2 (1984), pp. 125–141; and Michele Hilmes, *Hollywood and Broadcasting* (Urbana: University of Illinois Press, 1990).

13. "RKO 10% Cut Now General," *Variety*, 26 January 1932, p. 15.

14. Martin Quigley, "The Old Red Rooster," *Motion Picture Herald*, 13 February 1932, p. 7.

15. "RKO Quarter Loss Is $2,166,713.67," *Motion Picture Herald*, 14 May 1932, p. 35.

16. Martin Quigley, "David Hits Out," *Motion Picture Herald*, 30 April 1932, p. 7.

17. Mike Steen, "A Louis B. Mayer American Film Institute Oral History of Pandro S. Berman," American Film Institute Archives, Los Angeles, n.d., p. 15.

18. "RKO Radio to Issue 62 Features, 140 Shorts, Convention Is Told," *Motion Picture Herald*, 21 May 1932, p. 82.

19. Ibid., p. 83.

20. B. B. Kahane to David Selznick, 4 June 1932.

21. Ibid.

22. B. B. Kahane, telegram to M. H. Aylesworth, 11 July 1932.

23. Ibid.

24. Merian C. Cooper, memorandum to C. D. White, 18 July 1932.

25. B. B. Kahane, letter to M. H. Aylesworth, 25 July 1932.

26. Ibid.

27. "RKO Reports $1,375,170 Loss for Six Months Ended June 30," *Motion Picture Herald*, 27 August 1932, p.24.

28. "Changes in 34 RKO Theatres Raise Gross Profit 237 Per Cent," *Motion Picture Herald*, 27 August 1932, p. 19.

29. M. H. Aylesworth to B. B. Kahane, 21 July 1932.

30. David Selznick to B. B. Kahane, 21 July 1932. Sam Jaffe (not the actor) was later hired, though his RKO employment would not last long.

31. Ibid.

32. B. B. Kahane to M. H. Aylesworth, 26 July 1932.

33. M. H. Aylesworth, telegram to B. B. Kahane, 2 August 1932.

34. David Selznick, memorandum to B. B. Kahane, 4 August 1932.

35. Ibid.

36. B. B. Kahane to M. H. Aylesworth, 4 August 1932.

37. M. H. Aylesworth to B. B. Kahane, 17 August 1932.

38. Ibid.

39. B. B. Kahane to M. H. Aylesworth, 18 August 1932.

40. M. H. Aylesworth, telegram to B. B. Kahane, 12 October 1932.

41. "Radio's Smash Contest," *Motion Picture Herald*, 27 August 1932, p. 56.

42. "Radio to Start Unit Production Soon: Selznick," *Motion Picture Herald*, 19 November 1932, p. 15.

43. B. B. Kahane to M. H. Aylesworth, 1 November 1932.

44. Ibid.

45. Gavin Lambert, *On Cukor* (New York: G. P. Putnam's Sons, 1972), pp. 42–44.

46. Lee Marcus to David Selznick, 9 June 1932.

47. Lambert, *On Cukor*, p. 60.

48. David Selznick, telegram to Lee Marcus, 22 June 1932.

49. B. B. Kahane to M. H. Aylesworth, 31 October 1932.

50. David Selznick to Katharine Brown, 27 January 1933.

51. Fred Astaire, *Steps in Time* (New York: Harper & Brothers, 1959), p. 213.

52. B. B. Kahane to M. H. Aylesworth, 3 October 1932.

53. Selznick, *Memo from David O. Selznick,* p. 43.

54. David Selznick to B. B. Kahane, Ned Depinet, Harold Franklin, Robert Sisk, 1 September 1932.

55. David Selznick, memorandum to B. B. Kahane, 25 July 1932.

56. B. B. Kahane to M. H. Aylesworth, 27 September 1932.

57. David Selznick, memorandum to Ned Depinet, Robert Sisk, B. B. Kahane, 30 August 1932.

58. B. B. Kahane to Ned Depinet, 4 October 1932.

59. David Selznick, memorandum to B. B. Kahane, 20 October 1932.

60. Harold Franklin, memorandum to B. B. Kahane, 6 December 1932.

61. Okrent, *Great Fortune,* p. 206.

62. Ibid., p. 238.

63. "RKO Roxy Prices from 40c to $1.50; To Open Dec. 29," *Motion Picture Herald,* 26 November 1932, p. 26.

64. "Two Radio City Theatres Lavish," *Motion Picture Herald,* 31 December 1932, p. 26.

65. Myer Kutz, *Rockefeller Power* (New York: Simon & Schuster, 1974), p. 61.

66. Terry Ramsaye, "Static in Radio City," *Motion Picture Herald,* 14 January 1933, p. 11.

67. Ibid.

68. "Music Hall Starts Combination Policy as RKO Roxy Continues," *Motion Picture Herald,* 14 January 1933, p. 25.

69. Martin Quigley, "RKO's Autograph Album," *Motion Picture Herald,* 3 December 1932, p. 7.

70. The Rockefellers, however, would never acquire a controlling interest in RKO, as has been asserted in a number of different works. See, for example, Cary Reich, *The Life of Nelson Rockefeller: Worlds to Conquer, 1908–1958* (New York: Doubleday, 1996), p. 99.

71. "Selznick Out," *Time,* 26 December 1932, p. 36.

72. M. H. Aylesworth, telegram to B. B. Kahane, 2 February 1933.

73. Ibid.

74. Selznick, *Memo from David O. Selznick,* pp. 51–52.

75. Ibid., p. 53.

76. Ibid.

77. Fay Wray, *On the Other Hand: A Life Story* (New York: St. Martin's Press, 1989), p. 103.

78. Selznick, *Memo from David O. Selznick,* p. 44.

79. B. B. Kahane, telegram to M. H. Aylesworth, 6 February 1933.

80. Sid Grauman to M. C. Cooper, 24 March 1933.

81. Selznick, *Memo from David O. Selznick,* p. 48.

82. Ibid., p. 50.

CHAPTER 4

1. B. B. Kahane to Merlin Aylesworth, 23 January 1933.

2. "RKO Receivers Sought in Three Separate Actions," *Motion Picture Herald*, 28 January 1933, p. 16.

3. "Committees Named in RKO Suits," *Motion Picture Herald*, 4 February 1933, p. 26.

4. "Then Came the Dawn," *Business Week*, 8 February 1933, p. 12.

5. Louis Nizer, "The Magic of Equity Receivership," *Motion Picture Herald*, 25 February 1933, p. 28.

6. Ibid., p. 29.

7. "Reorganizing of RKO Underway," *Motion Picture Herald*, 11 February 1933, p. 16.

8. "Committees Named in RKO Suits."

9. Robert Sobel, *RCA* (New York: Stein & Day, 1986), p. 94.

10. Ibid., p. 99.

11. B. B. Kahane to M. H. Aylesworth, 13 February 1933.

12. Ibid.

13. Merian Cooper, telegram to Katharine Hepburn, 9 March 1933.

14. "Hollyday," *Time*, 20 March 1933, pp. 41–42.

15. "7 Companies on Full Pay," *Motion Picture Herald*, 15 April 1933, p. 9.

16. "Cooper Giving Free Hand to His Staff," *Motion Picture Herald*, 1 April 1933, p. 18.

17. B. B. Kahane to William Mallard, 10 May 1933.

18. "Cooper Giving Free Hand to His Staff."

19. B. B. Kahane to Merlin Aylesworth, 10 May 1933.

20. Ibid.

21. "RKO Reduces Theatre Holdings," *Motion Picture Herald*, 17 June 1933, p.27.

22. Harold B. Franklin to M. H. Aylesworth, 23 June 1933.

23. M. H. Aylesworth, memorandum to H. R. Lamb, 23 June 1933.

24. "RKO Roxy Second Run," *Motion Picture Herald*, 27 May 1933, p. 17.

25. "Westerns on Way Out as Public Taste Changes," *Motion Picture Herald*, 1 April 1933, p. 9.

26. "84 Features with Music Available for Booking in Next Few Months," *Motion Picture Herald*, 20 May 1933, p. 9.

27. "Radio Schedules 52 for 1933–34," *Motion Picture Herald*, 1 July 1933, p. 33.

28. Ibid.

29. W. L. Brown, report on Radio-Keith-Orpheum Corporation, 18 July 1933.

30. B. B. Kahane, telegram to M. H. Aylesworth, 10 October 1933.

31. B. B. Kahane to M. H. Aylesworth, 6 June 1933.

32. B. B. Kahane to Ned Depinet, 10 November 1933.

33. "J. R. McDonough, Realist," *Motion Picture Herald,* 12 August 1933, p. 17.

34. B. B. Kahane to J. R. McDonough, 5 October 1933.

35. B. B. Kahane to J. R. McDonough, 7 October 1933.

36. J. R. McDonough to B. B. Kahane, 16 October 1933.

37. B. B. Kahane to J. R. McDonough, 23 October 1933.

38. B. B. Kahane to J. R. McDonough, 10 November 1933.

39. "Fran," memorandum to J. R. McDonough, 17 November 1933.

40. David O. Selznick to Ned Depinet, 18 October 1933. Years later, with his eyes focused on posterity, Selznick would claim that the RKO theater proprietors had encouraged him to modernize the story. See Selznick, *Memo from David O. Selznick,* p. 415.

41. Merian Cooper to Ned Depinet, 28 July 1933.

42. B. B. Kahane, telegram to Ned Depinet, 31 October 1933.

43. "Little Women Sets Music Hall Record," *Motion Picture Herald,* 25 November 1933, p. 46.

44. Merian Cooper to David Selznick, 2 November 1933.

45. Robert Sisk to Ned Depinet, 18 December 1933.

46. B. B. Kahane to J. R. McDonough, 15 November 1933.

47. Throughout its early history, RKO was much more willing to allow its top talent to share in the profits of their pictures than were other companies. Besides Hepburn, Fred Astaire, Irene Dunne, John Ford, Irving Berlin, and others eventually became RKO profit participants. At MGM, on the other hand, Louis B. Mayer, Irving Thalberg, J. Robert Rubin, and other executives and producers had percentage deals, but the studio's numerous stars received straight salaries.

48. J. R. McDonough to B. B. Kahane, 17 November 1933.

49. J. R. McDonough to Katharine Hepburn, 22 January 1935.

50. "RKO Net Loss for Year Is Halved: 58 of 162 Owned Houses Dropped," *Motion Picture Herald,* 11 November 1933, pp. 56–60.

51. Ibid., p. 60.

52. Quotations in this and the following paragraph are drawn from Merian Cooper, memorandum to the Board of Directors, 18 December 1933.

53. Quoted in Thomas W. Bohn and Richard L. Stromgren, *Light and Shadows* (Port Washington, NY: Alfred Publishing, 1975), p. 236.

54. Merian Cooper, memorandum to the Board of Directors.

55. B. B. Kahane to Ned Depinet, 7 December 1933.

56. M. C. Cooper, memoranda to All Producers and Directors, 11 January 1934 and 16 January 1934.

57. "Irving Trust Report Notes RKO Gaining," *Motion Picture Herald,* 26 May 1934, p. 12.

58. Victor Shapiro, "The Hollywood Scene," *Motion Picture Herald,* 10 February 1934, p. 16.

59. "McDonough to Head RKO Radio; Cooper Again Production Chief," *Motion Picture Herald,* 24 February 1934, p. 19.

60. Ibid.

61. Fred Astaire to Leland Hayward, 9 February 1934.

62. Fred Astaire to Leland Hayward, 12 February 1934.

63. Leland Hayward to Fred Astaire, 16 February 1934.

64. Pandro Berman to Leland Hayward, 26 February 1934.

65. Katharine Hepburn to RKO Studios, Inc., 13 February 1934.

66. Merian Cooper to J. R. McDonough, 2 April 1934.

67. Merian Cooper to Merlin Aylesworth, 2 April 1934.

68. Merlin Aylesworth to Merien [*sic*] Cooper, 16 April 1934.

69. J. R. McDonough, memorandum of telephone conversation with A. H. McCausland, 17 May 1934.

70. J. R. McDonough, telegram to A. H. McCausland, 20 May 1934.

71. Pandro Berman to J. R. McDonough, 31 March 1934.

72. B. B. Kahane to J. R. McDonough, 22 March 1934.

73. Pandro Berman to Ned Depinet, 27 March 1934.

74. B. B. Kahane to J. R. McDonough, 22 March 1934.

75. Ibid.

76. Pandro Berman to B. B. Kahane, 12 June 1934.

77. Ibid.

78. B. B. Kahane, memorandum to Pandro Berman, 13 June 1934.

79. "Plots and Plans," *Time*, 25 June 1934, p. 40.

80. Broadcasters Organize Raid on Hollywood Film Talent," *Motion Picture Herald*, 14 April 1934, p. 9.

81. Ibid.

82. Victor M. Shapiro, "The Hollywood Scene," *Motion Picture Herald*, 2 June 1934, p. 31.

83. Pandro Berman, telegram to Ned Depinet, 10 April 1934.

84. B. B. Kahane, memorandum to Lou Brock, 25 April 1934.

85. Ibid.

86. B. B. Kahane to Ned Depinet, 14 July 1934.

87. Pandro Berman, telegram to Katharine Hepburn, 3 June 1936.

88. "Irving Trust Report Notes RKO Gaining," *Motion Picture Herald*, 26 May 1934, p. 12.

89. "RKO, Paramount Ask Reorganizing," *Motion Picture Herald*, 16 June 1934, p. 12.

90. "More than 8,000,000 Attended Radio City Houses in First Year," *Motion Picture Herald*, 20 January 1934, p. 27.

91. "Rothafel Resigns Post as Director of Music Hall," *Motion Picture Herald*, 13 January 1934, p. 22.

CHAPTER 5

1. "Irving Trust Is Named Permanent Trustee of RKO," *Motion Picture Herald*, 30 June 1934, p. 38.

2. Brock would return in the late 1930s, once again assuming command of the RKO shorts unit in 1939.

3. "RKO Schedules 50 for New Season," *Motion Picture Herald*, 23 June 1934, p. 12.

4. Ibid., p. 18.

5. "RKO Payments Await Agreement," *Motion Picture Herald*, 13 October 1934, p. 43.

6. "Reorganizing of RKO Is Started," *Motion Picture Herald*, 3 November 1934, p. 15.

7. Fred Astaire to Katharine Brown, 6 November 1933.

8. According to Berman, Brock was offered the property but turned it down to produce *Down to Their Last Yacht*. He told Berman, "I can blow better scripts out of my nose." See Bob Thomas, *Astaire the Man, the Dancer* (New York: St. Martin's Press, 1984), p. 94.

9. B.B. Kahane, memorandum to Pandro Berman, 25 September 1934.

10. Ned Depinet to J.R. McDonough, 22 October 1934.

11. Arlene Croce, *The Fred Astaire & Ginger Rogers Book* (New York: Galahad Books, 1972), p. 39.

12. J.R. McDonough to M.H. Aylesworth, 21 January 1935.

13. Ibid.

14. Perry Lieber, "History of RKO Radio Pictures," 27 May 1946, p. 6.

15. J.R. McDonough to M.H. Aylesworth, 18 January 1935.

16. Fred Astaire to Merian Cooper, 26 January 1934.

17. Ned Depinet to Jules Levy, 4 February 1935.

18. Jerome Kern to Pandro Berman, 8 February 1935.

19. "Improved Receipts and Product Lead the Parade in Review of 1935," *Motion Picture Herald*, 4 January 1936, p. 65.

20. "RKO Loss Cut to $310,575 in 1934," *Motion Picture Herald*, 15 June 1934, p. 63.

21. "RKO Admissions Up $46,065 Weekly," *Motion Picture Herald*, 20 July 1935, p. 54.

22. "RKO Loss Cut to $310,575 in 1934."

23. "RKO Admissions up $46,065 Weekly," p. 56.

24. "50 Color Attempts in 50 Years," *Motion Picture Herald*, 1 June 1935, p. 45.

25. Kenneth Macgowan to John Hay Whitney, 21 June 1934, The Kenneth Macgowan Collection, UCLA Theater Arts Library, box 9, file 14 (hereinafter referred to as Kenneth Macgowan Collection).

26. Ibid.

27. "Lowell Sherman, Actor, Director, Dies in Hollywood," *Motion Picture Herald*, 5 January 1935, p. 44.

28. "'Becky Sharp' in Color May Open Movies' Third Era," *Newsweek*, 22 June 1935, p. 22.

29. Kenneth Macgowan to John Hay Whitney, 16 May 1935, Kenneth Macgowan Collection, box 29, file 15.

30. John Speaks to Kenneth Macgowan, 29 June 1936, Kenneth Macgowan Collection, box 31, file 3.

31. A portion of the Orson Welles picture *It's All True* was shot in three-strip Technicolor in 1942, but that film would never be released.

32. Leland Hayward to B. B. Kahane, 16 October 1935.

33. Pandro Berman to B. B. Kahane, 14 March 1935.

34. Years later, Ford would recall the circumstances that surrounded the film's production in an entertaining but thoroughly fanciful manner. Among other things, he claimed Joseph Kennedy was running RKO at the time. See Peter Bogdanovich, *John Ford* (Berkeley: University of California Press, 1978), pp. 59–64.

35. Fred Astaire to Pandro Berman, n.d.

36. "Exhibitors Lose 'Top Hat' Fight," *Motion Picture Herald*, 9 November 1935, p. 24.

37. "Improved Receipts and Product Lead the Parade in Review of 1935," p. 67.

38. W. G. Van Schmus to Pandro Berman, 18 September 1935.

39. "The Biggest Money Making Stars of 1934–35," *Motion Picture Herald*, 28 December 1935, p. 13.

40. Twitchell, "Story Report on *She*."

41. Cooper was correct; the story has been filmed several times since he produced it.

42. Gahagan is remembered more for her career in politics than for her show business efforts. Under her married name, Helen Gahagan Douglas, she served three terms in the U.S. House of Representatives before losing to Richard Nixon in a bitterly fought campaign for a Senate seat in 1950.

43. J. R. McDonough, memorandum to Merian Cooper, 8 February 1935. Years later Cooper claimed that he had been promised a budget of $1 million for each picture, but RKO cut the budgets in half when *She* was deep in pre-production. This appears not to have been the case, and Cooper ended up spending more than $500,000 on each film anyway. See Mark Cotta Vaz, *Living Dangerously: The Adventures of Merian C. Cooper* (New York: Villard, 2005), p. 259.

44. Their effects work on *Son of Kong* was also substandard, though they had a reasonable excuse. The quickie sequel, released near the end of 1933, had a final budget of only $269,000.

45. RKO rereleased *She* and *The Last Days of Pompeii* on a double bill in 1949. They did well, recouping their original losses.

46. "Odlum and Lehmans Buy Large Part of RCA's Control of RKO," *Motion Picture Herald*, 19 October 1935, p. 54.

47. Kenneth L. Fisher, *100 Minds That Made the Market* (Woodside, CA: Business Classics, 1993), p. 153.

48. Ibid.

49. "Rathvon Named by Odlum to Handle RKO Revamping," *Motion Picture Herald*, 26 October 1935, p. 46.

50. "Rockefeller Claim Stirs RKO Action," *Motion Picture Herald*, 2 November 1935, p. 34.

51. "Vaudeville Sinks to Lowest Ebb as 'Back to Film' Movement Grows," *Motion Picture Herald*, 31 August 1935, p. 17.

52. "The Men Who Revived Paramount Go to Work on RKO," *Newsweek*, 16 November 1935, p. 30.

53. Ibid.

54. L. P Yandell, memorandum to David Sarnoff, 4 October 1938, folder 675, box 90, Business Interests series, Record Group 2 OMR, Rockefeller Family Archives, Rockefeller Archive Center, Sleepy Hollow, New York (hereinafter cited as RAC).

55. "Spitz Starts Duties with RKO; Says Depinet Will Retain Post," *Motion Picture Herald*, 16 November 1935, p. 24.

56. "Briskin at Radio," *Motion Picture Herald*, 28 December 1935, p. 9.

57. Samuel Briskin to Leo Spitz, 23 December 1935.

58. Samuel Briskin to Leo Spitz, 29 January 1936.

59. " 'Free Delivery' of Screen Talent Hailed at NBC Coast Opening," *Motion Picture Herald*, 14 December 1935, p. 15.

60. "Hollywood Back on the Air to Exploit Pictures and Players," *Motion Picture Herald*, 7 September 1935, p. 15.

61. " 'Free Delivery' of Screen Talent Hailed at NBC Coast Opening."

62. Martin Quigley, "Radio Competition," *Motion Picture Herald*, 14 December 1935, p. 29.

63. "Hollywood Back on the Air to Exploit Pictures and Players."

64. "Attendance, Revenues, Profits Continue Rising Survey Shows," *Motion Picture Herald*, 2 May 1936, p. 61.

CHAPTER 6

1. B. B. Kahane to Sam Briskin, 8 January 1936.

2. Frank Capra, *The Name above the Title* (New York: Macmillan, 1971), p. 90.

3. Samuel Briskin to Jules Levy, 6 April 1936.

4. Pandro Berman, letter to Leo Spitz, 9 April 1936.

5. Leo Spitz to Pandro Berman, 13 April 1936.

6. Samuel Briskin to Leo Spitz, 29 January 1936.

7. Samuel Briskin to Leo Spitz, 31 January 1936.

8. Ibid.

9. Alfred Wright to RKO Studios, Inc., 26 February 1936.

10. B. B. Kahane, telegram to Leo Spitz, 25 March 1936.

11. Emanuel Levy, *George Cukor, Master of Elegance* (New York: William Morrow, 1994), p. 88.

12. Lambert, *On Cukor*, pp. 96–97; Charles Higham, *Kate* (New York: W. W. Norton, 1975), pp. 77–78.

13. Ned Depinet to B. B. Kahane, 4 February 1936.

14. B. B. Kahane to Ned Depinet, 6 February 1936.

15. B. B. Kahane to Ned Depinet, 12 February 1936.

16. Quotations in this and the following paragraph are drawn from Sam Briskin, telegram to Leo Spitz, 28 May 1936.

17. Pandro Berman to Katharine Hepburn, 3 June 1936.

18. Frank O'Heron, memorandum to B. B. Kahane, 2 July 1934.

19. Max Steiner, memorandum to B. B. Kahane, 4 October 1934.

20. "B. B. Kahane at Columbia Pictures as Vice-President," *Motion Picture Herald*, 15 August 1936, p. 38.

21. Sam Briskin to Leo Spitz, 11 April 1936.

22. Pandro Berman to Leo Spitz, 25 May 1936.

23. Sadly, the Gershwin brothers would write only two scores for RKO films. After completing the music for *Shall We Dance* and *A Damsel in Distress*, both released in 1937, George Gershwin died of a malignant brain tumor at age thirty-eight.

24. "Jesse Lasky Joins Radio to Work as Unit Producer," *Motion Picture Herald*, 24 October 1936, p. 22.

25. Tino Balio, *United Artists: The Company Built by the Stars* (Madison: University of Wisconsin Press, 1976), p. 137.

26. "Agreement Between Walt Disney Productions, Ltd., and RKO Radio Pictures, Inc.," 2 March 1936.

27. Al Finestone, "Aylesworth Doubts Obstacle of Television to Box Office," *Motion Picture Herald*, 14 March 1936, p. 65.

28. Ibid.

29. "Aylesworth on the Disney Deal," *Motion Picture Herald*, 14 March 1936, p. 22.

30. "Rockefeller-RKO Claim Settlement Hits a Stalemate," *Motion Picture Herald*, 16 May 1936, p. 60.

31. "RKO Reorganized by January—Spitz," *Motion Picture Herald*, 27 June 1936, p. 40.

32. "'Street' and Broadway both Await RKO Plan," *Motion Picture Herald*, 24 October 1936, p. 48.

33. Astaire, *Steps in Time*, pp. 223–227.

34. Pandro Berman to Leo Spitz, 8 June 1936.

35. Maxwell Anderson to Harold Freeman, 28 April 1936.

36. Samuel Briskin to Leo Spitz, 16 September 1936.

37. Leo Spitz to Samuel Briskin, 22 September 1936.

38. "RKO Reorganization Plan Sets Capitalization of $33,000,000," *Motion Picture Herald*, 28 November 1936, p. 55.

39. Ibid.

40. Ibid., p. 56.

41. "Kennedy to Study RCA Structure; Lohr Succeeds Aylesworth in NBC," *Motion Picture Herald*, 4 January 1936, p. 31; "M. H. Aylesworth Quits at N.B.C., To Stay at RKO," *Motion Picture Herald*, 3 October 1936, p. 71.

42. James P. Cunningham, "Aylesworth 'On the Air' for Radio-Screen Understanding," *Motion Picture Herald*, 18 July 1936, p. 45.

43. "51 Million for Talent Is Radio Reply to Theatre," *Motion Picture Herald*, 5 September 1936, p. 13.

44. Pandro Berman to Fred Astaire, 18 May 1936.

45. Cunningham, "Aylesworth 'On the Air' for Radio-Screen Understanding," p. 46.

46. "Jack Cohn Answers Aylesworth; Urges War on Radio Appearances," *Motion Picture Herald*, 8 August 1936, p. 61.

47. "RCA Annual Report for 1936," pp. 10–11.

48. "Higher Grosses, Earnings Presage Great Year Ahead," *Motion Picture Herald*, 2 January 1937, p. 15.

49. Ibid.

50. "RKO Reports Net of $2,514,734 for 12 Months," *Motion Picture Herald*, 6 March 1937, p. 72.

51. "Aylesworth Joins Scripps-Howard," *New York Times*, 2 February 1937, p. 19.

52. Minutes of "A Special Meeting of the Board of Directors of RKO RADIO PICTURES," 19 March 1937, p. 16. The minutes also reveal that Aylesworth derived no compensation, beyond his NBC salary, for serving as corporate president of RKO from 1932 to 1935.

53. "Film Companies Blanket Radio with Exhibitor Aids," *Motion Picture Herald*, 30 January 1937, pp. 13–14.

54. " 'B' Films Become Issue of Studio and Theatre," *Motion Picture Herald*, 13 February 1937, p. 13.

55. Lou Lusty, memorandum to Sam Briskin, 28 January 1937.

56. Samuel Briskin, memorandum to Leo Spitz, 21 January 1937.

57. Samuel Briskin, memorandum to Lee Marcus, 12 May 1937.

58. Lee Marcus, memorandum to Sam Briskin, 14 May 1937.

59. Leo Spitz to Sam Briskin, 17 September 1937.

60. Ned Depinet to Leo Spitz, 29 November 1937.

61. Samuel Briskin, memorandum to Lou Lusty, 2 October 1937.

62. G. B. Howe, memorandum to Ross Hastings, 25 September 1937.

63. Lou Lusty, memorandum to Sam Briskin, 10 August 1937. See also my article, "How Howard Hawks Brought *Baby* Up: An *Apologia* for the Studio System," in Leo Braudy and Marshall Cohen, eds., *Film Theory and Criticism*, 7th edition, (New York: Oxford University Press, 2009), pp. 515–522.

64. Leo Spitz to Sam Briskin, 25 August 1937.

65. Ibid.

66. Lou Lusty, memorandum to Sam Briskin, 2 October 1937.

67. "RKO Radio Lists 56 features and 198 Short Subjects for 1937–38," *Motion Picture Herald*, 19 June 1937, p. 45.

68. Ibid., p. 46.

69. Lou Lusty, memorandum to Sam Briskin, 25 August 1937.

70. Ned Depinet to Sam Briskin, 19 August 1937.

71. Leo Spitz to Sam Briskin, 6 August 1937.

72. Ibid.

73. Sam Briskin to Leo Spitz, 26 August 1937.

74. Sam Briskin to Leo Spitz, 14 September 1937.

75. Leo Spitz to Sam Briskin, 16 September 1937.

76. "Special Master Named for RKO Report Hearing," *Motion Picture Herald*, 26 June 1937, p. 14.

77. "Only $21,176,694 of Claims against RKO Allowable," *Motion Picture Herald*, 26 June 1937, p. 14.

78. "Opposition to Plan for RKO Draws Attack," *Motion Picture Herald*, 3 July 1937, p. 38.

79. "Briefs Filed in Plan for RKO," *Motion Picture Herald*, 31 July 1937, p. 49.

80. N. Peter Rathvon to Sam Briskin, 4 August 1937.

81. Samuel Briskin, letter to N. Peter Rathvon, 9 August 1937.

82. Samuel Briskin to N. Peter Rathvon, 21 August 1937.

83. Harold Bruckner to Nelson Rockefeller, 16 July 1937, folder 675, box 90, Business Interests series, RG 2, OMR, Rockefeller Family Archives, RAC.

84. Harold Bruckner to Nelson Rockefeller, 24 July 1937, folder 675, box 90, Business Interests series, RG 2, OMR, Rockefeller Family Archives, RAC.

85. "Briskin Says He Will Quit RKO," *Motion Picture Herald*, 30 October 1937, p. 18.

86. G. B. Howe, memorandum to Leo Spitz, 17 January 1938. Briskin would soon return to his old home, Columbia Pictures, where he worked with B. B. Kahane as a studio executive under Harry Cohn. In 1942 he joined the U.S. Army Signal Corps and remained in the military until 1945. Shortly after his discharge, he formed Liberty Films, an independent company, with George Stevens, William Wyler, and Frank Capra.

87. "Briskin Says He Will Quit RKO."

88. Lillie Messinger to Pandro Berman, 15 November 1937.

89. "Cut in Claim of Rockefeller Center on RKO Proposed," *Motion Picture Herald*, 13 November 1937, p. 22.

90. "New Moves Point to RKO's Reorganization," *Motion Picture Herald*, 11 December 1937, p. 22.

91. "Withdraw Charge in RKO Hearing," *Motion Picture Herald*, 25 December 1937, p. 22.

92. Ibid.

93. "The Biggest Money Making Stars of 1937," *Motion Picture Herald*, 18 December 1937, pp. 13–15.

94. Fred Astaire to Pandro Berman, 25 November 1937.

95. Harry Brandt to Sam Briskin, 8 January 1937.

96. Pandro Berman, telegram to Ned Depinet and Barrett McCormick, 6 August 1937.

97. Pandro Berman to Katharine Hepburn, 14 August 1937.

98. Ned Depinet to Leo Spitz, 10 November 1937.

99. A. H. McCausland to Leo Spitz, 11 December 1937.

100. A. H. McCausland to Leo Spitz, 22 December 1937.

101. William R. Weaver, "Build-Up for 'Snow White' Opening Dwarfs Hollywood Predecessors," *Motion Picture Herald*, 25 December 1937, p. 21.

102. Ibid.

103. "'Snow White' Grosses Half of Production Cost at Music Hall," *Motion Picture Herald*, 12 February 1938, p. 16.

104. Ibid., p. 13.

105. "'Snow White' on Way to All-Time Domestic Gross," *Motion Picture Herald*, 28 September 1940, p. 85.

106. Sam Shain, "Grosses, Then and Now," *Motion Picture Herald*, 28 September 1940, p. 85.

107. Ibid.

108. George E. Morris, memorandum to Gunther R. Lessing, 30 April 1938.

109. "RKO Net Profit at $1,821,165," *Motion Picture Herald*, 23 April 1938, p. 51.

110. Roy Chartier, "The Year in Pictures," *Variety*, 5 January 1938, p. 11.

111. "Paramount Net $6,145,103 for '37," *Motion Picture Herald*, 30 April 1938, p. 41.

CHAPTER 7

1. "Slow Progress on RKO's 77B Reorg Brings Inside Stuff into the Open," *Variety*, 12 January 1938, p. 2.

2. Ibid.

3. Pandro Berman to Leo Spitz, 28 January 1938.

4. "RKO Management to Stay, Headed by Spitz," *Motion Picture Herald*, 26 February 1938, p. 18.

5. "Lengthy Delay in RKO Reorganization," *Motion Picture Herald*, 29 January 1938, p. 46.

6. "RKO's Creditors Study Amendments on Reorganization," *Motion Picture Herald*, 5 March 1938, p. 28.

7. O. C. Doering to J. R. McDonough, 12 April 1938.

8. J. R. McDonough to A. H. McCausland, 26 April 1938.

9. J. R. McDonough to A. H. McCausland, 24 May 1938.

10. "Revised RKO Plan Submitted, Court Orders Hearing," *Motion Picture Herald*, 21 May 1938, p. 24.

11. "RKO Plan Ready for Court on August 1st," *Motion Picture Herald*, 23 July 1938, p. 57.

12. "Atlas Option on RKO Stock Will Not Be Exercised," *Motion Picture Herald*, 30 July 1938, p. 33.

13. J. J. Nolan, memorandum to Ross Hastings, 8 January 1938.

14. Various sources have reported that Hepburn paid $220,000 to buy out her RKO contract, but I have found no evidence of this. See Todd McCarthy, *Howard Hawks* (New York: Grove Press, 1997), p. 258.

15. Pandro Berman to Katharine Hepburn, 3 May 1938. Berman and Hepburn would work together again at MGM in the 1940s.

16. "WAKE UP! Hollywood Producers," *Hollywood Reporter*, 3 May 1938, p. 3.

17. Leo Spitz to Pandro Berman, 28 April 1938.

18. Leo Spitz to Ginger Rogers, 4 April 1938.

19. J. R. McDonough, telegram to Leo Spitz, 16 April 1938.

20. Pandro Berman to Mark Sandrich, 21 April 1938.

21. J. R. McDonough, memorandum to file, 21 April 1938.

22. Pandro Berman to Mark Sandrich. Rogers's version of her difficulties with Sandrich can be found in Ginger Rogers, *Ginger: My Story* (New York: HarperCollins, 1991), pp. 195–197.

23. Ross R. Hastings, notes of meeting in J. J. Nolan's office, 17 March 1938.

24. J. R. McDonough to A. H. McCausland, 25 March 1938.

25. G. B. Howe, memorandum to Ross Hastings, 24 May 1938.

26. Leo Spitz to Pandro Berman, 17 May 1938.

27. "Dead Cats," *Time*, 16 May 1938, p. 57; "Hollywood in a Dither: Stars Scent a Pay-Cut Drive in Exhibitors' Attack," *Newsweek*, 16 May 1938, p. 24.

28. "The Biggest Money Making Stars of 1938," *Motion Picture Herald*, 24 December 1938, p. 13.

29. Jules Levy, memorandum to Leo Spitz, 16 May 1938.

30. Leo Spitz to Pandro Berman, 17 May 1938.

31. Leo Spitz to Pandro Berman, 25 May 1938.

32. Leo Spitz to J. R. McDonough, 17 May 1938.

33. Leo Spitz to Lee Marcus, 16 June 1938.

34. J. R. McDonough to Ned E. Depinet, 21 June 1938.

35. Ibid.

36. Lee Marcus to Ned. E. Depinet, 4 August 1938.

37. Lee Marcus, memorandum to J. J. Nolan, 7 March 1940.

38. "RKO Announces 54 Features and 199 Short Subjects for '38–'39," *Motion Picture Herald*, 13 August 1938, p. 66.

39. "RKO Will Release 54 Feature Films," *New York Times*, 11 August 1938, p. 12.

40. W. G. Van Schmus to Nelson Rockefeller, 2 June 1938, folder 679, box 90, RG 2 OMR, Business Interests series, Rockefeller Family Archives, RAC.

41. Nelson Rockefeller to Sidney Kent, 17 June 1938, folder 679, box 90, RG 2 OMR, Business Interests series, Rockefeller Family Archives, RAC.

42. W. G. Van Schmus to Nelson Rockefeller, 2 September 1938, folder 679, box 90, RG 2 OMR, Business Interests series, Rockefeller Family Archives, RAC.

43. Floyd Odlum, memorandum to Nelson Rockefeller and David Sarnoff, 30 September 1938, folder 679, box 90, RG 2 OMR, Business Interests series, Rockefeller Family Archives, RAC.

44. Ibid, "Exhibit A."

45. Nelson Rockefeller, memorandum to Thomas Debevoise, 4 October 1938, folder 675, box 90, RG 2 OMR, Business Interests series, Rockefeller Family Archives, RAC.

46. "Schaefer Will Head RKO When Reorganization Plan Is Approved," *Motion Picture Herald,* 15 October 1938, p. 16.
47. Leo Spitz to Pandro Berman, 7 October 1938.
48. Robert Sparks, memorandum to Sam Briskin, 9 April 1937.
49. Sam Briskin, memorandum to Robert Sparks, 14 April 1937.
50. "Daily Budget Reconciliation—*Bringing Up Baby,*" 6 January 1938.
51. "Shooting Schedule—*Bringing Up Baby,*" 27 December 1937.
52. Ligon Johnson to RKO-Radio Pictures, Inc., 16 June 1937.
53. Samuel Briskin to Leo Spitz, 20 August 1937.
54. Ned Depinet to Pandro Berman, 2 September 1938.
55. In 1943 Spitz would found International Pictures with William Goetz. Their company merged with Universal in 1946, and he became one of the leaders of Universal-International until 1953, when he retired from the film business.
56. "Republic, RKO Report 1938 Profits; Warner in $6,000,000 Refunding," *Motion Picture Herald,* 11 March 1939, p. 25.
57. "Pressures from Without Headline Film Year," *Motion Picture Herald,* 31 December 1938, p. 45.
58. Ibid.
59. "U.S. Sues Majors to Divorce Exhibition and End Block Sales," *Motion Picture Herald,* 23 July 1938, p. 12.
60. "George Schaefer Takes Over at RKO; Hearings Are Delayed to Nov. 22," *Motion Picture Herald,* 29 October 1938, p. 22.

CHAPTER 8

1. "Biography of George J. Schaefer" (publicity release), February 1939.
2. Dan O'Shea, telegram to Ned Depinet, 24 March 1936.
3. Howard Hawks, Ben Hecht, and Charles MacArthur to Sam Briskin, 27 October 1936.
4. Sam Briskin to Howard Hawks, 27 October 1936.
5. Sam Briskin, telegram to Howard Hawks, 2 November 1936.
6. Sam Briskin, telegram to Leo Spitz, 14 April 1937.
7. J.R. McDonough to Leo Spitz, 6 July 1938.
8. Mike Steen, "A Louis B. Mayer American Film Institute Oral History of Pandro S. Berman," American Film Institute Archives, Los Angeles, n.d., p. 28.
9. J.R. McDonough to Leo Spitz, 1 September 1938.
10. Steen, "Oral History of Pandro S. Berman," p. 28.
11. George Schaefer to Ned Depinet, 3 December 1938.
12. "Final Memorandum Showing Cost of '39–40' Program as Discussed at La Quinta by Messrs. Schaefer, Depinet, and Berman," 20 January 1939.
13. George Schaefer to Andrew Christensen, 23 January 1939.
14. George Schaefer to Lunsford P. Yandell, 6 February 1939.
15. "RKO and Wilcox Form Company to Produce in Hollywood and London," *Motion Picture Herald,* 17 December 1938, p. 11.

16. George Schaefer to Pandro Berman, 27 February 1939.

17. Pandro Berman to George Schaefer, 1 March 1939.

18. Steen, "Oral History of Pandro S. Berman," pp. 57–58.

19. J. R. McDonough to Ned Depinet, 21 October 1938.

20. Ibid.

21. Pandro Berman to Florence Lipkin, 14 April 1939.

22. Irene Castle [McLaughlin] to Pandro Berman, 4 April 1937.

23. Sidney Lipsitch, memorandum to George Haight, 23 June 1938.

24. Irene Castle [McLaughlin], memorandum to Pandro Berman, 5 October 1938.

25. Irene Castle [McLaughlin] to Pandro Berman, 16 December 1938.

26. J. R. McDonough, letter agreement with Irene Castle McLaughlin, 2 March 1939.

27. Astaire expert John Mueller argues that McLaughlin was right about Rogers and Plunkett's alterations, which, he asserts, were "mostly damaging" to dance sequences in the film. See John Mueller, *Astaire Dancing* (New York: Knopf, 1985), p. 151.

28. Croce, *The Fred Astaire & Ginger Rogers Book*, p. 165.

29. Abram Simon and Morton Garbus to R.K.O.–Radio Pictures, Inc., 27 February 1939.

30. J. R. McDonough, letter agreement with Irene Castle McLaughlin.

31. J. R. McDonough, telegram to George Schaefer, 15 June 1939.

32. "RKO Ends Convention Season, Announcing 58 in New Program," *Motion Picture Herald*, 24 June 1939, p. 58.

33. Ibid., pp. 59–60.

34. Lillie Messinger to Leo Spitz, 16 December 1937.

35. Ross R. Hastings, memorandum to M. B. Silberberg, 13 March 1941.

36. Ross R. Hastings, memorandum to G. B. Howe, 1 December 1939.

37. Ross R. Hastings, memorandum to Pandro Berman, 28 July 1938.

38. Ginger Rogers to Pandro Berman, 2 March 1939.

39. Pandro Berman to Ginger Rogers, 3 March 1939.

40. George Schaefer, telegram to Ned Depinet, 15 May 1939.

41. "War Halts Hollywood's Last Big European Mart," *Motion Picture Herald*, 9 September 1939, p. 15.

42. Ibid.

43. George Schaefer to Pandro Berman, 15 September 1939.

44. Steen, "Oral History of Pandro S. Berman," p. 34.

45. "Cameras Shoot Hollywood into Complete Product Preparedness," *Motion Picture Herald*, 9 September 1939, p. 18.

46. George Schaefer, memorandum to all RKO Employees, 25 September 1939.

47. George Schaefer to J. J. Nolan, 5 September 1939.

48. George Schaefer to J. J. Nolan, 14 September 1939.

49. Orson Welles, telegram to George Schaefer, 18 September 1939.

50. J. R. McDonough, memorandum to George Schaefer, 7 December 1939.

51. George Schaefer to J. J. Nolan, 11 December 1939.

52. J. R. McDonough, telegram to George Schaefer, 16 December 1939.

53. George Schaefer to J. J. Nolan, 31 October 1939.

54. "Judge Approves RKO Plan; Confirmation Now Awaited," *Motion Picture Herald*, 21 January 1939, p. 28.

55. Court to Hear Appeals on RKO," *Motion Picture Herald*, 25 February 1939, p. 32.

56. "Three Object to Plan for RKO," *Motion Picture Herald*, 24 June 1939, p. 64.

57. "Court Backs Bondy on His RKO Plan Approval," *Motion Picture Herald*, 22 July 1939, p. 65.

58. "Court Gets Details of New RKO Stock Plans," *Motion Picture Herald*, 5 August 1939, p. 81.

59. "Atlas RKO Offer Ends; SEC Joins Case; Stirn Loses," *Motion Picture Herald*, 9 September 1939, p. 26.

60. "Atlas in New RKO Plan; Change in Sales Staff," *Motion Picture Herald*, 14 October 1939, p. 57.

61. "Atlas in New Underwriting Offer to RKO," *Motion Picture Herald*, 16 December 1939, p. 52.

62. Ibid.

63. George Schaefer, telegram to J. J. Nolan, 28 December 1939.

64. Ross R. Hastings, memorandum to Pandro Berman, 30 March 1939.

65. J. R. McDonough to George Schaefer, 1 June 1939.

66. J. R. McDonough to George Schaefer, 13 July 1939.

67. Pandro Berman to George Schaefer, 15 December 1939.

68. George Schaefer to Pandro Berman, 15 December 1939.

69. George Schaefer, telegram to J. J. Nolan, 19 December 1939.

70. The 1938–1939 production year generated $1,909,000 in profits for RKO, as well as containing several high-quality pictures.

71. After leaving RKO, Pandro Berman spent more than twenty-five years as a producer for MGM, where his record of tasteful, intelligent, and profitable motion pictures would continue to grow. He received the Irving Thalberg Award from the Academy of Motion Picture Arts and Sciences in 1977.

72. Herb Golden, "Films' $1,739,000 for Scripts in '39," *Variety*, 3 January 1940, p. 7.

CHAPTER 9

1. Nelson Rockefeller became president of the Museum of Modern Art in 1939.

2. "President's Report, RKO Board Meeting—July 30, 1940, Memo Re: Policy of Distributing Independent Production," p. 2, attached to letter from George J. Schaefer to Nelson Rockefeller, 1 August 1940, folder 681, box 90, RG 2 OMR, Business Interests series, Rockefeller Family Archives, RAC.

3. "New RKO Tees Off Clear of Debt; Gross Up $8,000,000 from 1933," *Variety*, 31 January 1940, p. 5.

4. "RKO Reorg.; After 7 Yrs. in C't, Finally in Clear," *Variety*, 10 January 1940, p. 2.

5. Ibid.

6. "New RKO Tees Off Clear of Debt."

7. "Atlas Asks for 100,000 Shares," *Motion Picture Herald*, 20 April 1940, p. 29.

8. "RKO Asks Cut in Allowances," *Motion Picture Herald*, 22 June 1940, p. 16.

9. "Schaefer Asks Reduction on RKO Claims," *Motion Picture Herald*, 20 July 1940, p. 50.

10. "Bondy Takes SEC 'Tip,' Cuts RKO Fees to Bond," *Motion Picture Herald*, 24 August 1940, p. 54.Ibid.

11. "RKO's Manpower Move," *Variety*, 24 January 1940, p. 3.

12. "Joe Nolan New RKO VP and Studio Boss," *Hollywood Reporter*, 17 February 1940, p. 1.

13. "RKO's Important Script Buys for Its Name Talent Cues Edington and Schaefer's Co. Plans for '40–41," *Variety*, 21 February 1940, pp. 3, 18.

14. "53 Feature Films Scheduled by RKO," *New York Times*, 28 May 1940, p. 29. For more on the Audience Research Institute, see Susan Ohmer, *George Gallup in Hollywood* (New York: Columbia University Press, 2006).

15. "Keough, Schaefer Hit Neely Bill," *Motion Picture Herald*, 8 June 1940, p. 22.

16. "Industry Leaders Complete Setup in National Defense Cooperation," *Motion Picture Herald*, 9 November 1940, p. 47.

17. "Newsreel History," *Motion Picture Herald*, 28 September 1940, p. 11.

18. George Schaefer to J.J. Nolan, 4 March 1940.

19. Harry Edington to Leda Bauer, 16 April 1940.

20. "RKO Plans 61–66, Record Number; 30 from UA to Cost 29 Millions," *Motion Picture Herald*, 30 March 1940, p. 76.

21. Ibid.

22. George Schaefer to J.J. Nolan, 6 March 1940.

23. Ibid.

24. J.R. McDonough to Ned Depinet, 9 September 1939.

25. J.R. McDonough to George Schaefer, 31 August 1939.

26. George Schaefer to Max Gordon, 24 October 1939.

27. George Schaefer to Ned Depinet, 25 October 1939.

28. Lee Clair, telegram to George Schaefer, 23 January 1940.

29. Frank S. Nugent, "Abe Lincoln in Illinois," *New York Times*, 23 February 1940, p. 19.

30. George Schaefer to Harry Edington, 4 June 1940.

31. J.R. McDonough to George Schaefer, 5 April 1939.

32. Pandro Berman, telegram to George Stevens, 8 February 1939.

33. George Schaefer to Pandro Berman, 10 April 1939.

34. Pandro Berman to George Stevens, 22 April 1939. For more on Stevens's dispute with RKO, see Tom Kemper, *Hidden Talent: The Emergence of Hollywood Agents* (Berkeley: University of California Press, 2010), pp. 99–101.

35. Dan Winkler, memorandum to Ross Hastings, 1 April 1940.

36. "Rambling Reporter," *Hollywood Reporter,* 17 February 1940, p. 2.

37. "53 Features from RKO in 1940–41; A.W. Smith Named Sales Manager," *Motion Picture Herald,* 1 June 1940, p. 28.

38. Dan Winkler, memorandum to J.J. Nolan, 5 August 1940.

39. Ibid.

40. George Schaefer to J.J. Nolan, 8 April 1940.

41. George Schaefer to Harry Edington, 21 May 1940.

42. "53 Features from RKO in 1940–41; A.W. Smith Named Sales Manager."

43. "An Address Delivered by George J. Schaefer President of RKO on the occasion of the General Staff Luncheon Held in connection with RKO Radio Pictures, Inc. Ninth International Sales Convention, 28 May 1940," p. 2.

44. George Schaefer to J.R. McDonough, 2 July 1940.

45. George Schaefer to J.R. McDonough, 29 July 1940.

46. "New Season's Product Lineups, Costs, Reported to Date," *Motion Picture Herald,* 20 April 1940, p. 13.

47. Lee Marcus to J.J. Nolan, 7 March 1940.

48. Ibid.

49. George Schaefer to Lee Marcus, 16 December 1940.

50. William Fadiman to Edgar Peterson, 14 June 1948.

51. For more examples of the journalistic taunting of Welles, see Joseph McBride, *Whatever Happened to Orson Welles?* (Lexington: University Press of Kentucky, 2006), pp. 33–34.

52. "SMILER WITH A KNIFE, HEART OF DARKNESS or INVASION FROM MARS?" Audience Research Institute, Report XIII, 15 May 1940.

53. Harry Edington to George Schaefer, 27 May 1940.

54. George Schaefer to Harry Edington, 5 June 1940.

55. J.R. McDonough, memorandum to George Schaefer, 14 June 1940.

56. J.R. McDonough to George Schaefer, 18 June 1940.

57. Don Gordon, memorandum to Lillie Messinger, 19 February 1940; Ardel Wray, memorandum to Lillie Messinger, 19 February 1940.

58. Dan Winkler, memorandum to Ross Hastings, 2 March 1940.

59. Joseph Breen to J.R. McDonough, 25 March 1940.

60. George Schaefer to Joseph Breen, 8 April 1940.

61. J.J. Nolan, memorandum to Collier Young, 12 April 1940.

62. George Gallup to J.R. McDonough, 23 April 1940.

63. George Gallup to J.R. McDonough, 20 August 1940.

64. Ibid.

65. George Schaefer to Harry Edington, 7 October 1940.

66. Ned Depinet to George Schaefer, 31 October 1940.

67. Balio, *United Artists,* p. 171.

68. "Consent Decree Signing the Story of 1940," *Motion Picture Herald,* 4 January 1941, p. 36.

69. Ibid.

70. Ned E. Depinet, "Ralph Hanbury Victim of Nazi Bomb," *The Radio Flash,* 5 October 1940, p. 8, American Film Institute Library, Los Angeles.

71. Ralph Hanbury to G. J. Schaefer, 24 September 1940.

72. G. J. Schaefer to Phil Reisman, 10 December 1940.

73. Don Gordon, memorandum to Lillie Messinger, 15 September 1939.

74. George Schaefer to J. J. Nolan, 20 December 1939.

75. George Schaefer to J. J. Nolan, 27 December 1939 and 9 January 1940.

76. "Kitty Foyle," Audience Research Institute, Report XXXII, 29 October 1940.

77. This account of Parsons's phone call is drawn from Notes on a telephone conversation with Miss Louella Parsons, 9 January 1941. In her autobiography, Parsons states that Welles lied to her about the source of the Charles Foster Kane character and that her rival Hedda Hopper saw the film before she did and informed Hearst it was about him. See Louella Parsons, *Tell It to Louella* (New York: G. P. Putnam's Sons, 1961), pp. 131–132. Her account is corroborated in Hopper's autobiography. See Hedda Hopper, *From Under My Hat* (Garden City, NY: Doubleday, 1952), pp. 289–290.

78. "'U', RKO, Columbia Report Incomes; SEC Lists More Film Stock Deals," *Motion Picture Herald,* 14 June 1941, p. 45.

79. "George J. Schaefer Will Stay at RKO Studio for a Year; Edington Leaving?" *Variety,* 1 January 1941, p. 5.

80. H. Golden, "The Changing World," *Variety,* 7 January 1942, p. 26.

81. Lee Marcus continued to work in the industry. At Twentieth Century–Fox he produced *The Dancing Masters* (1943), *They Came to Blow Up America* (1943), *Roger Tuohy, Gangster* (1944), and other films.

82. "R.-K.-O. Pay Is Restored," *New York Times,* 3 February 1941, p. 13.

83. For an in-depth case history of *Citizen Kane* and the attendant controversy, see Robert L. Carringer, *The Making of Citizen Kane* (Berkeley: University of California Press, 1985).

84. "Miscellany," *Newsweek,* 16 September 1940, p. 12.

85. J. J. Nolan to George Schaefer, 6 September 1940.

86. "Hearst Dislikes 'Kane,'" *Motion Picture Herald,* 18 January 1941, p. 9.

87. "Decide Future of Welles' Pic by This Week," *Variety,* 12 February 1941, p. 4.

88. George Schaefer to Orson Welles, 15 February 1941.

89. "Hearst Opens Blast on RKO—Schaefer; 'Citizen Kane' Release Still Indef," *Variety,* 19 February 1941, p. 2.

90. Orson Welles to George Schaefer, 7 March 1941.

91. George Schaefer, telegram to Orson Welles, 7 March 1941.

92. Ross R. Hastings, memorandum to Mendel Silberberg, 13 March 1941.

93. "Mr. Welles, in Militant State, Phones RKO: 'I'll Be Suing You,'" *Motion Picture Herald*, 15 March 1941, p. 27.

94. "'Kane' Department," *Motion Picture Herald*, 22 March 1941, p. 9.

95. Ross R. Hastings, memorandum to Mendel Silberberg.

96. David Nasaw, *The Chief: The Life of William Randolph Hearst* (Boston: Houghton Mifflin, 2000), p. 568.

97. Bosley Crowther, *Hollywood Rajah: The Life and Times of Louis B. Mayer* (New York: Holt, Rinehart & Winston, 1960), p. 290.

98. George Stevens, Jr., ed., *Conversations with the Great Moviemakers of Hollywood's Golden Age* (New York: Knopf, 2006), p. 462.

99. "Kane Revealed," *Motion Picture Herald*, 12 April 1941, p. 9.

100. George Schaefer to C. B. McDonald, 14 April 1941.

101. "$10,000 Advance, $30,000 in Week for 'Citizen Kane,'" *Motion Picture Herald*, 10 May 1941, p. 18.

102. "'Kane' 2-a-Day Disappointing," *Variety*, 14 May 1941, p. 4.

103. Orson Welles, memorandum to George Schaefer, 3 July 1941.

104. George Schaefer, telegram to Orson Welles, 30 December 1941.

105. "RKO Exec Realignments Include Mallard, Donovan Resignations; Nolan, Youngman, Ullman Shifts," *Variety*, 9 April 1941, p. 5.

106. Reg Armour, memorandum on the Ginger Rogers negotiations, 12 March 1941.

107. Reg Armour, memorandum to George Schaefer, 18 July 1941.

108. Ross Hastings to Dan Winkler, 24 November 1941.

109. "Sol Lesser Post as RKO Studio Head Complicated by UA Contract," *Variety*, 23 April 1941, p. 5.

110. W. G. Van Schmus to Nelson Rockefeller, 26 February 1941, folder 676, box 90, RG 2 OMR, Business Interests series, Rockefeller Family Archives, RAC.

111. Barbara Hall, "Oral History of Albert E. Van Schmus," n.d., p. 8, Academy of Motion Picture Arts and Sciences Library, Beverly Hills, CA.

112. W. G. Van Schmus to Nelson Rockefeller, 28 April 1941, folder 676, box 90, RG 2 OMR, Business Interests series, Rockefeller Family Archives, RAC.

113. "Breen, O'Connor, et al.," *Motion Picture Herald*, 10 May 1941, p. 9.

CHAPTER 10

1. "Koerner Heads RKO Theatres," *Motion Picture Herald*, 17 May 1941, p. 18.

2. J. R. McDonough to George Schaefer, 27 June 1941, p. 18.

3. Douglas W. Churchill, "Screen News Here and in Hollywood," *New York Times*, 27 June 1941, p. 15.

4. Thomas Doherty claims the studio reorganization was Breen's idea and that the RKO "board of directors frustrated Breen's ambitions to consolidate

his power." This was not the case. See Thomas Doherty, *Hollywood's Censor: Joseph I. Breen and the Production Code Administration* (New York: Columbia University Press, 2007), p. 148.

5. W.G. Van Schmus to George Schaefer, 1 May 1941, folder 679, box 90, RG 2 OMR, Business Interests series, Rockefeller Family Archives, RAC.

6. Ibid.

7. George Schaefer to W.G. Van Schmus, 6 May 1941, folder 679, box 90, RG 2 OMR, Business Interests series, Rockefeller Family Archives, RAC.

8. "Breen Cues RKO Studio Staff Reshuffle," *Variety*, 25 June 1941, p. 5.

9. "Edington's RKO Washup; Nolan Out after 21 Years," *Variety*, 2 July 1941, p. 5.

10. Edmund Weisl to Joseph Breen, 29 July 1941.

11. George Schaefer to Joseph Breen, 16 September 1941.

12. "119 Features Already 'In the Can,' for '41–'42," *Motion Picture Herald*, 23 August 1941, p. 12.

13. "Breen Talks about Policy and Entertainment Product for RKO," *Motion Picture Herald*, 28 June 1941, p. 30.

14. Balio, *United Artists*, pp. 155–159.

15. "Goldwyn Likes RKO," *Motion Picture Herald*, 6 December 1941, p. 8.

16. According to biographer Scott Berg, Goldwyn needed desperately to strike a deal with RKO. He had failed in his negotiations with other studios and was facing the unappealing prospect of crawling back to United Artists if he and Schaefer had not come to terms. Thus, George Schaefer was in a stronger bargaining position than he realized. See A. Scott Berg, *Goldwyn* (New York: Knopf, 1989), p. 354.

17. "Goldwyn, Breen, O'Connor, Sisk, Meyers, Top Personnel Shufflings," *Motion Picture Herald*, 3 May 1941, p. 25.

18. Robert Sisk to George Schaefer, 15 February 1940.

19. Sisk then went to work for Paramount for a short period before relocating to MGM, where he remained a fixture for years thereafter.

20. M.B. Silberberg, memorandum to William Hinckle, 20 May 1941.

21. "RKO Asks Court to Sustain Dismissal of Ailing Pommer," *Variety*, 11 June 1941, p. 5.

22. Erich Pommer to Joseph Breen, 15 November 1941.

23. Erich Pommer to Joseph Breen, 25 November 1941.

24. "More Coin for B's at RKO; Schaefer Orders Quickies off the Lot," *Variety*, 28 May 1941, p. 6.

25. George Schaefer to J.R. McDonough, 31 March 1941.

26. Ibid.

27. Quotations in this and the following paragraph are drawn from J.R. McDonough, memorandum to Joseph Breen, 30 October 1941.

28. Quotations in this paragraph are drawn from George Schaefer to Joseph Breen, 31 October 1941.

29. Bob Dann, telegram to Dan O'Shea, 4 September 1935.

30. George Schaefer to Cliff Reid, 15 January 1940.

31. J. R. McDonough to Harry Edington, 3 June 1940. Later, Hitchcock would claim that RKO executives forced this conception and ending on him. See Francois Truffaut, *Hitchcock* (New York: Simon & Schuster, 1967), p. 102.

32. J. J. Nolan to George Schaefer, 15 June 1940.

33. J. R. McDonough, memorandum to George Schaefer, 25 January 1941.

34. George Schaefer to J. R. McDonough, 10 February 1941.

35. G. B. Howe, memorandum to Reg Armour, 18 April 1941.

36. Joseph Breen, memorandum to Harry Edington, 20 August 1941.

37. George Schaefer, memorandum to Perry Lieber, 17 February 1941.

38. David Ogilvy to George Schaefer, 13 August 1941.

39. Joseph Breen, memorandum to All Employees, 12 December 1941.

40. "Hollywood Adjusts to War and Extends Work in Nation's Service," *Motion Picture Herald,* 20 December 1941, pp. 12–13. The studio was unable to follow through on this announcement. *Bombardier* would finally go before the cameras more than a year later and be released in 1943.

41. Barton P. Turnbull, memoranda to files, 18 and 19 November 1941, folder 681, box 90, RG 2 OMR, Business Interests series, Rockefeller Family Archives, RAC.

42. Van Schmus had been advocating that Schaefer be given a new contract since April 1941. W. G. Van Schmus to Nelson Rockefeller, 28 April 1941, folder 676, box 90, RG 2 OMR, Business Interests series, Rockefeller Family Archives, RAC.

43. "Rathvon V-P of RKO in a General Exec Reorg; Kingsberg's Titles," *Variety,* 17 December 1941, p. 6.

44. Charles Koerner to George Schaefer, 23 December 1941.

45. "Holdovers Hearten Schaefer; Sees Big Yr. Ahead for RKO," *Variety,* 3 December 1941, p. 5.

46. "RKO Policy Reorganization May Be Disclosed Shortly," *Motion Picture Herald,* 29 November 1941, p. 17.

47. George Schaefer, memorandum to Gordon Youngman, 3 November 1941.

48. "RKO's Reorg Troubles Had Effect on Talent," *Variety,* 31 December 1941, p. 23.

49. Ned E. Depinet to Hugh L. Ducker, 19 July 1943.

50. "Sarnoff Angry over McDonough Shift, Threatens Action Blocking RKO Deal with Schaefer; Wants New Exec Setup," *Variety,* 25 March 1942, p. 5.

51. "RKO Washes Up Sked in 9 Mos.," *Variety,* 14 January 1942, p. 4.

52. "Rogell Leaves RKO; Shake Impends," *Variety,* 21 January 1942, p. 4.

53. George Schaefer to Joseph Breen, 23 January 1942.

54. Perry Lieber, memorandum to Joseph Breen, 28 January 1942.

55. Joseph Breen to George Schaefer, 24 January 1942.

56. Lesser went back to making independent pictures. His Tarzan films, starring Johnny Weissmuller and distributed by RKO, would be popular for years to come.

57. Sol Lesser to Joseph Breen, 30 January 1942.

58. J. R. McDonough worked in motion picture financing after he left RKO.

59. Gordon Youngman to Richard Hungate, 6 July 1943.

60. "RKO May Copy Universal in Culling Studio Production Manpower from Theatre Execs; Charlie Koerner Up," *Variety*, 4 March 1942, p. 5.

61. Ibid.

62. George Schaefer to Orson Welles, 10 September 1941.

63. Reg Armour to Joseph Breen, 8 September 1941.

64. Reg Armour, telegram to Joseph Breen, 7 October 1941.

65. George Schaefer to Orson Welles, 3 December 1941.

66. Quoted in Doherty, *Hollywood's Censor*, p. 148.

67. George Schaefer, telegram to Orson Welles, 27 February 1942.

68. Ned Depinet, telegram to George Schaefer, 18 March 1942.

69. George Schaefer to Orson Welles, 21 March 1942.

70. Ibid.

71. For more on the production and postproduction of *The Magnificent Ambersons*, see Carringer, *The Making of Citizen Kane*, pp. 121–134; and Robert L. Carringer, *The Magnificent Ambersons: A Reconstruction* (Berkeley: University of California Press, 1993).

72. In his autobiography, Douglas Fairbanks, Jr., describes his own "mission" to South America. Ostensibly there to "investigate the effects of Latin American public opinion of American motion pictures," Fairbanks claims his real task was to get in touch with certain influential national groups that were "believed to be veering toward Nazi ideology" and then submit an analysis of the situation and "what we could do about it" to the U.S. government. See Douglas Fairbanks, Jr., *The Salad Days* (New York: Doubleday, 1988), pp. 380–387.

73. John Hay Whitney to Orson Welles, 20 December 1941.

74. I have chosen to use the Brazilian spelling "Carnaval" throughout this section, though executives like Schaefer often employed the American spelling, "carnival," in their correspondence.

75. George Schaefer to Gordon Youngman, 27 February 1942.

76. Phil Reisman to George Schaefer, 11 February 1942. Walt Disney had visited Brazil and several other South American countries in the late summer and early fall of 1941.

77. Orson Welles to George Schaefer, 25 February 1942.

78. Lynn Shores to Walter Daniels, 24 February 1942.

79. George Schaefer, telegram to Orson Welles, 5 March 1942.

80. Orson Welles, telegram to George Schaefer, 18 March 1942.

81. Lynn Shores to Walter Daniels, 21 March 1942.

82. "Sol Lesser, McDonough Quit RKO; Studio Prod. Reorg Awaits Schaefer," *Variety*, 4 February 1942, p. 5.

83. Ibid.

84. "Lesser and Pascal Who Left UA to Join RKO Back into the Fold," *Variety*, 11 February 1942, p. 4.

85. "Hawks Exits RKO," *Variety*, 27 May 1942, p. 23.

86. Youngman to Hungate, 6 July 1943.

87. "Sarnoff Angry over McDonough Shift."

88. George Schaefer, telegram to Orson Welles, 14 April 1942.

89. Ibid.

90. Orson Welles, telegram to George Schaefer, 15 April 1942.

91. George Schaefer, telegram to Orson Welles, 16 April 1942.

92. Lynn Shores to Walter Daniels, 22 April 1942.

93. Reg Armour, transcript of telephone conversation with Phil Reisman, 27 April 1942.

94. George Schaefer to Orson Welles, 29 April 1942.

95. Earl Rettig to George Schaefer, 14 May 1942.

96. George Schaefer to Phil Reisman, 18 May 1942.

97. Phil Reisman to George Schaefer, 25 May 1942.

98. *It's All True* has become just as controversial in scholarly circles as it was for RKO in 1942. For a more detailed account, see my article, "Orson Welles, George Schaefer, and IT'S ALL TRUE: A 'Cursed' Production," *Film History* Vol. 2 (1988), pp. 325–335. For additional interpretations of the events, see Richard Wilson, "It's Not *Quite* All True," *Sight and Sound* Vol. 39 (1970), pp. 188–193; McBride, *Whatever Happened to Orson Welles?* pp. 65–79; and Catharine L. Benamou, *It's All True: Orson Welles's Pan-American Odyssey* (Berkeley: University of California Press, 2007).

99. "Breen Extends Vacash," *Variety*, 1 April 1942, p. 5.

100. "Breen Returns as Head of Code Administration," *Motion Picture Herald*, 16 May 1942, p. 18.

101. N. Peter Rathvon to Charles Koerner, 8 May 1942.

102. N. Peter Rathvon to Charles Koerner, 10 July 1942.

103. Burton Turnbull to Nelson Rockefeller, 20 April 1942, folder 679, box 90, RG 2 OMR, Business Interests series, Rockefeller Family Archives, RAC.

104. Nelson Rockefeller to Burton Turnbull, 22 April 1942, folder 679, box 90, RG 2 OMR, Business Interests series, Rockefeller Family Archives, RAC.

105. "Odlum May Take Personal Command of RKO in Order to Protect His $6,000,000; Schaefer Stepping Down," *Variety*, 10 June 1942, p. 5.

106. "Schaefer's RKO B.R. Quest," *Variety*, 3 June 1942, p. 5.

107. N. Peter Rathvon to Charles Koerner, 10 July 1942.

108. "RKO Seeks Unfreeze of $2,800,000 British Coin for Immediate Cash; Discuss Theatre Dept. Changes," *Variety*, 17 June 1942, p. 5.

109. "Schaefer Leaving RKO Post; Odlum to Take Over," *Motion Picture Herald*, 13 June 1942, p. 23.

110. George Schaefer, letter to Nelson Rockefeller, 12 June 1942, folder 679, box 90, RG 2 OMR, Business Interests series, Rockefeller Family Archives, RAC.

111. Susan Dalton and John Davis, "An Interview with John Cromwell," *The Velvet Light Trap*, no. 10 (Fall 1973), p. 24.

112. Roy Alexander Fowler, *Orson Welles* (London: Pendulum, 1946), p. 33.

113. During the remainder of World War II, Schaefer functioned as national chairman of the War Activities Committee of the Motion Picture Industry. Afterward, he became a consultant who assisted such independent producers as Stanley Kramer, Otto Preminger, and George Stevens in the negotiation of distribution agreements.

APPENDIX

1. F. Scott Fitzgerald, *The Last Tycoon* (New York: Charles Scribner's Sons, 1941), p. 3.

2. For an explanation of how profits and losses were determined for each film, see my book *The Golden Age of Cinema: Hollywood, 1929–1945* (Malden, MA: Blackwell, 2007), pp. 82–85.

3. The distribution office published a weekly house organ called *The Radio Flash* to keep its salesmen apprised of company developments and, more important, to stimulate their enthusiasm for RKO's new product. The *Flash* consistently described this product as "terrific," "sensational," "tremendous," and the like. The American Film Institute Library in Los Angeles holds a nearly complete run of the publication.

4. Paul N. Lazarus, "Distribution: The Changes to Come," in A. William Bluem and Jason E. Squire, eds., *The Movie Business* (New York: Hastings House, 1972), p. 188.

Selected Bibliography

Astaire, Fred. *Steps in Time*. New York: Harper & Brothers, 1959.

Balio, Tino. *Grand Design: Hollywood as a Modern Business Enterprise, 1930–1939*. New York: Scribner's, 1993.

———, ed. *The American Film Industry*. Rev. ed. Madison: University of Wisconsin Press, 1985.

———. *United Artists: The Company Built by the Stars*. Madison: University of Wisconsin Press, 1976.

Ball, Lucille, with Betty Hannah Hoffman. *Love, Lucy*. New York: G. P. Putnam's Sons, 1996.

Basten, Fred E. *Glorious Technicolor*. New Brunswick, NJ: A. S. Barnes, 1980.

Beauchamp, Cari. *Joseph P. Kennedy Presents: His Hollywood Years*. New York: Knopf, 2009.

Belton, John. *Widescreen Cinema*. Cambridge, MA: Harvard University Press, 1992.

Benamou, Catherine L. *It's All True: Orson Welles's Pan-American Odyssey*. Berkeley: University of California Press, 2007.

Berg, A. Scott. *Goldwyn: A Biography*. New York: Knopf, 1989.

Bergan, Ronald. *The United Artists Story*. New York: Crown, 1986.

Bergman, Andrew. *We're in the Money: Depression America and Its Films*. New York: New York University Press, 1971.

Bilby, Kenneth. *The General: David Sarnoff and the Rise of the Communications Industry*. New York: Harper & Row, 1986.

Bluem, A. William, and Jason E. Squire, eds. *The Movie Business*. New York: Hastings House, 1972.

Bogdanovich, Peter. *John Ford*. Berkeley: University of California Press, 1978.

Bohn, Thomas W., and Richard L. Stromgren. *Light and Shadows*. Port Washington, NJ: Alfred, 1975.

Bordwell, David, Janet Staiger, and Kristin Thompson. *The Classical Hollywood Cinema: Film Style and Mode of Production to 1960*. New York: Columbia University Press, 1985.

Braudy, Leo, and Marshall Cohen, eds. *Film Theory and Criticism*. 7th ed. New York: Oxford University Press, 2009.

Brownlow, Kevin. *The Parade's Gone By*. New York: Ballantine, 1968.

Capra, Frank. *The Name above the Title*. New York: Macmillan, 1971.

Carringer, Robert L. *The Magnificent Ambersons: A Reconstruction*. Berkeley: University of California Press, 1993.

———. *The Making of Citizen Kane*. Berkeley: University of California Press, 1985.

Chandler, Alfred, Jr. *The Visible Hand: The Managerial Revolution in American Business*. Cambridge: Harvard University Press, 1977.

Chandler, Charlotte. *I Know Where I'm Going: Katharine Hepburn; A Personal Biography*. New York: Simon & Schuster, 2010.

Crafton, Donald. *The Talkies: American Cinema's Transition to Sound, 1926–1931*. Berkeley: University of California Press, 1997.

Croce, Arlene. *The Fred Astaire and Ginger Rogers Book*. New York: Galahad Books, 1972.

Crowther, Bosley. *Hollywood Rajah: The Life and Times of Louis B. Mayer*. New York: Holt, Rinehart & Winston, 1960.

———. *The Lion's Share*. New York: E. P. Dutton, 1957.

Davis, Ronald L. *The Glamour Factory: Inside Hollywood's Big Studio System*. Dallas: Southern Methodist University Press, 1993.

Doherty, Thomas. *Hollywood's Censor: Joseph I. Breen and the Production Code Administration*. New York: Columbia University Press, 2007.

Eames, John Douglas. *The MGM Story*. London: Octopus Books, 1977.

———. *The Paramount Story*. New York: Crown, 1985.

Eyman, Scott. *Print the Legend: The Life and Times of John Ford*. New York: Simon & Schuster, 1999.

Fairbanks, Jr., Douglas. *The Salad Days*. New York: Doubleday, 1988.

Finler, Joel W. *The Hollywood Story*. New York: Crown, 1988.

Fisher, Kenneth L. *100 Minds That Made the Market*. Woodside, CA: Business Classics, 1993.

Fitzgerald, F. Scott. *The Last Tycoon*. New York: Charles Scribner's Sons, 1941.

Fowler, Roy Alexander. *Orson Welles*. London: Pendulum, 1946.

Francisco, Charles. *The Radio City Music Hall*. New York: E. P. Dutton, 1979.

French, Philip. *The Movie Moguls*. London: Weidenfeld & Nicholson, 1969.

Gabler, Neal. *An Empire of Their Own: How the Jews Invented Hollywood*. New York: Crown, 1988.

Gehring, Wes D. *Irene Dunne: First Lady of Hollywood*. Lanham, MD: Scarecrow Press, 2003.

Goldner, Orville, and George E. Turner. *The Making of King Kong*. New York: Ballantine, 1975.

Gomery, Douglas. *The Hollywood Studio System: A History*. London: British Film Institute, 2005.

————. *Shared Pleasures: A History of Movie Presentation in the United States*. Madison: University of Wisconsin Press, 1992.

Hampton, Benjamin B. *History of the American Film Industry*. New York: Dover, 1970.

Haver, Ron. *David O. Selznick's Hollywood*. New York: Knopf, 1980.

Hays, Will H. *The Memoirs of Will H. Hays*. Garden City, NY: Doubleday, 1955.

Hepburn, Katharine. *Me: Stories of My Life*. New York: Random House, 1991.

Higham, Charles. *Kate*. New York: W. W. Norton, 1975.

Hilmes, Michelle. *Hollywood and Broadcasting: From Radio to Cable*. Urbana: University of Illinois Press, 1990.

Hirschhorn, Clive. *The Columbia Story*. New York: Crown, 1990.

————. *The Universal Story*. New York: Crown, 1983.

————. *The Warner Bros. Story*. New York: Crown, 1979.

Hollis, Richard, and Brian Sibley. *The Disney Studio Story*. New York: Crown, 1988.

Hopper, Hedda. *From Under My Hat*. Garden City, NY: Doubleday, 1952.

Izod, John. *Hollywood and the Box Office, 1895–1986*. New York: Columbia University Press, 1988.

Jacobs, Lewis. *The Rise of the American Film: A Critical History*. New York: Teachers College Press, 1968.

Jewell, Richard B. *The Golden Age of Cinema: Hollywood 1929–1945*. Malden, MA: Blackwell, 2007.

————, with Vernon Harbin. *The RKO Story*. London: Octopus Books, 1982.

Jobes, Gertrude. *Motion Picture Empire*. Hamden, CT: Archon Books, 1966.

Kael, Pauline, Herman J. Mankiewicz, and Orson Welles. *The Citizen Kane Book*. New York: Bantam, 1971.

Kanin, Garson. *Hollywood*. New York: Viking Press, 1967.

Kemper, Tom. *Hidden Talent: The Emergence of the Hollywood Agents*. Berkeley: University of California Press, 2010.

Kennedy, Joseph P. *The Story of the Films*. Chicago: Shaw, 1927.

Kerr, Paul, ed. *The Hollywood Film Industry*. London: Routledge & Kegan Paul, 1986.

Kindem, Gorham, ed. *The American Movie Industry: The Business of Motion Pictures*. Carbondale: Southern Illinois University Press, 1982.

Kutz, Myer. *Rockefeller Power*. New York: Simon & Schuster, 1974.

Lambert, Gavin. *On Cukor*. New York: G. P. Putnam's Sons, 1972.

Lasky, Betty. *RKO: The Biggest Little Major of Them All*. Englewood Cliffs, NJ: Prentice-Hall, 1984.

Lasky, Jesse L., with Don Weldon. *I Blow My Own Horn*. Garden City, NY: Doubleday, 1957.

Levy, Emanuel. *George Cukor, Master of Elegance*. New York: William Morrow, 1994.

Lyons, Eugene. *David Sarnoff*. New York: Harper & Row, 1966.

McBride, Joseph. *Searching for John Ford: A Life*. New York: St. Martin's Press, 2001.

———. *Whatever Happened to Orson Welles?* Lexington: University Press of Kentucky, 2006.

McCarthy, Todd. *Howard Hawks*. New York: Grove Press, 1997.

———, and Charles Flynn, eds. *Kings of the Bs: Working within the Hollywood System; An Anthology of Film History and Criticism*. New York: E. P. Dutton, 1975.

Macgowan, Kenneth. *Behind the Screen*. New York: Delacorte Press, 1965.

Madsen, Axel. *Stanwyck*. New York: HarperCollins, 1994.

Maltby, Richard. *Hollywood Cinema*. 2nd ed. Malden, MA: Blackwell, 2003.

Miller, Don. *B Movies*. New York: Ballantine Books, 1973.

Mosley, Leonard. *Zanuck: The Rise and Fall of Hollywood's Last Tycoon*. Boston: Little, Brown, 1984.

Moss, Marilyn Ann. *Giant: George Stevens, a Life on Film*. Madison: University of Wisconsin Press, 2004.

Mueller, John. *Astaire Dancing*. New York: Knopf, 1985.

Nasaw, David. *The Chief: The Life of William Randolph Hearst*. Boston: Houghton Mifflin, 2000.

Ohmer, Susan. *George Gallup in Hollywood*. New York: Columbia University Press, 2006.

Okrent, Daniel. *Great Fortune: The Epic of Rockefeller Center*. New York: Viking, 2003.

Parsons, Louella O. *Tell It to Louella*. New York: G. P. Putnam's Sons, 1961.

Powdermaker, Hortense. *Hollywood, the Dream Factory*. Boston: Little, Brown, 1951.

Reich, Cary. *The Life of Nelson A. Rockefeller: Worlds to Conquer, 1908–1958*. New York: Doubleday, 1996.

Roddick, Nick. *A New Deal in Entertainment: Warner Brothers in the 1930s*. London: BFI, 1983.

Rogers, Ginger. *Ginger: My Story*. New York: HarperCollins, 1991.

Rosten, Leo C. *Hollywood: The Movie Colony, the Movie Makers*. New York: Harcourt Brace, 1941.

Sarris, Andrew. *"You Ain't Heard Nothin' Yet": The American Talking Film History and Memory, 1927–1949*. New York: Oxford University press, 1998.

Satchell, Tim. *Astaire: The Biography*. London: Hutchinson, 1987.

Schatz, Thomas. *Boom and Bust: The American Cinema in the 1940s*. New York: Scribner's, 1997.

———. *The Genius of the System: Hollywood Filmmaking in the Studio Era*. New York: Metropolitan Books, 1996.

Selznick, David O. *Memo from David O. Selznick*. Ed. Rudy Behlmer. New York: Viking Press, 1972.

Shindler, Colin. *Hollywood in Crisis: Cinema and American Society 1929–1939.* London: Routledge, 1996.

Sklar, Robert. *Movie-Made America.* Rev. ed. New York: Vintage Books, 1994.

Slide, Anthony. *The American Film Industry: A Historical Dictionary.* New York: Limelight, 1990.

Smoodin, Eric, ed. *Disney Discourse: Producing the Magic Kingdom.* New York: Routledge, 1994.

Sobel, Robert. *RCA.* New York: Stein & Day, 1986.

Staiger, Janet, ed. *The Studio System.* New Brunswick, NJ: Rutgers University Press, 1995.

Stanley, Robert. *The Celluloid Empire: A History of the American Motion Picture Industry.* New York: Hastings House, 1978.

Stevens, Jr., George, ed. *Conversations with the Great Moviemakers of Hollywood's Golden Age.* New York: Knopf, 2006.

Thomas, Bob. *Astaire, the Man, the Dancer.* New York: St. Martin's Press, 1984.

———. *Building a Company: Roy O. Disney and the Creation of an Entertainment Empire.* New York: Hyperion, 1998.

———. *King Cohn: The Life and Times of Harry Cohn.* New York: G. P. Putnam's Sons, 1967.

———. *Thalberg: Life and Legend.* Garden City, NY: Doubleday, 1969.

———. *Walt Disney: An American Original.* New York: Hyperion, 1994.

Thomas, Tony, and Aubrey Solomon. *The Films of 20th Century–Fox.* Secaucus, NJ: Citadel, 1979.

Thomson, David. *Showman: The Life of David O. Selznick.* New York: Knopf, 1992.

Truffaut, Francois. *Hitchcock.* New York: Simon & Schuster, 1967.

Vasey, Ruth. *The World According to Hollywood, 1918–1939.* Madison: University of Wisconsin Press, 1997.

Vaz, Mark Cotta. *Living Dangerously: The Adventures of Merian C. Cooper.* New York: Villard, 2005.

Vidor, King. *A Tree Is a Tree.* New York: Harcourt, Brace, 1952.

Vieira, Mark. *Irving Thalberg: Boy Wonder to Producer Prince.* Berkeley: University of California Press, 2010.

Wasko, Janet. *Movies and Money: Financing the American Film Industry.* Norwood, NJ: Ablex, 1982.

Welles, Orson, and Peter Bogdanovich. *This Is Orson Welles.* New York: Da Capo Press, 1998.

Wilcox, Herbert. *Twenty-Five Thousand Sunsets: The Autobiography of Herbert Wilcox.* London: Bodley Head, 1967.

Wood, Michael. *America in the Movies.* New York: Basic Books, 1975.

Wray, Fay. *On the Other Hand: A Life Story.* New York: St. Martin's Press, 1989.

Zierold, Norman. *The Moguls.* New York: Coward-McCann, 1969.

Index

Aalberg, John, 264
Abbott, George, 194
Abe Lincoln in Illinois, 172, 178, 185, 197–99, 203, 255
Abel, David, 97, 261
Academy Award, 75, 102, 106, 129, 144, 145, 175, 188, 233
Academy of Motion Pictures Arts and Sciences, 42, 219, 265
Accounting Department, 265
Acting Department, 156, 259
Action/Adventure films, 22, 74, 79, 98, 155, 157, 161, 169
Address Unknown, 200
Advertising, 33, 51–52, 55–56, 128, 171, 204, 208, 210, 213, 215, 217, 218–19, 269
Advertising Department, 55, 58, 202
The Affairs of Annabel, 161
After Tonight, 72
Alcott, Louisa May, 75
Alger, George W., 139–40, 142, 151
Alice Adams, 106, 113, 118, 120, 121, 128
Allegheny Uprising, 173, 203
Allen, Gracie, 144
All Quiet on the Western Front, 53
Allvine, Glendon, 94
Alperson, Edward, 253, 270
Ambassador Hotel, 137
Ameche, Don, 68

The American Way, 172, 178, 185, 197
Amos 'n' Andy, 27
Anderson, Maxwell, 128, 129
Andy Hardy series, 161
The Animal Kingdom, 59, 60
Animated shorts, 126
Anna Karenina, 64
Anne of Green Gables, 97, 98, 104
Anne of Windy Poplars, 178, 203
A Pictures, 50–51, 68–69, 72, 85, 98, 106, 116, 130, 134–35, 137–39, 157, 196–97, 203, 221, 223, 247, 252, 258–59
Applause, 38
Ardrey, Robert, 209–10
Argosy magazine, 140
Argosy Pictures, 72
Arlen, Richard, 44
Armour, Reg, 249–50, 252
Arms and the Man, 247
Armstrong, Robert, 47, 62, 135
Arnold, Edward, 153
Art deco style, 97, 260
Art Department, 260
Art direction, 97, 102, 106, 175, 260
Arthur, Jean, 127, 202
Astaire, Adele, 54, 82
Astaire, Fred: Astaire-Rogers formula, 107; Astaire-Rogers partnership at RKO, end of, 178; as auteur, 200; *The Barkleys of*

Astaire, Fred: *(continued)*
Broadway, 178; *Carefree*, 153–54, 163; collaboration with music department, 263; contract negotiations, 105, 117–18, 200; *A Damsel in Distress*, 143–44, 156, 200; declining reputation, 156, 159; disinterest in teaming with Rogers, 82–83, 117, 143, 175; displeasure with RKO instability, 105, 117–18, 151; emergence as top star, 94, 97, 108, 135; *Flying Down to Rio*, 81, 123; *Follow the Fleet*, 127; *The Gay Divorcée*, 96–97, 99, 107; and Irving Berlin, 104–5; and leading ladies, 117–18; leaves RKO, 200; and Leland Hayward, 74, 83; Lubitsch's desire to work with, 155; profit participation, 282n47; and radio, 131; *Radio City Revels*, 89, 107; *Roberta*, 98–100, 107; *Shall We Dance*, 143, 163; signs with RKO, 54, 71; *The Story of Vernon and Irene Castle*, 175–76, 178; *Swing Time*, 117, 127; *Top Hat*, 106–8, 109, 118, 127
Astor Theater, 22
A. T. & T., 13
Atlas Corporation, 101, 110, 139, 142–43, 151–52, 159–60, 167, 168, 186–87, 192–93, 235, 253
Audience Research Institute, 194, 206, 209, 212–13, 233. *See also* Gallup, George
August, Joseph, 261
Autry, Gene, 136
The Awful Truth, 155, 174
Aylesworth, Merlin Hall: as chairman of board, 111, 160; concern over A and B pictures, 50; conflict with Selznick, 48–50, 61–62, 64, 65; as corporate president, 40–43, 46–52, 149; leaves the company, 133; and the Legion of Decency, 95; and NBC, 60, 73, 131; and Radio City Music Hall, 59; radio-film harmony, 42–43, 51, 89, 112–13,

131–32, 134; and RKO reorganization, 82; and television, 126; and theater operations, 69; working with Kahane and Cooper, 84, 92

B Pictures, 9, 50–51, 68–69, 94, 98, 104–5, 134–39, 156–57, 197, 204, 214, 228, 230–31, 246–47, 258–59
Bachelor Mother, 180–83, 194
Bachrach, Ernest, 261
Baker, Graham, 172–73, 178, 179, 201, 226
Balaban and Katz theater chain, 111
Balio, Tino, 125, 211
Ball, Lucille, 99, 135, 161, 230, 259
Ball of Fire, 227, 253
Bank holiday, 67
Bank of America, 146
Bankers Trust Company, 237
Bankruptcy, 42–43, 66, 92, 192. *See also* receivership
Banks, Leslie, 70
Baravalle, Victor, 25
The Barkleys of Broadway, 178
Barry, Harold, 262
Barrymore, Ethel, 59
Barrymore, John, 11, 55
Bauer, Leda, 196
Baxter, Anne, 240
Beau Idea, 36
The Beachcomber, 202
Becky Sharp, 101–3, 104
Before the Fact, 231, 233
Behind the Headlines, 134
Benedict, Howard, 246–47
Benjamin Franklin, 194
Bennett, Constance, 31, 35, 47, 53, 56–57, 72–73, 259
Bennett, Joan, 75
Benny, Jack, 112
Berggren, P. J., 26
Berle, Milton, 135
Berlin, Irving, 59, 104–5, 106, 175, 263, 282n47
Berman, Henry, 262

Berman, Pandro S.: as associate
  producer, 44, 52, 69–70; and David
  Selznick, 44; and Fred Astaire, 83,
  96, 98, 107, 131, 163; and George
  Schaefer, 168, 173–75, 179–80, 225,
  230; and George Stevens, 200–201;
  and Ginger Rogers, 153–54, 163,
  175–77, 180–82; and *Gunga Din*,
  169–70; and *Hunchback of Notre
  Dame*, 183–84, 187–88; and
  Katharine Hepburn, 84, 91, 106,
  118, 121, 128, 152; leaves RKO, 187,
  201, 294n71; and lending stars,
  86–88; and *Mary of Scotland*, 128;
  as production head, 85–86, 89,
  141–42, 148, 149–50, 155–59, 162,
  189; resigns as production head, 88,
  187; and *Room Service*, 163–65;
  and *Stage Door*, 143–45; steps in
  for Cooper, 73, 82, 85; and Tech-
  nicolor, 101; as unit producer, 94,
  113–14, 116, 136, 189, 260
Berns, Mel, 263
Berst, J. A., 31
The Best Years of Our Lives, 33
Big Broadcast of 1936, 112
The Big Trail, 27
A Bill of Divorcement (1932), 53, 55–56
A Bill of Divorcement (1940), 203
Bill, Raymond, 253
Billy the Kid, 27
Bird of Paradise, 44, 55
Birth of a Nation, 8
The Bitter Tea of General Yen, 60
Blackface, 28
Blane, Sally, 24
Blind buying/selling, 211, 268
Block booking, 145, 147, 166, 190, 194,
  211, 225–26, 268
Blore, Eric, 96, 106, 259
Blumberg, Nate, 69, 238, 270
Boles, John, 28, 88
Bombardier, 234, 300n40
Bondy, Judge William, 65, 96, 139,
  142, 150–51, 186–87, 192–93
Borden, Olive, 24
Boretz, Allan, 164

Bowman, Patric, 59
"box-office poison" campaign, 153,
  156
Boyd, William, 31
Boyer, Charles, 174, 202
Boys Town, 161
Brady, Alice, 96
Brandt, Harry, 144, 156
Brandt, Jerrold T., 201
Breakfast for Two, 155
Break of Hearts, 106, 120
Breen, Bobby, 220–21
Breen, Joseph: as head of production,
  221–26, 228–30, 236–40, 252–53,
  255; Production Code Administra-
  tion, 77, 208–10, 221, 252–53
The Bride Walks Out, 127
Bring 'Em Back Alive, 55
Bringing Up Baby, 136–37, 140, 152,
  153, 155, 162–63, 169, 222, 239
Briskin, Samuel, 112, 115–17, 120–21,
  123–26, 130–31, 134–42, 147–48,
  159, 162–66, 169
Broadway, 12, 22, 25, 27, 58, 85, 143,
  163, 178, 266
Broadway Melody, 21–22
The Broadway Melody of 1936, 112
Broadway Melody of 1940, 200
Broadway Theater, 218
Brock, Lou, 81, 85, 86, 89–91, 94–95,
  96, 105, 260, 283n2, 283n8
Broderick, Helen, 106, 161, 259
Bronder, Lucia, 56
Brown, Harry Joe, 35
Brown, Hiram, 16–18, 22, 25, 30, 31,
  34, 37, 40
Brown, Katharine, 54, 96, 267
Brown, Tom, 89
Buck, Frank, 55
Bulldog Drummond series, 161
Bulwer-Lytton, Sir Edward, 109
Burns, George, 144
Business Week, 66
Butler, David, 225

Cabanne, Christy, 10
Cagney, James, 24

Call Out the Marines, 229
Camera Department, 261, 262, 264
Camera FX Department, 260, 261, 262, 264
Canutt, Yakima, 10
Capitol Theater, 58
Capra, Frank, 60, 68, 116, 234, 289n86
Carefree, 153, 157, 163
Carey, Harry, 32
Carthay Circle Theater, 146
Cartoons, 6, 101, 124, 126
Casablanca, 122
The Case of Sergeant Grischa, 28
Casting Department, 261
Castle, Edgerton, 140
Catholic Legion of Decency, 95, 157
C.B.C. Film Corporation, 112
Censorship, 77, 96, 158, 171, 194, 208, 210. *See also* Production Code Administration
Chandler, Chick, 89
Chaney, Lon, 187
Chang, 44
Chaplin, Charlie, 10, 59
Charlie Chan series, 161
Charteris, Leslie, 161
Chartier, Roy, 147
Check and Double Check, 27–28
Cheesman, Ted, 262
Chemical National Bank, 34
Chester Bennett Productions, 10
Christensen, Andrew, 171
Christopher Strong, 92
Cimarron, 33, 36, 47, 57, 233
Citizen Kane, 2, 5, 203, 207–8, 213, 214–20, 222, 241–42, 251, 254–56, 260
Clark, Carroll, 106, 260
Clark, William H., 265
Clearances, 211, 269
Clip Joint, 158
Cobb, Gerard, 168
The Cocoanuts, 22
Cohen, Maury, 136
Cohn, Harry, 68, 69, 80, 105, 112, 149, 152
Cohn, Jack, 132, 149

Colbert, Claudette, 24
Coldeway, Anthony, 36
Cole, Rufus, 8–9
Collier's, 12, 162
Collins, Ray—240
Collis, Maurice, 194
Colman, Ronald, 169
Color film, 26, 101. *See also* Technicolor
Colorado Public Utilities Commission, 41
Columbia: B. B. Kahane, 122, 289n86; B pictures, 69; cost consciousness, 68; Depression-era stability, 68; Disney, 125; Harry Cohn, 80, 149; Howard Hawks, 123; Jack Cohn, 132, 149; Katharine Hepburn loan, 152; major studio, 257; Samuel Briskin, 112, 116, 139, 289n86; Sid Rogell, 124
Comedies, 28, 54, 165, 190, 196
Commitments Department, 3, 265
The Common Law, 35
Compson, Betty, 24
Condemned Women, 204
Confessions of a Nazi Spy, 196
Connelly, Myles, 36
The Conquerors, 49, 57–58
Conrad, Joseph, 185
Consent decree of 1940, 194, 211, 225, 236, 256
Consolidated Film Industries (CFI), 261
Construction Department, 261
Cooper, Merian C.: and David Selznick, 44, 50, 55, 65; as head of production, 65, 67–71, 74–76, 79–82, 85, 92; illness, 73–74, 82, 84, 141; and *King Kong,* 55, 62–63; leaves RKO, 103, 109; and Pioneer Pictures, 101–3; as producer, 44, 94, 108–9, 110, 285n43; steps down, 85
Coordinating Committee on National Defense, 194–95
Cormack, Bartlett, 51
Corporate president, 2, 3, 16, 46, 61–62, 68, 116, 149, 157, 159–60, 168, 172, 220, 235, 258, 271

Correll, Charles. *See* Amos 'n' Andy
Corrigan, Lloyd, 102
Cortez, Ricardo, 47, 52
Cortez, Stanley, 240
Cost overages, 48, 49, 51, 175
Costello, Dolores, 240
Costume Department, 262, 264, 266
Cotten, Joseph, 240
The Covered Wagon, 146
Cowan, William J., 24
Coward, Noel, 59
Cox, Anthony Berkeley, 231
Cracked Nuts, 35
Cram, Mildred, 174, 175
Cramer, Claire, 264
Crawford, Joan, 131, 153
Crime films, 157
The Criminal Code, 123
Creelman, James, 109
Croce, Arlene, 97, 177
Cromwell, John, 77, 86, 87, 90, 95,
    198, 255, 260
Cronjager, Edward, 261
Cukor, George, 53, 55, 57, 72, 75–77,
    118, 152, 232, 260
Custer, Bob, 10

Daily Mirror, 218
A Damsel in Distress, 143, 144, 156,
    200, 287n23
Dance, Girl, Dance, 203, 227
Dance Hall, 22
Dance numbers, 96, 109, 117, 153,
    177, 200
The Dancing Masters, 297n81
Dancing Pirate, 104
Danger Lights, 27
Daniels, Bebe, 24, 25, 28, 36, 38
Darnell, Linda, 202
Daves, Delmer, 174
David Copperfield, 64, 76
Davies, Marion, 131, 219
Davis, Bette, 24, 86, 87
Day, Laraine, 202
Dee, Frances, 75, 104, 231
Del Rio, Dolores, 36, 55, 81
DeMille, Cecil B., 109

Denham, Carl, 62
Departments. *See names of individ-
    ual departments*
Depinet, Ned E., 36, 41, 48, 55, 76,
    81–82, 99, 107, 112, 134, 135, 138,
    149, 160, 168, 171, 196, 225, 227,
    267–69
Depression, 19, 28, 32, 34, 38, 43,
    58, 63, 68, 97, 133, 184, 186, 189,
    270
Derr, E. B., 10, 31
DeSylva, Buddy, 175, 180
The Devil and Miss Jones, 222,
    247
Dieterle, William, 188, 189, 215,
    226
Dietrich, Marlene, 195
Dinner at Eight, 64
Directors Department, 71, 105, 260
Disney, Roy, 125
Disney, Walt, 101, 124–26, 146–47,
    148, 201, 244, 301n76
Distribution, 1, 8–10, 15, 35, 48, 52,
    80, 103, 124–26, 147, 166, 192, 211,
    217, 257–58
Distribution division, 36, 63, 66, 107,
    146, 234, 241, 267–71, 303n3
Distribution exchanges, 268, 269
Divestiture, 66–67
Dix, Richard, 12, 24, 25, 28, 36, 38, 57,
    85, 95, 98, 121, 135, 259
Dixiana, 28, 32, 81, 101
Dmytryk, Edward, 262
Don Juan, 10
Donovan, Frank R., 220
Double features, 97, 111, 259, 285n45
Dove, Billie, 10
Down to Their Last Yacht, 85, 89–91,
    95, 284n8
Drake Hotel, 24, 95
Drama films, 10, 28, 86, 196
Dreiser, Theodore, 194
Dressler, Marie, 36
Duna, Steffi, 102
Dunn, Linwood, 261
Dunne, Irene, 27, 36, 38, 57, 85, 86, 95,
    98, 135, 174–75, 259, 282n47

Earhart, Amelia, 59

The Echo, 22

Eddy, Nelson, 195

Edington, Harry: concedes decisions to Schaefer, 203, 214, 255; as head of production, 187, 193, 195–96; "in name only," 195, 220; and Orson Welles, 206–7, 215; *Suspicion*, 231, 233; "washing up" his contract, 224, 236

Editorial Department, 262

Eglington, Bill, 261

"Eight major" studios, 19, 38, 166, 211, 257

Eilers, Sally, 135

Electrical Department, 262–63

Electrical Research Products, 13. *See* A. T. & T.

Ellison, James, 202

Enchanted April, 110

Enzinger, George, 177

Equity Pictures, 18

Ermolieff, Joseph, 216

Errol, Leon, 5

Espy, Reeves, 247

Estabrook, Howard, 33, 47, 57, 67, 260

The Ex-Mrs. Bradford, 127, 136

Executive producer for B films, 259

Exhibition, 22, 24, 146, 223, 238–39, 258

Exhibitors Herald and Motion Picture World, 17–18, 20, 25

Exploitation films, 157

Fadiman, William, 205

Fairbanks, Douglas, 10

Fairbanks, Jr., Douglas, 170, 171, 195, 301n72

Famous Players-Lasky, 12

Fan magazines, 31, 51, 266

Fanny Foley Herself, 36

Father Takes a Wife, 229, 230

Faulkner, William, 168

Faversham, William, 104

Faye, Alice, 68

Feldman, Charles, 200

Ferber, Edna, 33, 143

Ferguson, Perry, 260

Fidler, Jimmy, 266

Fields, W. C., 278n7

The Fight for Life, 226

Film Booking Offices of America, Incorporated (FBO), 9–10, 12–16, 18–20, 24, 31, 189, 274n23

Film Daily, 33

Film palace. *See* "picture palaces"

"Final production authority," 61, 188, 203, 224, 258

Fineman, B. P., 10, 94

First National, 9, 14, 15

The First Rebel. See *Allegheny Uprising*

Fisher, Kenneth L., 110

Fitzgerald, F. Scott, 258

Fitzmaurice, George, 56–57

Five Came Back, 204

Flight From Glory, 204

"Fly Away Home," 260

Flying Down to Rio, 71, 81, 82, 86, 90, 96, 123

Follow the Fleet, 116, 127

Fonda, Henry, 197

Fontaine, Joan, 135, 143, 156, 202, 231–34

Forty-Second Street, 71

Four Daughters, 161

The Four Feathers, 44

The Four Horsemen of the Apocalypse, 146

Ford, John, 95, 106, 120, 128, 129, 199, 234, 282n47

Foreign box office, 183–84, 196, 256, 269

Foreign Power Company, 110

Fort, Garrett, 194

Foster, Norman, 242

Four Jacks and a Jill, 252

Fowler, Roy Alexander, 255

Fox Film Corporation. *See* Twentieth Century-Fox

Fox Movietone News, 32

Frank Ross-Norman Krasna Productions, 201

Franklin-Blank Productions, 201
Franklin, Harold B., 41, 48, 55, 60, 70, 201, 270
Freckles, 98
Frederick, Pauline, 10, 52
Freeland, Thornton, 81
Friends and Lovers, 36

Gable, Clark, 121, 131, 169
Gahagan, Helen, 108, 285n42
Gallup, George, 194, 209–10, 213. *See also* Audience Research Institute
The Gang's All Here, 278n7
Gangster genre, 38, 76
Garbo, Greta, 56, 153, 155, 195
Garnett, Tay, 225
The Gay Diplomat, 44
The Gay Divorce, 82, 83, 96
The Gay Divorcée, 96–97, 99, 106, 107
General Electric Company, 12, 66
Genre. *See names of individual genres*
Gershwin, George, 123, 124, 263, 287n23
Gershwin, Ira, 123, 263, 287n23
Gilbert, John, 25
Girl Crazy, 49
Girl From Mexico, 204
Girl of the Rio, 55
"give-away" nights, 97
Glade, Coe, 59
Gloria Productions, Incorporated, 18
Goetz, Harry, 172, 178, 179, 192, 197–99, 226
Goetz, William, 292n55
Goldwyn, Samuel, 33, 125, 140, 155–56, 191, 226–27, 253, 299n16
Gone With the Wind, 64, 121, 122, 147, 189, 218, 243
Good Housekeeping, 241
Gordon, Don, 208, 212
Gordon, Max, 172, 178, 179, 192, 197–99, 226
Gosden, Freeman. *See* Amos 'n' Andy
Gower Street studio. *See* RKO Studio

Graham, Martha, 59
Graham, Sheilah, 266
Grainger, Dorothy, 89
Grand Hotel, 50
Grand National Pictures, 257
Grant, Cary: *Bringing Up Baby*, 162–63; *Gunga Din*, 169, 171; and Harry Edington, 195; *Holiday*, 152; nonexclusive contract, 202; *Once Upon a Honeymoon*, 247; *Suspicion*, 231, 233; *Sylvia Scarlett*, 119
Grass, 44
Grauman's Chinese Theater, 22, 63
Grauman, Sid, 63
Green Hell, 195
Green, Lawrence, 253
Griffith, D. W., 103
"grooming" talent, 53, 156, 267
Guiol, Fred, 169
Gunga Din, 123, 145, 155, 156, 158, 168–71, 174, 175, 176, 200

Haggard, H. Rider, 108
Haight, George, 176
Haldane of the Secret Service, 10
Half Rogue, 194
Hall, John, 3–4
Hamilton, William, 97, 262
Hamlet, 102
Hammerstein, Oscar, 176
Hanbury, Ralph, 211
Happy Days, 27
Harbach, Otto, 99
Harbin, Vernon, 3–4
Harding, Ann, 31, 47, 53, 55, 57, 72, 86, 95, 98, 110, 123, 195
Hardwicke, Cedric, 188, 215
Harris, Jed, 226, 247
Harrison, Joan, 231
Hart, Moss, 185
Hart, William S., 8
Hawks, Howard, 123, 136–37, 141, 154–55, 162–63, 168–70
Hawks, William, 154, 201, 215, 247
Hayakawa, Sessue, 10
Hays Office, 77, 157

Hays, Will, 59, 112, 208, 209
Hayward, Leland, 74, 82–83, 105, 120, 154, 200, 215, 220
Hayward, Louis, 161
Head of Production, 258, 261, 267, 268; B. B. Kahane, 122; B. P. Schulberg at Paramount, 53; Charles Koerner, 238; Charles Rogers at Pathe and Universal, 32, 35, 277n64; Darryl Zanuck at Twentieth Century-Fox, 68, 189; David Selznick, 35, 40, 44–46, 50, 53, 62; Edwin King, FBO, 10; Hal Wallis at Warner Bros., 189; Harry Edington, 195, 220; Irving Thalberg at MGM, 189; Joseph Breen, 238, 252; Merian C. Cooper, 74, 84, 85; Pandro Berman, 85, 148, 162, 165, 175, 189; Samuel Briskin, 125, 130, 140, 141, 169; William LeBaron, 15, 29
Hearst, William Randolph, 59, 208, 213–19, 254, 297n77
Heart of Darkness, 185, 190, 205–6, 207
Hecht, Ben, 24, 169
Hell and High Water, 140
Hempstead, David, 212, 215, 225, 260
Hepburn, Katharine: Academy Award, 75; Alice Adams, 105–6; "box office poison," 153; Bringing Up Baby, 136–37, 152, 162–63; contract negotiations, 83–84; contract termination, 152, 156; debut, 55; disenchantment with RKO, 120–21; and George Stevens, 106; The Little Minister, 97; Little Women, 75–77; public disenchantment with, 90; signing, 53–54, 267; Spitfire, 77–78, 90–91; Stage Door, 143–45; Sylvia Scarlett, 118–20; as top star, 95, 98; waning reputation, 118, 128, 135; A Woman Rebels, 121, 128
Herbert, A. P., 194
Herman, Al, 175
Hertz, John, 111

Herzbrun, Henry, 228
High Flyers, 135
Hit the Deck, 22, 24
Hitchcock, Alfred, 231–34, 300n31
Hitting a New High, 155, 162
Hively, George, 262
Hodges, Douglas, 25
Hold 'Em Jail, 49
Holden, Lancing C., 108
Holiday, 152
Hollywood on the Air, 89, 113
Hollywood Reporter, 76, 152, 201
Holmes, Phillips, 56
Holmes, Taylor, 59
Holt, Tim, 203, 228
Hook, Line and Sinker, 28
Hoover, Herbert, 38
Hopkins, Miriam, 102–3, 135
Hopper, DeWolf, 59
Hopper, Hedda, 266, 297n77
Horror films, 235, 247
Horton, Edward Everett, 96, 106
Houdini, Harry, 10
Houdini Picture Corporation, 10
Howard, Leslie, 56, 86, 87
Howard, Sidney, 208, 209
Howe, G. B., 265
Hoyt, Harry, 36
Hughes, Howard, 2, 4
Hugo, Victor, 187
Hull, Cordell, 212
The Hunchback of Notre Dame, 178, 180, 183–84, 185, 187–88, 190, 226, 233, 259
Hunt, J. Roy, 261
Hunt Stromberg Productions, 10
Hurst, Fannie, 59

Idiot's Delight, 116
I Dream Too Much, 110
Iles, Francis. See Cox, Anthony Berkeley
Imperator-Radio Pictures, 173
Independent producers, 174, 179, 191–92, 202, 226
Independent Theatre Owners Association, 144, 153, 156

The Informer, 106, 122, 129, 130
Institute of Public Opinion, 194
"intermediates," 134, 138–39, 156
Intermezzo, 64
International Pictures, 292n55
Irene, 203
Irving Trust Company, 65, 66, 110,
    145, 149–50, 171, 192
Italian Superpower Corporation,
    110
It's a Gift, 278n7
It's All True, 241–46, 248–52,
    285n31
Ivanhoe, 173, 178

Jaffe, Sam, 48, 67, 170
Jalna, 110
Jamaica Inn, 202
The Jazz Singer, 11, 102
Joan of Arc, 102
Joan of Paris, 252
John, Graham, 36
Johnson, William, 262
Jolson, Al, 11, 112
Jones, Robert Edmond, 59, 60, 102
Jordan, Dorothy, 84, 90
Journal-American, 218
Joy of Living, 162, 173
Julius Caesar, 178

Kahane, Benjamin Bertram (B. B.): at
    Columbia, 122–23; and contract
    negotiations, 54, 61, 72; cost-
    cutting, 67; and David Selznick, 44,
    46–50, 57–58, 62; and FBO, 18;
    Flying Down to Rio, 81; and
    Katharine Hepburn, 78, 84, 119–20;
    and Lou Brock, 85–86, 90; and
    Merian Cooper, 69, 73–74; and
    Pandro Berman, 88, 101; as
    president of RKO Studios, 82; as
    president of production, 41, 46–52,
    61–63, 65, 70; as production head,
    89, 94, 104, 105, 112–15; as RKO
    general counsel, 36–37
Kalmar, Bert, 24
Kalmus, Herbert, 101

Kanin, Garson, 156, 160, 180, 182,
    208–10, 215, 227
Kaufman, Edward, 104, 136, 155, 164,
    260
Kaufman, George S., 143, 185
Keene, Tom, 71
Keith, B. F., 8, 14
Keith-Albee-Orpheum, 13–16,
    18, 41
Kennedy, Edgar, 105
Kennedy, Joseph P.: FBO, 10, 12, 15,
    18, 274n23; Pathe, 13, 30–31; and
    Queen Kelly, 18; Robertson-Cole,
    9; rumored FBO merger, 15; sound
    conversion, 10–12, 14
Kennedy, Rose, 59
Kent, Sidney, 159
Kentucky Kernels, 105
Kern, Jerome, 99, 263
King, Edwin, 12
King Kong, 55, 61, 62–63, 76, 79, 103,
    110, 122, 261, 263
King Solomon's Mines, 98
Kingsberg, Malcolm, 254, 270
Kipling, Rudyard, 123, 168
Kismet, 9
Kitty Foyle, 212–13, 234
Koerner, Charles, 223, 235, 238–39,
    247, 253, 270
Kramer, Stanley, 303n113
Krasna, Norman, 180, 194
Kreutzberg, Harold, 59
Kyser, Kay, 203, 215, 222

Labor unions, 138–39
La Cava, Gregory, 143, 155, 173
La Cucaracha, 95, 102
Laddie, 98
The Lady Consents, 116
A Lady to Love, 208
Laemmle, Carl, 69
Laemmle, Junior, 69
Lang, Fritz, 173
Lasky, Jesse, 44, 123, 136, 155
The Last Days of Pompeii, 85, 95, 103,
    108–10, 285n45
The Last of the Mohicans, 102

Latin American market, 212
Laughton, Charles, 178, 188–89, 194, 202, 208–10
Law of the Underworld, 204
LeBaron, William, 25, 28–29, 31, 33, 34; and coming of sound, 14–15; FBO, 12, 18, 19; as head of production, 22–24, 29, 31, 33–36, 80; at Paramount, 41, 278n7; playwright, 22; Rio Rita, 24–25
Lederer, Francis, 71, 89, 98
Leeds, Andrea, 145
Legal Department, 117, 216, 265
Legion of Decency. See Catholic Legion of Decency
Lehman Brothers, 101, 110
Lessing, Gunther, 151
Lesser, Sol, 220–21, 223–25, 228, 230, 236–39, 246, 255, 300n56
Let's Try Again, 85
Letty Lynton, 50
Levy, Jules, 99, 116, 135, 156
Lewton, Val, 247
Liberty Films, 289n86
Lieber, Perry, 237, 266
Life, 146, 217, 241
The Life of the Party, 155
The Lights of New York, 11, 102
Lindi, Aroldo, 59
Literary properties, 34, 85, 173, 178, 190, 193–94, 199, 255
Little Caesar, 38
The Little Foxes, 227, 253
Little Men, 222, 226
The Little Minister, 97, 106, 121
Little Women, 72, 75–77, 79, 92, 104, 118, 152
Lloyd, Harold, 10, 173, 179, 201
Loew's, Inc., 19, 68, 110, 111, 270
Lombard, Carole, 178, 194, 208–10, 212
Look Magazine, 241
Look Who's Laughing, 230
Lord, Robert, 57
Lorentz, Pare, 226
Los Angeles Times, 76
The Lost Patrol, 71

The Lost Squadron, 44
Love Affair, 158, 174–75, 247
The Love Parade, 38
Lubitsch, Ernst, 53, 155
Lubitsch touch, 210
Luce, Claire, 96
Luce, Henry, 217
Lucky Partners, 203
Lusty, Lou, 136, 137

MacArthur, Charles, 169
Macgowan, Kenneth, 53, 75, 86, 94, 102, 103, 104, 260
Mackaill, Dorothy, 32
Mackenzie, Compton, 118
The Mad Miss Manton, 156
Madison Square Garden, 235
The Magnificent Ambersons, 239, 241–42, 248
Majestic Pictures, 257
Makeup and Hair Stylists Department, 263, 264
Mallard, William, 212
Mamoulian, Rouben, 103, 104
Man of Two Words, 89
A Man to Remember, 156, 160–61, 204
Man Without a World, 195–96, 204
Management. See corporate president; executive producer for B films; head of production
Mankiewicz, Herman, 207, 219
March, Fredric, 120
March of Time, 5, 145
Marcus, Lee: on Katharine Hepburn, 53; liaison between studio and home office, 41; as president of RKO Pathe Pictures, 32, 34, 38; as producer at Twentieth Century-Fox, 297n81; quits RKO, 214, 227; supervision of B pictures, 104, 134–37, 157–58, 173, 183, 195–97, 204–5, 230; as vice president, FBO, 18
Markert, Russell, 59
Marx Brothers, 24, 164–65

Mary of Scotland, 116, 119–20, 121, 128

Mascot Pictures Corporation, 257

Massey, Raymond, 178, 198, 199

Maugham, Somerset, 86

Max Gordon Plays and Pictures, 172, 198

Mayer, Louis B., 63, 69, 73, 149, 169, 217, 254, 282n47

Maynard, Ken, 32

The Mayor of 44th Street, 229

McCarey, Leo, 155, 158, 173, 174–75, 247

McCausland, A. H., 66, 84, 145, 151

McCrea, Joel, 56–57, 70, 195, 202

McDonough, Joseph R. (Mac): appointment to board, 150; and B. B. Kahane, 113–14, 115; B films, 157, 228–30; budgeting, 170, 173, 175, 207, 214, 228–30, 232–33; conflicts with Pandro Berman, 86, 88; corporate president, 82; forced resignation from RKO, 237–38, 246; as general manager RKO, 73; and George Schaefer, 179, 228–30, 238, 247–48; and Ginger Rogers, 153–54, 212; and Howard Hawks, 154–55; and Katharine Hepburn, 78; management shake-up, 112, 123, 150, 193; and Merian C. Cooper, 73–75, 84–85, 108–9; and Radio City Music Hall, 92; resigns VP title, 223; RKO studios, 94, 97–98; *They Knew What They Wanted*, 208–9

McGaffey, Elizabeth (Bessie), 266

McLaglen, Victor, 106, 129, 170, 171

McLaughlin, Irene Castle, 175–77

Meira, Manuel Olimpio, 252

Melodrama, 157, 161, 190

Melody Cruise, 71, 75, 81, 86, 90

Mercury Productions Company, 178–79, 192, 206, 216, 219, 242

Meredith, Burgess, 164

Messinger, Lillie, 142, 163, 178–79, 208, 212, 267

Metro-Goldwyn-Mayer (MGM): A picture budgets, 203; Astaire-Rogers, 178; borrowing George Fitzmaurice from, 56; David Selznick, 35, 63–64, 72, 73; Depression-era profits, 26, 68, 147, 237; Ernst Lubitsch, 155; Floyd Odlum, 110; Fox merger rumors, 32; George Cukor, 72, 75, 118; *Hunchback of Notre Dame* rights, 187–88; Katharine Hepburn, 153; Lou Ostrow, 247; as "major" studio, 1, 10, 257; offer to buy *Gunga Din*, 145; offer to buy *King Kong*, 63; Pandro Berman, 187, 294n71; "Realife" process, 27; Sam Wood, 212; sound, 14; and stars, 259; theater acquisition, 19, 270; unit production, 69, 94; widescreen, 26–27

A Midsummer Night's Dream, 116

Miller, Earl, 262

Mitchell, Langdon, 102

Mitchell, Margaret, 121

Mitchell, Silberberg, and Knupp, 117

Monogram Pictures, 257

Monte Carlo, 38

Montgomery, Douglass, 77

Montgomery, Lucy Maud, 97

Moore, Grace, 104–5

Moorehead, Agnes, 240

Morley, Christopher, 212

Morley, Karen, 52

Morning Glory, 75, 76, 92, 103, 121, 144

The Mortal Storm, 200

Moss, Jack, 239

Mother Carey's Chickens, 152, 153, 156, 161

Motion Picture Herald, 32, 43, 51, 71, 76, 89, 101, 108, 110, 113, 126, 131, 184, 196, 211

Motion Picture News, 12, 13

Motion Picture Producers and Distributors of America (MPPDA), 76–77. *See also* Hays Office

Movie palace. *See* "picture palaces"

Movietone, 15
Movietone sound newsreels, 12, 32
Mr. and Mrs., 194
Mr. and Mrs. Smith, 231
Mulhall, Jack, 32
Muni, Paul, 24
Murder on the Blackboard, 85
Murdock, J. P., 13
Murfin, Jane, 260
Murray, John, 164
Museum of Modern Art (MOMA), 191, 195
Music Department, 22, 263
Music for Madame, 143, 155
Musicals, 22, 24, 26, 28, 38, 71, 75, 81, 93, 98, 105, 127, 190, 200, 221, 244, 263
Musuraca, Nicholas, 261
Mutiny on the Bounty, 106
My Favorite Wife, 203
My Man Godfrey, 143

National Board of Review, 33, 62, 106, 219
National Broadcasting Company (NBC): David Sarnoff, 21; Merlin Aylesworth, 40–42, 60, 73, 131–32; NBC studio, 112; radio-movie symbiosis, 89; "Red" and "Blue" networks, 21; Rockefeller Center, 29
The NBC Revue of 1934. See *Radio City Revels*
National Electric Light Association, 41
Neagle, Anna, 173, 203
Neely bill, 194
Negri, Pola, 208
Nero Wolfe series, 161
The New Deal, 166
New Faces of 1937, 140, 143
Newman, Alfred, 188
Newsreel, 5, 12, 27, 31, 32, 34, 43, 66, 268
Newsweek, 111, 156, 214–15
New York Stock Exchange (NYSE), 133

The New York Times, 199
The New Yorker, 241
Nichols, Dudley, 106, 128, 162, 169, 260
Nicholls, Jr., George, 262
Ninotchka, 155, 210
Niven, David, 183
Nizer, Louis, 66
Nolan, J. J.: assistant secretary of RKO, 220; *Citizen Kane*, 215; production schedule, 196; rehiring, 247; resignation, 224; studio commitments, 184, 247, 265; "VP in charge of RKO studios," 193, 223; waste prevention, 186
Nugent, Frank S., 199
Nurse Edith Cavell, 173

Oakie, Jack, 135, 161, 164
Obliging Young Lady, 252
O'Brien, Edmund, 188
O'Brien, George, 171, 197, 203
O'Brien, Willis, 109–10
O'Connor, John J., 223, 270
O'Day, Dawn. *See* Shirley, Anne
Odlum, Floyd B.: Atlas investment trust, 101, 110; declines purchase of RCA stock, 151–52; and George Schaefer, 160, 221, 234–35, 248; and Joseph Breen, 221; postpones purchase of RCA stock, 143, 146, 150; RKO management shake-up, 111–13, 115, 131–33, 159; RKO performance, 147, 150; underwriting RKO shares, 187; willingness to sell interest in RKO, 254
Office of Inter-American Affairs, 242–43
O'Flaherty, Liam, 106
Ogilvy, David, 233
Of Human Bondage, 85–86, 87
O'Hara, Maureen, 188, 212
Oliver, Edna May, 36, 161, 259
Olivier, Lawrence, 55, 231
Once Upon a Honeymoon, 247
One Hour With You, 53

One Man's Journey, 75
One Night of Love, 105
Orpheum theaters, 13, 41
Oscar, 33, 106, 212–13, 219, 232, 233–34. *See also* Academy Award
O'Shea, Daniel T., 265
Ostrow, Lou, 201, 247
The Other Man, 209
Ouspenskaya, Maria, 175

Pan, Hermes, 97, 100, 200
Pantages Theater, 24, 171, 270
Parachute Battalion, 229
Paramount: David Selznick, 35, 44; Depression-era profits, 26, 147, 237; Ernst Lubitsch, 155; Floyd Odlum investment, 110; George Cukor, 53; George Schaefer, 168; Jesse Lasky, 44, 123; Leo Spitz, 111; "major" studio, 1, 257; Merian C. Cooper, 44, 53, 75; Radio-Keith-Orpheum (Canada) Ltd., 22; receivership, 66, 99; reorganization, 101; 77B, 92; sound conversion, 14; studio lot, 9; theateracquisition, 19, 24, 270; upper management, 149; widescreen, 26; William LeBaron, 41, 278n7
Parker, Jean, 75
Parkyakarkus, 135, 164, 178
Parsons, Louella, 213–15, 266, 297n77
Pascal, Gabriel, 226, 247
Passage from Bordeaux, 228
Pathe Film Company: facilities, 97, 259; Joseph Kennedy, 13, 15, 30–31; Pathe News, 31–32, 132, 195, 220; RKO merger, 5, 30–32, 123; RKO Pathe Pictures, Incorporated, 32–36, 38, 43, 56, 123, 130
Penner, Joe, 89, 135, 164, 178
The Perfect Crime, 15
Perkins, Grace, 194
Perry Mason series, 161
The Peter B. Kyne Story, 204
Peterson, Edgar, 205
The Petrified Forest, 116

The Phantom of Crestwood, 51–52
Photophone, 13, 15–16, 29–30, 132
Piazza, Ben, 267
Pichel, Irving, 70, 108
Pickford, Mary, 8, 125
"picture palaces," 14, 58, 108, 270
Pin-Up Girl, 278n7
Pioneer Pictures, 71, 95, 101–4, 243
Pitts, Zasu, 135
Pittsburgh Calcium Light & Film Company, 18
The Play's The Thing Productions, 173
The Plow That Broke the Plains, 226
Plunkett, Walter, 176
Polglase, Van Nest, 97, 106, 175, 260
Pommer, Erich, 202, 208, 209, 227–28, 237
Pons, Lily, 104–5, 110, 135, 178
Porter, Cole, 263
Portrait of a Rebel, 128
Potter, H. C., 176–77
Poverty row, 93, 257
Powell, Eleanor, 200
Powell, William, 44, 127
Power, Tyrone, 68
Powers, Pat, 9, 10
Pre-editing, 71
Preminger, Otto, 303n113
Prison pictures, 157, 161
The Prisoner of Zenda, 64
Proctor theaters, 23
Producers Department, 86, 94, 134, 136, 260
Producers Releasing Corporation (PRC), 257
Production Code Administration (PCA), 77, 208–10, 221, 252
Production Department, 86, 263
Production head/Production chief. *See* Head of Production
Profit participation, 55, 69, 78, 120, 265, 282n47
"programmers," 134, 228
Property Department, 22, 263–64
The Public Enemy, 38

Publicity Department, 104, 133, 145, 197, 213, 227, 237, 238, 247, 265–66
Pyramid Pictures Corporations, 201

Quality Street, 143
Queen Kelly, 18
Quigley, Martin, 17–18, 21, 113

Radio, 13, 15–16, 21, 27, 30, 42–43, 51–52, 75, 89, 111, 112–13, 126, 131–34, 206
Radio City Music Hall, 29, 51, 58, 60, 63, 70, 76, 79, 81, 92, 95, 99, 102, 107, 127, 130, 146, 159, 188, 217, 221
Radio City Revels, 89, 107, 162
Radio Corporation of America (RCA): antitrust suit, 66–67; David Sarnoff, 17, 19, 40, 152, 167, 247–48; Depression-era losses, 67; J. R. McDonough, 73; merger, 14, 20; Photophone, 13, 15–16, 29, 132; profits, 29; radio-film symbiosis, 21; RKO reorganization, 152; RKO stock buyout, 110, 142–43, 150–51; Rockefeller Center, 29, 58; sound on film, 12–13, 15, 19; television, 126; underwriting RKO, 37, 100–101
The Radio Flash, 303n3
Radio-Keith-Orpheum Corporation: bankruptcy relief, 92; birthday, 16; board of directors, 16, 40, 49, 51, 79–80, 98, 133, 140, 152, 186, 215, 236, 238–39, 253; corporate profits, 26, 33, 79, 91, 101, 113, 133, 147, 166; cost-cutting, 43, 46–47, 67–68, 186; creditors, 66, 127, 139, 142, 150–51, 186–87; financing, 34, 37, 101, 151, 237; "great purge," 246–47; management instability, 2, 88–89, 92, 112, 115, 142, 149, 160, 220, 225; merger rumors, 22–23, 30–31; net losses, 38, 43–44, 48, 65, 81, 99, 214; Pathe merger, 30–32; recapitalization, 37, 130, 187; reorganization, 40–41, 70, 96, 110,

127, 130–31, 139, 142, 150–52, 167, 186–87, 192; stockholders, 37, 139, 142, 186; subsidiary merger, 130; theater acquisition, 23–24, 34. *See also* corporate president; Radio City Music Hall; RKO Pathe Pictures, Incorporated; RKO Radio Pictures; Rockefeller Center; receivership
Radio-Keith-Orpheum (Canada) Ltd., 22
Rainbow on the River, 221
Rainbow Parade, 126
Ramsaye, Terry, 60, 74
Ranger the dog, 10
Rapee, Erno, 59
Raphaelson, Samson, 231
Rathvon, N. Peter, 110, 126, 140, 149–50, 159, 235, 237
Raymond, Gene, 81, 127
Rebecca, 64, 213, 232
Rebound, 36
Receivership, 37, 61, 63, 65–67, 79, 91–93, 95–96, 99, 111, 130–31, 139, 149, 150–51, 166, 186, 192–93
Ree, Max, 25
Reed, Luther, 24, 25, 260
Regent Theater, 58
Reid, Cliff, 94, 136, 137, 162, 246, 260
Reisman, Phil, 244, 249–52
Reissue/Re-release, 63, 171, 222, 285n45
Reliance Pictures, 123, 168
Republic Pictures, 257
Research Department, 266
Reville, Alma, 231
Rhodes, Erik, 96, 106, 259
The Rialto Theater, 58
Rice, Elmer, 194
Rickaby, H. C., 139
Rin-Tin-Tin, 201
Rio Rita, 20, 22, 24, 25, 28, 33, 101, 169, 188
The River, 226
Rivoli Theater, 15, 58
RKO 281, 254
RKO Pathe News, 31–32, 132, 195, 220

RKO Pathe Pictures, Incorporated, 32–36, 38, 43, 56, 123, 130

RKO Radio Pictures: birthday, 20; contract negotiations, 47, 61, 83–84, 112, 117, 179, 200, 220; "Hollywood's most mismanaged studio," 88; improving product, 110; improving reputation, 183; lending stars, 86, 88; logo, 20, 133; "major" studio, 1, 257; pay cuts, 67–68, 184, 214; poor quality, 28, 92, 141, 222; production schedule, 44–46, 50, 69, 80–81, 130, 138, 171, 178, 196–97, 226; profits, 99–100, 133; talent acquisition, 24–25, 27, 52, 71, 104, 135, 155, 202; weak male talent, 98, 164, 169; widescreen, 26–27. *See also* A pictures; B pictures; Head of Production

"RKO Radio's Little Theatre on the Lot," 260

RKO "Ranch," 22, 97–98, 188, 259

RKO Roxy, 58–60, 63, 70, 92

RKO Studio: Colegrove, 8; expansion, 22, 98; Gower Street, 9, 31, 98, 259; RKO PatheStudio, 31, 43, 97, 259

RKO Theatre of the Air, 89

Roach, Hal, 105

Roadhouse Murder, 49

Roar of the Dragon, 49

Roberta, 85, 98–100, 107, 113

Robertson-Cole (R-C), 8–10, 18, 94

Robertson, Harry, 8–9

Robinson, Edward G., 24

Robson, Mark, 262

Robson, May, 112

Rockabye, 56–57

Rockefeller Center, 29–30, 33, 58, 61, 110–11, 126, 130, 139, 142, 151, 159, 192. *See also* Radio City Music Hall; RKO Roxy

Rockefeller family: Abby Aldrich Rockefeller, 191; and George Schaefer, 160, 255; John D. Rockefeller, Jr., 29, 59; Nelson Rockefeller, 159–60, 191, 195, 234–35, 242–43, 249, 253; and Radio City Music Hall, 59, 95; and RKO Roxy, 70, 92; as RKO stockholders, 60, 130–31, 139–42, 151–52, 280n70; unhappiness with Floyd Odlum, 159, 235

Rogell, Sid, 123–24, 237, 246, 263

Roger Tuohy, Gangster, 297n81

Rogers, Charles R., 32, 34, 35, 277n64

Rogers, Ginger: Astaire-Rogers decline in popularity, 156, 159; Astaire-Rogers formula, 107; *Bachelor Mother*, 180–83; *The Barkleys of Broadway*, 178; *Carefree*, 153–54, 163; conflict with Mark Sandrich, 153–54; contract expiration, 220, 236; *A Damsel in Distress*, 143; emergence as a top star, 94, 98, 135, 202; end of Astaire-Rogers partnership at RKO, 178; *Flying Down to Rio*, 81; *Follow the Fleet*, 127; *The Gay Divorcée*, 96–97; *Kitty Foyle*, 212–13, 234; *Once Upon a Honeymoon*, 247; Oscar, 212–13; *Radio City Revels*, 89, 107; *Roberta*, 98–99, 107; *Top Hat*, 106–9, 127; *Shall We Dance*, 143; *Stage Door*, 143, 153; *The Story of Vernon and Irene Castle*, 175–78; *Swing Time*, 127; teaming with Astaire, 82–83, 117, 143, 200; *Tom, Dick and Harry*, 227

Rogers, Lela, 154, 259–60

Rogge, Florence, 59

Room Service, 157, 158, 163–65

Roosevelt, Franklin D., 33, 67, 92, 199

"Roosevelt recession," 166

Rose, Ruth, 109

Rosenberg, Nathan, 151

Ross, Frank, 201, 247

Rothafel, Samuel Lionel "Roxy," 58–59, 60, 92

Rowland, Richard A., 94

Roxy Theater, 58, 92

Rubin, J. Robert, 282n47

Ruby, Harry, 24

Ruffo, Titta, 59

Ruggles, Wesley, 10, 24, 25, 32, 47, 260
Ryskind, Morrie, 143

Sacco and Vanzetti, 129
The Saint in New York, 161
Salary cuts, 43, 47, 67–68, 184, 212, 237–38
Sales conventions, 24, 44–45, 71, 95, 127, 137, 158, 178, 202, 226, 268–69
Sanda Mala, 194
Sanders, George, 161, 231
Sandrich, Mark, 54, 95, 96, 105, 106, 109, 124, 153–54, 260
Santell, Al, 10
Sarecky, Louis, 260
Sarnoff, David: as chairman of the board, 16, 35, 40, 111; and David Selznick, 35–36, 62, 64, 74; and George Schaefer, 160, 235, 247–48; and Joseph Kennedy, 18–19, 31, 274n23; and J. R. McDonough, 73, 74, 247–48; and Merian C. Cooper, 84; renewed interest in RKO, 150; Pathe purchase, 31–32; radio-film symbiosis, 21, 27, 132; RCA, 13, 15, 17, 19, 29, 67, 101, 150, 152, 167; RKO corporate profits, 26; Rockefeller Center, 29, 30, 58–60; sells RCA shares in RKO, 110; takes control of RKO, 37, 40
Saturday Review of Literature, 212
Sayre, Joel, 169
Schaefer, George J.: acquiring "important" properties, 171–72, 190, 194, 199, 208–11; "appointments from within the ranks," 193; B films, 229–30; block booking, 194; and Charles Koerner, 239; concerns about WWII, 183–84, 194, 195–96, 211–12; conflict with Lee Marcus, 204, 214; Coordinating Committee on National Defense, 194–95; as corporate president, 160, 166–68, 172, 178, 189; cutting costs, 184–86, 203, 214, 229–30, 237; deal with Sam Goldwyn, 227; and Ginger

Rogers, 212–13, 220; growing lack of confidence in, 253–54; *Gunga Din*, 180–81; interference with production decisions, 173–74; and Joseph Breen, 221–23, 225, 226, 228, 238; legacy, 254–56; McDonough report, 238, 247–48; negotiations with Astaire, 200; Orson Welles, 178–79, 185, 205, 206–7, 213–20, 239–46, 248–52; and Pandro Berman, 162, 173–74, 179–80, 188–89; portrayal by Roy Scheider, 254; precarious position, 234–35; prestigious productions, 188, 190, 197–99; production schedule, 196–97, 226, 228; release of George Stevens, 201; resignation, 254; signing independent producers, 174, 179, 191–92, 202, 226; and Sol Lesser, 224–25, 237–38; *Suspicion*, 231–33; unfreezing foreign money, 254; at United Artists, 159–60; working with Harry Edington, 195, 203, 236
Scheider, Roy, 254
Schenck, Joseph, 68
Schenck, Nicholas, 149
Schnitzer, Joseph I., 18, 22, 25, 26, 28–29, 33, 34, 40–41, 278n3
Schoedsack, Ernest B., 44, 53, 62, 70, 110
Schulberg, B. P., 41, 53
Schwarz, Vera, 59
Scollard, Pat, 10
Scott, Alan, 107, 260
Scott, Randolph, 99
Screen tests, 53–54, 267
Screwball comedy, 136, 163, 231
Scripps-Howard, 133
The Searchers, 122
The Secret Hour, 208
Seiter, William, 10, 164–65
Selznick, David O.: and B. B. Kahane, 44, 46–50, 58; borrowing Joan Fontaine from, 231; contract renegotiation, 55, 58, 61, 63; *Gone With the Wind*, 121, 243; as head of

production, 35–36, 40–41, 44–46; as independent producer, 191; and Merian C. Cooper, 44, 65, 69, 75, 76; at MGM, 63–64, 72, 73; report card, 55–57; resignation, 61–62, 64; Selznick International Pictures, 104, 243; talent acquisition, 52–55
Selznick, Lewis J., 35
Serials, 9, 52
Set design, 97, 102, 260
Shall We Dance, 124, 143, 163, 287n23
Shapiro, Victor, 89
Shaw, George Bernard, 226
She, 103, 108–9, 128, 285n43, 285n45
She Done Him Wrong, 103, 278n7
Shelley, George, 136
Shelton, John, 202
Sheridan, Ann, 202
Sherman Antitrust Act, 66
Sherman, Lowell, 102–3
Sherwood, Robert, 197, 199
Shirley, Anne, 97, 231, 259
Shores, Lynn, 244–46, 249, 252
Short films, 5–6, 11, 31, 32, 69, 95, 102, 104, 126, 171, 211, 250, 259, 268, 270
Shorts division, 81, 95, 105
Show Boat, 22, 27
Shurlock, Geoffrey, 252–53
Sidewalks of London, 202
The Sign of the Cross, 109
Silberberg, Mendel, 228
Silent films, 14, 21, 24–25, 34, 38, 208
Silly Symphonies, 101
Silvera, Darrell, 263–64
Sing Your Worries Away, 229, 252
The Singing Fool, 146
Sino-Japanese War, 183
Sisk, Robert, 55, 76, 104, 136, 137, 227, 260
Sister Carrie, 194, 203
Sisters of the Skillet, 59
Sistrom, Joseph, 136, 137
Sky Giant, 204
Sloane, Paul, 90
Small, Edward, 123, 136, 155, 168

The Smartest Girl in Town, 127
Smashing the Rackets, 157–58
The Smiler With a Knife, 185, 205–6
Smith, Courtland, 32
Snow White and the Seven Dwarfs, 126, 146–47
So Red the Rose, 121
Sobel, Robert, 67
The Soldier and the Lady, 216
Son of Kong, 285n44
The Son of the Sheik, 56
Sothern, Ann, 127
Sound revolution, 10–15, 19, 21, 25–26, 31, 53
Sound Department, 262, 264
Spanish Civil War, 183
The Spanish Main, 103
Sparks, Robert, 162, 163, 164
Special effects, 55, 62, 109
Special effects department, 263
Spitfire, 77–78, 90–91, 106, 120
Spitz, Leo: B films, 134, 137, 139, 157; as chairman of the board, 134, 150; as corporate president, 111–13, 115–17, 127, 130, 131, 147; exit from RKO, 159–60; and exploitation films, 157–58; and Orson Welles, 179; and Pandro Berman, 149–50, 153, 155–56, 165–66; *Room Service*, 163–64; series pictures, 161; *Stage Door*, 143, 145; stars, 135; "substandard productions," 138; Universal-International, 292n55
Spoor, George K., 26
St. Clair, Mal, 24, 25
Stage Door, 138, 143, 144–45, 153, 155
Stanley theater circuit, 19
Stanwyck, Barbara, 98, 127, 135
A Star is Born, 64
Star system, 73
Steen, Mike, 174
Stein, Paul, 36
Steiner, Max, 97, 106, 122, 263
Step-deals, 34
Stevens, George: *Alice Adams*, 106; *A Damsel in Distress*, 144; directors department, 260; *Gunga Din*, 155,

Stevens, George (continued)
169–70, 176, 200; Liberty Films,
289n86; promotion to A features,
95, 105; rift with RKO, 200–201
Stevenson, Bob, 215
Stevenson, Edward, 262
Still Department, 261
Stingaree, 85–86, 89, 95
Stirn, Ernest, 186
Stock market crash, 19, 25, 26
Stokowski, Leopold, 59
Story Department, 53, 108, 140,
266–67
The Story of Louis Pasteur, 116
The Story of Vernon and Irene
Castle, 175–78
The Strand theater, 58
Strip Tease, 158
Studio manager, 123, 124, 237, 261,
263
Sturges, John, 262
Sullivan, Charlie, 10
Suspicion, 231–34, 239, 253
Sutton, Grady, 105
Swamp Water, 235
Swanson, Gloria, 12, 18, 56. See
also Gloria Productions,
Incorporated
Swanson, H. N., 94
Swing Time, 117, 127, 128, 130
Swiss Family Robinson, 173, 178,
203, 226
Sylvia Scarlett, 116, 118–20, 128
Syncopation, 22, 252
Syrett, Netta, 128

A Tale of Two Cities, 64
Talent Department, 267
Talent scouts, 30, 54, 267
Talking motion pictures ("Talkies"),
12, 14, 15, 19, 21, 24, 28–29, 38,
102, 111, 208
Tarkington, Booth, 106
Taylor, Dwight, 107
Technicolor, 71, 101, 243, 245–46, 250;
three-strip, 95, 101–3, 104, 285n31;
two-color process, 101

Television, 19, 21, 42, 99, 124, 126,
132
Temple, Shirley, 68, 131
Tevlin, C. J., 4
Thalberg, Irving, 69, 73, 126, 189,
282n47
That's Right, You're Wrong, 203
Theater division, 41, 95, 238, 270
They Came to Blow Up America,
297n81
They Knew What They Wanted,
208–11, 227, 255
They Met in Argentina, 222
Thompson, Major L. E., 270
Thomson, Fred, 10, 12
The Three Musketeers, 102
Tiffany Productions, 10
Tim Holt Westerns, 203, 228
Time Magazine, 61, 88, 145, 156, 241
The Toast of New York, 140, 143, 155
Tom, Dick and Harry, 227
Tom Brown's School Days, 178, 203,
226
Tone, Franchot, 169
Too Many Girls, 194, 222
Too Many Wives, 134
Topaze, 62, 104
Top Hat, 106–8, 109, 113, 118, 127,
269
Towne, Gene, 172–73, 178, 179, 201,
226
Tracy, Lee, 135, 259
Tracy, Spencer, 24, 169
Trade papers, 10, 15, 21, 25, 27, 82, 134,
146, 208–9, 215, 221, 237–38, 266
Trevor, Claire, 178
Trigger, 90
Tristan and Isolde, 102
Tunney, Gene, 59
Turnbull, Burton, 253
Tuskegee Choir, 59
The Tuttles of Tahiti, 252
Twelvetrees, Helen, 31, 47
Twentieth Century, 123
Twentieth Century-Fox: Depression-
era losses, 65, 68, 214; Depression-
era profits, 26, 147; Floyd Odlum

investments, 110; Ginger Rogers, 220; "major" studio, 1, 257; management, 68, 149, 189; merger rumors, 32; newsreels, 12, 32; sound conversion, 12, 132; theater acquisition, 19, 24, 270; uncertain future, 166; widescreen, 26–27; WWII profits, 236–37; *Young Mr. Lincoln*, 197, 199

Twist, John, 260

Two on an Island, 194

Two Thoroughbreds, 204

Tyler, Tom, 10

The Unbreakable Miss Doll, 194

Underworld, 24

Unexpected Uncle, 230

Unit production, 52, 61, 69, 94, 174, 178–79, 199

United Artists, 52, 123–26, 159–60, 168, 190–92, 221, 223, 226, 247, 257, 299n16

United Fruit Company, 110

United Producers Corporation, 201

United Studios, 9

U.S. Department of Justice, 66, 166

Universal: *Bachelor Mother*, 180; B Pictures, 69; Charles Rogers, 277n64; Depression-era losses, 68, 114; George Cukor, 53; Howard Benedict, 247; *The Hunchback of Notre Dame*, 187; International Pictures merger, 292n55; John Wayne, 136; Joseph Schnitzer, 18; as "major" studio, 1, 257; Ned Depinet, 36; profits, 190, 238–39; war years, 149

Upperworld, 24, 275n18

Vagabond Lover, 24, 27

Valentino, Rudolph, 10, 56

Vallee, Rudy, 24, 27

Valley of the Sun, 252

Van Beuren Corporation, 126

Van Doren, Carl, 194

Van Schmus, W. G., 95, 108, 159–60, 221, 223, 225, 234, 300n42

Van Wagner, Garrett, 235, 265

Vanity Fair, 102

Variety, 27, 28, 37, 76, 147, 192, 236, 238

Vaudeville: performance, 14, 19, 30, 59, 267; in RKO theaters, 28, 48, 58, 111; theaters, 8, 13–14, 23

Veiller, Anthony, 129, 143, 169

Vertical integration, 1, 15, 192, 225, 257, 270

Vidor, King, 52, 215

Vigil in the Night, 180, 201, 203

Village Tale, 110

Vivacious Lady, 222

Voco Productions, 201

Vogue Pictures, Ltd., 201

Vollmer, Lula, 90

Von Stroheim, Erich, 18, 195

Vorkapich, Slavko, 67

Votion, Jack, 201

Waldorf Astoria Hotel, 169, 202

Wall Street, 26, 100, 110, 254

Wallis, Hal, 189

Walker, Vernon, 261

Walking on Air, 127

Walt Disney Pictures, 132, 151

Wanger, Walter, 52

War Activities Committee, 303n113

War of the Worlds, 207

"War of the Worlds" radio broadcast, 179, 206

Wardrobe Department, 22, 264

Warner Bros.: anti-Nazi films, 196; borrowing Bette Davis from, 86, 87; borrowing William Dieterle, 188; cost cutting measures, 68; Depression-era profits, 26, 147, 237; Floyd Odlum, 110; Fox merger rumors, 32; Hal Wallis, 189; as a"major" studio, 1, 257; Max Steiner, 122; net corporate losses, 65; Sid Rogell, 124; sound, 10, 12, 26, 132; theater acquisition, 19, 24, 270; "Vitascope" process, 27; widescreen, 26–27

Warner, Jack, 149

Warsaw Incident, 204
Wasserman, Lew, 215
Water Gypsies, 194
Way Back Home, 44
Way Down East, 103
Wayne, John, 124, 136, 178
Weaver, William R., 146
Weber & Fields, 59
Wednesday's Child, 104
Weekend for Three, 230
Weisl, Ed, 221
Weissmuller, Johnny, 300n56
Welles, Orson: *Citizen Kane*, 207–8, 213–19, 255, 256, 297n77; deal with RKO, 178–79, 206; *Heart of Darkness*, 185, 190, 205–6; *It's All True*, 241–46, 248–52, 285n31; *The Magnificent Ambersons*, 239–41; *Smiler With a Knife*, 185, 205–6
Wellman, William, 57
Wells, H. G., 207
We're Rich Again, 85
West, Mae, 76, 103, 153, 278n7
Western Costume, 264, 278n3
Western Electric, 13, 15, 29–30, 132
Westerns, 10, 22, 32, 71, 124, 136, 171, 196–97, 203, 228, 259
Westinghouse Electric and Manufacturing Company, 12, 66
Westward Passage, 49, 55
Wheeler and Woolsey, 35, 36, 54, 95, 105
Wheeler, Bert, 25, 28, 135, 259
Whelan, Tim, 36
Where Sinners Meet, 85
Whitney, Cornelius Vanderbilt (Sonny), 101–3
Whitney, John Hay (Jock), 69, 71, 101–3, 243
White, Thelma, 89
Whittaker, Charles, 36
Widescreen, 26–27
Wilcox, Herbert, 173, 179, 201
Wilde, Hagar, 162
Wilkinson, Jim, 262
Withers, Hildegarde, 161

Wilson, Richard, 244–45, 252
Winchell, Walter, 266
Winkler, Dan, 202, 231
Winterset, 129–30
Wise Girl, 155, 156
Wise, Robert, 217, 241, 262
Without Orders, 204
The Witness Chair, 116
Woit, C. F., 265
The Wolf Man, 235
Wolfson, P. G., 136, 155, 260
The Woman Between, 36
The Woman I Love, 143
A Woman Rebels, 121, 128
The Women, 232
Wood, Sam, 10, 212
Woodruff, Frank, 247
Woolsey, Robert, 25, 28, 135, 259
Work, Cliff, 69, 238
World Film Company, 168
World War II, 3, 38, 69, 72, 183, 192, 196, 198, 214, 234
Wray, Ardel, 208, 212
Wray, Fay, 62
Wright, Alfred, 118
Writing Department, 260, 266
Wyler, William, 234, 289n86

Yellow Dust, 135
Yost, Dorothy, 260
You Can't Take It with You, 161
You Only Live Once, 172–73
You'll Find Out, 222
Youmans, Vincent, 24, 81, 123
Young April, 140
Young Bride, 49
Young, Collier, 267
Young Mr. Lincoln, 199

Zanuck, Darryl F., 68, 72, 189
Ziegfeld, Florenz, 20, 25
Zohbel, Herman, 34
Zoning, 269